RETURN FROM
THE ARCHIPELAGO

RETURN FROM THE ARCHIPELAGO

Narratives of
Gulag Survivors

Leona Toker

INDIANA UNIVERSITY PRESS
BLOOMINGTON & INDIANAPOLIS

This book is a publication of

Indiana University Press
601 North Morton Street
Bloomington, IN 47404-3797 USA

http://www.indiana.edu/~iupress

Telephone orders   800-842-6796
Fax orders   812-855-7931
Orders by e-mail   iuporder@indiana.edu

The paper used in this publication meets the minimum
requirements of American National Standard for Information Sciences—Permanence of Paper for Printed
Library Materials, ANSI Z39.48-1984.

Manufactured in the United States of America

Library of Congress Cataloging-in-Publication Data

Toker, Leona.
    Return from the Archipelago : narratives of Gulag
survivors / Leona Toker.
        p.   cm.
    Includes bibliographical references and index.
    ISBN 0-253-33787-9 (cl : alk. paper)
    1. Russian literature—20th century—History and
criticism. 2. Concentration camps in literature.
3. Concentration camps—Soviet Union. 4. Prisoners'
writings, Soviet—History and criticism.   I. Title.

PG3026.C64 T648 2000
891.709'355—dc21
                                                    00-037040

    1 2 3 4 5   05 04 03 02 01 00

TO

Dana

AND

Jonathan

CONTENTS

Acknowledgments

Almost every national, ethnic, or professional group on either side of the border of the former Soviet Union has its own favorite Gulag memoir, one that speaks in the language of its own culture. Readers may therefore be disappointed at opening this book and not finding references to the books that have been important in their lives. No apology for the omission might suffice here, but I must offer some explanations: the vastness of the corpus, the inaccessibility of many books, the language barrier. I have, for instance, gained access to some memoirs by Lithuanian Gulag survivors, but not books written in Latvian, Estonian, or the Transcaucasian and Central Asian languages. The plight of the prisoners of World War II in the Soviet Union has been similar to, yet also significantly different from, that of Gulag inmates. Their books remain, regrettably, outside the scope of this study—despite the gracious help of Professor Emiko Ohnuki-Tierney of the University of Wisconsin in Madison concerning the Japanese POWs. It has likewise proved nearly impossible to keep track of all the new publications that have appeared, both in Russian and in foreign languages, since the so-called Second Russian Revolution. I have endeavored to study the landmark works of the corpus and record the conclusions of this fourteen-year-long process in the present book, with various degrees of brevity, hoping that the periodization of the Gulag corpus suggested here as well as the description of the Gulag memoir genre might, in principle, accommodate the sources that for one or more of the above reasons have not been examined.

The idea of this book was born in long and fruitful conversations that it was my good fortune to have with Anatoly and Irina Khazanov, now of the University of Wisconsin in Madison. To the Khazanovs I also owe my friendship with Bronia and Avram Ben-Yakov, who have generously shared with me great amounts of otherwise inaccessible information. I am glad to have this opportunity to publicly thank them for their patient advice and loans of books from their unique collection. Bronia Ben-Yakov's dictionary of Gulag slang was also my first systematic introduction to the Gulag corpus.

Profound changes have taken place in Russia since I first began working on this book. I therefore had to revise and complement the manuscript with large portions of new materials several times. Throughout this process I had the rare good fortune to be able to rely on both the support and the uncompromising criticism of a great scholar. Professor H. M. Daleski read the whole of one of the versions of the book and numerous other fragments. As has been the case in the almost three decades of our teacher-student relationship, he made extremely valuable detailed comments. I am also grateful to Professor Michael Scammell of Columbia University for a timely critique of one of the versions, for remarks on parts of another, and for calling my attention to what might have been unpardonable lacunae. A number of friends have read separate parts of the manuscript and amended them in important ways: Emily Budick and Ilya Zakharovich Serman of the Hebrew University, writer Ruf' Zernova, Meir Sternberg and Zephyra Porat of Tel Aviv University, Avram Ben-Yakov of the University of Bar Ilan, and Alvin Rosenfeld of Indiana University in Bloomington, whose own work on the literature of the Holocaust has stimulated much of my thinking. The highly professional textual and structural comments of Janet Rabinowitch of Indiana University Press have helped the present version to take its final shape.

My thanks go to Gene Barabtarlo of the University of Missouri at Columbia, translator Sima Veksler, and mathematician Vladimir Gershovich, a former dissident, for several useful leads. To Alla Barabtarlo of the University of Missouri, Columbia, I am grateful for generous help and advice with sundry bibliographical matters. Shalamov scholars Michael Brewer of Pittsburgh University and Laura Kline of the University of Michigan in Detroit have generously shared their work and their research materials. Some of their brilliant insights have provided further stimulus for my work. I am also deeply grateful to people who have shown interest in the project and kindly sent me materials that I otherwise could not have obtained: writer Phil Casoar; Pekka Tammi of the University of Tampere; Christine Raguet-Bouvart of the University of Bordeaux III; Gavriel Shapiro of Cornell; Charles Lock of the University of Copenhagen; Stuart Tave of the University of Chicago; Herbert Grabes of Giessen University; Matthias Bauer and Christiane Lang-Graumann of the University of Münster; and my Hebrew University colleague Nita Schochet. Encouragement was at times needed more urgently than at other times; and I am glad to have this opportunity to thank my colleagues, Lois Bar Yakov, Ruth Nevo, Shlomith Rimmon-Kenan, Sanford Budick, and Menakhem Brinker, as well as Geoffrey Hartman of Yale and

Matei Calinescu of Indiana University at Bloomington, for their moral support.

Research grants from the Hebrew University's Faculty of Humanities allowed me to benefit from the energetic and intelligent help of research assistants Haym Dolgopolsky, Joseph Osinsky, and, in particular, Natalia Cherepashenets-Druker, now at UCLA.

I also thank the Rockefeller Foundation for a grant that gave me a month in Bellagio with ideal conditions for completing research of the background materials for the book.

Owing to the specificity of the project, the active encouragement and assistance of my family has been vitally important. Despite his own over-loaded schedule, my husband, Gregory (Tsvi) Toker, read and discussed with me much of the material. The insights of my father, Aba Strazhas, are inextricably interwoven with my own thoughts. My children, Dana and Jonathan, pitched in with technical help. Yet the person to whom I owe the greatest gratitude is my mother, Nedda Strazhas, whose unwavering belief in the value of this research supported me at difficult moments, who read this book and all its spin-offs, chapter by chapter and version by version, giving me the benefit of her memories, ideas, and critical suggestions.

Different portions of the material of this book were first published in *Hebrew University Studies in Literature and the Arts; Poetics Today; Studies in Short Fiction;* the collections *In Honour of Professor Victor Levin: Russian Philology and History,* ed. W. Moskovich, J. Frankel, I. Serman, and S. Shvarzband (Jerusalem: Praedicta, 1992); *Commitment in Reflection: Essays in Literature and Moral Philosophy,* ed. Leona Toker (New York: Garland, 1994); *Literature and Philosophy,* ed. Herbert Grabes (special issue of *REAL,* Germany); *Jews and Slavs,* vol. 4, ed. W. Moskovich, S. Shwarzband, and A. Alekseev (Jerusalem: FPL, 1995); and *Critical Ethics: Text, Theory and Responsibility,* ed. Dominic Rainsford and Tim Woods (Basingstoke: Macmillan, 1999). I thank the publishers of these journals and collections for permission to reprint material here.

A Note on Sources

This book contains frequent references to two sources. Aleksandr Solzhenitsyn's *The Gulag Archipelago: An Experiment in Literary Investigation* is abbreviated as *GA*, with an addition of the number of book and chapter (when it is necessary to note page numbers, I refer to Thomas P. Whitney's translations of Parts 1–4 and Harry Willetts's of Parts 5–7 (New York: Harper and Row, 1973, 1975, 1978). In discussing Varlam Shalamov's short stories I usually refer to the cycle to which a story belongs, with the following abbreviations: *KR* for *Kolymskie rasskazy* (the first cycle in the larger collection bearing the same name), *AL* for *Artist lopaty*, *LB* for *Levyi bereg*, *VL* for *Voskreshenie listvennitsy*, and *KR-2* for *Perchatka, ili KR-2*. The distribution of the stories among the collections is based on that of the two-volume *Kolymskie rasskazy*, ed. I. P. Sirotinskaya (Moscow: Sovremennink, 1991), but page references, unless otherwise indicated, are given according to the first book-length edition of Shalamov's *Kolymskie rasskazy*, ed. Mikhail Geller (London: Overseas Publications Interchange, 1978). The titles of the stories are given in English when a published English translation is available, and in Russian if this is not, so far, the case. Quotations from Shalamov, as well as from several other authors (see introductory note in Works Cited), are given in my own translation. In the cases of other Russian authors, titles of as yet untranslated works are most often given in English in the text and in the original, accompanied by a translation, in Works Cited.

A Note on Transliteration

In Works Cited, I have used a slightly modified version of the Library of Congress system of transliteration for Russian names and titles. In the body of the work, however, I have used the more popular spellings, such as "Dostoevsky" rather than "Dostoevskii," as well as spellings that convey a better sense of pronunciation, such as "Aksyonov" rather than "Aksenov." In many cases, moreover, the single and double apostrophes that represent the Russian soft and hard signs, respectively, have been deleted to ease the reading of those not familiar with Russian spelling. For the same reason, throughout the text discussion I have omitted some doubled vowels, using, for example, "Lidia" instead of "Lidiia." Cross-references have been added to the bibliography to guide those not familiar with Russian to the proper listings.

RETURN FROM
THE ARCHIPELAGO

Introduction

Looking through the window of a railway car at the Katyn station on April 29, 1940, Stanislaw Swianiewicz, an expert on the Soviet economy, was unable to figure out what was going on at that very moment, on that lovely spring day, in the forest three kilometers away. He caught strange signs and wondered at their meaning: soldiers had bayonets fixed to their rifles (what for?); the windows of the bus that carried away his fellow Polish POW officers in groups of thirty were painted over (who should not see what?); the bus came back for new consignments every half hour, which meant that the prisoners were not taken far (why were they not plainly marched to their destination?); the NKVD colonel had an air of being in charge of a complex operation (of what kind?). Professor Swianiewicz knew that the Soviet Union had not signed the international conventions on prisoners of war; therefore anything was possible. Later, on his way to prison in a Black Maria, he expected to be shot—he alone; he was still spared the unthinkable though logical realization that his comrades were being shot, methodically and matter-of-factly, just out of earshot, while the bus was dispatched for more (1989: 114–20).

The canon of liberal education has since been opened to a study of the hard facts of recent history, supplied by reports of Amnesty International, academic research, or narratives of atrocity survivors. We often defer this study out of self-protection, believing that we know enough about evil and heroism and can imagine the rest. Actually, however, we don't and we can't—but this is not an instant discovery.

On a visit to a museum in 1940, the speaker of Auden's "Musée de Beaux Arts" notes how well the "Old Masters" understood the "human position" of suffering: it "takes place / While someone else is eating or opening a window or just walking dully along." In the right-hand lower corner of Brueghel's *Icarus,* referred to in the poem, the legs of the boy who has fallen into the sea can still be seen above the water; but the sun is shining, and the peasant in the foreground has his furrow to plow. The "expensive delicate ship" from whose deck Icarus could have been seen keeps on its course: it has "somewhere to get to and sail[s] calmly on."

Auden's poetry displays a seismographic sensibility to contemporary moods. Most of us are vaguely aware that "even the dreadful martyrdom must run its course / Anyhow in a corner." We live, work, love, walk dully along, learn, plan, sympathize, control, pay insurance premiums—all the while quite well aware of "some untidy spot / Where dogs go on with their doggy life and the torturer's horse / Scratches its innocent behind on a tree." In the global village, such untidy spots are not too remote, and the tendency to look away from them conflicts with the pervasive belief that, once illuminated, they have a better chance of being set right. Citizens of the modern world find themselves on the "expensive delicate ship" of state that can—but does not always choose to—respond to calls of distress.

The lines about "the torturer's horse" scratching "its innocent behind on a tree" implicitly juxtapose the ordeal of the victims, which Auden prefers not to visualize, with the trivial discomfort of the animal involved in the infliction of torture (cf. Améry 1980: 35). Concrete details of gas chambers, interrogation dungeons, punishment cells, execution cellars, and killing fields surpass the worst dystopian imagination. One of the few mechanisms that make it possible to read firsthand accounts of atrocities is the balance between the emotional impact of the materials and the cognitive activity of the reader. Concentration-camp empires, in particular, have created new semiotic systems, and our efforts to decode them distance the pain of reconstructive imagination that could otherwise have been overwhelming.

The ability to read accounts of atrocities is not necessarily a sign of a more advanced stage of individual ethical development. One may, perhaps, have been kinder precisely at an earlier stage when one mapped the road to the private chambers of horror but fearfully avoided taking it. Opting for a study of atrocities is not a reason for self-congratulation, yet it is an ethically positive act, if only because the victims usually *want* the world at large to know of their plight.

Yet the appropriateness of *artistic* texts for the transmission of such knowledge is not unproblematic. Lawrence Langer, for instance, notes that "art's transfiguration of moral chaos into aesthetic form might in the end misrepresent that chaos and create a sense of meaning and purpose in the experience of the Holocaust."[1] But then narrative art does not necessarily endow death with a meaning. What most survivor accounts seek to make poignantly meaningful is not the death but the individual *lives* of the victims whose worth is denied by totalitarian regimes.[2] History books or archival materials are of little help here—one needs more effective aids to imagination and thought. Quality writing about atrocities is ethically significant not only because it captures potentially reluctant audiences, but also because it stages and mediates a closer engagement with its material.

* * *

Soviet concentrations camps, the so-called Gulag,[3] are, as some of the most influential contemporary philosophers (Rorty 1989: 173; MacIntyre 1981: 33) have acknowledged, an integral and prominent part of what a modern intellectual has to know about the history of the twentieth century. The present study is devoted to *literary* reflections of the Gulag, mainly to survivor narratives, both fictional *and* memoiristic.

I believe that not only the general reader but also professional historians must be exposed to these narratives. This imperative has not been made less urgent since the doors of the formerly secret archives of various Soviet institutions, including those of the KGB, came ajar in the 1990s. Enlightening as the discovered documents have proved to be, they do not, by themselves, reveal the nature of the human predicament in which the victims of the Stalinist penitentiary system found themselves. Indeed, even the franker of the secret police reports on camp conditions use an official newspeak that needs both semantic and pragmatic gloss: an outsider can, perhaps, guess that "alimentary dystrophy" means deadly slow starvation, but it takes a veteran to explain to us that "absence of drying facilities" translates into death by freezing in the padded clothes that had not dried on the prisoner's body overnight (Razgon 1994: 9–42).

Survivor evidence also warns us against the reliability of the *statistical* information provided by official archival materials. The exact number of the victims of the Gulag is still unknown. In the eighties, a sharp academic debate on the subject in the pages of the journals *Slavic Review* and *Soviet Studies* was triggered by Steven Rosefielde's estimate that during peak years Soviet penal institutions must have held 10 million prisoners (1980, 1981).[4] Rosefielde was challenged by Stephen G. Wheatcroft (e.g., 1981, 1983, 1990) and other like-minded authors—eventually dubbed "revi-

sionist" (by an imprecise analogy with the deniers of the Holocaust)—
who pointed to the absence of documented statistical evidence and
waived memoir literature as biased and impressionistic. In the eyes of the
majority of Russian readers and many Western scholars, the latter school
did not win the day even when the studies of the available KGB archives
seemed to suggest that the actual numbers fell even below Wheatcroft's
1981 estimate of 4–5 million prisoners in the sample peak year of 1939
(see Bacon 1994).

Indeed, the phenomenon of near-exclusive reliance on official archives looks disconcertingly similar to the erstwhile uncritical acceptance
of the proud optimism of the Soviet media and to the jamming of the
discordant voices that insisted on the underside of the achievements of
the socialist state. Only the justification of the jamming is, these days,
epistemological: individual memory is distrusted because it is expected
to be partial, subjective, and self-serving. The resulting neglect of personal narratives often leads to a naive overemphasis on statistical confirmation of long-known facts, an unapologetic inclusion of data from
Stalin's made-to-order 1939 census,[5] an almost fetishistic attitude to official documents, and the style of circumlocution and understatement
that borders on misrepresentation.[6] No doubt, some memoirs can be self-
serving and narrow; yet the truth-value of official records is no less problematic—and it is firsthand narratives that tell us about such strategies of
falsification as, for instance, recourse to the "ten-years-of-imprisonment-
without-correspondence" formula to conceal death verdicts, conviction
of political offenders on criminal charges, omission of transit prisoners
from employment records, or ex post facto fabrication of medical records
for hundreds of the dead.[7] It is also from the memoirs that we learn about
the different standard deviations in different types of accounting. Thus,
on the basis of reports on the workforce available in the camps, Edwin
Bacon calculates the grand total of 3.96 million prisoners in 1945 (1994:
122); by a striking contrast, Anton Antonov-Ovseenko, son of the Bolshevik leader executed in 1937 and himself a Gulag survivor, states that,
judging by the number of food rations for places of detention, there were
16 million prisoners that year (1991: 3). As is well known, officials in
charge of forced labor tended to understate the manpower at their disposal: they had to account for the low output, especially since the production quotas were so unrealistically high that individual convict workers
could hardly fulfill 30 or 50 percent of the daily tasks. Conversely, officials
in charge of camp administration tended to inflate the numbers of prisoners: in order to claim maximum amounts of provisions (insufficient to
begin with and further diminished by theft) they counted those who had
recently died or been transported to other camps. J. A. Getty et al. (1993:
664–67) are aware of the poetic license of statisticians in the latter case;

what they disregard is the difference between the scope of the hyperbole and the litotes. To wit, the grafting of "dead souls" could amount only to a small percentage, whereas it was both expedient and ideologically correct to have only a *fraction* of camp inmates counted as the available work force.

The bureaucrats who drew up the documents contained in the KGB archives were not concerned with the sum total: each was in charge of his own piece of the jigsaw puzzle and did not have to fit it to other fragments.[8] The documents are too numerous for a prompt evaluation in terms of comprehensiveness; some documentation, moreover, has most probably not been declassified (Pipes 1996: 3, 13);[9] and much paperwork has apparently been destroyed—in the best Russian tradition dating at least from the sixteenth-century Times of Trouble.[10] The danger of disinformation that incomplete records can cause is smaller when a well-informed researcher traces separate personal files; this procedure, practiced, for instance, by Maggs (1996) and Razgon (1994: 5–42, 84–113), also doubles as a commemoration of the individual victims of the regime. The question of the number of victims nevertheless remains unanswered, which in itself is a reflection on the moral essence of the Gulag phenomenon.

One can argue that for a literary study of Gulag narratives the question of numbers is not important, since the emotional outrage and its intellectual sublimation do not diminish in ratio to the statistics. For a victim, however (and the victims must be the focus of such a study), there are worse things than turning into statistics—and one of them is *dropping out* of statistics (see Diamond 1994: 195–221). Familiarity with survivor memoirs partly reduces or compensates for these insults to the memory of the dead.

The basic truthfulness of firsthand accounts of atrocities requires outside confirmation, either by historical research or by related testimonies. Hence, even memoirs devoid of artistic merit are needed. In the sketch "Through the Snow" that opens Varlam Shalamov's *Kolymskie rasskazy* [*Kolyma Tales*], one of the greatest works of the Gulag corpus, prisoners are shown trampling down the snow to make roads for cars and tractors. Unexpectedly, the last sentence of the sketch tells us that the tractors would be driven by "readers" rather than by "writers." The scene is thus turned into an allegory: the snow becomes a blank page on which even "the smallest and the weakest" can help leave a trace if only they do not always walk in the footsteps of others but trample down some untouched portion of the snow. Shalamov sought to write his own stories in such a way that they should have a liberating effect on other survivors—other witnesses had to be enabled to tell what they knew without being hampered by literary conventions. Even "the smallest and the weakest" had to be encouraged to support, modify, complement, or correct Shalamov's own testimony, take the readers where he himself had not been, challenge his memories and opinions, and, by evoking the experience of more victims, rescue more from oblivion.

* * *

Most Gulag narratives were written for consciousness-raising purposes. At the present stage in the history of their reception, the need for that practical goal is considerably reduced, and it is the artistic merit of these texts that claims attention. Yet the terms of any discussion of the aesthetic facet of the texts of testimony must be adapted to their persistent historical and admonitory significance. Between prisons, chain gangs, forced-labor settlements, the Gulag, the Chinese *laogai* and the Nazi *Lagers,* imprisonment has become "*the* experience of the century" (Böll 1973: 227)—or rather, *the recorded* experience, since the "true witnesses" (Levi 1988: 63) of the century's mass murders cannot speak. If one's vision is to be well attuned to modern cultural life, it must have a place (Auden's "untidy spot") for the human consequences of the variously re-emerging totalitarian terror and for the ways in which they dwarf the tragic predicaments explored in the literature of the past.[11]

According to Shalamov, "the man of today tests himself and his actions not against the actions of Julien Sorel, Rastignac, or Andrei Bolkonskii, but against events and people of real life—the life whose witness and participant the reader himself has been."[12] It would be more accurate to say that we test ourselves *not only* against the heroes of classical novels; but what Shalamov also implies is that the modern demand for documentary literature stems not so much from the need for knowledge as amenity[13] as from the need for self-scrutiny. On being shown what kinds of things were happening at the time when we were insulated by an illusion of security, on being told the inside stories behind the events of which our memory has retained only formalized official images, we examine ourselves and rethink our past. Our scale of values is modified and our lives are placed into perspective. The self-testing often takes the shape of a sympathetic identification with the memoirists and of surmises about how we would have acted in their place, whether we would have been able to endure their experience, and whether we might not have found ourselves on the side of the hammer rather than of the nail. By describing human behavior in extreme situations, concentration camp literature provides us with a testing ground for political ideologies as well as for psychological, ethical, and even aesthetic theories. It helps us dismantle stereotypes, calls our attention to the suffering of individual victims, gives faces and names to statistical figures, and engages us in the ritual of commemoration. It also reminds us—insofar as we tend to forget—what it is like to have to live under totalitarian regimes.

* * *

Unlike the literature of the Holocaust, the Gulag *literary corpus* has not yet been given sufficient literary critical attention. A number of Gulag memoirs are referred to, alongside books about Nazi camps, in Terrence Des Pres's *The Survivor* (1977 [1976]), but this thought-provoking sociological study of the structure of survival behind barbed wire treats its primary sources as testimony and does not examine their artistic features. The same is true of Tzvetan Todorov's more recent *Facing the Extreme: Moral Life in the Concentration Camps* (1996). Alain Parrau's comparative literary study, *Écrire les camps* (1995), examines only two works out of the vast Gulag corpus; a limited number of Gulag works are also discussed in Bernadette Morand's 1976 study of the writings of political prisoners. So far only Mikhail Geller's *Kontsentratsionnyi mir i sovetskaia literatura* [*The World of Concentration Camps and Soviet Literature*] (1974) is wholly devoted to numerous literary images of Soviet penal justice, yet it dwells more extensively on the official Soviet misrepresentations of Gulag realities than on the writings of survivors; moreover, even its chapters on Solzhenitsyn and Shalamov deal almost exclusively with the subject matter. Geller's approach was appropriate for a pioneering study written during the so-called stagnation period, when political imprisonment in later versions of the camps, alias "corrective colonies," was still widely practiced. Now that the topical significance of Gulag testimonies is (one hopes) largely a matter of the past, the time is ripe for a closer examination of the art of this body of documentary writing.

Gulag narratives are bifunctional objects whose informational and aesthetic functions become "marked" at different periods of reception (see Mukařovský 1970; Toker 1997):[14] they can be read as historical documents or publicistic statements *and* as works of art. I do not claim more urgency for Gulag narratives than for the literature about other mass atrocities: each historical phenomenon must be studied in its specificity. It would be misleading, for instance, to draw a sustained analogy between the Gulag and the Nazi *Vernichtungslager*s: there are no parallels to the Nazi denial to whole nationalities of the basic human right—to live; nor are there parallels to the Nazi patent of the factory-type production of death. Yet the literature of the Holocaust and that of the Gulag refer to fully developed semiotic systems that shed light on each other's veiled aspects, either through analogies or through contrasts. The history of the

Gulag is also the most relevant background for that of the still existing Chinese *laogai*, established on the basis of similar ideological assumptions and perhaps more efficient in the dehumanization, brainwash, and economic exploitation of millions of victims.[15] Yet China's "labor reform camps" are not yet a matter of the past; they should still be a target of international protest activities rather than a subject of a literary-critical study.

Some of the early discussions of Aleksandr Solzhenitsyn's work (see Howe 1963: 19; Erlich 1973: 16–17), reflected an uneasiness about engaging in a formal analysis of discourse whose primary function was consciousness-raising. This anxiety was mainly due to the fact that in the seventies the Gulag was not yet an encapsulated phenomenon of the past. Now, at the turn of the millennium, Soviet concentration camps are no longer news; political imprisonment has been abolished in the former Soviet Union; and the issue of the Gulag, including the post-*glasnost* revelations, has passed from the domain of journalists to that of historians. It is now ethically possible and, I believe, necessary to consider the writings of former prisoners as *artistic works* and to analyze not just the testimony that they present but also their formal features—with due apologies for the artificiality of the unavoidably implicated provisional distinction between content and form. Yet even this will be done with some sense of remorse in view of the fact that the conditions of *criminal* convicts in Russia and many other countries are still so harsh that prisons are liable to propagate crime rather than control it.

I limit this study to memoirs and prose fiction, leaving aside poetry and drama. Because of the difference in the circumstances of composition, the history of Gulag poetry does not quite coincide with that of Gulag prose. Gulag poetry was often composed while the authors were still behind barbed wire; prose works were usually written upon release—committing them to paper in the camps was practically impossible,[16] and mnemonic devices that would preserve them in the authors' memory could not compete with those used to memorize verse. The creative impulse behind the composition of poetry is less closely associated with the imperative to testify; moreover, like drama, poetry presupposes a dynamics of reception different from that of the "epic" genre. For all these reasons, possible methodologies for the study of Gulag poetry and drama are not coextensive with those applicable to prose narratives.

The corpus of Gulag prose has a history of its own, and there is no one-to-one correspondence between its landmarks and those of the history of the camps themselves. After Chapter 1 sketches the history of the Soviet camp empire, Chapter 2 surveys the development of Gulag testimony, describes its main periods, and places its prominent issues and most significant works in a historical perspective. Chapter 3 offers a detailed genre analysis of Gulag memoirs, and Chapter 4 discusses the centrally important work of Gulag documentary prose, Aleksandr Solzhenitsyn's *The Gulag Archipelago*.[17]

Chapter 5 considers the elements of fictionalization in factographic works, in preparation for showing in what way works of fiction, whose material is, by definition, not amenable to public verification, can double as historical sources. Chapters 6 and 7 discuss fictional narratives conceived expressly as vehicles of historical testimony. Chapter 6 is devoted to the life and work of Varlam Shalamov, a subtly philosophical artist whose short stories erase the borderlines between historical testimony and an imaginative construction of the past and provide an example par excellence of narratives as bifunctional objects. Chapter 7 analyses Solzhenitsyn's novel *The First Circle* and his seminal novella *One Day in the Life of Ivan Denisovich,* both based on his camp experience. Chapter 8 deals with works that include images of the Gulag but that largely disown the testimonial function.

Works of the latter group signify a reabsorption of Gulag writing into the Russian literary tradition, as well as a reshaping of this tradition. Indeed, since the atrocities of the twentieth century are vastly different from whatever has been represented in the literature of the previous ages (cf. Hoffman 1964: 23–24), the literature of the Gulag, like the literature of the Holocaust, often highlights the asymmetry of traditional cultural schemata and unprecedented new realities. It has been observed (Ezrahi 1980: 13) that Holocaust narratives constitute a break with the traditions of the national literatures in whose languages they are written, so that Primo Levi's *If This Is a Man* is not really Italian literature or Elie Wiesel's novels are not really French. This is also true of Gulag testimonies by non-Russian authors. Yet even the testimonies of sophisticated Russian writers like Solzhenitsyn, Shalamov, or Sinyavsky, steeped in three centuries of Russian letters, could not be accommodated by the inherited patterns of genre and thought. And it is through further literary experiments that the writers who had not been imprisoned attempt to process the unwieldy heritage of labor-camp lore.

Recent interdisciplinary studies of literature and ethical theory (see, for instance, Booth 1988; M. Nussbaum 1986 and 1990: 125–47; Diamond 1991: 367–81) argue that the *form* of a literary work has an ethical aspect. Gulag literature is unique material for the study of the ethics of form, of the way the content of ethically oriented writings may be "implicated in their literary structure, not only as it happens or by an author's deliberate choice but intrinsically" (Lang 1990: 120). Literary critical writing about camp narratives is necessarily riddled with ethical caveats in respect to both its statements and its language. In discussing Gulag narratives I have attempted both to distance the inevitable brutality and coerciveness of their subject matter and to avoid intellectualizing this subject matter beyond recognition. I kept reminding myself that the history of atrocities is recidivistic—and that foregrounding the artistic merits of concentration-camp literature may, but should not, obliterate its admonitory aims.

1 Soviet Labor Camps: A Brief History

In a recognizable modern form, concentration camps were first introduced in 1896 by the Spanish troops in Cuba (Kaminski 1990: 34–35) and then in 1900 by the British in the Boer War in South Africa. They functioned as administrative measures against potential rather than actual opponents: the population of whole villages was interned. Though concentration camps were both symptomatic and productive of large-scale misery and loss of life, in their infancy they were sometimes perceived as signs of progress in moral practice, especially in comparison with the "take-no-prisoners" civil-war principles or what is euphemistically called "ethnic cleansing." Eventually, however, it became apparent that the camps were not necessarily an *alternative* to slaughter: at their worst they were easily transformed into instruments of mass murder—relatively swift mass murder in Auschwitz and relatively slow in Kolyma and some of the Chinese *laogai*.

In Soviet Russia, as elsewhere, concentration camps were established in order to repress a wider resistance than could be contained by available prisons (whose capacity in the whole of the Russian Empire had barely exceeded 200,000). They were born of a power struggle and adopted by ideology, yet they soon developed a self-sustaining dynamic of their own. Their further history was shaped by the interaction of this internal

11

dynamic with the expediencies and the theory-based policies of an ideo-cratic regime.

On seizing power in October 1917, the Bolshevik leadership made the splendid ideological move of dismantling the old prison administration. According to Marxist beliefs, crime was a product of social injustice; it would disappear when the triumph of socialism abolished the exploi-tation of one class by another. Meantime, crime showed every sign of persisting; moreover, political resistance ("counterrevolution"), private trade ("profiteering"), and accidents at work sites ("sabotage") were rein-terpreted as crime. While the People's Commissariat of Justice was taking over the management of prisons, a new agency was established in Decem-ber 1917. It combined the investigative and the punitive functions and was called the "Cheka" (abbreviated acronym for "The Extraordinary Commission for Combating Counterrevolution, Sabotage, and Specula-tion"). The word "extraordinary" (*chrezvychainaia*) was meant to suggest emergency measures, yet it soon came to be perceived as referring not to the temporary character but to the extraordinary mandate granted to this first political-police force by the Soviet state (see Wolin and Slusser 1957: 4–8).

By the summer of 1918 the social basis of the Bolshevik government had drastically contracted. The hopes of the democratic intelligentsia had been smashed by the suppression of the Constituent Assembly and the ousting of members of non-Bolshevik parties from the government; the support of the peasants, won by the distribution of confiscated es-tates, was lost when, owing to the collapse of industry, the government could not provide proper compensation for the requisitioned agricul-tural produce. It was under these conditions, when the military action of an organized body—the White Guards or the Czechoslovak POWs—had a reasonable chance of toppling Bolshevik rule, that the idea of concen-tration camps came to the fore. In an order of June 4, 1918, Leon Trot-sky demanded that all Czechoslovaks who refused to lay down their arms be detained in "concentration camps"; later the same month he pro-posed such internment for all former officers who refused to join the Red Army (see Geller [Heller] and Nekrich 1986: 66). Upon the outbreak of several local uprisings against the Soviet regime, on August 9, 1918, Len-in too recommended "merciless mass terror against the kulaks, priests and White Guards" and the "locking up of suspects in concentration camps outside the city" (Lenin 1970, 50:143–44). This was a blueprint for the prophylactic use of concentration camps to incapacitate the *potential* opponents of the regime—whereas the *active* opponents and members of the a priori marked groups ("kulaks, priests and White Guards") were to be subjected to the "merciless terror" of summary executions.

In this context, the term "concentration camps" was less frightening than it would become later (Bezsonov 1928: 37).[1] Yet concentration camps were also used for Civil War hostages, whose incarceration was open-ended and often terminated by their execution in revenge for victories of the White Guard armies or for assassinations of Bolshevik leaders.

On August 30, 1918, Fanny Kaplan shot at and wounded Lenin; the same day Leonid Kanegisser assassinated M. S. Uritsky, head of the Petrograd Cheka. The government retaliated with the "Red Terror," proclaimed by the cabinet's decree of September 5, 1918. The decree expanded the powers of the Cheka and, among other things, practically legalized the camps (Conquest 1990: 310). In the months that followed, the camps were still a relatively minor issue, because the Cheka made prompt use of its new license not only to make arrests but also to pass and execute death sentences. About 60,000 death sentences were meted out between September 1918 and January 1920 (M. Jakobson 1993: 25); the number of people shot or hanged summarily, especially in the territories swept by the Civil War was, apparently, much larger.

Since the right to make arrests was also exercised by other government agencies, the prisons were becoming overcrowded. There was a lack of funds to pay their staff and supply the prisoners with clothing, soap, or even sufficient amounts of food (M. Jakobson 1993: 36). For reasons both ideological (the expected waning of prisons under socialism) and economic (small budget, housing shortages), new prisons could not be built in the post-Revolution years. Instead, people formally sentenced to imprisonment, as well as those held on an administrative basis, were often transferred to supposedly temporary camps organized in available monastery or private estate buildings or in hastily constructed barracks. Whereas the makeshift character of the facilities seemed to point at the impermanence of the camps, the relative cheapness of setting them up encouraged their proliferation.

In addition to using the "places of confinement" under the jurisdiction of the Commissariat of Justice, the Cheka maintained camps of its own. The two agencies entered into a competition for funds, facilities, and inmates. In this power struggle (traced in M. Jakobson 1993), the Cheka stood for the expediencies of repression, whereas the Commissariat of Justice laid emphasis on Marxist legal ideals, such as re-education.[2] The continued existence of crime after the revolution was now attributed to "relics of the capitalist past"; the agenda of the Commissariat of Justice was to "re-educate" the inmates through labor. For this reason, as well as in the hope of financing the prisons and camps at least partly by deductions from the prisoners' wages, the Commissariat of Justice recommended labor, especially physical labor, for all prisoners; lighter offenders were even sentenced to forced labor without imprisonment.[3]

The Cheka and the NKVD (the People's Commissariat of Internal Affairs), which ran most of the prisons and camps from 1922 through 1930, had more practical concerns. Whereas the NKVD favored prison labor not so much for its "educational" value as for the prospect of making the camps economically self-sufficient, the main concern of the Cheka lay with incapacitation of the "socially dangerous," especially since the widespread unemployment in the whole country in the early twenties was a stimulus for the free workers' productivity and an obstacle to the systematic development of convict labor.

In most camps from 1918 through 1920 the discipline was perfunctory, the regulations were lax (see Doubassoff 1926: 192–250; Pipes 1996: 119–21), and successful escapes were numerous. The death toll was large, mainly owing to neglect and privation; in 1922 great numbers of prisoners plainly starved. In camps situated near larger cities prisoners fared better than in more distant locations, since the possibilities of interaction with the local population were greater, the mail and the provisions more regular, and the rule of the guard commanders less arbitrary. In the camps themselves manufacture was difficult to organize, and since taking the prisoners to work outside the enclosures promoted escapes, the Cheka often chose not to enforce the convict labor. The logistics lessons were, however, assimilated: in 1920, on the initiative of Felix Dzerzhinsky, head of the Cheka, "special concentration camps" were created (Bacon 1994: 44) in the northern regions, mainly around Arkhangelsk. The remote location and rugged terrain made escape even from the work sites unpromising. The first of the camps to leave a grim trace in popular memory was set up in Kholmogory in 1921 to hold the Kronstadt sailors who had survived the brutal suppression of their rebellion.[4]

The Cheka was officially abolished by a decree of February 6, 1922, as a hint at a liberalization following the end of the Civil War. Its functions and its leader, however, were transferred to the State Political Administration (GPU).[5] This new agency was supposed to run only one prison in Moscow and one in Petrograd, but Dzerzhinsky managed to keep the "special" camps as well.

In 1922–23 the inmates of the Kholmogory and Pertominsk camps near Arkhangelsk were transferred to the venerable monastery grounds of the Solovetsky Islands in the White Sea; the so-called Solovki then became the largest single concentration camp in the country.[6] The prisoners included former members of the upper classes or the intractable intelligentsia, members of the suppressed political parties, White Guard soldiers and officers, clergymen, peasants who had opposed the grain requisitions, workers who had gone on strike, black-market traders, and engineers or technicians charged with "wrecking." There were also common and professional criminals; their numbers eventually grew.

Recruiting camp guards and commanders from captive White Guard officers and Chekists who had committed punishable offenses solved the question of staffing. Aware of the precariousness of their position, the former officers sought to ingratiate themselves with the new regime by emphatic zealousness; most were eventually shot anyway. The numerical disproportion between the cadre and the prisoners led to sadistic ways of maintaining control: a church on Sekirnaia Hill was converted into a torture prison and the monastery basements into execution chambers. The penal function of the Solovki was not secret, and there were rumors of atrocities; but with little concrete information in print, the threat represented by the camps was enhanced by their mysteriousness.

In the Solovki prisoners categorized as "political" were exempt from labor. This status was granted only to members of the Social Revolutionary (SR) Party, Mensheviks, and anarchists; all the other actual or "platonic" opponents of the regime were classed as "counterrevolutionaries" (later as "enemies of the people") and held together with the criminal offenders. Eventually, even members of socialist parties were denied the status of political prisoners, and the notion itself went out of official circulation.[7] Labor became mandatory throughout the camp system.

In the northern camps opponents' and delinquents' isolation from society was more efficiently combined with forced labor. Camp maintenance soon stopped being the main form of employment. Lumbering for export (much in demand) and infrastructure projects turned camp inmates into a slave labor force. The locations of new camps were now determined not by the available facilities but by the sites where such labor was needed. From the Solovki, camp metastases (Solzhenitsyn's famous metaphor) spread to the mainland.

The expansion of the network was spurred by Stalin's collectivization of agriculture, which brought hundreds of thousands of peasants into the camps, and by the great leap toward industrialization, which created a huge demand for labor. The concept of "re-education through labor" was now given a new meaning: the degree to which the prisoners were "reforged" was now measured by their production output. Certain work teams, usually made up of criminal convicts, were granted conditions that allowed them to claim miraculous productivity. Thus, ideology ceased competing with expediency and became its instrument. The shift to the so-called reforging campaign was preceded by a typically Stalinist scapegoating: in the fall of 1929 hundreds of the White Guard officers who had served as warders in the Solovki were shot, along with great numbers of their fellow officers and intellectuals from among the prisoners.

The darkest side of reforging was the new policy of using hunger as incentive. Up to 1930 the starvation of the prisoners was a by-product of the lack of funds, of the difficult food situation in the whole country, of thefts, and of plain neglect. Reforging transformed it into a disciplinary and motivational measure. Robert Conquest notes that "Stalin was well aware of Marx's economic objection to slavery" as inefficient because slaves, who got minimal subsistence irrespective of their production results, had no incentive to work; consequently, "with his usual refusal to accept precedent," he resorted to "the simple but untried method of *not* giving the slave a flat subsistence, but linking his rations to his output" (1990: 332). The prisoners were divided into categories according to the percentage of the output quotas that they fulfilled, which determined the diets (the place on the food scale) that they were assigned.

In 1930–1931 Britain and the United States boycotted Soviet lumber because it was produced by prison labor (Dallin and Nikolaevsky 1947: 217–31). To maintain the source of income, the Soviet authorities replaced export-lumber camp inmates by "free settlers" (people sentenced to exile and forced labor but not to incarceration) and transferred hundreds of thousands of prisoners, at a great cost in life because of the hastiness of the operation, to various capital investment projects, the first major one being the construction of the White Sea–Baltic Sea canal from September 1931 to April 1933. Since these projects were financed by the government,[8] the issue of the economic self-sufficiency of the camps went off the agenda; conversely, the propagandistic build-up around the ennobling effect of labor reached new heights.[9] The White Sea–Baltic canal, dug by convicts through a rocky terrain, with manual tools, in just twenty months, was widely publicized as one of the miraculous achievements of Stalin and the socialist system. Ironically, the collection of essays and sketches entitled *The Stalin White-Sea–Baltic Canal* (1934; recently reprinted in Russia) to which some of the prominent intellectuals and writers, such as Maxim Gorky, Aleksei Tolstoy, Valentin Kataev, Vera Inber, Victor Shklovsky, and M. Zoshchenko, contributed with various degrees of willingness, was soon banned and became a bibliographical rarity, since many of its Chekist heroes and its eminent authors (such as Bruno Jasienski) fell in the Great Purge, and their names were destined to obliteration.[10]

What the government did endeavor to keep secret was the unbearable living conditions of the prisoners, the scantiness of food, the insufficiency of medical aid, the deaths by freezing in the work sites. Between 200,000 and 300,000 prisoners participated in the project, at least 100,000 at a time; the mortality rate among them reached at least 25 percent, the total estimates ranging from 50,000 to 200,000 dead (Rosefielde 1980: 571). As in most cases of slave labor, the operation proved to be a failure in the long run. Owing to the shortness of the time assigned, the poor supplies of proper building materials, and the exhaustion of the workers, the canal was dug too shallow for larger-scale navigation. But this did not become apparent until later.

The needs of labor organization and technical expertise led to the transfer of some of the surviving intellectuals from hard labor to lifesaving white-collar jobs. It is at this point in the history of the Gulag that the concept *vytashchit'*, "to drag someone out" (from the general duties to easier jobs), came into use. Another lifesaving procedure was the artful padding of worksheets—paradoxically, reforging involved teaching the intelligentsia in the camps to reject honesty as a prima facie value. But the greatest corruption stemmed from the policy of privileging criminal offenders: deemed socially close to the working class, they became the ones most likely to benefit from amnesties as well as soft jobs and power positions in the camps. The code of the Russian criminal underground forbade the so-called "honest thieves" to work; those who worked, and especially those who collaborated with the authorities, were termed "bitches" and punished at the slightest opportunity. The pressures of the reforging increased the numbers of the "bitches"; and when the "bitches" became leaders of work teams, their defensiveness and lack of moral scruple led to the most cruel abuse of other inmates. Confronted with the "no work, no food" scheme, the "honest thieves" kept themselves in provisions by terrorizing their political campmates, appropriating their belongings, and getting part of the production output of the "contras" recorded as their own. Political prisoners would work themselves to death, yet their food rations, insufficient even if fully provided, were based on only a part of their output (and then further reduced by regular in-camp theft).

In the early thirties labor camps spread over the territory of the USSR, especially its arctic regions. The prisoners built railways, roads, industrial complexes, and cities around them; they manned the construction works and coal, lead, and gold mines, as well as the development of whole regions, like the gold-rich frigid Kolyma. The worst lot was that of forced-labor pioneers sent to set up brand new camps and work sites: they did not have even minimal accommodations until they had built them themselves. The mortality rate on such new projects was much higher than in veteran camp sites.

The "corrective-labor" publicity experiment did not last long: disclosures of the amount of convict labor systematically used in the development of the country's economy could undermine claims about the superiority of the socialist system. Stalin was intent on fostering an untroubled image of socialist well-being, a vast Potyomkin village that beguiled Lion Feuchtwanger, Bernard Shaw, H. G. Wells, Walter Benjamin, and other visitors from the West. By the mid thirties the network of labor camps disappeared from public view, hidden like a sewage system, to which Sol-

zhenitsyn compares it in *The Gulag Archipelago*. The need for conceal-
ment increased when the politics of terror and the economics of slave
labor became mutually supportive, though the weight of the secrecy lay
not with the existence of the camps but with their centrality for the functioning of the regime. On the "ideological front," on the eve of the Great
Terror (see Conquest 1990) the attribution of criminality to the "relics of
the capitalist past" was largely replaced by Stalin's creative contribution
to Marxism—the theory of the intensification of the class struggle in the
period of socialist construction.

Having demolished the left and the right opposition to the "party line"
by the mid thirties, Stalin sought to destroy the very possibility of opposition to his rule. As the Hungarian writer and Gulag survivor Jószef
Lengyel would remark, the common denominator of the repression of
the White Guards and the Kronstadt sailors in the twenties and of the Old
Bolsheviks or the foreign Communist refugees in Russia in the thirties
was "the principle that 'He who once dared lift his hand against any . . .
authority, can be expected to dare to do so again'" (1973: 48). The arrests
of the late thirties were the result of vengeful and prophylactic purges
—yet the fact that they swept away ordinary apolitical people was not
unrelated to the demand for slave labor. Each unit of the secret police
had its quotas of arrests just like every industrial plant had its production
quotas. A significant percentage of arrests was made on the basis of voluntary denunciations: a person could perish in the camps because someone wanted his apartment, or her job, or a victim for career-oriented
"vigilance." Yet after Kirov's assassination in December 1934, the inflow
of victims was intensified by the exponential proliferation of new dossiers: each detainee was pressured (and since the summer of 1937 routinely tortured) to make depositions against several others still at large.[11]

The dynamic of the ensuing developments in the Gulag was shaped by
the fluctuations in the supply and demand of slave labor: a deadly regime
periodically depleted the labor force, and since the set production targets had to be reached, the camp authorities would attempt to conserve
the remaining labor force by improving the prisoners' lot. In the years
of the most intense terror, 1938–1939, there was no shortage of prison
labor—hence the conditions of the camp inmates were at their worst. A
significant percentage of the people arrested at that time were shot in
the cellars of the NKVD; a wave of in-camp trials and executions swept
through the "Archipelago" as well. In many camps, however, hard labor
and starvation were sufficient instruments of a somewhat slower extermination.

In 1939, after Nikolai Yezhov was replaced by Lavrenty Beria at the
head of the NKVD, the number of arrests decreased, and there was even
a small wave of pre-trial releases. The life of the camp inmates became

somewhat less precarious: in-camp executions were discontinued, and a whole generation of their perpetrators fell, together with Yezhov himself. The attempts of the medical personnel and the more liberal of the camp authorities to keep people alive improved the balance between conservation of the work force and fulfillment of the plan.[12] Yet the camps soon received replenishments from the eastern regions of Poland annexed to the USSR in 1939, and in 1940 from the newly annexed Baltic States and Romanian territories. After Hitler's assault on the USSR in 1941, the critical demand for an immediate output in the lumber camps led to a maximum exploitation of the labor force and a total disregard for the disabled, who were often left to die of exhaustion and pellagra (Razgon 1994: 341–46). A relative relaxation followed the first Soviet victories, and American lend-lease flour improved the diet of the inmates of the Far Eastern camps. Yet during and after the war several whole nationalities were transferred to Kazakhstan and Siberia, with the weaker dying and the more prominent put behind barbed wire in the process (Conquest 1960). Great numbers of younger people were sentenced to camp terms for breaches of labor discipline. Toward the end of the war came German, Alsace-Lorrainian, Japanese, Italian, Austrian, and other POWs,[13] and the "Vlasovites" (former Soviet soldiers who had allowed the Germans to recruit them and had served under General Vlasov); new consignments arrived from the Baltic states and Western Ukraine. At the same time many of the Soviet officers and soldiers were arrested, lest the weapons of those who had defeated Hitler should be turned against Stalin.[14] The camps also swallowed the *Ostarbeiter* returning from forced labor in Germany, Cossack migrants turned back in accordance with the Yalta agreement (see Bethell 1974 and Tolstoy 1977), and veteran emigrants from Russia captured by Soviet agencies amidst the post-war chaos in Middle and Western Europe (Stalin must have feared the growth of the Russian diaspora). A number of foreign citizens, such as Raoul Wallenberg,[15] were arrested or kidnapped for various reasons by the Soviet forces in East European countries or detained by the local Communist governments and handed over to the Soviet police; many of them proceeded to the camps. At the end of the war with Japan in August 1945, there were massive arrests in the Northern Chinese territories, especially in the city of Kharbin, until then one of the main centers of the Russian emigration.[16]

In the first year after World War II, the principle of extermination by labor was again put into practice in special-regime *katorga* camps (*GA* 5: 1; Conquest 1978: 60, 102) for people who had in various ways, willingly or unwillingly, collaborated with the Germans. After twelve working hours the prisoners were locked up in overcrowded tents or barracks, often without blankets in the coldest weather: everything was done in this closed space rather than in lavatories, dining rooms, or medical wards. A part of their rations, insufficient to begin with, was appropriated by the criminal convicts in charge of the delivery, and the time for whatever sleep their conditions allowed was reduced by roll calls and searches. On their clothing each wore an identification made up of a letter and three numerical digits. Solzhenitsyn writes that the first "alphabet" in Vorkuta (about 28,000 prisoners) was dead within a year (*GA* V: 1); it must have contained particularly strong people to have lasted that long. This was the darkest hour of the Archipelago since 1938.

In other camps of the late forties, the balance between the production plans and the mortality toll was similar to that of 1939–40 and 1942–43. Most of the victims of the Great Terror were by now sick or dead. The post-war arrests had brought in people who had had contacts with foreigners,[17] including ex officio contacts with the American personnel in charge of the wartime lend-lease transfers of the American equipment to Russia. There were great numbers of former "collaborators," both in the narrow and in the broad sense of the word, the latter including anyone who had held any job—down to street-sweeping—under the German occupation. The largest post-war "wave" was made up of Lithuanians, Latvians, Estonians, Moldavians, and Western Ukrainians.[18] The most prominent members of the upper and middle classes of the pre-war Baltic republics had been deported in the spring of 1941; the purge was resumed after the war and extended to former members of unions, parties, and even student corporations.[19] There was also a hunt for alleged or actual Ukrainian Banderovites (followers of national resistance leader Bandera) and Lithuanian "forest brothers" ("bandits" in the Soviet vocabulary), who had been waging an armed struggle against Soviet rule and who nowadays, in their newly independent countries, are regarded as heroic freedom fighters—despite the known brutality of their erstwhile practices. A minor but suggestive wave of arrests brought in second-generation victims, such as Zayara Vesyolaya or Irina Maevskaya, who had been too young in 1937: if, upon accession to the throne, a Sultan kills his brothers in a seraglio, he might well be apprehensive about their offspring. The prophylactic terror continued until Stalin's death in March 1953, with a high in 1949, the year of the second-round arrests and massive official anti-Semitism.

The 1934–53 period is the one most thoroughly documented in memoir literature because of the significant proportion of intellectuals imprisoned in those years. By the late thirties, when the camps already dotted the whole territory of the country, clustering particularly densely in the northern regions, the Urals, and Kazakhstan, their functioning had become relatively standardized. Therefore, the memoirs pertaining to these two decades paint a more or less uniform picture of the inmates' conditions, one that most often provides a basis for comparison with the state of the art at other periods or in rival camp systems.

Here is a sketch of this default case. When not executed by the authorities or murdered by the criminal convicts, purge victims faced a lethal combination of chronic hunger, overwork, and neglect. About half of their calorie intake consisted of bread (on the average, about a pound a day); the rest came from trash soup (*balanda*) cooked from calculated amounts of potatoes, groats, fish, sugar, and fats; sometimes they would also get a few spoonfuls of lean porridge. The portions of cooked foods were usually shrunk by theft; the bread rations were cut and the porridge denied if a prisoner did not meet the production quotas. Few could possibly meet the quotas since these were too high even for skilled, able-bodied laborers: as the prisoners got less food, they had even less strength to work and thus entered a "vicious spiral" (Ekart 1954: 60). According to Shalamov, in Kolyma a prisoner could reach the stage of lethal exhaustion in three weeks (the time span is more often given as closer to three months, but much depended on the season and political constellations). The drop in the output enraged the overseers, who would then send the prisoners to deadly punishment cells, subject them to beatings, or, in 1938, charge them with "sabotage," which was punished by death. Prisoners were now divided into "brigades," and the rations were calculated in accordance with a whole "brigade's" production. Thus fellow inmates were induced to police one another, demand output from even the weakest, and help drive each other to death. As noted above, a drastic increase in the mortality rate sometimes led to a temporary improvement in the prisoners' conditions since production "deadlines" could have a "literal meaning" for the authorities as well (Stajner 1988: 77). Yet the prisoners could not afford to wait for such contingencies any more than they could rely on their physical stamina; salvation could come from being "dragged out" from the general duties, such as mining, construction, or lumbering, on which the overwhelming majority of the camp inmates were employed, to camp-maintenance and white-collar jobs. At the "general works" the amount of calories expended always exceeded the amount of calories received; this deficit, with the addition of scurvy and pellagra, was the main reason for the death toll. The number of prisoners who died in the Gulag between the beginning of the Great Terror in 1934 and Stalin's death in 1953 is usually estimated at 20 to 25 million (see Panin 1976: 92–93n; Conquest 1990: 485–89; Rosefielde 1981: 51–83).

At the worst times, unlike common criminals and people with lighter charges (such as "anti-Soviet propaganda"), the "enemies of the people" were denied the possibility of extricating themselves, at least temporarily, from the "vicious spiral" by being transferred to medical, engineering, administrative, or maintenance work. Yet even when access to softer jobs was not officially banned, the availability of such employment was very limited.

In the thirties and forties the situation was exacerbated by the policy of keeping the political prisoners[20] together with the criminal offenders, whom the authorities treated more leniently even though the notion that they were "socially close" to the "working class" was wearing out. Against the background of cynical lip service to "re-education," the criminal convicts both served and corrupted the camp authorities. They were the first to get the softer jobs and power positions, which they seldom failed to abuse. Thus the purge victims were trapped between the authorities, the criminals, and the climate.

In 1947 the special hard-labor regime of the punitive camps was partly relaxed; the conditions in the other camps were likewise slightly improved. To some extent this may have been associated with the international publication of witness accounts and their impact on influential figures such as Eleanor Roosevelt (see Zernova 1990: 150). However, the main reason must have lain in the need for convict labor, which prevailed over the drive to eliminate the undesirables: the war with Germany had considerably reduced the labor force in the whole country.

In the post-war years new kinds of brutalization spread over the camps. The so-called "honest thieves" regarded those professional criminals who had served in the army during the war as supporters of the regime: due to the resulting abuse, many of the latter were now converted into "bitches" (see p. 17 above) with a grudge against their former associates. This led to a ruthless in-camp warfare between the "bitches" and the "honest thieves" (see Shalamov's 1959 sketch "'Such'ia' voina" ["The 'Bitch' War"] 1998, 2:56–76). The sociology of the political prisoners had also undergone changes: the place of a large percentage of the meek victims of the Great Terror was taken by yesterday's tough soldiers and by people from the recently annexed territories. The loyal supporters of the regime still remaining behind barbed wire were now outnumbered by active non-conformers. Moreover, according to Solzhenitsyn (*GA* V: 2), at a certain point in the late forties the terror regime overshot its aims: the newly introduced twenty-five-year sentences left people no hope of living until their release and created a devil-may-care attitude. The massive presence of war veterans in the camps intimidated the professional criminals, and, largely under the influence of the Western Ukrainians, who tended to reject the humanistic inhibitions of veteran inmates, prisoners began to assassinate stool pigeons, thus facilitating organized disobedience. In 1952–54 strikes broke out in many camps, often leading to rebellions; they were brutally suppressed, sometimes with the use of tanks,[21] though "diplomacy" was resorted to in moderate cases (Filshtinsky 1994: 170–80).

In 1952–53 Stalin was planning a new wave of mass terror, and it is quite possible that his closest associates—Beria, Kaganovich, Molotov, Khrushchev—were slated for scapegoating. Yet these people, unlike the Old Bolsheviks purged in 1937–39, knew their boss's methods. According to one theory (Avtorkhanov 1976), they may have helped him off the stage —whether immediately before or, more likely, after his stroke in early March 1953 (see also Malia 1994: 311–12). If these conjectures are right, then despotism was destroyed by its own inner dynamics. One should not derive comfort from such a thought, yet one may find it supported by a partial analogy from the history of the Gulag. The improvement of the prisoners' diet in the early fifties (when the supply of the convict labor dwindled) actually enhanced their resistance: "Freed from the urgent day-to-day worry over food, the prisoners had time to think about other things that were wrong, and started considering their position as a whole. They quickly realized that though certain marginal improvements had been made, their fundamental predicament remained the same. . . . The government had, quite literally, given them food for thought" (Scholmer 1954: 232–33). One can only speculate whether this process would have been impeded by the new mass influx of slave labor. The scenario consisted in provoking pogroms, and, in an act of, as it were, protection, deporting the Jewish population to Birobidzhan and Siberia.[22] Instead, on March 27, Beria gave amnesty to prisoners sentenced to five years or less, thus releasing huge numbers of common criminals. The sentences of political prisoners were, at the time, seldom shorter than eight years, and the "Beria amnesty" further promoted the unrest among them.

In a bid for power, Beria also initiated the first de-Stalinization move: on April 4 the country awoke to the news that the doctors arrested during the loud anti-Semitic campaign ostensibly directed against "murderers in white gowns"[23] were exonerated and, if still alive, released from prisons. This was generally taken for a sign that the terror would subside. In a brief struggle among Stalin's heirs, Beria was defeated and, in July 1953, executed. The victorious Khrushchev continued the liberalization. Though uprisings in the camps were suppressed with the usual brutality, it became obvious that the Gulag was facing a crisis (see also Werth 1997: 258–68); the uprisings were therefore followed by a dramatic improvement in camp conditions as well as by releases of individual political prisoners, especially in 1955.[24] After the Twentieth Communist Party Congress in 1956, where Khrushchev made his Secret Speech about Stalin's crimes, great numbers of Communist purge victims were exonerated. Special release commissions came to the camps: it is estimated that 8 million of the 12 million inmates were set free (Conquest 1990: 478). A large proportion of those left behind had actually been Nazi collaborators in the wartime years (the "*polizei*")—they would be encountered, and disdained (usually for good reason), by the dissidents imprisoned in the sixties. In the years 1956–61 the camp regime was the most humane in Gulag history.

The years of "the thaw" (1953–64) and the so-called stagnation (1964–86) have been aptly redescribed as "enlightened Stalinism" (Avtorkhanov 1959: 343): the bureaucratic party dictatorship continued with fewer "excesses." Food shortages were no longer allowed to turn into famines: if harvests were poor, Khrushchev preferred to buy grain abroad, whereas Stalin had exported it while millions of peasants were starving in the Ukraine. The ratio of terror and goal-oriented propaganda was reversed —propaganda took priority and terror became punitive instead of prophylactic.[25] The remaining "excesses" mostly pertained to deadly repression of "economic opposition" (Bukovsky 1979: 189–93)—not just embezzlers but also official proponents of economic reform, traders in foreign currency, and individuals whose business initiatives represented ideologically premature sprouts of a free market system (see also Geller [Heller] and Nekrich 1986: 633–34).

The removal of the brutal and unpredictable Stalinist terror led to a revival of an intense intellectual and cultural life in the big cities and to renewed hopes for the future of the country, the rule of law, and human rights. These hopes were premature. The year 1956 also saw the Soviet invasion of Hungary. And 1961, the year of the open de-Stalinization campaign at the Twenty-Second Congress of the Communist Party, was also the year when the regime in concentration camps was again considerably tightened. Here the "thaw" yielded to the "squeeze" (*zazhim* [the background of Felix Roziner's novel *A Certain Finkelmeyer*]) earlier than in the media.

In several ways the regulations became more stringent than before 1956; for instance, the prisoners' rights to buy food in camp kiosks and to receive food parcels from relatives were severely restricted. The pressures of "political re-education" and the attempts to recruit individual prisoners into cooperation with the KGB were intensified almost beyond endurance. Though the working hours were now not so long as under Stalin and the diet was no longer deadly, the prisoners were still deliberately subjected to chronic undernourishment. The "prescribed hunger" (Levi 1990: 42), no longer an incentive for work, turned into a torture instrument, along with untreated diseases. It sapped the energy that could have gone into active resistance and served as a means of revenge for any show of independence.[26] Judging by Marchenko's *My Testimony,* the main cause of the prisoners' death now lay in medical neglect. Indeed, in 1972 the dissident poet Yury Galanskov died in the Barashevo camp as a result of medical malpractice (Galanskov 1980: 10); Marchenko himself died of a mistreatment in the Chistopol prison on December 8, 1986.

In 1961 the political prisoners were transferred to the camp complex in the Mordovian autonomous republic, near the town of Potma. The new policy was to separate them from the criminal convicts in order to protect the latter from political infection.[27] The segregation was not always maintained, if only because rowdies sometimes deliberately committed "political" offenses in order to be transferred from the camps in which they had come into conflict with fellow inmates. Where the presence of the criminal convicts was more massive, the authorities could inflict additional suffering on a recalcitrant political prisoner by inciting the criminals against him and having him badly beaten (Voinovich 1993: 64; cf. Wat 1990: 368–76).[28] In general, however, the new political prisoners of the "stagnation" period were no longer the confused chance purgees; they were actual dissidents, members of national movements or human-rights activists, and they often commanded the criminals' respect for their courage. The attitude of the rowdies to the more eminent among the dissident convicts, to those of whom they had heard in the media, was particularly friendly. In the prison narratives of dissidents, the main criticism of the criminal communities of these less hungry times concerns not their "foreign relations" but the extreme cruelty of their homosexual laws, according to which the passive homosexuals were forever stigmatized, mistreated, and turned into sexual slaves (see Amalrik 1982: 187–88; Guberman 1990: 77–88; Kuznetsov 1979: 53–105; Abramkin 1992: 96–106).

In 1972 political prisoners, especially those able to maintain a contact with foreign media, often with the help of bribed guards, would be moved further from Moscow, to the Perm district in the Urals. The function of political imprisonment was now perceived not as "corrective" but as *incapacitating* and *punitive* (cf. *GA* 7: 2). Since extensive political repression was not supposed to be necessary at the stage of developed socialism, in the mid sixties the practice of incarcerating some of the dissidents in psychiatric institutions gained momentum (see Gluzman 1989); in the seventies it threatened to expand (see Bukovsky 1996: 144–61).

Camp officials who had lost their jobs in the mid fifties were now partly reabsorbed into the cadre of the penal system; and their often wantonly malicious petty persecution of individual prisoners was, to a large extent, motivated by the reduction of their power. The changed ratio between the numbers of prisoners and of KGB operatives left the latter the leisure and the motivation to subject practically *every* political prisoner to recruitment pressures. The ideology of re-education was reduced to abstract lip service combined with concrete attempts to persuade dissidents to renege, "live like everyone" (Marchenko 1987), and cooperate. Forced-labor output considerations played a smaller role in the post-Stalin years. Taking advantage of the housing shortage in the big cities and of the residual romantic enthusiasm of urban youth, Khrushchev had succeeded in manning new construction and agricultural projects in Siberia with free workers. Yet convict labor continued to be used, and may still be used even now, in uranium mines.

By the eighties the long-term ineffectiveness of slave-labor economics had been reconfirmed. As a result of propaganda-related monumentalism, inflexible central planning, disregard for ecology, and, in particular, the deadly waste of know-how and intellectual resources in the Stalin years followed by a partial suppression of creative intelligence under "tired totalitarianism," the Soviet Union found itself facing an economic impasse. Stalinist terror controls over efficiency in workplaces might have delayed the decline, yet the country's growing dependence on trade relations with the West made the regime's insistence that human rights were an internal affair progressively less tenable. The dissidents of the sixties, starting with Andrei Amalrik, had learned to establish contacts with foreign journalists and diplomats; writers had found ways of publishing their works abroad; and millions of ordinary people throughout the country started listening to foreign radio broadcasts despite the government's attempts to jam the transmissions. The KGB could now get away with quietly destroying only those opponents of the regime who had remained unknown to the public: links with foreign media went a long way toward safeguarding individual dissidents' lives.

The losses in Afghanistan heightened the public discontent. Many of the returning veterans of the Afghanistan war bitterly and fearlessly rejected conformism. The nuclear disaster at Chernobyl, and the impossibility of concealing it, provided the decisive stimulus for reform favored by Mikhail Gorbachev, who, however, did not expect his wary changes to develop their own momentum and end in what is now known as the Second Russian Revolution.[29]

The beginning of Gorbachev's *glasnost* and *perestroika* in 1986 meant also a gradual end to political imprisonment in the Soviet Union. One of the last retribution/incapacitation "model-muddle" (Sommer 1976: 16–34) camps for political prisoners, Perm-35 in the Urals, seemed to be surviving on a day-to-day basis when the journalist David Remnick (1994: 270–76) visited it in 1987. He found its cadre embarrassed at their dwindling prestige and looking out for their pensions.[30]

At first, individual case revisions and pardons took place in response to "contrite" appeals; later, almost any letter of appeal or any protest from the West could lead to an individual's release; the process was completed by Yeltsin in 1992. Which is not, however, to imply that since the present convicts in Russian and the former Soviet Republics are common criminals, public opinion need no longer be concerned with the conditions in their penal facilities, especially those for juvenile delinquents.

The events of 1989–92 put a belated end to the gigantic experiment in imposing an artificial social system on a reluctant population. It has not entirely discredited the Communist ideals: what Arthur Koestler (1945) called "the Yogi and the Commissar," the Change from Within and the Change from Without, are still the magnetic poles of our imagination. Yet in 1917 the population of the Russian empire had neither a viable democratic tradition nor a secular ethical practice sufficiently rooted to offset Lenin's emphasis on the "class morality" conception of "good" as whatever serves the cause. The Marxist dogma of the need for the dictatorship of the proletariat after a socialist revolution was used to justify the Bolsheviks' uncompromising drive for total control; the ideal of the Change from Without was contaminated by the expediencies of power politics. Humanist ethics was easier to dispense with when renamed "bourgeois morality" (paradoxically, the mid thirties saw the return of the worst aspects of "bourgeois" morality in family life). The replacement of justice and law by the principle of expediency (*tselesoobraznost'*) as well as the Trotskian mot juste about not entering the socialist state in "white gloves" (cf. Shteppa 1957: 78) were routinely resorted to for defusing moral dilemmas, sympathy, guilt. The principle that the end justifies the means was publicly criticized yet widely practiced. "The end" was all too readily confused with "the means of production": the building of the heavy industry and of the social structures that would support it justified, as it were, the "temporary" abuse of living people,[31] replaceable "cogs" in the state machine. The forced-labor camps were an ultimate expression of this attitude; the search for alternative values in present-day Russia may be considerably impeded by residual habits of dehumanizing thought.

Yet though the Gulag grew out of specific socio-political and ideological circumstances, it was a complex of moral liabilities of a general nature that allowed it to rise. Consensus-based democratic institutions can restrain the effects of such tendencies as a blank disregard for individual dignity, the treatment of people as instruments or as obstacles, a single-minded drive toward a maximization of immediate profits, blind political faith, and psychological defenses against sympathy. Yet to *reverse* these tendencies one needs "the Yogi," the individual commitment to sensitive interpersonal respect. *Sub specie aeternitatis,* literary explorations of the Gulag experience create conditions for the formation and refinement of this commitment. In their immediate social and historical context, however, these literary works played a significant role in accelerating the erosion of the Archipelago and, with it, the system that it had buttressed for seven decades.

2 The Literary Corpus

The memoir literature about the Gulag published over the past seventy years now forms a considerable library. To trace the historical development of this corpus, I focus on the ideological positions of landmark works as well as on their responses to the pressures created by the reception context. I base the periodization on the time of writing and the time when the narratives were made public; these are not always the same, but both are linked to the time of the authors' release.[1] Testimonies that belong to the same period usually share a number of ethical goals or shades of attitude, which influence their selection of materials in similar ways and generate similar topoi. By contrast, each book's structure and tone are associated less with the common concerns than with the individual experience and personality of the author. Yet the literary merit of an individual memoir does not rest on its formal features alone. As William Wordsworth has shown in his study of epitaphs (1974: 48–99), it is the congruence of the content and the stance that lays the foundation for the aesthetic appeal of multi-functional texts.

* * *

From the very beginning, narratives that dealt with political imprisonment in Soviet Russia bifurcated into the predominantly factographic materials in émigré publications and the predominantly fictional ones in official Soviet literature.[2] The latter downplayed the extent of the Bolshevik terror and vindicated its acts by highlighting the iniquities of counterrevolutionaries. The bad guys were the first to attack; the "contras," the "wreckers," and the "kulaks" showed "their true colors" and were removed from the stage in accordance with the principle of "the liquidation of the bourgeoisie as a class." The formula "as a class" denoted "not as individuals" and implied dispossession, yet owing to its categorical accent and sword-swishing onomatopoeia, it quite truthfully evoked an out-of-the-limelight physical clean sweep (cf. Leggett 1981: 113–15). What happened to the deported after the curtain fell, where they were taken, whether they lived or died, was of no concern to the authors: the "hostile elements" were supposed to be getting what they deserved.

The reflections of the earliest purges in Soviet fiction played on conventional humanistic expectations: the inner conflicts required for the attenuation of the good-guys-versus-bad-guys pattern were provided by the tension between personal sympathies and the ideological *soznatelnost'* ("political consciousness"; see Hosking 1980: 13). Tellingly, what a "repentant Chekist" would regret was not the atrocities that he had perpetrated but the moments of compassion or kinship that he had felt for an individual "enemy" who was to be brought to justice (see Geller 1974: 95–108).

In the Western press the roles of the goats and the sheep were reversed. In the contemporary British press Cheka prisons were endowed with "a sinister glamour and a tragic halo," like the images of "the Paris prisons under the Reign of Terror" (Sarolea 1926: vii). In the Nazi Germany of the thirties, stories of Soviet *Strafarbeitkolonien* doubled as anti-Semitic propaganda (Kaminski 1990: 38; Dallin and Nikolaevsky 1947: 313–14), yet the material was carefully studied, with a view to "improvement," by the officials in charge of building a rival camp empire.

Sober firsthand accounts of the Soviet prisons and camps by emigrants (e.g., Melgunova-Stepanova, 1928) had to compete with these market-friendly schemata. The actual situation in the first Soviet camps was for the most part both simpler and grimmer. The prisoners suffered from dirt, cold, lice, typhus, crowding, hunger, uncertainty, indignities, and occasional sadistic humiliation; yet in the Solovki there were also reprieves, lighter jobs, amateur theatricals, and (propagandistic) in-camp newspapers (see Gorcheva 1996). Employment in these frameworks saved many a human life.

Yet in most cases, not for very long. Though vast numbers of educated people were imprisoned in the first decades of the Gulag, few got a chance to tell their story. Hundreds fell in the wave of executions that swept the Solovetsky camp in 1929; thousands perished owing to torture in the Sekirnaia, typhus, deadly conditions at the White Sea canal works in 1931–33 (*GA* 3: 3; Geller 1974: 135–57), or unalleviated hardships at "pioneering" northern camps. Nor could the prisoners released in the twenties and thirties publish their memoirs at that time, unless they emigrated or escaped abroad.[3]

Stalin's administration was reluctant to allow camp graduates to leave the country. However, in the early thirties, when hard currency was needed for industrial expansion, people whose foreign friends or relatives paid their travel and "passport expenses" were sometimes allowed to emigrate. In early 1934, a former English governess of an affluent Russian family thus ransomed her favorite ward, Iulia de Beausobre, the future author of *The Woman Who Could Not Die* (1938), who had been released (*aktirovanna*) from the camps owing to ruined health.[4] In the thirties protests abroad could still lead to the repatriation of foreign nationals even if they had seen the inside of Soviet prisons, as did the Croatian Communist Ante Ciliga and the Belgian-born Trotsky supporter Victor Serge.

For fugitives, the only feasible choices before World War II were China and Finland, neighboring countries that would not extradite them. The Chinese option was taken by the White Guard officer I. M. Zaitsev[5] and by the defector N. I. Kiselev-Gromov; both published memoirs. One of the first to take the Finnish option was the White-Guard officer A. Klinger (see 1990 [1928]), who had escaped, with the help of forged documents, from the Solovki transit station on Popov Island. Crossing the Finnish border was at first possible with the help of smugglers (Doubassoff 1926: 276–305); by the later twenties this ended. A group escape from Kem on the White Sea to Finland is recorded in the shrewd 1926 memoir by J. D. Bezsonov. One of the four participants of Bezsonov's group of fugitives, S. A. Malsagoff, a Chechen, gave the first systematic description of the Solovetsky island camps.[6]

Two fairly distinguished prisoners made spectacular escapes to Finland from camps near Kem. After arduous trekking through marshes and hills, biologist Vladimir Tchernavin crossed the border with his wife and child in 1932; sports writer Ivan Solonevich, with his son Yury and his brother Boris, who was escaping from a neighboring camp, crossed in August 1934. Tchernavin's *I Speak for the Silent* (1935) is a factually rich memoir that produces the impression of total reliability. In addition to describing the camps, it sheds light on the regime's assault on scientists accused of "wrecking" for their opposition to the ecologically ruinous expansion of the Murmansk fishing industry.[7] The flamboyant *Rossiia v kontslagere* [*Russia in the Concentration Camp*] by Solonevich is probably the best-written camp narrative of the pre-war years. First serialized in the

Parisian émigré newspaper *Poslednie novosti* in 1936, it was reissued many times and translated into a number of languages. The title of the 1938 British version was *Russia in Chains.*

Whereas Tchernavin sought to mobilize Western public opinion against the Soviet regime, Solonevich mainly addressed the Russian émigré audience, to warn the enthusiasts who considered going to the "motherland of the international proletariat" in order to participate in the "socialist construction." His message was that Soviet economic activities were wasting national resources, that the fruits of dedicated work were appropriated by the hollowly careerist new ruling class, and that any efforts to promote the public good would be ultimately futile. Solonevich describes, for instance, being sent to a colony for juvenile delinquents where the club director persuaded him to organize the construction of athletic grounds for the children (otherwise kept in deprivation, hunger, and idleness). The boys welcomed the chance to work in the forest outside the camp, yet a few took this opportunity to run away, and some of these drowned in the swamp: thus, in the particular situation, the best intentions led to dire results.

For Solonevich the Soviet society is a giant "drinking house," *kabak,* a rhyming euphemism for a not-quite printable Russian synonym of "whorehouse." Here, as in Zola's *Assomoir,* energies are wasted, family life is perverted, lower-class children go hungry, and predators feast. Joining the system in order to beat it, in Svirlag, a centralized system of camps around the river Svir and the town of Medvezhegorsk, Solonevich exploits the residual reforging publicity campaign. His masterstroke is a bid to organize an in-camp athletics competition, a Potyomkin-village event with a great propaganda and prestige potential. The preparations for the show involve improved rations for himself and his "athletes" and give him the freedom of movement that facilitates his escape.

The success of his memoir among the émigré readership placed Solonevich in a position of influence in the Russian diaspora. Having moved to Bulgaria, he founded a monarchist publishing house, Golos Rossii (Voice of Russia), and launched a newspaper by the same name. In the late thirties, because of some oddities in their behavior, the near miraculous escape of the Solonevich trio *after* the passing of the June 7 law (which made attempts to flee abroad punishable by death) gave rise to rumors that they were Soviet agents *allowed* to get abroad in order to monitor émigré communities (see Prianishnikov 1979: 336–44). It stands to reason that Solonevich might not have told the whole truth about his collaboration with the camp authorities and that the secret police may have condoned his escape in exchange for promises. Indeed, a streak of the authorial persona's all-too-flexible opportunism does show in *Russia in Chains,* and the adventure-story flavor of its account of the escape is almost Hollywoodian. Yet if there was a deal, Solonevich must have refused to keep the terms. "Lubyanka"[8] retaliated: in February 1938, shortly after Solonevich received the news of his father's death in a Soviet concentration camp, a bomb was brought into his office inside a mock package of books; the explosion fatally wounded his wife and killed his editorial secretary.

In Germany, where Solonevich moved with his son, he became a Nazi supporter, believing that Hitler would free Russia from Stalin. This expectation was widespread at the time; the killings of Jews was not considered too high a price—on the contrary, the propaganda pamphlets published by Solonevich on the eve of the war display an ideological anti-Semitism (not evident in his camp memoirs). After the war he made his way to Argentina and launched the monarchist newspaper *Nasha strana* [*Our Country*]. Eventually he was deported to Uruguay, where he died in 1953, after a stomach operation, under circumstances that his followers regarded as suspicious (see Foreword to Solonevich 1968: 5–7).

Outside Russian émigré circles, the consciousness-raising effect of the early Gulag testimonies was severely limited. Sometimes it was subverted by the individual features of the book, such as Bezsonov's self-portrait (prior to his religious conversion in prison) as a dissolute, supercilious, and brutal White Guard officer, or de Beausobre's emphasis on the mystical religious experience that sustained her. Solonevich, who places images of human suffering into high relief, still inadvertently creates the impression that the camps, located—almost symbolically—at the outer geographical limits of the country, were a marginal, though inevitable, phenomenon. For this reason, *Russia in Chains* may have been less detrimental to Soviet propaganda than the 1938 memoirs of Ante Ciliga, who presented the Soviet regime, with its achievement of economic growth through an unprecedented exploitation of the people by the bureaucracy, as a betrayal of the October revolution. Ciliga was the first to say that an understanding of "the Russian Enigma"[9] can be attained only through prison experience. However, he was never held in the camps, and much of his information about them is imprecise. Indeed, one of the intrinsic reasons for the limited effect of early Gulag memoirs on Western readers' imagination was lack of mutual confirmation: a uniformity of practice had not yet been achieved in the camps, and they were already too numerous for any veteran to command an overview.

Indeed, since the victims of punitive treatment in the Sekirnaia prison had almost as little chance to survive as those on the execution lists, most memoirists had only hearsay information about the worst atrocities. Their wish to present comprehensive information led to occasional inaccuracies. These, especially if combined with touches of sensationalism, allowed Soviet propaganda to discredit the accounts.[10] As to successful escapes, they were usually possible only if one was not totally depleted: most of the fugitive authors had been spared the lower rungs of the "vicious spiral." For all the verve of *Russia in Chains* and all the wisdom of *I Speak for the Silent,* the absence of personal experience of a prolonged confrontation with death limited their power. To keep himself fit for the escape, Solonevich consistently evaded the general works and remoter camps: unlike Solzhenitsyn after 1949, he did not feel obliged to immerse himself in that destructive element. His book contains acute observations, soul-searching dialogues, hilarious incidents, strident accounts of individual fates, and details of excellently masterminded adventure; yet it does not contain what Charlotte Delbo (1995: 115, 225) has called the "useless knowledge" of extremity.[11] It lacks—and (to its credit) does not attempt to simulate—the eschatological depth that characterizes the memoirs of people who did have an intimate and lengthy knowledge of the rock bottom of survival.[12]

Having disapproved of the Soviet regime a priori, most of the early memoirists regarded the camps as its natural extension and were not surprised by the abuses they witnessed. Their tone of weary sarcasm (and what is sometimes read as a "bittersweet" sagacity "peculiar to Eastern Europe" [Lourie 1975: 100]) was not suited to elicit an intense emotional response. However, the main reasons for the relative ineffectiveness of the consciousness-raising function of their books lay not so much in their own features as in an unfavorable reception-context. Western left-wing ideologues tended to protect their illusions by treating the testimony of the former prisoners as the private grievances of disgruntled individuals. The business world was mainly interested in the opportunities presented by the timber-dumping, tractor-buying young Soviet Union. The contrast between the newsreels of the achievements of Stalin's first Five-Year Plan and the newsreels of the burning of foodstuffs to maintain prices in the USA sufficed to distract public attention from the signals that Soviet economic growth had a grim underside. The discordant voices of camp veterans seemed as marginal as the out-of-the-way camps they had left behind.

* * *

While World War II temporarily removed the Gulag from the public agenda in the West, a group of people, mainly of Polish origin, made it their major concern. The Polish contingent of the Gulag had consisted of Communists arrested during Stalin's Grand Charades and a six- or seven-digit number of victims of the Molotov-Ribbentrop agreement. Seventeen days after Hitler's invasion of Poland on September 1, 1939, Stalin moved his troops across the Polish eastern border and, in accordance with the pact, occupied the territories up to the Bug River. The Soviet forces took hundreds of thousands of POWs, even though the Polish army showed almost no resistance on the eastern front. About 15,000 Polish officers,[13] including some of the country's intellectual élite (considered not amenable to Communist re-education) were massacred in 1940 near Katyn; several thousand more were executed near Starobelsk and Kalinin.[14] Trainloads of middle-class citizens, members of various political parties, and just conspicuous personalities were deported from the Soviet-occupied territories to the camps. The people who had fled eastward from the Nazis entered a high-risk category if they refused to accept Soviet citizenship. Many of the Poles and Polish Jews (including future Israeli prime minister Menachem Begin) who had sought refuge in Lithuania were arrested after the de facto annexation of the Baltic states in 1940.

In the camps, the luckier of the Poles fought the calorie deficit by bartering their clothes for food. Their possessions and bodies were thinning down when, in August 1941, because of the panic caused by the initial Soviet defeats in the war against Germany, Stalin decided on an amnesty for Poles, a gesture to the Sikorski government in exile and its British hosts. General Wladyslaw Anders was then released from a Soviet prison and authorized to form a Polish military force to help the Soviet army fight Germany. Polish evacuees and amnestied prisoners made their way, often with enormous difficulties, to his recruiting centers. Yet Stalin treated the Polish Corps with suspicion; their supplies were reduced and Anders's activities obstructed. Anders was eventually allowed to take his soldiers to Persia, where they obtained international assistance; later they distinguished themselves in the battle of Monte Cassino (see Anders 1949). The Polish citizens who had not managed to leave the Soviet Union with Anders were allowed to repatriate in the first years after the war. In 1946 an anonymous collection of exile and camp memoirs, *The Dark Side of the Moon* (with, for the record, some clearly anti-Semitic touches), was published in England with T. S. Eliot's preface. The reports of ex-prisoners to the Documentation Office of Anders's army also led to a number of publications concerning the Soviet penal system, in particular to Zamorski and Zwierniak's *La Justice Soviétique* (1945), some materials of which were also used in David J. Dallin and Boris I. Nikolaevsky's *Forced Labor in Soviet Russia* (1947), the first full-length academic study of the camps and the first systematic argument that the camp system was an *organic* element of the Soviet social structure. Memoirs were also written by several Jewish beneficiaries of the Sikorski amnesty (Gilboa, Ekart), who were not, however, accepted into Anders's Corps.[15]

About four thousand Jews had left Russia with Anders's army (Anders

1949: 112–13). Among them was Menachem Begin, liberated from a camp near Medvezhegorsk in 1941. Owing to the urgencies of his involvement in the Zionist struggle, his *White Nights,* a memoir of Soviet prisons and camps, would come out only in 1957.

The most significant *literary* product of the Sikorski amnesty for the Gulag corpus was *A World Apart* by Gustav Herling-Hrudzinski. A student with Communist affiliations, Herling had fled from Warsaw after the German invasion. Arrested by the NKVD in an attempt to cross the border to the still independent Lithuania, he was imprisoned for about a year and a half in the camp of Yertsevo of the Kargopol group.[16] Released in 1942, exhausted by a hunger strike in protest against the authorities' sabotage of the Sikorski amnesty, he joined Anders's army. His book *Inny swiat. Zapiski sowieckie,* written in 1949–50, was published in 1951 in English (*A World Apart*) and later in other languages. The epigraph is a quotation from Dostoevsky's *The House of the Dead:* "Here there is a world apart, unlike everything else, with laws of its own, its own manners and customs, and here is the house of the living dead—life as nowhere else and a people apart."[17]

Herling's narrative oscillates between emotionally charged authorial discourse and elegantly laconic reportage. The former is often heavily metaphoric. Herling was one of the first to suggest that the goal of torture at the interrogation period was, first and foremost, not to discover any "truth" but to break the prisoner's personality, "dismantle" it, and "reassemble" it, prior to dispatching him to the camps. This process is described through a combination of engineering and surgical metaphors. For example:

> thoughts and emotions become loosened in their original positions and rattle against each other like the parts of a broken down machine; the driving belts connecting the past and the present slip off their wheels and fall sloppily to the bottom of the mind. . . . The prisoner is now willing to admit that he had betrayed the interests of the proletariat by writing to his relatives abroad, that his slackness at work was sabotage of socialist industry. . . . In feverish haste the surgeon cuts out the heart, his probing instruments transplant it to the body's right side, strip flakes of infected tissue from the brain, graft small patches of skin, change the direction of the blood flow, repair the torn network of the nervous system. The human mechanism, arrested at its lowest ebb and taken to pieces, is reconstructed and altered; those gaps between disjointed ideas are filled by new connections . . . the next morning he wakes feeling empty as a nut without a kernel and weak after the inhuman strain to which his whole organism has been subjected during the last few months, but dazzled by the thought that everything is already behind him. When a prisoner walks between the bunks without saying a word to anyone, it is easy for the others to guess that he is a

convalescent with rapidly healing scars and a newly-assembled personality, taking his first uncertain steps in a new world. (67)

By contrast, Herling's scenic unfolding of camp semiotics is economical and invites the reader to infer what is happening behind the closed doors, who reports on whom and for what purpose, what is passing in the minds of the victims or traitors. The authorial persona is strangely passive during the scenically rendered episodes—apparently, he is as powerless to change the course of events as a spectator is at a play. Yet Herling's theory that this play is set in a different moral universe is subverted by his inclusion of such literary topoi as the prodigal son, the kiss of Judas, physical martyrdom to stifle moral anguish, the conflict between heterosexual desire and homo-social bonds, and chess as the game of life: in the camp versions of such situations, values are distorted but not beyond recognition.

Most of Herling's grim anecdotes share the motif of betrayal. In the Vitebsk prison, a few cigarettes are a sufficient motive for juvenile delinquents to inform on a fellow inmate; an imprisoned Cossack is disowned by his son; a criminal convict consigns his girlfriend to six buddies; the secret police expose one of their own to the revenge of the prisoners; a squealer's report leads to a prisoner's execution for a reckless remark; and Herling himself is denounced by his closest camp friend. All this takes place against the background of scurvy-caused night-blindness that makes people helpless after dark and pellagra-caused dementia that destroys their human image.[18]

Herling views camp experience as a moral disease from which one recovers only gradually. In the epilogue he speaks of a young Jewish prisoner who had succumbed to the NKVD pressure and made a false deposition about four German Communists, whereupon they were killed. After the war the man seeks out Herling and (in an implicit reversal of the remorse of the Germans after the Holocaust)[19] asks him for sympathy. Herling does not oblige, yet he thinks that if the meeting had taken place immediately after his release from the camp, he might have been more pliable. The three years that have elapsed are presented as the period of his moral recuperation:

> I might have been able to pronounce the word that was asked of me, on the day after my release from the camp. . . . In 1945 I already had three years of freedom behind me, three years of military wondering and battles, of normal feelings, love, friendship, and sympathy. . . . The days of our life are not like the days of our death, and the laws of our life are not like the laws of our death. I had come back among people, with human standards and conceptions, and was I now to escape from them, abandon them, voluntarily betray them? The choice was the same: then

it had been his life or the lives of the four Germans, now it was his peace or mine. No, I could not say it.[20] (247)

Herling thinks that no matter what course he chooses, he will betray someone: either his new associates in their "normal" life or a fellow ex-prisoner who, like himself, has lived in a world governed by special laws. Strictly speaking, it is for his peace of mind rather than out of a duty to the dead that Herling refuses to comfort his visitor. Despite the pensive elegance of his style, the sense of his ethical confusion is reinforced by the fact that even the plight of the "Roman 'lazzaroni,' small ragged war-children" in the streets beneath his windows seems "normal" to the author after the reawakened memories of the camp. Herling thinks of his visitor as "a bird with a broken wing" (248), nostalgic for his lost decency. Herling himself seems unhappy at not having lived up to a prima facie code of honor, but there is a sense of relief about having the most moral-ly disastrous kind of camp experience relegated to a man in whom he refuses to acknowledge a secret sharer.

Though parts of the book are narrated in the present tense, the past tense predominates, even in the generalized accounts of camp condi-tions: it is obviously difficult for Herling, who had lived a different life for several years, to realize that the world of the camps still exists. While re-living his camp experience, he seems to wish to live it down, instead of thinking about it as still the fate of millions. Paradoxically, it is partly for this reason that these days his book has a more contemporary ring.

* * *

The late forties and early fifties saw the publication of memoirs by a group of authors who went public as witnesses not only in the literary but also in the *juridical* sense of the word, people who testified at one or both of the Paris trials that put the issue of Soviet concentration camps on the public agenda.

In 1946 a sensation was produced by the publication of *I Chose Free-dom* by Victor Kravchenko, a Soviet *apparatchik* who had defected in 1944 while on a trade mission in the USA. Kravchenko had narrowly escaped imprisonment in 1937 but had observed Stalin's terror at sufficiently close quarters. His book vividly describes the underside of the Soviet economic expansion, the famine in the Ukraine, and the purges; among other matters he records the chilling glimpses that, as a high-ranking functionary, he caught of forced-labor convicts during his visits to indus-trial sites. Kravchenko was vilified in the Western left-wing press and re-sponded by bringing a libel suit against the Communist newspaper *Les Lettres françaises*. The well-publicized trial took place in 1949; the hair-raising stories told on the witness stand turned it into a trial of the Soviet regime (see Berberova 1990; Izard 1949; Terrée 1982; and Kravchenko's own less successful second book, *I Chose Justice,* 1950). Kravchenko won the suit, yet was awarded insulting token damages.[21]

The other Paris trial took place from November 25, 1950, through January 6, 1951. The plaintiff was David Rousset, formerly a Resistance fighter who had survived the Nazi camps and described them in a passionate poetic essay, "L'Univers concentrationnaire,"[22] and the novel *Les Jours de notre mort* [*The Days of Our Death*]. On learning about the still-functioning camps in the USSR, Rousset started a public campaign for their abolition. He too was attacked by the Communist press, in particular by *Les Lettres françaises* (the editor, Pierre Daix, a prisoner under the Nazis, has since repented his denial of the Gulag), which he then sued for libel.[23]

Most of the ex-prisoners whom Rousset called on to testify to the existence of Soviet camps had been Communists (Buber-Neumann, Weissberg, Lipper, El Campesino, Leonhard), or socialists (Gliksman), or Communist sympathizers (Margolin); most were known to him through their published memoirs. Rousset avoided witnesses who could be suspected of a *prior* anti-Soviet bias;[24] indeed, Susanne Leonhard would claim to have remained faithful to her Marxist ideals even in her 1959 memoir. The Jews among the witnesses were even less likely to be suspected of willfully maligning the Soviet Union: they owed it gratitude for its role in defeating Nazi Germany.

One of the Jewish witnesses was Julius Margolin, an Israeli intellectual of Russian origin, with a doctoral degree in philosophy from the University of Berlin. Margolin had emigrated from Poland to the British-mandate Palestine in 1936. He was visiting Lodz in 1939 when the German invasion sent him fleeing to his native Pinsk, soon occupied by the Soviet army. Arrested for not holding a Soviet passport and sentenced to five years in the camps, he was in a large group of Poles sent to the camps in the Karelian woods, around Medvezhegorsk and Kotlas, previously described by Solonevich.

The title of Margolin's book, *Puteshestvie v stranu ze/ka* [*Journey to the Country of the Z/K*][25] evokes associations with travel and fantastic literature, such as *Gulliver's Travels*. A gullible bespectacled "astonished ram" finds himself in a foreign land whose language he speaks but whose customs he has to learn (cf. Margolin 1960/62 on intellectuals in the camps). His relatively light charge makes him eligible for an office job, which, unable to toady and intrigue, he promptly loses. Though as a Zionist he esteems manual labor and feels honor-bound to prove himself at the general works, the calorie deficit soon produces the usual vicious-spiral effect. Pronounced an invalid, he is put on starvation rations but transferred to lighter jobs and at a crucial point hospitalized, which helps him survive to the end of his five-year term.[26]

Margolin's narrative concentrates on a prisoner's inner life. A Kant and Husserl scholar (1952: 62), he shows himself attempting "to turn reality into a subject of investigation" (207); as a narrator, he relives this phenomenological investigation and presents reality as the content of a prisoner's consciousness. Jobs like woodcutting, gardening, or railway construction, as well as camp topography, the logistics of adaptation in the barracks and overcrowded camp hospitals,[27] the handling of starvation rations, confrontations with criminals, and a gamut of interpersonal relationships are all placed in the context of the *zek*'s (the term "z/k" was pronounced *zek*) inner life, alongside his plights, intentions, calculations, afterthoughts, and emotional responses to contingencies. Margolin restrains idiosyncratic touches by concentrating on *the public facet* of his inner life; he thus universalizes the account of his experience—though not at the expense of authenticity. His persona is not just any *zek* but one who combines a Zionist affiliation with the self-consciousness of the fussy, puny, alien-looking Jew, vociferously but helplessly protesting against injustice. Yet as starvation and depletion progress, the individual features of his character fade, and his consciousness begins to contract. Margolin is probably the first memoirist to describe the prisoners' "dehumanization" (ch. 6) as a consequence of the vicious spiral: the prisoners are stripped of such identity props as status, profession, family ties, real and makeshift homes, possessions, camp friends,[28] outward dignity, strength, flesh.[29] The final stage of "dehumanization" is the loss of mental balance. The chapter "Camp Neurosis" deals with different forms of hunger-related irrationality, later also catalogued by Marchenko in *My Testimony*. Margolin's own neurosis, which stopped short of pellagric dementia (more fully described by Herling), took the shape of an insistence on warming his soup and drying his bread on the barrack stove instead of eating them as they came.[30]

In tune with his persona's desperate confrontations with his jailers and his criminal campmates, Margolin concludes his memoir with a voice-in-the-wilderness plea for international control over the Soviet penal policies. Writing the book in 1946–47, immediately after his return to Palestine via Poland, he appeals to the public opinion in the West, attacks the double standard of the intellectuals who protest against the social injustice in democratic societies yet make attempts ("pusillanimous and treasonable" [413]) to hush up Soviet abuses. Among the conditions of the aesthetic appeal of his memoirs is this perfect congruity of the content of his book and its agenda.

At Rousset's trial Margolin managed to silence the lawyers of *Les Lettres françaises* and preempt accusations of venting personal grievances. Later the same year he persuaded the congress of cultural workers in Bombay to pass a resolution condemning Soviet concentration camps. In the mid fifties, when the Archipelago was largely depopulated, Margolin turned more to other issues. He wrote—lucidly, from an original angle, and with a touch of estrangement—on politics, history, and literature; his 1965 autobiographical memoirs of childhood astonished his readers by their frankness. A Zionist Jew in Russia, he remained a somewhat alienated Russian writer in Israel. Having joined the followers of Jabotinski, he placed himself in opposition to the mainstream Israeli discourse dominated by Ben Gurion's policies; nor did he identify with all of Menachem Begin's views. His posthumous *Povest' tysyacheletii* [*A Tale of Millennia*] was the first book on Jewish history for many immigrants from the USSR; it circulated in Moscow in the late seventies. Margolin's most numerous readers were among the intellectuals who emigrated from the Soviet Union after his death in 1971.

"The Nazis had taught us to comfort ourselves with comparisons," notes Koestler describing his 1939 internment in France (1941: 62). Margolin believed that as a historical phenomenon the Soviet camps were more dangerous than the Nazi *Lagers* because they were hidden from outsiders and masked by humanistic slogans; yet he knew that an individual prisoner's experience was far worse in the German camps (1975: 247–54). Margarete Buber-Neumann was in a unique position to compare the two.

Her most passionate criticism was directed against the Gulag, because it was still functioning at the time when she was writing her memoir. She had fled Nazi persecution together with her second husband Heinz Neumann,[31] a German Communist leader who had fallen into disgrace with his Central Committee for opposing Hitler at the time when Stalin's policies were conciliatory.[32] In Moscow they worked as translators and lived at the Hotel Lux, which housed Comintern workers and foreign Communist refugees. Neumann fell victim to Stalin's crackdown on the Comintern in 1937. He was heard of in prison shortly after the arrest but never again—most of the prominent Comintern leaders were shot within a year. Buber-Neumann was arrested several weary months later[33] and sent to the Karaganda camps in Kazakhstan. In the fall of 1939 she found herself in the group of German Communists brought from different Soviet camps to be handed over to the Gestapo in accordance with a clause in the Molotov-Ribbentrop agreement (some of them had been sentenced to death in absentia in Germany; some were Jews[34]). Buber-Neumann's lot was the Ravensbrück concentration camp. She was relatively lucky: Karaganda was less deadly than the northern camps; and Ravensbrück was not an extermination camp—for the latter purpose its prisoners were usually transported to Auschwitz. Readiness to muster inner resources for unfamiliar activities and the ability to rise to unforeseen occasions helped her to survive. Nevertheless her body almost succumbed to illness or exhaustion at least once in each camp; and in Ravensbrück she narrowly escaped execution.

Buber-Neumann's *Under Two Dictators* displays clear and direct insight and firmness of ethical stance. It was written, she claims, not out of the desire to give vent to her feelings but because of her duty "to let the world know on the basis of first-hand experience what can happen, what must happen when human dignity is treated with cynical contempt" (xii). Accordingly, she treats the conditions in prisons and camps first and foremost as *indignities* and only then as hardships. In Russia, the overcrowding, vermin, bad and scanty food, male guards in women's bathhouses, excessive output quotas, and like conditions are caused by a disdain and non-recognition of the prisoners' basic needs—by neglect rather than malice. In Ravensbrück, however, the assault on one's dignity is active. When Buber-Neumann first comes to this camp, it is clean and well kept. Yet here the imposition of order and hygiene is as insulting as their absence in Russia. The women have their hair shaved off on the slightest suspicion of lice, undergo the daily humiliation of perverse "bed-building," are slapped on the face for any infringement, and have to attend—or suffer—public whippings. Toward the end of the war cleanliness is increasingly difficult to maintain, and Ravensbrück becomes as chaotic as the filthy Russian camps, with the addition of its specific atrocities.

Yet though one's outward dignity is stripped away, one's inner dignity is maintained through anger, refusal of inner consent, a search for constructive ways of helping oneself and others, and a rejection of pathos and despair. At brick-making near Karaganda, a Kazakh prisoner refuses to ask free shepherds for food since it is undignified for a Moslem woman to approach men—but she gets their attention by singing an ethnic song (120–21); in Ravensbrück, a former prostitute who had catered to masochistic clients refuses to execute corporal punishments on fellow prisoners and is sent to Auschwitz (208): dignity is an aid in survival and a motivation for heroic self-sacrifice.

In post-war West Germany, where she died on the last day of the Berlin Wall (Todorov 1996: 75), Buber-Neumann sought to come to terms with her past and claim justice for her generation. She testified at both Kravchenko's and Rousset's trials and wrote a number of works not only on her own experience but also on the fates of the German Communist movement.[35] She also wrote *Milena,* a biography of her beloved friend, Kafka's Czech translator Milena Jesenska, who had died in Ravensbrück.

The very first of Rousset's witnesses to be called to the stand was a thin,
pale, black-clad woman in her late thirties. Struggling to overcome acute
stage fright, she tried to recount her experience of Kolyma camps. The
attorneys of *Les Lettres françaises* loudly insisted that her private misadventures were irrelevant; she still managed to make a few strong statements
before being dismissed from the stand.[36] Elinor Lipper, a Swiss citizen of
Dutch Jewish descent and one of the numerous idealistic victims of the
Soviet propaganda of the thirties, had been arrested in 1937, two months
after arriving in the country that she expected to have achieved social
justice. Ten years later, the Swiss government, one of the few to stand up
to Stalin for its own citizens, obtained her release; it took her another
year and a half to make her way through transit prisons from Kolyma to
the border.

Lipper's memoir, *Eleven Years in Soviet Prison Camps,* refers to the stages
of her own ordeal in prisons and camps only in the outline necessary to
present the credentials of a firsthand witness. It is written mostly in the
present tense in order to emphasize that the described state of affairs still
obtains at the time of composition. Yet the richly informative synoptic
narrative is punctuated with inset stories in the past tense, dealing with
the destinies of usually unnamed individual prisoners—a nursing mother torn away from her baby or a woman denied her son's forgiveness
for having publicly repudiated him after his arrest. Contrasting with the
starkly sarcastic frame narrative, these strident insets achieve a direct
emotional appeal.[37] They seem to continue tormenting the author: her
"soul labours" (Wordsworth 1974: 71) as she writes. Yet in the second half
of the book the pathos is restrained even in the inset narratives, as if reenacting the weariness of a veteran prisoner who is no longer astounded
by the sight of suffering. Some aspects of Lipper's method of composition
would eventually be given a masterful development in Solzhenitsyn's *The
Gulag Archipelago,* for which her book would also provide a factual source.

A tendency to self-effacement also characterizes the narrative of Jerzy
Gliksman, a Sorbonne-educated lawyer and an important member of the
pre-war Warsaw Jewish community. Gliksman had fled eastward from the
German invasion and was arrested by the Soviet border patrol when he
tried, like Herling and Ekart, to cross the border to the still independent
Lithuania. He was one of the few fortunate Jews to be released through
the Sikorski amnesty in the fall of 1941 and to be taken into Anders's
army. The amnesty was neither comprehensive nor automatic—in some
camps only separate individuals were set free; in others, whole groups. In

the latter, Polish Jews stood better chances to benefit from the amnesty; this was the case of Menachem Begin and of the future memoirists Joshua Gilboa and Antoni Ekart, who, unlike Gliksman and Begin, were turned down by Anders's officers and eventually swept back into the camps. Gliksman's half-brother, the Bund leader Victor Alter, was, together with his colleague Henryk Erlich, executed in a Soviet prison in 1941.

Private grief is not allowed into Gliksman's book. Like Lipper, Gliksman believes that he will be one of the first to "tell the West" about the Soviet camps. He devotes separate chapters to the different aspects of prison and camp life, such as starvation, lack of air, bad sanitary facilities, and exposure to frost, and explains the corresponding logistics of adaptation, such as trading one's clothes for food, washing improvisation, delousing. Owing to the matter-of-fact calmness of the tone and the abundance of systematically arranged details, *Tell the West* presents the conditions of the prisoners not as horrors or indignities but as bleakly logical consequences of the authorities' aim to minimize the costs and maximize the profit from prison labor. Gliksman faithfully follows a campmate's injunction: "'If you really tell in the West about what you saw here, do not fail to add that the suffering Russian people is inherently good'" (352).

A similar view of the prisoners' predicament is presented, through a diametrically opposite narrative method, by the most celebrated among Rousset's witnesses, Valentin Gonzalez, alias El Campesino, a hero of the Spanish Civil War. This is the very same El Campesino about whom Ernest Hemingway had made the following prophetic remark:

> He was a brave, tough man; no braver in the world. But God, how he talked too much. And when he was excited he would say anything no matter what the consequences of his indiscretion. . . . He was a wonderful Brigade Commander though in a situation where it looked as though everything was lost. He never knew when everything was lost and if it was, he would fight out of it. (1940: 230)

The autobiographical *El Campesino: Life and Death in Soviet Russia*, written in collaboration with Julian Gorkin, starts with El Campesino's anarchist version of Robin-Hood-style noble banditry in Estremadura, his service in the Spanish Foreign Legion, his conversion from anarchism to communism, and his role in the Civil War. Like many Spanish Communists, upon the defeat of the Republic El Campesino found refuge in the USSR. He was told that his wife Juana Rodriguez and their children had been killed by the fascists.

Owing to his rejection of opportunistic conformism, El Campesino slid from high privilege in Moscow to destitution in the wartime Near East.

He preferred the latter, since the former amounted to a luxurious imprisonment and complicity in injustice. On the outskirts of Kokand in Uzbekistan, he reverted to banditry and, he claims, used the spoils to help other Spaniards and make reconnaissance trips to the border. He then escaped to Persia but was recaptured by the NKVD forces that operated freely in vast regions on both sides of the border. He was jailed and tortured: in Stalin's Russia a prominent public figure was the more likely to become a victim of moral and physical abuse.[38]

Having refused to make false confessions, El Campesino was sentenced to three years' imprisonment. Though camp realities are described only in the second half of his book, they form its center of gravity: the book contains a particularly passionate indictment of the Gulag and of the social phenomena that it reflects. Like most of the veterans of Stalin's camps, El Campesino reports on the cold, hunger, long hours of slave labor, scurvy, pellagra, absence of hygiene, and terrible living conditions. Yet he also emphasizes the glaring insufficiency of safety precautions that augmented the death toll in the coal mines of Vorkuta.[39] He survived the initial period there by becoming one of the privileged, "exemplary," shock workers. This could not last: sooner or later, despite the larger rations, even "Stakhanovites" began to "slide down the inexorable slope" (182). A mine explosion sent him to the hospital and thence on the route to his second escape from the USSR—not without a spell in a Bukhara prison, or the sight of guards shooting wounded prisoners after an earthquake in Ashkhabad.

One of the main concerns of El Campesino's memoir is the regime's attempt to deface individual identities. Despite the diabolical torture to which the author has been subjected, he chooses to emphasize not the sadism of separate officers but the bland callousness of the regime that leaves evacuees to starve and beg and turns prisoners into dispensable tools not worthy of the investment in safety precautions. This callousness is a logical extension of the attack on individuality as a source of value. Yet though El Campesino wishes to restore the stature of the people whose deaths are denied tragic grandeur, he partly defeats his purpose by allowing his own personality to dwarf the portraits of the ordinary prisoners by his side.

El Campesino's later life is sketched in the final chapter of his second book of memoirs, *Jusqu'à la mort* (1978), written in collaboration with Maurice Padiou. In post-war France he lived by manual labor. His aborted involvement with a group of militant anti-Francoists led to his arrest and banishment to the island of Bréhat in 1961; in 1963 he settled in Metz. After the death of Franco, he called on his countrymen to vote for Felipe Gonzalés. In 1977, owing to an interview in a Spanish newspaper, his wife Juana, who had been imprisoned and tortured but not killed, found out that he was alive. They were reunited. The appendix to *Jusqu'à la mort* says that on February 18, 1978, in the city hall of Metz, he was married to Juana Rodriguez, mother of his three children. The elderly couple was seen walking hand in hand along the city streets. In the mid eighties El Campesino returned to Spain.

Rousset's witnesses had been in the Gulag at its worst times and had known near-lethal starvation: their first-hand experience of the "vicious spiral" lends depth to their writing. Keenly aware that at the time of composition the deadly Soviet camps still thrive, they make passionate appeals on behalf of their fellow sufferers left behind and, being more careful than their pre-war precursors, avoid endangering them by naming names or disclosing the subterfuges of their struggle for survival. They tend to regard the camps not as an *extension* of the general state of affairs in the USSR but rather as its *systematic underside*. In view of their left-wing antecedents, this attitude places their books not only in the Gulag corpus but also in that of the literature of disillusionment—the testimonies of a generation that eventually rebelled "against its own youth" (Kundera 1981: 13), its Communist faith crushed by the directly observed realities (Koestler's *Darkness at Noon* and *Scum of the Earth*, Kundera's *The Book of Laughter and Forgetting*, Panaït Istrati's *To Another Flame*, memoirs by Kravchenko, Serge, Kopelev, Berger, Ciliga, Scholmer, and those collected in Crossman's *The God That Failed*). Yet the target of their attacks is not the Soviet regime as such but its concentration camps. This may be a matter of urgencies, or the consequence of the impression of Stalin's invincibility after World War II. In retrospect, however, the relaxation of the Soviet penal system and of the secrecy around it emerges as one of the central factors in the erosion of the Soviet monolith.

Largely unaware of each other's work while writing their own, Rousset's witnesses felt like messengers in Job 1—"and I only am escaped alone to tell thee." Hence their tendency to downplay individual touches and their attempts to present detailed and comprehensive accounts of the topography and routine of the camps. Hence also the ambivalent cumulative effect of their work: they are mutually supportive[40] but also repetitive. The element of redundancy in their historical evidence is, however, contained by the interest each presents to the specific ethno-political community of the author.

* * *

In 1946–47 Dallin and Nikolaevsky processed the still unpublished testimonies of Russian emigrants of the so-called second wave, that is, former Soviet citizens who made their way or were deported to Western Europe during the German occupation and evaded forced repatriation.

A few years later, the second-wave emigration produced its own books on Soviet prisons and camps, such as Vladimir Petrov's trilogy (including a Gulag version of the adventure story, 1950), Nicholas Prychodko's sober *One of the Fifteen Million* (1952), Ivanov-Razumnik's leisurely *Prisons and Exile* (1953), Boris Shiriaev's pious and somewhat aestheticizing *The Unfading Light* (1953), Sergei Maksimov's fictionalized and at times dreamily poetic *Taiga* (1952).[41] The latter three works came out in Russian; their publication, as well as that of K. Petrus's *The Prisoners of Communism* (1953), Julius Margolin's memoirs, and other Russian-language materials, had been made possible by the establishment of the Chekhov Publishing House in New York.

The Gulag testimonies of the second-wave writers were usually less passionate than those of most of Rousset's witnesses. In some cases the emotional intensities may have subsided during the several years between the release and the writing; in other cases (Shiriaev's and Ivanov-Razumnik's), the imprisonment had not been of the harshest kinds. Moreover, whereas Buber-Neumann, Margolin, and El Campesino see themselves as bearers of urgent responsibility conferred by the privilege of having shared a painful alien lot, the writers of the second wave present themselves as fugitives from a hopeless and homely dystopia.

* * *

Gulag testimonies of the late forties and early fifties may have played a role in the slight easing of the camp inmates' lot in Stalin's last years. Moreover, they contributed to the creation of the climate in which Khrushchev felt obliged not only to release the majority of the political prisoners in 1954–56 but also to allow a more or less inconspicuous repatriation of a number of foreign citizens among them. As a result, in the interim period between Stalin's death in 1953 and Khrushchev's de-Stalinization move of 1956, there appeared a number of Gulag memoirs written by foreigners and published in Western Europe and the USA.

These memoirs generally carry a reduced emotional appeal, mainly because their authors have already seen the beginning of the "thaw." Their consciousness-raising drive is not as prominent as that of their pre-1953 precursors. The authors are already aware of not being the first to bear witness. Hence, their main emphasis is not so much on the camp regulations and routine as on concrete historical particulars, personal discoveries, and the tower-of-Babel demographic complexity of the postwar Gulag (which the Soviet old-timers tended to perceive as a marginal deviation from the patterns established in the thirties).

Mixed origins and German citizenship facilitated the 1955 repatriation of Georgy Tregubov, a member of the NTS, the anti-Soviet *Natsional'no-*

Trudovoi Soiuz (National Labor Union),[42] who had been lured to East Berlin in 1947 and brought over to the Soviet Union. Tregubov survived the interrogations by assuming a personal insignificance and faking an erratic mysticism. His 1957 camp memoir also describes the workings of the Soviet secret police, such as four-stage interrogations with the use of torture (the first stage yields a general evaluation of the prisoner, and the fourth is applied only to prominent figures who show resistance), and on techniques of self-protection against it. An imaginary enemy likewise lured to East Berlin, accused of espionage, and released in 1955, was Erica Wallach, whose book *Light at Midnight*[43] records, among other things, her amazement at her own strength and resilience, at the amount of physical and moral suffering that she could endure without breaking.

Among the more common concerns of the foreign prisoners repatriated in the fifties is the fate of their countrymen. Thus Unto Parvilahti (1959) is particularly interested in the fate of the Finns,[44] Jean Nicolas (1958) in that of the French, John Noble (1958, 1959) in that of the Americans, and Joseph Scholmer (1954) in that of the Germans in the Gulag.

Scholmer's *Vorkuta* is perhaps the shrewdest memoir of the 1953–56 batch. A Communist who had been imprisoned under the Nazis and who served as a health official in East Berlin after the war, Scholmer was already disillusioned by the time of his arrest in 1947. Soon after his arrival in Vorkuta, his health deteriorated, and as an "invalid" he was given maintenance jobs that provided him with a good vantage point for observing the conditions in a variety of camps, the relations between different national and political groups of prisoners, the fluctuating moods of the guards, and the first strikes. Scholmer's discourse calmly eschews conventional pieties. Tortured at the interrogations in East Germany and required to reveal the names of his "associates," he turned the revolutionary principle of "robbing the robbers" upside down by falsely naming some of the most orthodox Communists who, he thought, "would benefit" from the kind of treatment he was getting in prison (16).[45] In the camps, not allowed to work as a doctor, he supplemented his starvation rations by practicing his own kind of medicine—helping prisoners *not* to recover from various diseases so that they might be released from work, as well as advising prisoners on ways to simulate illness so that they might extricate themselves from tight spots: these people were ill anyway, since overwork and starvation caused far graver physical conditions than the diseases of the officially recognized kind. Scholmer's quietly creative, cagey wisdom underneath ethical paradoxes is conveyed in an ironically reflective tone that gives the reader a sense of total credibility.

Scholmer's style is to a large extent representative of the emotionally subdued but richly informative narratives of most repatriated foreigners.

Exceptional in this sense are, alongside the angry narrative of Erica Wallach and the astounded one of Bernhard Roeder (1956), the reminiscences of Nikolai Krasnov (1957). Krasnov was the son of White emigrants; he grew up in Yugoslavia and at the beginning of the war fought against the Germans in the ranks of the Yugoslav Royal Army. Upon capture, he followed his father and uncle—and his great-uncle, the Cossack general Peter Krasnov—in throwing in his lot with the Cossacks who had gone over to the German side and moved westward, families, livestock, bag, and baggage. Krasnov's is one of the few vivid accounts of the maneuver by which the British military rounded up this community at Lienz and handed them over to the Soviet forces. A few witnesses of this operation managed to escape, but Nikolai Krasnov was probably the only one who also saw what happened to the Cossacks after their capture and survived a ten-year imprisonment, some of it in special-regime camps, to tell the story.[46]

In addition to its emotionally charged account of the Lienz affair, Krasnov's book contains materials on some aspects of Gulag history seldom reflected in other memoirs:[47] the guards' premeditated shooting of prisoners on fake pretexts of escape attempts; the plight of the Kharbin and Shanghai Russians who left Communist China after Stalin's death to join their camp-veteran relatives in post-release Siberian exile; and the selective liberation of Yugoslavs, depending on their relationships with Tito's circles.

Krasnov attacked the Soviet regime from a priori White Guard positions, and his rigid disbelief in the permanence of the Communist rule —a prophetic attitude, as we know now—sounded naive to many of its readers. Yet the KGB may have held a different attitude. In 1960, the year of the publication of the slightly revised English translation of his memoirs, Krasnov died suddenly,[48] on the threshold of a new life in Argentina, having rejoined his wife, who had escaped the round-up at Lienz. It seems that for a long time, publication of Gulag memoirs endangered the authors even outside the socialist bloc.

* * *

Khrushchev's secret speech about Stalin's crimes at the Twentieth Communist Party Congress in 1956 gave a new impetus to the "thaw" that had started shortly after Stalin's death. The released political prisoners were allowed to move from their places of exile to large cities, and their mutual-support social groups created a favorable context for the writing of memoirs, even if with little hope of publication. After the Twenty-Second Party Congress (1961), that brought the critique of Stalinism out into the open, the prospects for publication no longer seemed unrealistic. A literary event of tremendous importance was the appearance of Solzhenitsyn's novella *One Day in the Life of Ivan Denisovich* in the journal *Novyi mir* in November 1962: the voice of the *zek* seemed to be finally admitted to Soviet literature (see Zhores Medvedev 1973: 4–29). Manuscripts dealing with the camp theme began to flood editorial offices.

Yet only a small and selective sprinkling of these works appeared in print between 1962 and 1966. Within a couple of years after *Ivan Denisovich*, it became clear that the chances of publication were reserved only for those camp materials that observed the ideological constraints of the "thaw."

The shock value of Khrushchev's attack on Stalin, its apparent courage, and its promise of relief after the reign of terror hid the slant of the official scapegoating of Stalin from the immediate notice of the broad public. The deployment of the emphases encouraged an uncritical acceptance of a series of presuppositions. Stalin's assault on "Lenin's Old Guard" (with the aim to remove his actual or potential rivals and usurp the credit as Lenin's invaluable associate during the October Revolution) was presented as his greatest crime. The repression suffered by much greater numbers of non–party members and the "physical liquidation" of people who had belonged to different socio-political categories were consistently downplayed.[49] The press emphasized that loyal Communists had been slandered, implying that if the accusations against them had been true, their fate would have been justified—and further implying that the camps were a necessity because there still existed "enemies." Political persecution as such was neither condemned nor eliminated.

Khrushchev admitted that the slander against old Communists had been deliberate but, launching the neologism "personality cult" as an all-purpose catchword, placed the blame entirely on Stalin and a handful of his accomplices. The role that most members of the Central Committee, including Khrushchev himself, had played in the purges was covered up. A return to justice and to the Leninist principles of "collective leadership" was proclaimed. While revealing only the tip of the iceberg, Khrushchev sought to produce an impression that the whole truth was being brought to light; his lip service to the necessity of telling the truth veiled the attempt to de-energize further inquiries. At the time, indeed, camp graduates could obtain pensions, yet were often intimidated and kept away from public life; to the foreigners among them it was suggested that they should stay inconspicuous on repatriation. The amount of camp material in the press was monitored,[50] and absolute priority was given to the "loyalist" (*blagonamerennye*) narratives (see *GA* 3: 11; Geller 1974: 272–81), which emphasized the Communists' fidelity to their ideals in adversity and at the same time underplayed this adversity. The writer who gave this formula the most systematic development is Boris Dyakov, whose camp memoirs came out as a book as late as 1966, after Khrushchev's fall.[51] They merit attention as a case of a made-to-social-order narrative, mendacious in its implications if not in its facts.[52]

In Dyakov's camp setting, his fellow Communists keep feelingly averring that they are true Leninists, that they have been slandered and wrongfully expelled from the party but still consider themselves its members (124), that they have never doubted the party's right and might, have never heard of any Communists reneging while in the camps (159), that one day the truth will come out and justice will triumph, and that not everyone in the camps is as innocent as themselves—one must still "defend the Soviet power" (45) against "blackguards" (22). They piously mark the anniversaries of the October Revolution (17) and "run" to the clubhouse when the prisoners are "allowed" to sign requested government loans (71).[53] At night Dyakov and his friend Todorsky study the history of the Communist Party and console themselves by Lenin's brief praise of Todorsky's pamphlet (74–75).[54] Their concern for the output exceeds that of the camp authorities; they write life-asserting poems and, given official permission, retire to write a novel; they profess hatred of the "Banderovites" and various German collaborators held in the camps, and Dyakov is surprised to see that medical assistance is not denied to the "Vlasovites" and other "enemies."

Dyakov's apparatus of would-be factual precision—his use of people's real names, scholarly reservations, footnotes—actually helps him to subvert the evidence of the scale and nature of the camps. "The horror is not the camp. It must be strict for criminals" (*dlia prestupnikov*), he writes, obviously including political offenders as well. "The horror lies in another thing—there are people here who have been punished without a crime. There are hundreds of them, or perhaps . . . it is terrible to think about it . . . there are thousands and thousands" (62): a crass understatement is thus passed for a momentous revelation. The distortion is buttressed by a few true-ringing notes, such as memories of the cultural policies geared to Stalin's rewriting of history or perplexity concerning the causes of the present injustice ("whose malicious power is at work here?" [13]). After Stalin's death the matter receives a conveniently standardized explanation: "Now we have understood: intoxicated by absolute rule, suspiciousness, and cruelty, Stalin took his friends for enemies and punished his own people" (260–61). The happy ending confirms the correctness of the loyalists' prophesies. The footnotes show that most of Dyakov's camp friends have been released and given special pensions or jobs in their own fields. Only a few seem to have died, almost none while still in the camp. The book ends with a former prisoner's remark, "The sun—how bright it is!" and a "broad smile."

Dyakov saw camp life in the years 1950–53, when the conditions had somewhat improved. Upon arrival he had hernia surgery and developed a fistula, which kept him off the "general works"; he spent the whole of his term in the Taishet region working as a hospital statistician, librarian, bookkeeper, or storage man. Thus, the soft jobs, which other camp survivors obtained after having repeatedly slid down the vicious spiral, were Dyakov's from the start, and he managed to keep the advantage.[55] In a typically Soviet depersonalized touch of private emotion, he bewails the injustice of his imprisonment, the fence, the submission to petty tyrants, the separation from his wife and from "habitual forms of life." These are obviously the sorrows of even the mildest forms of imprisonment; they suggest nothing about the specificity of the Gulag. Dyakov practically admits that he refused to see the disconcerting things: when an emaciated prisoner is brought in for examination, Dyakov leaves the room, unable to look at "a human mummy" (125).[56]

Glimpses of the truth (which in the eyes of some readers might have sufficed to justify the book) are cushioned in Dyakov's text. Thus he tells about a harassed young man who suddenly dashes away from the column of prisoners, shouting "I am escaping!" He is shot by the guards without warning, in accordance with instructions. The narrator wonders, irrelevantly: "Who killed Koroliov? . . . Who sanctions provoking people to escape? . . . Who has sanctioned the instruction of death?" (131). At issue here is not an escape attempt but suicide by taking advantage of the guards' readiness to shoot;[57] yet spelling this out would damage the general impression that life in the camps was quite bearable.[58] Similar rhetoric defuses one of the central topical issues of the sixties: whether the blame for Stalinist atrocities lay with individuals or with the system. Here the meaning of the words is distorted: "the individuals" means not top party figures (purge-start careerists now in the "collective leadership") but anonymous villains, "schizophrenics and conscious criminals" in the ranks of the police; "the system" means not the socio-political structure that denies people civil rights and economic independence but the scheme of incentives according to which "the police interrogator gets a bonus for each promptly obtained 'confession'!" (207).[59]

Lowering one's intellectual profile is the safest course in any totalitarian state (cf. Bettelheim 1960: 153–57); Stalin, in particular, was known to dislike having brilliant people around him. Dyakov's book is well suited not only to disinfect the camp theme but, owing to its insipidity, also to reduce public interest in it. Under Khrushchev, who fostered an impersonal formulaic style in political discourse[60] and favored writers who were proficient in handling the proper formulae in "human-interest" contexts, Dyakov's children's-literature tone was politically suitable (as was the absence of reference to the fallen Khrushchev). Dyakov's Todorsky claims that he started his work on the Lenin-praised pamphlet by wondering "where one could find a sample" of that type of writing (139) and then succeeded in "correctly formulating" the "problem task." Dyakov likewise built what might have become a model for "loyalist" memoirs. Fate, however, was against him: soon after the publication of his book the stream of camp narratives, no matter how "correct," was dammed up—even Galina Serebriakova, another notorious loyalist, did not succeed in getting her memoirs into print in the Soviet Union. By the time the floodgates were reopened under Gorbachev, the stencil offered by Dyakov had become obsolete.

* * *

In 1964, Stalin's apprentices in "the collective leadership" decided that the disclosure had gone too far,[61] and a conservative about-face put an end to the "thaw."

When journals stopped accepting materials on the "personality cult," the rejected typescripts started passing from hand to hand. The process gained momentum in 1966—it marked the beginning of the narrative-prose Samizdat, the hand- or type-written "self-publication."[62] Symptom-atically, among the first works that circulated in this way was the anony-mous "Memoir of a Bolshevik-Leninist,"[63] by one of Stalin's victims who claimed to have remained loyal to the Communist ideals. Such materials set Samizdat apart from anti-Communist propaganda as well as from the more radical discourse of the *glasnost* period. Nevertheless, it took a great deal of personal courage and confidence in the value of one's work for a Gulag survivor to risk the long-awaited personal safety by making his or her memoir public while staying within easy reach of the KGB.

Ivan Denisovich had paved the way for camp narratives; the ban lent them the additional attractiveness of the forbidden fruit. One of the best-written and best-known books that circulated in Samizdat and was even-tually published in the West (this procedure was humorously referred to as Tamizdat, "publication *there*") is Evgenia Ginzburg's *Krutoi marshrut.*[64] Written with energy and flair, this vivid camp testimony doubles as a story of a former Communist's disillusionment and remorse.

The title of Ginzburg's memoirs means "steep route" or "tough march-ing" and connotes moral elevation. When H. D. Thoreau described the soldiers' marching "against their common sense and consciences" as "very steep marching indeed" (225–26), he referred to the morally wea-risome effect of conformity. By contrast, Ginzburg's "steep march" led to a clarity of moral vision and a rejection of false innocence.

A journal editor, university lecturer, and wife of a high-ranking official in Kazan,[65] prior to her arrest in 1937 Ginzburg had belonged to the Soviet "priviligentsia." Stalin's "eighteenth Brumaire" (1967: 74) of 1937–38 decimated this class, removing most of the people who were making visible careers without collaborating with the NKVD, without secretly or openly denouncing colleagues or baiting the marked victims of the regime. Ginzburg was sentenced to ten years' imprisonment for "counter-revolutionary Trotskyite terrorism" on the basis of not having informed on a colleague who had been incautious on the question of "the permanent revolution." In 1939, after two years in prison, she was transferred to the camps in Kolyma, where she went down the vicious spiral at lumbering, was three times on the verge of death, got lucky breaks, learned the skills of hospital attendance and poultry work, was tossed from soft berths to punitive camps, narrowly escaped rape, made friends, fell in love, managed to survive her full ten-year term, and got permission for her surviving son, the future writer Vasily Aksyonov, to join her in Kolyma's capital, Magadan (her elder son perished in the Leningrad blockade). In 1949, less than two years after her release, she was again briefly imprisoned in Magadan during the wave of the second-round arrests; her temporary banishment to Kolyma was then commuted to permanent exile. During the "thaw," in the mid fifties, she was allowed to return to European Russia.

In an ironic reversal of the reforging theory, Ginzburg's book traces the process of her re-education as disillusionment with the party dogma. In her account of the news of Kirov's murder she writes: "Had I been ordered to die for the Party—not once but three times, that very night, in that snowy winter dawn, I would have obeyed without the slightest hesitation. I had not the shadow of a doubt of the rightness of the Party line" (1: 3). Completing the first volume of her memoirs soon after the Twenty-Second Party Congress, Ginzburg submitted to a degree of self-censorship in the hope of having her book published: "after all, a sentence or so was not much sacrifice for the sake of publication, of reaching people at last" (2: 419). She deplored this at the end of the second volume, written in the seventies, during the "stagnation." Her expressions of happiness at having lived to see the Twentieth and the Twenty-Second Congresses (Stalinism is "over and done with" and the "great Leninist truths" have been re-established in the party [1967: 417]) in the Introduction to the Russian edition of the first volume,[66] make her sound like a Dyakov-type entrenched loyalist. Yet, like her first cellmate, who suspects her of being a stool pigeon but soon changes her mind, the reader is persuaded otherwise[67] while watching how the conflicts between Ginzburg's conscience and party discipline are immediately resolved in favor of the former. Eventually Ginzburg accepts her ordeal as a punishment for not having resisted evil in her happier days:

When you can't sleep, the knowledge that you did not directly take part in the murders and betrayals is no consolation. After all, the assassin is not only he who struck the blow, but whoever supported evil, no matter how: by thoughtless repetition of dangerous political theories; by silently raising his right hand; by faint-heartedly writing half-truths. *Mea culpa* . . . and it occurs to me more and more frequently that even eighteen years of hell on earth is insufficient expiation for the guilt. (2: 153)

In the mid forties, Ginzburg's break with Marxism took a religious form: judging by Aksyonov's Introduction to the 1985 Possev edition of *Krutoi marshrut*[68] and by remarks in her own narrative, at a certain point, in spite of the residue of Soviet patterns of conduct and thought, she turned to Christianity. This was largely under the influence of Dr. Walter, the Catholic ethnic German whom she married in Kolyma. Bald, middle-aged, blind in one eye due to an untreated disease, with legs perpetually swollen from years of scurvy and starvation in the gold mines (his scurvy sores reopened and he died soon after they left Kolyma), Dr. Walter is the "jolly saint" of her memoir, wise, strong, devoted, irreverently facetious, and comically sentimental.

Owing to the vividness of the remembered scenes, the intensity of the rekindled emotions, and the re-enactment of the suspense caused by the uncertain prospects of survival, Ginzburg's narrative brings home to the reader the flavor of a woman's Gulag experience. Yet it produces the misleading impression that after Stalin's death and the improvement of the ex-prisoners' conditions in Magadan, the world of the camps ceased to exist, like a whirlwind that had exhausted its fury.[69] The new forms of abuse of slave labor, the procrastination in the release of prisoners, the strikes, the rebellions, and their gory suppression find no place in Ginzburg's narrative. The veil of secrecy around them was dense yet not impenetrable, and one may surmise that after 1953 she relapsed into a semi-conscious blindness to things that threatened to disrupt her picture of reality.

Implicit in Ginzburg's narrative, with its socio-political protest combined with a lingering love for the idea of a Marxist revolution, is the Prague-spring formula "socialism with a human face." Indeed, it was only in the nineties that the bulk of the Soviet intelligentsia began to shed their "foundational" beliefs. Up to the nineties, they regarded socialist economy as intrinsically more advanced than the one based on the free market, the world destroyed by the October Revolution as decadent beyond regeneration,[70] and the socialist system as invincible and inevitably bound, after some childhood diseases, to lead to a Golden Age of justice, equality, and plenty. Independent thinkers like Solzhenitsyn, Amalrik, and Bukovsky, who did not share this essentially millenarian view (cf. Cohn 1957: 307–19, 185–86), formed a small minority.

Ginzburg's book also reflects another mythical pattern: a good ruler (Lenin) has been replaced by a pseudo-savior (Stalin) under whose reign society deteriorates; when the bad ruler is removed and the erstwhile values are restored ("the great Leninist truths have again come into their own in our country and Party!" [1: 417]), one expects regeneration, dawn after darkness, thaw after a winter of discontent. The ideology of the "thaw" had left the cult of Lenin intact, presenting the years 1928–53 as a temporary deviation: it was not until the very late eighties that disconcerting comparisons between Stalin's crimes and the policies initiated by Lenin became current in Russia.[71] Ginzburg stopped short of this reorientation. Though her ideological position was too radical for her memoirs to be published in Russia under Brezhnev, it was tame enough for them to come out at an early stage of *glasnost,* considerably earlier than the main works of Solzhenitsyn and Shalamov. Yet even before that, in the late sixties and early seventies, the moderateness of her political stance precluded suspicions of an a priori anti-Soviet tendentiousness and widened the appeal of her memoirs both at home and abroad. Less than three decades after the trials of Kravchenko and Rousset, Ginzburg was fêted by the French PEN Club and warmly acclaimed by the broad public; terminal cancer cut short her work on an account of a Kolyma inmate's Paris experience.

Written and propelled from Samizdat to Tamizdat at approximately the same time as Ginzburg's book but striking a different ideological keynote was *Moi vospominaniia* [*My Recollections*] by Ekaterina Olitskaya, a member of the Socialist Revolutionary (SR) party, which had, up to 1917, fought against czarism alongside the Bolsheviks. The book traces the antecedents of prison and camp conditions that Ginzburg came to know in the late thirties and records the fate of non-Bolshevik socialists up to 1939.

The SR ideology that permeates Olitskaya's memoir is inseparable from her character and life, creating the impression of a perfect correspondence of the content and the stance. In a grim reversal of the SR slogan "In Struggle Shalt Thou Gain Thy Right," the structure of the narrative reflects the stages in the political prisoners' *losing* struggle for human rights. The account of Olitskaya's first imprisonment, in the Solovki, is the story (used by Solzhenitsyn in *GA* 3: 2) of the political prisoners' doomed protests against the gradual tightening of the camp regime. In the succession of prisons through which Olitskaya passed after her second arrest during the Great Terror, she notes the relentless reduction of the inmates' amenities and the decrease in the effectiveness of their resistance.

Olitskaya admits that for all the traditional SR virtues of stamina, mutual help, loyalty, and adherence to principle, their solidarity was not extended to the prisoners held on the "general" rather than the "political" regimen or to members of other parties, especially the Communists. An unmistakable ruthlessness to others and to themselves transpires in her admiring portraits of her SR associates. The SR principles demanded the sacrifice of private life for the sake of the common struggle; indeed, in the mid thirties Olitskaya and her common-law husband decided that they had no right to private happiness under the oppressive regime. They sent their five-year-old daughter to her grandmother and went underground ("How dare I not leave my girl now? How can I demand disobedience, implacability, courage, and sacrifices from others if I myself do not decide to enter the struggle?" [2: 81]). The little girl died of pneumonia; and Olitskaya was left with the belief that the death occurred at the moment when she seemed to hear the child's anguished cry for help (2: 98).[72] Olitskaya also mentions the last time when she had a sense of her husband's physical presence after they were separated in prison. The date of his execution is not known. One of the most touching places in the book is the unwonted outcry that interrupts the story of her brief reunion with her brother: "*Why did they all have to perish, and only I was to survive, I who cannot even properly describe them?*" (2: 64). Notes like this are infrequent in the work. Olitskaya's narrative is dry and her portrait gallery relatively flat, stylistically reflecting, as it were, an East European ascetic model of a woman revolutionary's mandatory self-discipline and self-suppression.

The major biographical consequence of this model of identity is a sense of alienation from the people for whose sake the sacrifices are made. The book probes Olitskaya's frustrated populism, her failure to identify with the life, dreams, and hopes of the people.[73] During the period of exile following her first imprisonment, she rejected the optimism promoted by the relative comfort of the years of the New Economic Policy (1921–29), when some private initiative was allowed. Where most of her contemporaries saw an apparent normalization of life after years of unrest and privation (2: 54),[74] she saw the consolidation of tyranny and the spread of ideological control, oppression, and hypocrisy (2: 20). She condemned the submissive wound-licking search for private happiness, defensive strategies such as pride in economic expansion, deliberate disregard for social ills, and an a priori support of the policies of the regime. Like the other SR activists, she found herself in both emotional and ideological isolation. After talking to her on the prison transport to Vladivostok, the novelist Zinaida Tulub exclaimed: "But you are an ichthyosaurus! *Please*, don't be hurt. I do not think badly of you. I am just so surprised to meet an archeological find" (2: 206).[75]

Eventually, however, the predicament of an undaunted minority turns out to be the general fate of "the people," in so far as "the people" is traditionally regarded as synonymous with "the oppressed." During the Great Terror alienation becomes the order of the day: provincial city dwellers close themselves up in their homes; and life itself seems to go underground at nightfall (2: 56). The persecutions endured by the SR party likewise become a version of the common fate: the SR form one of the "streams" (*GA* 1: 1) that flow into the camps in the late thirties. Olitskaya's dream of solidarity with the oppressed is, ironically, fulfilled by her second arrest and five-year camp term. She is sent to Kolyma (in the same freight car as Ginzburg, whose poetry recitals she recollects [2: 213]). The image of a Kolyma mass grave at the end of her book is a grim symbol of an individual identity's merging with the common lot.

* * *

Samizdat of the mid sixties was part of a new phenomenon in Soviet history—the dissident movement. By contrast to the Opposition activities of the late twenties, this was a non-party movement; by contrast to sporadic conspiracies, it prioritized not the deposition of the regime but its democratization. It demanded compliance with the Constitution and the laws on the part of the authorities (the main ideologue of this approach was Aleksandr Esenin-Volpin, a son of the poet Sergei Esenin) and insisted on the legality of its own actions, including its open appeals to public opinion at home and abroad (cf. Grigorenko 1982: 289–90). It gained impetus from cultural and literary activities, such as the spontaneous poetry readings in Moscow's Mayakovsky square that started in 1958. In the Caucasus, the Ukraine, and the Baltic republics (see Alekseeva 1984: 7–236) the movement was associated with the struggle for national independence. In Moscow, a group headed by Pyotr Yakir became the focus for links with clandestine organizations throughout the country, yet itself was not clandestine. Dissidents like Grigorenko, Chalidze, and Sharansky turned the openness and legality of their activities into a principle, which was eventually epitomized by Andrei Sakharov. In 1968, to ensure that the protest activities should be accurately recorded and made known to the world, Natalia Gorbanevskaia launched the Samizdat journal *Khronika tekushchikh sobytii* [*Chronicle of Current Events*], a landmark in the history and historiography of the movement.[76] The logistics of self-publication became practically the only conspiratorial activity of the dissident movement: paradoxically, the movement had to take recourse to underground practices in order to come into the open.

At the peak of the "thaw,"[77] Khrushchev, who had already sanctioned the persecution of Pasternak for the foreign publication of *Doctor Zhivago*, launched an attack on the freedom of experimentation in literature and the arts—in particular, on abstractionism in painting and sculpture. Literature too was expected to remain within the officially recognized bounds. In 1964 the young poet Joseph Brodsky was arrested, tried, and sentenced to exile for "parasitism," that is, for devoting himself entirely to his literary work—a privilege reserved only for the members of the Union of Soviet Writers. In 1965 Yuly Daniel and Andrei Sinyavsky were arrested for having published allegedly slanderous works abroad. Instead of terrorizing the dissident movement into self-effacement, their 1966 trial gave new impetus to new protests[78] and enlisted the energetic aid of the foreign media.[79] The government struck back, arresting most of the prominent dissidents, yet the protest campaigns and Samizdat were no longer to be stopped.

In 1967 a new bombshell exploded in Samizdat—*My Testimony* by Anatoly Marchenko. This was the first sustained narrative about the camps not of the Stalin but of the Khrushchev-Brezhnev era. It showed that contrary to the impression produced by the official literature of the thaw as well as by many Samizdat memoirs, there were still great numbers of political prisoners in the forced-labor camps and that the prison regime was still near deadly. Marchenko described the kinds of people held behind bars in the sixties; the way of life in the strict-regime camps and in the grim Vladimir prison, where people were deliberately subjected to chronic starvation, oppressive political and KGB controls; and a malicious administration that was nostalgic for the vaster powers it had wielded in the Stalin days. He also described the mutual respect and solidarity among most of the prisoners and the servile opportunism of former Nazi collaborators.[80]

A blue-collar worker from Siberia, Marchenko had been unjustly imprisoned on a criminal charge. Angered, he attempted to flee the Soviet Union, was caught, and was sentenced again, this time on political charges. In a Mordovian camp he made friends with the writer Yuly Daniel, who helped him contact dissident circles upon release. With the editorial assistance of Larisa Bogoraz, he wrote memoirs remarkable for purity of form and intense though restrained emotiveness.

After his release from the camps in 1966 Marchenko was not allowed to reside in Moscow. In retaliation for *My Testimony* and a letter to *Rude Pravo* about the threat of the Soviet invasion of Czechoslovakia, he was rearrested in 1968 and spent three years in strict-regime camps (1968–71).[81] In 1975, arrested again and banished to Chuna, he wrote an account of his recent hunger strike, *Ot Tarusy do Chuny* [*From Tarusa to Chuna*]. His work on *Zhivi kak vse* [*Live Like Everyone*] (1987), describing mainly the plight of a released prisoner, was interrupted by his fifth arrest; the completed part deals with the years 1966–69. To his death in Chistopol prison[82] in 1986, Marchenko remained an uncompromising champion of justice and human rights.

* * *

In the seventies, owing to outer and inner pressures, the Soviet Union allowed the emigration of several hundred thousand people. Those who sought emigration at the time did so either for ideology-related reasons such as Zionism, for economic reasons, or in quest of more favorable conditions for creative self-actualization; the latter motivation included the possibility to publish one's work. In the same decade, considerable numbers of the politically "undesirable" were either *forced* into exile or left no viable alternative to emigration. As a result, various aspects of the cultural history of the USSR emerged from the pens of Solzhenitsyn, Brodsky, Sinyavsky, Vladimov, Aksyonov, Dovlatov, Voinovich, Sasha Sokolov, Aleshkovsky, Kandel, Vladimir Maksimov, Amalrik, Alekseeva, Bukovsky, Grigorenko, Chalidze, Plyushch, Zinoviev, and others. The seventies and early eighties saw a considerable increase in the number of Russian-language books and periodicals in the USA, France, Germany, and Israel. This was the heyday of Tamizdat, a spontaneous convergence of the works of brilliant though not like-minded intellectuals into a near-comprehensive cultural history of the USSR, in which the semiotics of penal institutions had the pride of place (owing, first and foremost, to the Western publication of *The Gulag Archipelago* and of Shalamov's stories, about which more later).

Foreign publications by writers who had left the Soviet Union in the seventies and eighties are usually classified as the work of the "third-wave" Russian emigration, the term "Tamizdat" often being reserved for the banned works by writers still living in the Soviet Union. The grand opening of Tamizdat in this narrower sense was the 1957 publication of Pasternak's *Doctor Zhivago,* followed by a violent campaign against Pasternak in the Soviet media. The second major event was the foreign publication, under pseudonyms, of the works of Sinyavsky and Daniel. Despite the show trial in which the two writers were convicted for slander of Soviet life, manuscripts by Soviet authors started making their way across the border in increasing numbers. Tamizdat publications included not only literary works but also open letters by dissidents and speeches made at trials. At times they were transmitted back to the Soviet Union by the BBC, the Voice of America, or Radio Liberty. The broadcasts of these stations provided an alternative to the Soviet official monopoly on literature and information while doubling as a partial safe-conduct to the dissidents: the KGB was less free to destroy a dissident whose activities had been reported by the foreign media.[83] The smuggling of manuscripts abroad was also a way to ensure that they should not perish if confiscated by the KGB. It was after the KGB had seized a copy of *The Gulag Archipelago* hidden in the USSR[84] that Solzhenitsyn gave the signal for publishing the book by the YMCA Press in Paris.

The seventies also saw the publication of a number of Gulag memoirs by foreigners who had been released in the "thaw" years. Some of them were written earlier but withheld from publication for various biographical or political reasons. *Seven Thousand Days in Siberia* by Karlo Stajner, a prominent member of the Yugoslav Communist Party arrested in Russia during the Great Terror and repatriated in 1955, was not allowed into print in Belgrade until 1971, and then only, it seems, with Tito's own sanction. The same year saw the publication of *Magadan* by Michael Solomon, who had been repatriated to Rumania in 1955 only to be jailed there for another nine years. Stajner's book is, with the exception of a few passages dealing with the author's private emotions, characterized by a considerable leveling of intensities; Solomon's is a chronological chain of grim incidents with the authorial persona's emotional responses and ethical qualms either elided or standardized. Between them, however, these two books contain a huge amount of concrete factual information on the topography of the Archipelago: unlike their literary merit, their value for historians has proved to be of the first order.

* * *

Camp memoirs written after the 1973 watershed publication of Solzhenitsyn's *The Gulag Archipelago* bear the mark of belatedness and have to define their position vis-à-vis Solzhenitsyn's materials, methods, or ideas.

Perhaps the only group of writers for whom this predicament did not really exist were the people of the younger generation who had been imprisoned during the "stagnation" period. However, these writers do not always focus on the camps: a more prominent part of the experience described in Amalrik's *Involuntary Journey to Siberia* is exile; at the center of Eduard Kuznetsov's *Prison Diaries* is prison; and the nadir of the experience dealt with in Grigorenko's *Memoirs* and Vladimir Bukovsky's *To Build a Castle* is the psychiatric ward.[85] Indeed, for political prisoners of the sixties and the seventies, labor camps were a less harsh form of incarceration than prisons (such as the Vladimir isolator), let alone psychiatric institutions.

In comparison with their Stalin-time precursors, dissident memoirists tend to devote more attention to the political struggle that led to their arrest. However, in the works of some of them such issues recede into the background when it comes to the description of their prison experience. Thus, in the memoirs of Zionists, such as Eduard Kuznetsov (*Mordovskii marafon* [*The Mordovian Marathon*]), Natan Sharansky (*Fear No Evil*), Hilel Butman (*From Leningrad to Jerusalem, the Gulag Way*), and Vladimir Markman (*Na kraiu geografii* [*At the Edge of Geography*]), the conditions of Soviet convicts become a no less important target of attack than the regime's national policies. Amalrik, Sharansky, and Kheifitz[86] comment on the power struggle between the dissident prisoners and the KGB, the dynamics of hunger strikes, the influence of the Western media, and the complex codes of resistance to Lubyanka's force and fraud. Kuznetsov's *Mordovian Marathon* contains, among other issues, heartrending accounts of the social and psychological consequences of homosexual practices in the camps. The victimization of passive homosexuals and male victims of rape as well as sundry power games of juvenile delinquents are also among the subjects extensively explored in Igor Guberman's slightly fictionalized 1990 collection of sketches *Progulki vokrug baraka* [*Strolls around the Barrack*].

In contrast to veterans of post-Stalin camps, the writers who had been imprisoned under Stalin but whose works appeared in print only in the seventies and eighties were well aware of the limited novelty of their materials. Whereas the earliest Gulag memoirists had to confront the suspicion and hostility of large segments of the Western audience but, like the dissidents of the seventies, knew that they were carrying unprecedented news, the belated witnesses of the Stalin years were likely to be waved off as offering "more of the same." They were writing into an already established context and had to develop strategies of interacting with it. Some used the context, explicitly or implicitly, as a proof of the importance of their own testimony, in a firm and usually quite justified belief in the value of their individual perspective; most of these authors were non-Russians writing in their own languages (Maloumian in French, Vinitski in Hebrew, Fisher in Yiddish). Another strategy (Badash, Rozanov 1979, Konson) was to supplement and amend the information presented by Solzhenitsyn and other precursors; a third was to describe encounters with well-known personalities as well as locations and aspects of camp life that had not yet been covered. Some of the less honest works also engaged in a version of "competitive suffering." A fourth practice, artistically the most significant, consisted in placing emphasis on individual experience. Belatedness could be turned to aesthetic advantage since it sanctioned an artistically selective approach to the material: one was exempt from the duty of dealing with the basics.[87] Among the clearest examples of the erasure of borderlines between late testimony and modernist art[88] as well as of the artistic potentialities inherent in the memoirs purged of biographical trivia is *Kratkie povesti* [*Brief Tales*] by Lev Konson, part of which circulated in Samizdat prior to the author's emigration to Israel.[89]

The issue of the individual voice was actually thematized in the works of people whose stories, factual or fictionalized, had already been told by Solzhenitsyn. The two most striking of these "real people" are Lev Kopelev and Dimitri Panin, prototypes of, respectively, Rubin and Sologdin of *The First Circle*. The title of Panin's memoirs published in Paris about a year after his emigration in 1972 is *The Notebooks of Sologdin:* while praising the general accuracy of Solzhenitsyn's vision, Panin wished to put on record the difference between himself and Sologdin, whom he viewed as a careerist and skirt-chaser.[90] Solzhenitsyn was angry with Panin for thus "capitalizing" on his work (Scammell 1984: 895). The posthumous Moscow 1991 reprint of Panin's memoirs came out under the title *Lubianka-Ekibastuz: Lagernye zapiski* [*Lubyanka-Ekibastuz: Camp Notes*].

Panin was a descendant of an upper-class family and a convinced anti-Communist. He rejected even the most idealistic versions of Marxism: from where he stood, the power over his country had been seized by a band of criminals. His critique of the Soviet rule is passionate and sweeping; and he analyses not the prevailing state of affairs but the ways of struggling against it. An engineer by training, he turns reflections on social, historical, and metaphysical matters into problem-solving procedures and presents his solutions in the shape of rules or "theses." This creates a sense of intellectual closure that, while unfavorably contrasting with Panin's emotional openness to individuals with different creeds, reconfirms the empowering effect of strong convictions in adversity.

Panin's narrative also probes the issue of a talented person's self-actualization under a totalitarian regime. The predicament of scientists torn between their love for their work and their reluctance to collaborate with the regime or become too visible reached a kind of tragic purity in his life. He sought a compromise with his conscience by working on technological projects that he deemed to be of greater benefit to the people than to the regime. However, his skills would soon make him conspicuous, a natural target for squealers. The problem of self-actualization was aggravated by the tension between a freedom fighter's readiness for self-sacrifice and a healthy, vigorous body's life-drive. Facing the gray zone, Panin recollects the occasions when hunger drove him to acts that fell short of his ethical principles. Despite an asceticism bordering on self-flagellation, hunger remains one of the most frequently recurrent motifs of his book and one of the pledges of its authenticity. The theme of the life-drive reaches its climax in Panin's account of his near-fatal forty-days' pellagra followed by a miraculous recovery. One does not need to share Panin's belief in the healing power of faith to be profoundly moved by the story of his sliding toward death, of his joy on being turned back from its threshold (164–69), and of his bursting into tears at the gift of a piece of bread from a fellow prisoner (171–72).

In the context of Panin's later writings, *The Notebooks of Sologdin* function as a presentation of credentials. Panin became the center of an intellectual circle in Paris. His friends published seventeen issues of the journal *Choix* devoted to his views; a number of his philosophical and publicist works appeared as supplements to this journal as well as in other frameworks. Whereas the ideas presented in Panin's treatises[91] may not be acceptable to most of his readers, his memoir will retain its interest not so much for the philosophical and practical convictions that it expresses as for its story of the origin of these convictions.

The "real person" behind Sologdin's flamboyant friend Lev Rubin, the literary scholar Lev Kopelev,[92] likewise wrote memoirs, and they lend support to the reader's impression of Solzhenitsyn's loving exasperation with this large and brilliant person who remained, too long and too obstinately, a victim of ideological calcination. If Olitskaya's memoirs reflect the ambiguities of self-sacrifice for the sake of political struggle, those of Solonevich the ambiguities of opting out, and those of Panin the ambiguities of self-actualization, Kopelev's autobiographical trilogy displays the ambiguities of the wish to belong, as well as the strange workings of intellect, benevolence, and generosity caught up in a closed system of political thought. In the camps, Kopelev could live with himself only by an adamant adherence to Communist ideals. His memoirs deal with the conflict between ethics and ideology; in contrast to Evgenia Ginzburg's story of an awakening to the realities, they trace an obstinate yet losing struggle against disillusionment.

The middle book of the trilogy, *To Be Preserved Forever* (the title alludes to the words stamped on the prisoners' NKVD files, meant to be kept in perpetuity) was written first, in 1968,[93] after Kopelev had undergone a reorientation[94] toward "socialism with a human face" yet before he emigrated to Germany. The vividness with which *To Be Preserved Forever* explores an entrenched Communist's dogmatism and casuistry is matched only by Koestler's *Darkness at Noon*. A victim of Stalin's 1944–45 purge of middle-rank army officers, Kopelev believed that he was arrested as a result of a merely local intrigue. The charge brought against him rested on his outspoken disapproval of the conduct of Soviet troops on German territories and of the tacit official permissiveness toward pillage and rape. The book describes the life and activities of a Soviet propaganda unit during the last year of World War II, prison scenes, scenes of the Volga-region camp life in the shadow of the "bitch war," and the workings of the Stalinist legal process. It traces the history of Kopelev's "file" through multiple juridical procedures and juxtaposes his memory of the events that led to his arrest with the official versions: extensive flashbacks are placed at points where this material is alluded to by interrogators or attorneys. In tune with the dissidents' policy of invoking the Soviet Constitution in their struggle against the arbitrary power of the regime, Kopelev responds to the fabricated accusations as seriously as if they had really been the cause of rather than the justification for his imprisonment. At the time, indeed, by treating the letter of the charges as if it were their spirit, he managed to win his acquittal at the trial and an "interlude" at liberty before the court judgment was reversed.[95]

The first part of the trilogy, *The Education of a True Believer* (1960–77) deals with Kopelev's early life. Its Russian title, *And One Made Oneself an Idol,* is an allusion to the breaking of the second commandment. Kopelev presents his adoption of Communist ideology as a teenage rebellion against the middle-class atmosphere of a home dominated by the egotistic, expansive, emotional, and opinionated mother. The mother's portrait, however, becomes much more attractive in the story of Kopelev's moral crisis during the artificial famine of 1932–33 in the Ukraine—she is the one person who weeps over the tragedy of the peasants. The scenes pertaining to the collectivization and the famine are the most intensely painful in the book.[96] Kopelev witnessed the activities that led up to the peasants' starvation and the period that followed it: during the worst months he was laid up sick—his bodily strength undercut, as it were, by a moral impasse.

The third book, *Ease My Sorrows,* dealing with the life in the prison institute, the *sharashka* described by Solzhenitsyn in *The First Circle,* is less emotionally charged: it seems to owe its origin not to the things that the author *must* say but to those he still has in stock. Here Kopelev seems to be fatigued and subdued, which probably reflects his attitude as a narrator at the time of the composition rather than his moods as a prisoner at the time of the events themselves. Though he refers to having participated in numerous quarrels, in the book he is most often cast in the role of listener, ironically in keeping with his work as a sound analyst, which like so much else in his life, eventually went down the drain. In fact, the gap between the attitudes of Kopelev the narrator and Kopelev the protagonist of his tale is evident throughout the trilogy. Kopelev recollects, with some embarrassment, his occasional acceptance of the Bolshevik belief that "subjective" sympathy for individuals was to be superseded by classifying them with the "objectively" hostile social groups. At the time of composition he opts for "spontaneity" rather than "class consciousness"; and his warm and tolerant attitude to people transpires in his reproduction of the whole spectrum of stylistic registers, dialects, and professional idioms. Like Solzhenitsyn's works and, to a smaller extent, Ginzburg's, Kopelev's trilogy is a heteroglot feast.

At least one issue, however, forms a common denominator of the content and the stance of Kopelev's memoirs: his thematized tendency toward belatedness, in both awakening to realities and telling the story. According to Kopelev's report, the captain of the *sharashka* volleyball team characterized his three able players, Solzhenitsyn, Panin, and Kopelev, in a quite symbolic manner:

> He explained to Panin that he played beautifully, bravely, but he hit the ball too hard, not caring where it might go. He asked Solzhenitsyn not to scurry up and down the court, not to give orders instead of the captain, and not to intercept his partner's ball, worrying that he might miss it. And he rebuked me: "You're a born volleyball player—you have the height, the stroke, the jump. But your reactions are delayed. You're always a half-step behind: you wave your arms when the ball is already behind you." (113)

The emigration of the *perestroika* period would eventually lead to the publication of one more perspective on the splendid trio, the 1995 memoir of the American-born Morris Hershman, which includes an account of his stay in the Marfino prison institute (1995: 158–73)—the Mavrino *sharashka* of *The First Circle*.

* * *

Some of the "real people" referred to in Solzhenitsyn's *The Gulag Archipelago* likewise published their memoirs abroad. One of the first to speak in her own voice soon after emigration was Lyubov Bershadskaya, whose narrative *Rastoptannye zhizni* [*Trampled Lives*] (1975) came out on the heels of the third volume of *The Gulag Archipelago,* where she is mentioned as a participant in the Kengir rebellion (5: 12). Another was Solzhenitsyn's "Alexander D.," believed to be the only sane survivor of two notorious torture prisons, Lefortovo and Sukhanovka (*GA* 1: 2).[97] In 1975 the identity of this person was disclosed: he was Alexander Dolgun, formerly an American citizen who repatriated in 1971 and wrote *Alexander Dolgun's Story: An American in the Gulag,* in collaboration with Patrick Watson. Solzhenitsyn uses Dolgun's case as a link in a chain of gradually escalating examples of torture; Dolgun himself supplements the paradigm with an inside story of the experience of torture, recovery, and struggle for survival. The tone of his narrative is unexpectedly cheerful, colored by the somewhat incredulous joy of an ordinary person's discovery of his strength and of the richness of his spirit. Dolgun's book provides, among other things, an account of the mass release and its multiple snags in 1955, making it clear that things were not completely set right in 1956 or even two decades later.

* * *

Dolgun's narrative belongs to the batch of memoirs published in the late sixties and the seventies by foreign ex-prisoners (Victor Herman, Aino Kuusinen, Dante Corneli, the Lithuanians Stefanija Rukienė and Elena Juciutė, and others) who had been released during the thaw but could not leave the country until much later. At the time, the subject of the Gulag regained increased relevance because of the persecution of the dissidents and the struggle for human rights in the Soviet Union.

One of the more strident voices of this period belongs to Victor Herman, another American who had gone to Russia in the thirties.[98] Arrested in 1937, Herman was savagely tortured because he had nothing to confess (prisoners who actually had something to confess had an easier time at the interrogations).[99] In the special wing of the Gorky (Nizhny Novgorod) prison, he was among those forced to sit, silent and motionless, for months, in an overcrowded airless cell. It is for the reader to decide whether the uniqueness of the experience described in his *Coming Out of the Ice* (1979)[100] undermines his credibility or supports his claim to having endured because of his professional athlete's outstanding physical fitness and spirit of competition.[101] Herman notes that at a certain stretch of his imprisonment his sanity was impaired—during the interrogation period he was subjected, among other things, to a mock execution.[102] At a certain point, in a peripheral camp of the Viatka region, being too weak to work, he survived by eating rats—not on an impulse but in a planned systematic way. For Herman, the memories of this deliberate transgression of a taboo, and of his daughter's hunger in the forest dugout, are unhealed wounds. Nothing is altogether incredible in the vastness of the Gulag, and Herman's self-portrait convincingly shows what it may have taken to live through suffering beyond ordinary human endurance.

* * *

In the late eighties, Gulag memoirs started appearing in the Soviet press. Their release was part of the general process of the liberalization of the Soviet literary market and of the convergence of the broad domestic audience with Samizdat and Tamizdat readers. The process (see Brown 1993: 3–4) began with the publication of the formerly banned writers of the first decades of the century, for example, the 1986 publication of Nikolai Gumilyov's poems (Marsh 1995: 13). This was followed by the extensive publication of writers whose separate works had already been printed before—Akhmatova, Bulgakov, Mandelstam, Pilnyak, Pasternak, Platonov, Zamyatin. At about the same time the works of major émigré writers like Aldanov, Berberova, Khodasevich, and Nabokov were published in the Soviet Union for the first time. Next came the formerly suppressed works of more recent writers, such as Lidia Chukovskaya, Yury Dombrovsky, Venedikt Erofeev, Vasily Grossman, Anatoly Rybakov, and others. Only then came the turn of the works by the more recent émigrés like Aksyonov, Vladimov, Sinyavsky, Sasha Sokolov, and, of course, Solzhenitsyn. Tantamount to the fall of the Berlin wall was the discovery that Tamizdat publication of a book no longer precluded its publication in Russia itself.

A closer context for the *glasnost*-era Gulag narratives was provided by the publication of more general memoirs about the times of Stalin— memoirs already known in the West (Nadezhda Mandelstam, Aleksandr Orlov), or retrieved from secret "desk-drawers" and revised (Kamil Ikramov) or left intact (Dimitri Likhachev), or else recently composed (Filshtinsky, Rapoport). At first, attempts were still made to monitor the flow of revelations—up to 1987, the depth of the public openness signified by the term *glasnost* could have been measured by the degree of the subversiveness of the published materials: Ginzburg's work preceded that of Solzhenitsyn, and the full edition of Shalamov's *Kolyma Tales* had to wait still longer. Oleg Volkov's *Pogruzhenie vo t'mu* [*Sinking into Darkness*] (1987),[103] whose early version had been provisionally (and belatedly) accepted by Tvardovsky for *Novyi mir* in 1965, was published in full abroad: its first domestic publication was still slightly censored (see Volkov 1990: 54–64).

By mid-1988, Soviet publications of camp literature came in an avalanche (see Marsh 1995: 17–22, 84–97). All the major journals, and most of the minor ones, printed materials pertaining to the Gulag; even scientific journals devoted sections to scientists who had been jailed. The situation had the marks of the massive resurgence of Holocaust testimonies thirty years after the event: a new generation was growing up, for which the major atrocity of Russian history was neither a living presence nor a subdued background. It was therefore necessary to introduce this atrocity into the canon of national education—partly in the hope that if the lessons of history were remembered, they would not repeat. The people who knew Stalin's camps firsthand were now old; their testimony had to be recorded and their memoirs made public before it was too late. An important role in this endeavor was played by the "Memorial" society founded in 1988 (see Remnick 1994: 100–119) and by the historical-literary society *Vozvrashchenie* (Return) that grew out of the social interaction of former prisoners. In 1988, the chairman of *Vozvrashchenie*, the poet Semyon Vilensky, editor of the journal *Volia* (Freedom), which focuses on imprisonment under totalitarian regimes, put together a seminal collection of women's memoirs of imprisonment, *Dodnes' tiagoteet* [*It Still Weighs Heavy*], later also published in the United States as *Till My Tale Is Told* (1999). Since 1991 the society has been able to print its own materials: poetry brochures, collections of documents, memoirs by individual ex-prisoners, and the anthology *Soprotivlenie v Gulage* [*Resistance in the Gulag*] (1992). It has also organized international conferences and extended its activities into the sphere of welfare.

The future-oriented ethical drive behind the new wave of camp materials was combined with the past-oriented drive—the wish to commemorate and honor the victims of the regime and to fill in gaps in historiography. This motivation was particularly strong in the case of second-generation victims, that is, people whose parents had perished in the purges and who themselves eventually endured imprisonment and other forms of punishment: for example, Zayara Vesyolaya, daughter of the writer Artyom Vesyoly, who perished in 1937 (see her "7–35" in Vilensky 1988: 539–88); Kamil Ikramov, son of Akmal Ikramov, condemned in the same 1938 show trial as Bukharin; and Pyotr Yakir, son of the general Yona Yakir, purged together with Tukhachevsky.[104] To a similar group also belong the Medvedev brothers, Zhores and Roy, whose father perished in Kolyma.[105] An urgent need for reviving the subject of the Gulag[106] converged with the removal of censorship.

Unfortunately, by the early nineties the previous information-hunger of the reading public was followed by a sense of surfeit. It is as if the public interest in the Gulag was killed not by banishing the subject (an expedient that failed in the late sixties) but by creating its overdose. Yet the surfeit also promoted the shift of critical attention from the historical disclosures to the literary value of the best of Gulag writings.

The most recent wave of Gulag materials falls into two parts: the "delayed" (Brown 1993: 2) or "desk-drawer" works, written long before and kept hidden during the "stagnation" period (e.g., *Nepridumannoe* by Lev Razgon, 1989),[107] and the "belated" new works, written in response to the new interest in the subject (e.g., *My shagaem pod konvoem* by I. Filshtinsky, 1994). The works of the first group are in many ways similar to those of Samizdat fame, but they evince a less powerful urge to speak up or else less confidence in the quality of their writing. Some of them (e.g., the memoirs of Sliozberg, Surovtseva, and Grankina) had been placed at the disposal of Solzhenitsyn and were used by him as sources for *The Gulag Archipelago*.[108] The ethical and artistic motivations behind them seem weaker than those of Samizdat works circulated at great risks in the times of "stagnation." Moreover, the memoirs written in the fifties and sixties (e.g., Olga Adamova-Sliozberg's "Put'") or even earlier (e.g., Dimitri Likhachev's notes smuggled out of the Solovki in 1930) but published only under *glasnost* faced a reception-context different from the one for which they had been intended. The most useful sub-genre for such delayed narratives turned out to be that of "autobiographical stories"—a form chosen, for instance, by Lev Razgon, who claims that he did not make revisions in his old narratives but elided parts of his material in order to avoid common-knowledge redundancies (see 1989: 35). And though the tone of the opening pages is reminiscent of children's literature (Razgon had, indeed, worked in that field), the material, selected on the principle of "what still *has to* be put on record"), progressively grows in seriousness of insight. This tendency is further enhanced in the 1994 expanded version of the book, *Plen v svoem otechestve*, which includes chapters written after Razgon got access to some of the KGB archive files.

The memoirs of the second group overlap with the vast new corpus of the *glasnost*-period autobiographies (see Balina 1992: 13) intended for those readers of the new generation who had had little or no knowledge of the literature forbidden in the previous decades. Unlike the "belated" Tamizdat works of the seventies and early eighties, these new books do not presuppose that their audience is steeped in Solzhenitsyn, or Margolin, or Ginzburg, or Marchenko, though allusions are often made to the works of Shalamov, whose Russian readership has been growing since 1987. They therefore often explain the camp realia well known to the readers of the earlier works.[109] The goal shared by most of the new Gulag books is pedagogical clarity. As if to sustain the interest of their elusive readers, many of the works structure their descriptive material around strong narrative kernels, with paradoxical twists of fate, lives of extraordinary people, or striking episodes of the authors' experience. And though according to earlier witnesses camp experience often exploded conventional moral norms, these narratives emphasize conventional ethical attitudes as a counterweight both to the *homo-homini-lupus* type of camp individualism and to the Communist value-framework. The conceptual processing of the moral practice of the camps is here considerably milder than in the works of earlier memoirists. Private-domain materials tend to be played down; the emphasis is placed on privileged-access insights and on corrective or gap-filling public-domain information.

* * *

In retrospect, one can say that the development of the Gulag-memoir corpus from the twenties to the nineties was associated with a change of perspective: from the view of the Gulag as a peripheral phenomenon to the recognition of its centrality in the Soviet system. Works of this corpus achieved the greatest philosophical depth and literary merit in the sixties and seventies. Throughout its history, and particularly in the "stagnation" years, the Gulag literary corpus was an integral part of the struggle against Soviet totalitarianism. It was also a factor in the history of the socio-political ideas within and beyond the borders of the former Socialist bloc.

Now that the political force of Gulag memoirs has spent itself in the changes that it has promoted, the works of the corpus still retain a composite value as historical documents and aesthetic objects of a peculiar kind. I shall end this chapter with a brief discussion of one of the later works of the corpus, the memoir *Chernye kamni* [*Black Stones*] (1989) written by the poet Anatoly Zhigulin in 1984 on the basis of old notes.

In about the middle of the book there is a chapter entitled "The Cemetery in Butugychag," which, the foreword tells us (6), was composed first. It starts with the words "I am the last poet of Stalin's Kolyma. Unless I tell, it will remain untold." The staccato sentences convey a pent-up emotion, which in the previous years had gone into Zhigulin's poems on his prison and camp experience. Yet the poems often needed clues to their submerged hints, or a framework in which their subject could be recognized; their import was diluted in seemingly innocuous verse collections. Zhigulin's memoir, however, is an exception from the calmer narratives of the *glasnost* period: it often matches the emotional pitch of the testimonies of the fifties and sixties. Yet—not without reason—it lacks the purity and confidence of their ethical stance.

The memoir was written when Zhigulin was ill and had reason to fear that he would not live long enough to tell his story with total openness. Hence, he encoded parts of it. "The Cemetery in Butugychag" tells of his work in a Kolyma mine; it takes up just a fraction of the book's total textual space, but the "black stones" of the title (which can, deceptively, make one think of coal) pertain to this part of the narrative and point to its centrality. The mine produces a metal. Gold, as everyone knows, was the main production of Kolyma, usually referred to as "the metal," but Zhigulin's 1964 poem about the mine, printed toward the end of the book (218–19), refers, rather, to "silver." The chapter contains some technical language and several puzzling points that the reader may attribute to stylistic imperfections, or a not-untypical hastiness. A description of the lode of ore is followed by the remark "We tried to avoid the drifts, and begged to be assigned to the cross-cut. The dust from the drilling was there too. And the ground was the hardest and the heaviest—pure granite. Yet granite! Pure!" (162)

It would take a trained geologist to understand the hints embedded in the chapter, recognize the "black-brown" lode with silvery-gray and rusty-ochre margins as the streak of uranium, and to read the "silver" pit Butugychag of the 1964 poem as a coded reference to a uranium pit. In 1988 *glasnost* was not yet ripe for revelations of this kind; the truth about

Butugychag was "declassified" a few years later. Nor was it in a Soviet journal, but in the Frankfurt-based émigré *Grani* that Zhigulin published the explanatory postscript article "Uranovaia udochka" ["The Uranium Rod"] in 1990. In 1988, a censor-editor of the journal *Znamia* had wondered, Zhigulin recalls, at his insistence on the (boring?) details about the mine.[110]

The seeming illogicality of the references to the hard soil of the cross-cut, "Yet granite! Pure!" becomes clear when one realizes how vastly preferable it was to have to work with pure granite than with the softer soil contaminated by radioactive substances. Another stylistic stumbling block later in the passage produces a similar delayed effect. Zhigulin refers to the health hazard of working in the Butugychag ore-dressing plant, especially in its drying room: the work was easy—just stirring the concentrate in the warm room rather than outside in the frost, in only six-hour shifts; one would also get better food, "even milk." The job was readily undertaken by young Western Ukrainians. "This is probably why in those dreams I think in Ukrainian," writes Zhigulin in a parenthetic reference to his nocturnal nightmares of Butugychag. An educated person, he had made every effort and paid every price (including punishment cells and a near-lethal escape attempt) to avoid working with uranium, but, short of inciting a suicidal rebellion, he could evade this work only if someone else was left behind to do it—and to die of radiation illness in the hospices of Butugychag—and to be buried without a cross or headstone in the frozen mausoleum of the hills. The Ukrainian of his dreams is the language of remorse. The passage is a clue to the understated thematic concern variously explored throughout the memoir and the poems that supplement it: one could not avoid getting somehow, directly or indirectly, implicated in the pervasive evil of the system; one kept running the risk of losing one's moral bearings, making ethical mistakes, slipping into unobtrusive forms of betrayal and corruption.

The discovery of the meaning of the hints planted in *Black Stones* is akin to an aesthetic experience. Zhigulin's strategy of coding is aesthetic insofar as it imposes a conceptual unity on an ostensibly fragmented narrative. Moreover, its large-scale effect reproduces some of the narrative's local effects. Though the self-consciously belated author ("I am the last poet of Stalin's Kolyma") is exempt from repeating what has been said by others, he still does have something to add to the general prison lore beyond the details of his particular case. In his lengthy account of the interrogation period, he deciphers for us the interrogator's order that he should be given "a nice fifth corner": the "fifth corner" is a beating of a helpless prisoner by four guards, each standing, as it were, in or for a corner of the cell, leaving it for the prisoner to seek an escape to the non-existent fifth corner. The epithet "nice" is not a sarcastic euphemism; it means that the prisoner is to be dealt with "nicely"—he is needed for further interrogations and so should not be killed or permanently maimed (61–63). The force of Zhigulin's account of the "fifth corner," "nice" or otherwise, lies in its implicit socio-linguistic point: the fact that the practice had been codified by a special metaphoric term tells us volumes about the work of the NKVD at that period.[111] Likewise, the understanding of Zhigulin's coding strategy itself, its "how" and "wherefore" as well as "what," gives us an immediate sense of the moral climate of the early stages of *glasnost,* a sense more vivid than insights obtained by historical analysis. Both a sympathetic and a cautiously critical reading of a narrative of this kind are ethically determined activities. Both have an occasional aesthetic bonus—yet in the case of the narratives whose stance re-enacts their content, the aesthetic and the ethical facets of the reader's experience are not easily told apart.

3
Gulag Memoirs as a Genre

"Gulag memoirs" as a genre are memoirs that are centrally concerned with camp experience. Works of this genre are but a part of the whole corpus of factographic firsthand accounts of the authors' imprisonment in Soviet concentration camps. For example, Boris Gorbatov's 1964 autobiography does not really belong to the Gulag memoir genre: though shaken by his brief term in Kolyma camps, the author had taken it in stride as one of the hardships encountered in the course of a staunch Communist's life.[1] By contrast, El Campesino's or Olitskaya's memoirs do belong to this genre: though the bulk of their texts presents an account of their pre-camp experience, the camps occupy the pivotal place in their concerns, with the other narrative details leading down to that nadir. Of the memoirs dealing with prisons rather than with the camps, Weissberg's *The Conspiracy of Silence* is, for analogous reasons, closer to Gulag narratives than, for instance, the 1983 memoirs of Avtorkhanov, which bear a closer affinity to the literature of disillusionment.[2]

Gulag memoirs have been perceived as a codified new narrative genre since approximately the late sixties. Most of them, just like Puritan spiritual autobiographies, slave narratives, or memoirs of disillusioned Communists, are written either by non-professional writers or by authors whose artistic talents are revealed in this—their first—literary endeavor. Yet even in the case of the former, high artistic merit often results from the harmony of the content and the stance: the narrative act seems to be an extension of the author's life, and that life acquires an aesthetic dimension of its own.[3] Referring to his NKVD file in Kolyma, full of squealers' reports, interrogators' memoranda, and other "data," Shalamov, perhaps the most exquisite professional writers among Gulag memoirists, combines the traditional metaphor of writing in blood with a photographic term: "the letters have not faded—human blood is a good fixing agent" (1990a: 212). The mixed metaphors[4] here co-laminate theories of art as a transformation of suffering, as a document, and as a means of arresting the flow of reality. Life seems to be writing itself, imprinting traces on white sheets of snow, memory, paper, in a continuum of the ethics of camp experience and the aesthetics of its record.

Because of similarities in their subject matter and in the writers' motivation for the narrative act, Gulag memoirs tend to display the following common morphological features: (1) tension between the *ethical* drive and an *aesthetic* impulse, closely associated with the bi-functionality of Gulag narratives as acts of witness-bearing and as works of art, (2) interconnection of *individual* and *communal* concerns, (3) inclusion of specific topoi as morphological variables, and (4) a modal scheme that can be described in terms of *Lent*.

* * *

In Gulag narratives, *ethical concerns* tend to prevail over psychological or socio-political ones. The main motivation for the narrative acts is ethical: giving evidence is the survivors' duty to those who have perished or are "still at sea" (Dolgun 1976: 343). The sense of this imperative is sometimes reflected in the titles (Tchernavin's *I Speak for the Silent*, Gliksman's *Tell the West*), in the dedications (*GA*), in the explicit appeals to public opinion (Margolin, Lipper, Buber-Neumann), in the comments on the survivor's obligation to testify (Ekart, Buber-Neumann, El Campesino, Ginzburg, Sliozberg), or in the references to friends who had asked the potential survivors to tell the story (Dolgun, Gliksman). The risk of becoming conspicuous targets for the KGB that the authors faced even abroad[5] enhanced the ethical significance of their testimony.

As noted above, the artistic merit of Gulag memoirs is associated with the congruence of the content and the stance. Memoirs published soon after the authors' release often have a heightened aesthetic appeal. The experience was still fresh for the authors, still fraught with emotion; moreover, the act of going public could mean, among other things, that the author had no reason to fear having his or her past acts exposed by fellow veterans. A memoirist's sense of the basic ethical integrity of his or her conduct at interrogations and in the camps (Ginzburg, Panin, Marchenko, Sharansky) can irradiate upon the text and become a source of aesthetic appeal in its own right; attempts to feign integrity (Dyakov) seldom remain undetectable. A memoirist's compunctious admission of the gray areas in his or her conduct in difficult circumstances (Panin, Solzhenitsyn, Ginzburg, Herling) adds to the aesthetic appeal of the narrative even when (or perhaps because) many aspects of the author's camp experience seem to have remained unprocessed. By contrast, in memoirs written long after the experience of imprisonment, the emotions of the past seem to have subsided and errors of the past to have been lived down: the authors (Volkov, Razgon) have, apparently, come to terms with them not in the course of but prior to writing. However, some of the early memoirists likewise needed a belief in their infallible rectitude (Buber-Neumann) or were not above boasting of their exploits (Petrov), whereas some of the belated memoirists (Konson, Herman, Zhigulin) seemed to relive the scenes from the past with unabated emotions and uneased outrage or remorse.

Not all the details of the memoirs are ethically oriented; some are there for the pleasure of narration. Whereas Lipper and Marchenko use autobiographical facts as a framework for organizing the general information that they were in a position to collect, Dolgun, Solonevich, and Petrov seem to enjoy the opportunities to incorporate good adventure stories into their account of the camps. To some extent, the story-telling impulse asserts itself in all the writings of survivors, whether essayistic, historiographic, or lexicographic. Thus, the 1968 journalistic report by Valentin Moroz from the camps of the sixties opens with a well-visualized scene of a manhunt; and *The Time of Stalin,* the historical monograph by A. Antonov-Ovseenko, draws on the author's camp recollections for insights into the criminal psychology behind Stalin's modes of operation (1981: 8, 9, 30–31, 50–51, 200, 220). Even the invaluable reference work *The Gulag Handbook,* by Jacques Rossi, is occasionally punctuated with miniature stories of his own experience. Such narrative moments often enhance ethical points.

In the selection of material for camp memoirs the ethics of reticence is balanced by the need for narrative freedom. Early Gulag authors (e.g., Doubassoff) were not always sufficiently aware of a possible clash between the story-telling impulse and the wish not to endanger those left behind; later memoirists were more cautious. Solonevich already knew that his work would be read not only by its target audience but also by the secret police and therefore tried to restrict himself only to those aspects of his escape that, he believed, could not be reproduced.[6] Lipper and Buber withhold the real names of the fellow prisoners left behind; Konson refuses to disclose his methods of facilitating communication between prisoners; and Kheifitz tells only of those prison subterfuges that, he claims, the turnkeys have already understood. Yet until very recently the ethical situation was complicated by the authors' weary disgust with the self-censorship prevalent in Soviet journalism and their resentment of the need for discretion even in the West—a reminder that the NKVD could still hold them under remote control. Telling a good story, complete with striking particulars, was, moreover, pragmatically justified by the consciousness-raising agenda—it promised wider audiences.

Short-term effects of Gulag testimony may have been similar to those of medicine that aggravates a patient's condition before curing it. Behaviorist psychology tells us that "the literature of freedom," including the literature of protest against incarceration, often leads to an intensification of punitive controls. An individual prisoner's struggle for inner freedom has rich aesthetic potential, and stories of subterfuges and escapes have entertainment value; details of both, however, are instructive and challenging to the so-called organs of repression. While camp regulations were still evolving through trial-and-error, the accounts of the prisoners' canny exploits in the memoirs of the first fugitives supplemented the data obtained from interrogators and informers, thus aiding the authorities to tighten the camp regime, perfect the training of the guards, and invent new preventive and punitive measures. When almost no more loopholes were available for alleviating their lot, the prisoners could still insist on their inner freedom in the face of outward helplessness. It was in response to this ultimate challenge—no less, perhaps, than in response to the ideological pressures regarding the growing statistics of imprisonment for opposition to the regime—that Big Brother eventually learned to put these prisoners into psychiatric institutions, where their personalities would be assaulted by drugs.[7] The double-edged effect of Gulag literature—raising the consciousness of the target audience and presenting free instruction to the Lubyanka—distinguishes the history of this corpus from that of the Holocaust literature, which came into being after the Nazi *Lager*s had been turned into museums.

* * *

The sense of one's obligation to testify on behalf of the collective is often intertwined with a specific personal motivation for telling the story. Ginzburg recollects how she explained the past to her surviving son, from whom she had been torn away: her first major memoir was the oral one offered to the teenage Vasily Aksyonov after he joined her in Kolyma.[8] The written memoir likewise seems to address the younger generation, which, she fears, may still be under the "hypnotic power of the monstrous accusations" (1981: 420) that had been brought against the purge victims. Thus the wish to counteract the systematic Stalinist distortions of history combines with the personal impulse of self-justification.

On arrival at each penal facility, most prisoners investigated the lay of the land: collecting facts was necessary for practical adaptation. Yet collecting *maximum* data, in excess of what was needed for daily survival, was also a form of resistance to the authorities' control of information. One ceased being a victim and turned into a subversive intern, a witness-in-training. Curiosity was also a psychological aid to endurance.[9] "Many a time," writes Ginzburg, "my thoughts were taken off my own suffering by the keen interest which I felt in the unusual aspects of life and of human nature which unfolded around me" (1967: 417). Storing material for prospective testimony enhanced the motivation for the struggle for survival; the writing of memoirs would be a natural sequel to this struggle.

As noted above, the main motives for writing memoirs were often supplemented by subsidiary personal objectives, such as placing things on record for an imaginary court of justice (Kopelev), presenting one's credentials as a public figure (Panin), engagement in soul searching (Konson), probing the reasons for one's failure to live up to codes (Herling), or locating camp experience in one's political or philosophical system (Margolin).[10] Personal aims frequently endow the memoirs with features of such literary genres as the *Bildungsroman* (Ginzburg), apologia (Kopelev), and confession (Konson), whereas communal aims are responsible for the features that these memoirs share with protest declarations (Lipper, Buber-Neumann, El Campesino), political satire (Solonevich, Solzhenitsyn), and *conte philosophique* (Margolin, Herling).

The interconnection of the communal and the individual concerns is also reflected in the components of the material. Since Dostoevsky's *The House of the Dead*, narratives of imprisonment have tended to combine stories of individual experience with accounts of the "shared suffering and common shame" (Ginzburg 1981: 122), that is, of the representative experience of the prisoners. Conditions in the Gulag are, indeed, seldom treated as grounds for personal grievance. Here the attitude of the memoirist as the *narrating voice* is different from the attitude of the memoirist as the *focal character* of the text, the prisoner who has witnessed the events and situations described: the *focalizer*[11] was a sharer of the *common* lot, yet the retrospectively narrating *voice* belongs to a concrete historical *individual* with his or her private memory, antecedents, and affiliations. Solzhenitsyn the author is a distinct personality; Solzhenitsyn the protagonist of the autobiographical chapters of *The Gulag Archipelago* is a regular *zek*,[12] one of many—especially when he nearly loses his life during the rebellion at Ekibastuz:

> I remember very well my state of mind; a nauseated indifference to my fate; a momentary indifference whether I survived or not. Why have you fastened your hooks on us, curse you! Why must we go on paying you till the day we die for the crime of being born into this unhappy world? Why must we sit forever in your jails? The prison sickness which is at once nausea and peace of mind flooded my being. Even my constant fear for the as-yet-unrecorded poem and the play I carried within me was in abeyance. In full view of the death which was wheeling towards us in military greatcoats, I made no effort at all to push through the door. This was the true convict mentality; this was what they brought us to. (*GA* 5: 11, 256)

Shalamov's focalizers have practically no distinctive personal features apart from intellect, decency, and the wish to live: it is the personality of Shalamov the narrator rather than of Shalamov the prisoner (or of his avatars Krist and Andreev) that dominates his tales.[13] Under Stalin, collective protests were forbidden;[14] solidarity between prisoners was felt, quite correctly, to threaten the order of things; and in the country at large, criticism of mass abuses was possible only under the guise of reports on local negligence or on individual mistakes (cf. Grigorenko 1982: 43). The memoirists' emphasis on the common concerns can, to some extent, be a form of resistance to the "divide and rule" strategy of the authorities, whereas their filtering of these concerns through the prism of subjective narration constitutes their answer to the regime's assault on the inner autonomy of its victims.[15] And since the uniqueness of the individual vision is often a matter of emotional coloration, an author's (e.g., Gliksman's) attempt to subdue emotion, to keep the self out of the story, makes the memoir largely redundant as soon as the evidence that it presents is confirmed by other sources and assimilated by historiography.

In most cases, however, it is the opposite temptation, that of foregrounding the self, that mars the effect of a memoir: V. Petrov's narrative, for instance, all too often lapses into a story of individual adventure. Indeed, solidarity with one's fellow prisoners is not always automatic and instantaneous. The uninitiated person tends to be shocked by the first sight of concentration-camp inmates and to distance himself from them:

> People of mouse-gray color. All their clothes were mouse gray: some sort of jackets, hanging rags, shapeless footwear on naked feet, mouse-gray caps with ear-flaps that flew around and endowed faces with a wild expression. And the faces were also mouse-gray, earth-hued—as if all of them were covered with dust. They seemed to wear everything in a

clownish fashion: things were either too wide and long or too narrow and short. They all kept together, and at their side there stuck a man with a gun who wore military dress and obviously belonged to "a different race." (Margolin 1952: 17)[16]

It takes time to distinguish personal untidiness from unavoidable effects of regulation-issue clothing and signs of advanced dystrophy; in the meantime, the newcomer tends to blame the prisoners themselves for their appearance and endeavors to remain different. Indeed, many survivor narratives tell of the focalizers' oscillation between the impulse to identify with fellow sufferers and the wish to avoid the common fate, that of wasting away at the "general works." Contrary to Kant's categorical imperative, escapes—whether from the camp or from hard daily labor— could succeed only if one chose a course emphatically different from that taken by the majority. One could, in rare cases, be saved by one's unique prowess (Solonevich, Petrov) or stamina (Herman, Dolgun); yet much more often it was directly or obliquely at the expense of others that one extracted oneself from the vicious spiral. An accountant's or a librarian's job, for instance, was available to one out of many; moreover, it existed only if there still were the many on "general duties." A long-term holder of such a privileged job in the camp might have paid for it by various shameful compromises. By contrast, as one blended with the others in the common lot, one's body was gradually ruined—and there is contradictory evidence on what became of one's soul. Some authors (Margolin, Herling, Marchenko) emphasize the ill effects of hunger neurosis on a person's character and state of mind; others (Solzhenitsyn, Panin, and —despite his own on-record remarks—even Shalamov) suggest that relinquishing dubious methods to improve one's condition could have a purifying effect. The reader senses a near-mystical depth in the memoirs of those survivors (Shalamov, Panin, Marchenko, Ginzburg)[17] who had at least once found themselves totally immersed in the destructive element of the common fate. The focalizers seem to be at peace with themselves on the downward slope, all their past errors sufficiently expiated by their present suffering; yet this peace is, in its turn, joyfully relinquished when, by a lucky chance, their movement towards death is reversed.

The emphasis on the common lot is stronger in the works of those memoirists who believe in the pioneering status of their disclosures. Tchernavin, for instance, excludes an account of his escape from *I Speak for the Silent* since a successful escape is not part of the communal experience;[18] Gliksman preserves impersonality in his discourse on camp logistics; and Lipper attempts to suppress personal matters to the extent of leaving out obvious autobiographical lacunae. On her way back from Kolyma, Lipper was placed in a ship's hold with another woman and a number of male prisoners. She tells the reader that the male scarecrows spent the night "mounting" the other woman (gang rape was so common a phenomenon in and around the camps that there was a slang term for it—"in chorus"). Lipper herself was huddling aside, trying to reduce her contact with the scene; she does not explain why the men left her alone. The explanation is provided in Margolin's *Paris Report* (1970): at the time Lipper was eight months pregnant. She gave birth to a daughter in a transit camp and, more than a year later, managed to take her to Switzerland;[19] the father, a doctor, had remained in Kolyma. Thus Lipper almost demonstratively elides the one detail that can account for her special sensitivity to the plight of mothers and children. By leaving a conspicuous biographical gap she partly defeats her purpose of concentrating on the communal issues; at the same time she signals the need for privacy, of which she was deprived in the camps and which she had to forgo in order to bear witness.

Ginzburg adopts a less radical and more complex strategy. Her later life in the camps is shaped by her relationship with Dr. Anton Walter, and her memoirs would have been incomprehensible without the story of their love. To maintain the communal nature of her concerns, Ginzburg presents this personal story as subsumable under the general "love-in-the-camps" rubric. She explains the range of attitudes to this issue: at one extreme, the austere SR belief that sex should be forgone amid the squalor of camp life; at the other extreme, the prostitution to which many women prisoners were reduced (see *GA* 3: 8); in between one could still encounter ardent friendship and genuine love.[20]

The possibility of entering into a romantic relationship was a symptom of an improvement in one's condition. The sexual urge, known to be prominent in milder forms of imprisonment, was suppressed at "general duties" by exhaustion and the "prescribed hunger" (Levi 1990: 42). The topos of the camp-romance emerges most frequently in accounts of lucky breaks, such as work in hospitals. In the milder post-Stalinist camps, sexual hunger would again become an issue.

The distinction between individual and communal concerns is canceled when the memoirists attempt to save the images of separate individuals from oblivion—opposing the authorities' drive towards the erasure of the names of their victims from history. Yet each memoir produces a specific new tension between a number of highlighted portraits and the undifferentiated mass of people who both remain at the background and press in upon one in overcrowded cells, trains, or barracks. *Shipwreck of a Generation* by Joseph Berger is exclusively devoted to the portraits and stories of different categories of people whom the author encountered in prisons and camps.[21] A. Vaneev's "Two Years in Abez" concentrates on the portraits of prominent fellow prisoners, such as philosopher

Lev Karsavin and scholar Nikolai Punin (husband of Anna Akhmatova), against a camp hospital setting.[22]

Ginzburg does not classify her camp acquaintances, yet each social group, including the guards and the criminals, is represented by at least one person colorfully drawn in her memoir. By contrast, in the memoirs of Olitskaya, few persons apart from the SR party members stand out from the mass. The number of people an author has befriended in the camps is sometimes in inverse proportion to the vividness with which they are recollected. Gustav Herling's eighteen-month camp experience being relatively limited, the prisoners who populate his memory are relatively few and do not have to compete for the author's retrospective attention; it is partly for this reason that each portrait, charismatic or otherwise,[23] is presented with a forceful emotional engagement.

The tension between individual identity and common cause is thematized in the memoir of El Campesino. Even before his arrest, the Soviet authorities, aided by the leaders of the Spanish Communist party in exile,[24] attacked his "Spanish individualism" and attempted to deprive him of his independence, his freedom of movement and speech, and even his names, the real one and the nom de guerre. In ethical theory the term "individualism" means regarding the individual rather than the social structure as the source of moral values, laws, and duties. Yet in popular usage "individualism," an ideology of respect for every particular person, is often confused with "egoism." El Campesino would not give up his intuitive adherence to ethical individualism in the former sense of the word, yet he sought to avoid the latter when he joined the Communist party and accepted its belief in giving up individual claims for the good of the cause:

> We Spaniards, and especially we of Estremadura, are individualists. Anarchism comes more naturally to us than communism. But little by little Joseito replaced my individualistic notions with the collective doctrines of the Communists. He roused my enthusiasm for the Russian Revolution. He convinced me of the need for a Communist Party and International, with disciplined members who were willing to sink their personalities in the common cause and obey orders from above without a question. (1952: 10)

El Campesino does not present himself as blameless, yet he believes that the course he chose was morally not the worst:

> Throughout the Spanish War, I held power over life and death in my hands. I do not say I always used it wisely or even justly. I do not apologize for anything I have done. It was a bitter war. It was not pretty on either side. But Republican excesses, such as they were, were nothing

compared with Franco's. It was Franco who mobilized Moorish troops against his countrymen, and gave them free rein. And the excesses of which I may have been guilty myself were nothing compared with those of the Moscow Communists. I did not slaughter my comrades in arms for disagreeing with my political opinions. (1952: 22–23)

El Campesino's thoughts of the deaths inflicted by him or because of him are in keeping with a heroic version of individualism: "I am a Spaniard. We look upon life as tragic. We despise death. The death of a bull in the ring, the death of a man in war, seems a fitting end to us. We do not torture our consciences about one or the other" (1952: 22). Whatever criticism may be leveled at this attitude, it lends tragic grandeur to the death of an individual, enemy or friend. El Campesino exposes the callous dismissiveness with which the camp authorities treat the routinized and almost anonymous deaths of the prisoners.

El Campesino's stance of a man of the people granted him a closer view of social phenomena that the intelligentsia deemed marginal. Incapable of painting sufficiently individualized portraits of his associates, he presented the common plight, the destitution, and the death toll with brush strokes whose vigor has remained unmatched.[25] Yet despite his passionate solidarity with his associates, he did not dissolve in the collective: time and again, the communal suffering boosted him into the position of leadership as onto the crest of a wave.

Owing to its dialectics of the individual and the communal, it is not easy to determine whether El Campesino's narrative is an "autobiography" or a "memoir." Yet for the very same reason, a watertight distinction between these two genres (the former placing its emphasis on the author's identity and experience and the latter on the public-interest data that the author has been in a position to store) is not necessary for the genre definition of Gulag witness-narratives. As noted above, most of the works that belong to this corpus are, in any case, hybrid forms that incorporate and rework elements of a variety of traditional narrative genres.

* * *

Gulag memoirs contain a specific set of topoi, which connect the selection of material with recurrent structural features. Of the nine topoi listed below, an individual narrative usually displays no less than seven.

The Arrest. Most of the early Gulag memoirs (Kopelev, Ginzburg, Solonevich, Petrov, Dolgun, Begin, Solomon, Scholmer, Tregubov, Ekart, Parvilahti, Lipper) begin with an account of the author's *arrest* or the period shortly preceding it; the author's previous experience is eventually sketched in flashbacks—as a portion of life that has been cut away.[26]

The Gulag Archipelago opens with an account of arrests in general and Solzhenitsyn's arrest in particular; and even Nadezhda Mandelstam's *Hope against Hope,* a companion piece both to her husband's poetry and to the Gulag corpus, starts with the day of Osip Mandelstam's first arrest. This type of opening effectively captures, "arrests" the attention of the reader (cf. Andrew Nussbaum 1990: 253). A few other authors (de Beausobre, Petrus, Shapiro, Wallach, Herling, and Krasnov) start with a brief but striking scene from their prison or camp life (most often pertaining to the first prison cell), but presently include flashback accounts of their arrest.

A narrative may also open with the motif of arrest rather than a scenic account of one. Margarete Buber-Neumann begins her *Under Two Dictators* with the aftermath of her husband's arrest: she recollects how she sallied outdoors after two days of total numbness: alienated and stunned, she threaded her way through Moscow throngs while huge portraits of Stalin were being hoisted above the merry streets in preparation for the anniversary of the October Revolution. The narrative ends with another symbolic episode: an exhausted ex-prisoner, she tries to cross over to the American zone in Germany; when an American sergeant tells her to wait she fears that she might be held up and so recaptured by the Soviet forces. Yet the sergeant returns with a horse-drawn cart: "'Get in,' he said. 'You've walked enough by the look of you. You're going to ride now'" (324). Margolin's narrative likewise ends with the released prisoner, exhausted, with an almost useless stiff leg, getting a lift on a passing locomotive. The last image of Lev Kopelev's *Ease My Sorrows* is that of children who offer to carry the released prisoner's bag to the train station. The images of carts, ships, trains, and airplanes recur in the endings of Gulag stories: having started with arrest, or with ensuing stasis, the narratives end with motion. Thus, though the motif of official cruelty at the beginning is often balanced by that of personal kindness in the end, the sense of stable closure is usually not produced.

The belated memoirs, especially those composed in the *glasnost* period, do not routinely start with an account of the arrest, the issue having been sufficiently explored in precursor works. Their initial response to arrest, especially the trauma of former convinced Communists ("Why me? It must be some mistake! *Me* with all these contras?!"), may still be a rankling embarrassment to some of the authors. Nor is overt moral introspection characteristic of most of the *glasnost*-period Gulag memoirists, possibly owing to the intervening time. Thus Razgon chooses to devote much more space to his *second-round* arrest and interrogations in 1950 (1994: 388–407) than to his first round in 1938 (1994: 84–91). In 1950, having already served one camp term, he was better "educated" than his interrogators, and his unhappiness at falling into their clutches once again was partly compensated by the enjoyment of his well-informed resistance—a grateful subject for a "belated" memoir.

Dignity. Though political imprisonment is an ancient phenomenon, the actual daily experience of a prisoner, unlike the ideas and acts that have led to the arrest, has only rather recently stopped being regarded as a shameful interim episode of a personal past and has turned into subject matter significant in its own right (see Morand 1976: 10–11). The main reason for this development is the unprecedented statistics of imprisonment in the twentieth century. A concomitant cultural reason is the change in the concept of dignity. The Socratic realization that true dignity does not depend on external props and consists in deserving rather than in being given credit ("nothing they did could humiliate me. I could only humiliate myself—by doing something I might later be ashamed of" [Sharansky 1988: 8]) has only recently seeped through into the consciousness of the broader public.

Concentration-camp inmates had to unlearn conventional physical shame: the communal character of camp life made it impossible to hide one's body from the eyes of the others; accordingly, their memoirs tend to reject decorous reticence. Narrative coyness about the body and its functions would risk belying the flavor of the actual experience. As some survivors believed, it was necessary to inform public opinion not only about the brutality of the interrogators and the callousness of the guards but also about the disgraceful sanitary conditions (see Ivanov-Razumnik 1953: 157), which to a large extent characterized the ethical culture of the captors. Thus the concept of dignity is not merely an issue raised but also a factor in the selection of material, in the deliberately sustained attention paid to the minutiae of the daily hardships in the camps. Not surprisingly, however, belated memoirists seem to have felt exempt from the narrative equivalent of latrine duty: the job had largely been done by their precursors. In the works of the particularly well-informed dissidents, such as *History's Carnival* by Leonid Plyushch (1979) or the memoirs of Grigorenko and Amalrik, the focus of interest has shifted back from the conditions of imprisonment to the paths that have led to prison.

Stages. Gulag memoirs written under the influence of the Russian literary tradition are usually divided into graphically separated units (chapters or sections) that deal with well-defined periods of the authors' stay in different prisons and camps. This text division re-enacts the "transport" stages of a Gulag prisoner's life. The word "transport" is an approximate translation of the Russian *etap,* meaning (a) a stage in a line of development, (b) a span of traveling between two transit prisons, and (c) a group of convicts shipped together from one transit point to the next. Transporting prisoners "by stages" (*po etapu*) along special routes with traditional stop-over stations had been practiced in Russia for centuries. In the Stalin period it turned into "perpetual motion" of immense scope (*GA* V), and it forms one of the main statistical hurdles for present-day historians.[27]

Being transferred from one camp to another entailed parting with friends and making a painstaking adjustment to a new place. In between there were overcrowded train carriages, thirst, lice, dirty or inaccessible toilets, robbery by professional criminals, the unconcern of lazy guards, orders to sit in the snow or mud at train stations (thus fixing oneself to the spot by the weight of one's own body), and the rudeness of nervous convoy commanders.[28] If the distance was long, the journey sometimes included weeks in various transit prisons, each with its own regulations.

Gulag narratives tend to literally "start a new chapter" at every such relocation. This narrative division often suggests that the experience is *relived* at the time of writing, with the consciousness of calendar time replaced by vivid memories of a place.[29] In retrospective accounts of the penal facilities, the notion of the "stage" is spatial rather than temporal. Though the temporal "chapters" in an individual prisoner's experience are also distinguished from each other by different associates and jobs, terminal points are always directly linked with a redeployment: oneself or one's cherished friend is sent off on a transport, or one is hierarchically or topographically repositioned within one's camp. Insufficient attention to the spatial/temporal "staging" of the recollected experience reduces the impact of a narrative: in the memoirs of Tregubov and Stajner, for instance, different camps seem to merge into a continuum of hardships. By contrast, the narratives where each stage is recollected separately, especially as a new educational experience, are more memorable and often more profound. In the memoirs of Solzhenitsyn, Panin, Kopelev, Ginzburg, Herling, Margolin, Herman, Dolgun, Marchenko, and Sharansky, and in the stories of Shalamov, each prison and camp becomes a station of an inner journey, a separate landscape of the mind.

Escape. Primo Levi writes that in the countries where the elementary needs of the population are satisfied, "young people experience freedom as a good that one must in no case renounce"; for them

> the idea of imprisonment is firmly attached to the idea of flight or revolt. The prisoner's condition is perceived as illegitimate, abnormal: in short, as a disease which must be healed by escape or rebellion. In any case, the concept of escape as a moral obligation has strong roots. According to the military code of many countries, the prisoner-of-war is under the obligation to free himself at all costs, to resume his place as a combatant, and, according to the Hague convention, the attempt to escape must not be punished. In the common consciousness, escape cleans and wipes out the shame of imprisonment. (1988: 122–23)

However, in the Nazi camps, the conventional moral obligation to escape[30] was often replaced by the obligation to endure, especially since successful escapes were followed by lethal retaliation upon the remaining prisoners.[31] In the Soviet Union, the authorities' revenge on the remaining inmates of the camps was less devastating, yet the chances of making a successful escape, or of surviving the recapture, were small. In Gulag literature the notion of escape eventually underwent the same modifications as it did in the literature of the Holocaust.

Escapes from the Gulag were easier in the twenties, while the fine art of camp management was in its infancy. By the late thirties, the sophistication of the NKVD had increased. As if in answer to Dumas's *The Count of Monte Cristo* (a most popular book among prison inmates), new regulations established the routine of smashing the skulls or piercing the chests of corpses with spokes to make sure they were quite dead. Camp "zones" were encircled by off-limit areas inside the barbed wire; in many places there were ambush traps (*sekrety*) outside. The population of the neighboring settlements was rewarded with foodstuffs for capturing fugitives —soon only the indomitable Chechens, deported by Stalin from their native Caucasus to Kazakhstan, could be fully relied upon to help escapees. Most prisoners, moreover, were reduced to physical exhaustion and emaciation before they could devise viable escape plans. Still, for many, escape remained an immediate ideological imperative or an irresistible temptation (cf. *GA* on Georgii Tenno, 5: 7). That some escapes succeeded after the mid thirties can be explained statistically: with the number of camp inmates throughout the country running in millions, some miraculous exploits could be expected to take place.

In "The Green Procurator" (*KR* 428–79) Shalamov presents a historical survey of escapes in Kolyma. Solzhenitsyn reports on ideologically motivated escapes (*GA* 5: 6–8) as well as on escapes undertaken as a last resort (*GA* 3: 14). A recaptured prisoner would be removed from the specific camp in which he had reached despair: "changing one's fate" had been a synonym for escape in czarist prisons as well.

Plans or fantasies of escape usually characterize the early period of imprisonment (Marchenko, Solonevich, Sharansky); later they fade out as a result of exhaustion and entrenchment in the camp routine. Preoccupation with escape is more frequent in the memoirs of men than of women, yet before the leveling exhaustion set in, both men and women would also "escape" in the figurative sense of the word—into dreams, imagination, memories, or poetry. Cultivation of friendships would create haven enclaves amidst the filth and vexation of camp life. The ultimate escape consisted in relinquishing the hold on one's sanity. Dementia, however, was most often a lethal symptom of advanced pellagra.

While looking for ways to escape, a prisoner studies the details of the functioning and topography of the camp. Thus, paradoxically, in pursuit of a private aim one gains a better awareness of the common conditions and perfects one's training as a potential witness.

Failed escapes and, in particular, escapes contemplated but not undertaken characterize the experience of a fair proportion of the prisoners;[32] a successful escape is, as mentioned above, an unusual achievement and signifies a break with the common lot. The break is most radical in the cases of cannibalism during escape attempts: if a group of famished fugitives in a Siberian forest contained professional criminals, hardly any member of the group could afford a quiet sleep. Konson (1983: 43–52) records the experience of a fellow prisoner under conditions where the killing of an accomplice fugitive for food became a "thinkable" eventuality. By contrast to Ginzburg, who treats a similar issue (1981: 124–25) with traditional outrage,[33] Konson attempts to reconstruct the dynamics of relationships under the sign of impending cannibalism, showing the way in which virtues such as courage, loyalty, and love of freedom could become horrifyingly perverted in a war of all against all.

Moments of Reprieve. The narrative counterpart of escape is sustained attention to the more pleasant moments in camp life—significant conversations, snatched opportunities to read, occasional freedom of movement, occasional solitude, a hot bath, ripe berries, little acts of kindness, extra pieces of bread, which, as Solzhenitsyn shows in *Cancer Ward,* would be devalued by the first *shashlik* in more affluent times. An important rhetorical consequence of such details is that they neutralize the danger of inuring the audience to atrocities. It is well known that after an uninterrupted series of violent or pathetic scenes, the readers' emotional response loses intensity, eventually leading to a re-enactment of the callousness of the unconcerned bystanders described in the text. One solution to the problem is to arrange the accounts of atrocities in an escalating sequence, as in Kosinski's novel *The Painted Bird* or in Dolgun's memoir.[34] Yet, though the escalation keeps our psyche under continuous siege, eventually it produces a cumulatively desensitizing effect. Most Gulag authors use a different method to prevent the blunting of the reader's response: they alternate the accounts of suffering with those of reprieve (cf. Primo Levi's *Moments of Reprieve*) or with informative or analytic passages. Hence the *pulsation method* of prison narratives: the rise and fall of emotional intensity in Herling's book, the poignant glimpses of individual tragedies amidst the picaresque or the satire of Solonevich, or Ginzburg's references to the specific compensations available at different stages of her camp life. The tug-of-war between suffering and respite is thematized by Marchenko in *My Testimony,* which records the authorities' pettily malicious struggle against all possible "reprieves" in the prisoners' daily life.

There may be a reverse view of the pulsating structure of memoirs of atrocity: critics of literary testimony sometimes suggest that expositions of vicious social systems can be deliberately punctuated with graphic images of cruelty—if these images appeal to the sado-masochistic voyeurism in reader response, they ultimately elicit an outraged reaction that helps individual readers to re-establish the sense of their own decency.[35] Yet in consciousness-raising discourse it is often hard to distinguish deliberate sensationalism from systematic factography. Whereas, as is well known, scenes of suffering can be exploited pornographically as would-be illustrations of the crimes of some recognized enemy. In the case of bona fide consciousness-raising narratives, it is the reader who must take the responsibility for elements of voyeuristic response.

Gulag authors are, in fact, usually quite reluctant to describe acute suffering; and when they do so, they usually emphasize not the pain or the cruelty per se but some additional aspect of the situation. Thus Herman and Dolgun present torture at interrogations as their competition with the torturers; El Campesino views it in the context of other massive assaults on his identity; Weissberg and Tregubov emphasize its pragmatic purposes. Gulag narratives contain little evidence of torture for the sake of torture, as at the hands of the Nazis (cf. Améry 1980: 21–41). Moreover, Gulag memoirists occasionally seem to *force* themselves to dwell on the suffering of the prisoners;[36] they implicitly demand that the reader should remain aware of the general background of misery while having a narrative reprieve between records of inevitable excesses.

Not infrequently, the narrative reprieves are comic.[37] In the best American tradition of the tall tale, Dolgun describes the impertinence that made his reputation in the camp and his ingenious strategies of secondary adaptation; yet he also makes an effort to set these "adventures" aside and do the real work of bearing witness:

> Incidents like these comic ones, moments of success in the operating room or in the illicit commerce of spoons and beds and flatirons, these are the pleasures that come to mind when people say, "What was it like in camp?" But these were rare moments—small bright spots almost obliterated by the gloom and terror out of which each day was built.
>
> Years later, sitting around with the Trade Union, which was how the former inmates referred to themselves to save embarrassment in the presence of the uninitiated, we would drink a sad toast to "all those still at sea," and then talk about the good aspects of those terrible days. We would recall the long and fascinating conversations with men of character and intellect whom we had had the good fortune of knowing through the misfortune of camp. We would remember every joke, every bottle of home brew, every funny song and every odd character: that was easy. To recall the horrors was work, and we usually avoided it.

> Working now over these pages, I avoid it until I cannot any more, be-
> cause that is the real fabric of my story. I take a holiday page after page
> to recall the funny things, and then remember that I must go back to
> work. (1976: 343)

Thus, the relative duration of the suffering and the reprieves tends to
be reversed in the written records, which is one of the reasons why, as it
is generally thought, it is impossible to imagine the taste of camp life on
the basis of the testimonies of others. Literature has practically no resources for an adequate presentation of the interminable hours of hard,
monotonous, and humiliating slave labor. Even if an author (e.g., Margolin) fills a page or two with minute descriptions of lumbering or railway
construction, the reader can still maintain defenses against imagining
what it would be like for a starving and aching body to have to perform
such work for over twelve hours a day, often in rain or frost, or amid
vicious gnats.[38] And since human communication, a subject that is more
readily amenable to narrative representation, cannot really take place
during hard work, Gulag literature allots a great deal of textual space to
lucky respites, smoking or meal breaks, days off, and after-hours. Eventually, however, accounts of these respites yield to stories of assaults by camp
bosses and criminal convicts, of disasters wreaked by new twists of policy
in high places, of the ravages of disease, and to the tragic stories of fellow
prisoners. These are, in their turn, followed by the logistics of adjustment
to new circumstances. The narrative *pulsates,* downward to exhaustion
and upward to recuperation, downward to acute suffering and upward to
relief. Whether its rhetorical orientation is intuitive or deliberate, the
pulsation method stems from the very nature of the Gulag experience.

Room 101. Though Gulag memoirists have witnessed atrocities that
they could never have imagined, there usually remains some "untidy
spot" where they fear to tread, some Orwellian room "one-oh-one" (Orwell 1949: 232). Each author is reluctant to face some special type of
suffering, depravity, or horror. This reluctance is sometimes conveyed
through the focalizer's averting his or her eyes from the most disturbing scenes, either in desperate self-preservation (as when Panin cannot
bear to see the degraded appearance of women prisoners) or because of
partial complicity (as when Dyakov chooses not to observe a starved patient).[39] The narrative consequence of these psychological mechanisms
is an alibi-like reticence that often leaves the reader vaguely aware of
the gap.

A terror gap in the work of one memoirist can be filled in the work of
another. Ginzburg chooses not to think about the treatment of the infants in the children's shelter when criminal convicts are appointed to
replace its "politically untrustworthy" personnel. As it happens, Hava

Volovich does take a closer look at the way criminal convicts run a Komi Republic camp shelter—blankets, instead of covering the children, are hung above the cots "for cleanliness"; mealtimes take the following form:

> The nurse brought burning-hot porridge from the kitchen. Having distributed it over bowls, she snatched, at random, a child from a cot, twisted his hands backwards, tied them to his body with a towel, and started pushing the hot porridge, spoonful by spoonful, into his mouth as if he were a turkey, not leaving him time to swallow. She was not embarrassed by the presence of a stranger, which meant that such "efficient methods" were legitimate. So this was why, despite the relatively high number of births, there were so many vacancies in this infant shelter. Three hundred infant deaths a year, yet in the pre-war times! And how many were there during the war![40] (Vilensky 1988: 481)

The luckier a prisoner, the less comprehensive the testimony. In the hospital Ginzburg sees men who have been worked to death in the gold mines, but it is Shalamov who takes us into the gold mines themselves. Dolgun and Herman take us where Shalamov has not been—into special prisons and torture chambers; and Konson gets quite privileged glimpses of criminal etiquette and cannibal ethos. This is one of the reasons Gulag memoirs are never felt to be self-sufficient, finished works: there is always a seepage between their texts and their contexts. Some gaps are never filled in: in the history of the Archipelago there were times and places from which there seem to be no survivor reports;[41] much as one learns about the camps, one never learns the worst.

At times, however, it is the author rather than the focalizer who prefers to keep out of Room 101. Thus, in his account of the murderous camps of Viatlag and Vorkuta, where he held the privileged position of a skilled laborer, Panin refrains from giving detailed descriptions of the horrors of death and depletion at the general duties. He mentions statistics, such as the 90–100 percent mortality rate during the winter season, but refuses to dwell on the gruesome forms of slow starvation. Precursor works exempt him from the obligation to do so; yet one is left with a lingering sense that, as an elderly man with broken health, Panin did not wish to relive his response to the harrowing sights of the past.

Chance. In ancient Greek literature chance emerged as inimical to the heroes' best-laid plans. In the classical European novel and drama it was resorted to as a deus ex machina resolution of otherwise inevitable tragic developments: in a grimly determinate state of affairs, virtue was felt to be so radically severed from its reward that the fortunate peripeteia came, as it were, by way of a rare exception. In the realistic fiction of the late nineteenth and early twentieth centuries, as a result of the demand for the average rather than the extraordinary, the benevolent play of chance was partly discredited. Gulag survivor memoirs rehabilitate chance as an integral aspect of human life.

Behind this attitude lies an awareness that statistical odds are strongly against individual survival and that ill fortune is not something that "can" happen but the general state of affairs. Accounts of sophisticated adaptation, of creative alertness, of individual feats of survival, and of common strategies (rules of thumb such as "it is better to be on openly hostile rather than on friendly terms with a squealer"[42] or "it is the full rations, not the partial rations, that kill") are overshadowed by the awareness that great numbers of prisoners had died before their initiation was complete or as a consequence of unforeseeable disasters. The logistics of adaptation could, moreover, merely postpone the descent along the vicious spiral. Survival was a matter of luck no less than of moral or physical strength: recognition of the role of chance tempers the Gulag survivors' sense of being intrinsically exceptional individuals (see also Suleiman 1996: 652–55).

The chance in question was that of being "dragged out" from the general duties, even if it meant staking one's survival on untoward employment—Buber-Neumann as an ox-cart water-carrier or Ginzburg as a poultry hand. One had to be prepared for a lucky break, recognize it, and use it to the best advantage. Intellectuals were a special target of Stalin's wrath because they were not easily amenable to thorough indoctrination, yet mutual help (see Kopelev 1975: 390–91 on "Society for the Preservation of the Intelligentsia") reduced the rate of their extermination. Memoirs record cases of national solidarity:[43] Herman's life was saved by a fellow American, Buber-Neumann was significantly helped by fellow Germans, Margolin was "dragged out" from the transport to Vorkuta by a Polish Jew, Solomon was often assisted by fellow Rumanians. Skilled specialists whose position in the camps was relatively strong could extend protection to friends: Panin thus got Kopelev brought to the prison institute (the *sharashka*) and Solzhenitsyn to a specialized workshop in Ekibastuz.

The Zone and the Larger Zone. The whole area of the camp, inside the barbed wire, was commonly referred to as the "zone." Many Gulag memoirists view the whole of the USSR as the "Larger Zone" (*GA* 3: 21, 564), a giant prison house with but different degrees of illusory freedom of movement. The relationship of the camp (the "zone") and life in the "Larger Zone" begins with the interaction with the camp guards, who live on the borderline between the two; those of them who are enlisted soldiers actually share part of the *zeks'* bondage. Gulag memoirists almost unanimously point to the guards' laziness and inefficiency, as well as to their relative non-maliciousness combined with an unquestioning obedience to orders, including orders to shoot. The convoy guards from Vologda were known to be brutal disciplinarians, but this group, as well as occasional individual sadists, were rather exceptional. The general laxness of the guards on many everyday occasions compares favorably with the efficiency of the SS in German *Lager*s. Yet the situation changes when the guards become economically interested or when, in their own turn, they come under threat from the higher authorities; in such cases they exhibit impenetrable callousness and even wanton cruelty.

J. Scholmer (1954: 168–69, 255–56) writes that, in Vorkuta, the prisoners who contemplated an uprising sounded out the conscripted soldiers among their guards about possible support and found that a large percentage sympathized with the prisoners; nevertheless, most soldiers said that they would shoot the prisoners, no matter how reluctantly, if given such commands. Bershadskaya notes that before the tanks were called in to suppress the uprising in Kengir, a note was thrown to the prisoners, encouraging them to go on because shooting had not been planned: she believes that it was written by a sympathetic soldier. Later, when soldiers were ordered to beat her up behind closed doors, they only pretended to do so, loudly cursing and clapping their palms. N. Krasnov (1957: 104–5) mentions a compassionate act on the part of a guard even in the Lefortovo military prison. And Sergei Dovlatov's 1982 *Zona* [*The Zone*] actually presents a camp for criminal offenders from the perspective of one of those sympathetic conscripted guards.

By contrast, in the memoirs pertaining to the post-Stalinist years (Marchenko, Sharansky), the salaried camp and prison officials are presented as pettily malicious: their livelihood is threatened by the reduction of the numbers of prisoners and their self-respect by the reduction of their power.

Likewise close to the "zone" are the people in nearby villages and towns, encountered at work or on the way there, or upon release, or during escapes. The traditional topos of the kindness of Russians to individual prisoners combines with the motif of callousness bred by the new social system. In a tribute, as it were, to Dostoevsky, Herling describes a poor woman's charity to a hungry ex-convict:

> At dawn we had to leave the station and we went begging through the town. I found a small street in the working-class district, where every day about noon a grey-haired old woman beckoned to me, first having made certain that no one was looking, and took me into her kitchen, where she gave me a mugful of unsweetened herb tea and a slice of stale bread. We never exchanged a word beyond my "spasibo"—"thank you," and her "idi z Bogom"—"God be with you." (1987: 230)

Yet this moving episode is sandwiched between the image of multitudes sleeping on the floors of railway stations and the story of the rudeness of people in a bread queue to a crippled soldier ("the contempt for a damaged machine which is out of circulation has permeated all strata of the Russian people and has polluted fundamentally honest hearts" [1987: 231]). According to Herling, the world of the camps is sick, and its outskirts are infected.

The last scenes of Kopelev's *To Be Preserved Forever* and *Ease My Sorrows* tell of the kindness and tacit understanding of ordinary people whom the author met on his way to and from imprisonment. Margolin's memoir ends on a similar note. Stories of unsolicited kindness on the part of strangers grace most Gulag testimonies. They are balanced, however, by stories of the recapture of fugitives with the help of the local population, of denunciations, and of blank insensitivity to suffering and injustice— phenomena that are almost unanimously attributed to the terror controls and the corrupting influence of the regime. The *zone-within-a-zone* motif expresses the general attitude to the relationship between the "zone" and the "Larger Zone": the camp is but a *more condensed* expression of the tendencies at work in the country as a whole. The uniqueness of its semiotic system, accountable for turning the camp into "another kingdom" or "a world apart," can be seen as a result of the dialectic leap from quantitative changes to a qualitative difference.

End-of-term fatigue. Most memoirs end with the author's being set free or, in the case of foreigners, repatriated. The homecoming part of the concentration-camp epics is usually either contracted or suppressed, or left for another book.[44]

Panin's memoirs do not include his release: he meant to write a sequel, but at his sudden death in 1987 the intention remained unrealized. Yet the somewhat premature ending of *The Notebooks of Sologdin* displays another characteristic feature of Gulag memoirs: the last days, or weeks, or months before the release tend to be poorly remembered and sparsely described. Kopelev likewise skips over his last year in the camp before sketching the story of his trudging to the railway upon release. Toward the end of the term, the prisoner is weary, has nothing new to learn from camp life, and can think of little but release. The narrative counterpart of this lassitude is the relative paleness of the accounts of the last months of imprisonment. Whereas the first impressions of prison and camp are remembered in detail, the last months are remembered in terms of impatience, hope for release, or anxiety that one's sentence may be arbitrarily extended or that amnesty may pass one by. The hollow days of expectation merge into a blurred stretch: a monotonous span of time that seems endless while one is living it appears empty, and therefore short, in retrospect. The memoirs of Olitskaya end in the middle of her stay in Kolyma—as if, having told the main things, she waived the final periods of her imprisonment. Lipper telescopes her memory of her moral fatigue in the following dramatized exchange:

> Slave and starve, slave and freeze, work faster, faster,
>   get going, get going!
> "Hello there, Elinor, I have a book that would
>   interest you."
> "Interest me? The devil with your book. I want
>   freedom."
> "Elinor, there's a movie at the club tonight."
> "The devil with your movie. I want freedom."
> "Elinor, they say overtimers are going to be released
>   soon."
> "The devil with your fairy stories. I don't believe
>   anything they say any more." (1951: 274)

In Lipper's case, however, the moral nausea is rendered vividly: she could not allow her narrative energies to flag because she still had to describe the tribulations in the transit prisons on her way from Kolyma.

Unlike the liberation from Nazi camps, release from the Gulag before 1953 was not a collective experience. It came closest to being a communal event in 1955–56; indeed, the last months in the camp are given the most concentrated attention by the memoirists (Dolgun, Zernova) who participated in that exodus.

* * *

Most of the Gulag narratives are written in what, by analogy with the carnivalesque mode described by Bakhtin,[45] can be called "*the Lenten mode.*" Lent is not the opposite of the carnival but its second self; the antithesis of both is the quotidian state of affairs.[46]

Lent, variously defined at different times in different places, is an institutionalized and circumscribed period of voluntary asceticism, with a fast undertaken for physical and spiritual purification. Gulag prisoners do not starve voluntarily: they are *denied* sufficient food, yet Gulag literature repeatedly suggests that *the answer to hunger is fasting.* Fasting was one of the ways of maintaining personal dignity in the camps. Literal fasting took the shape of hunger strikes held in the earliest and the latest periods in the history of the Gulag,[47] of occasional Jewish observances of the Day of Atonement,[48] and of punishment-cell privations incurred by devout Christians for refusing to work on religious holidays.[49] Mainly, however, the Lenten abstention from carnivorousness is to be understood in a figurative sense: it means a refusal to become a cannibal, that is, to prolong one's own life at the expense of others (in the language of the criminals, "you die today and I tomorrow"), or to hold jobs that involve bending the will of others. Shalamov, Olitskaya, Ginzburg, and Solzhenitsyn repeatedly suggest that the demands of the moral self are almost naturally stronger than one's biological needs; Panin describes a conscious acceptance of asceticism, a deliberate suppression of the needs of the healthy life-loving body. A hedged-in habit of self-limitation that preserved individuals from degradation enhanced the resistance of their bodies to the inroads of hunger and disease; by contrast, fighting other prisoners for morsels of food may have been symptomatic of or conducive to a lethal loss of the moral powers of endurance. According to Solzhenitsyn, the injunction "not to lick the bowl" was not so much a matter of dignity as of survival; Shalamov, however, claims that he was not above licking the bowl or rummaging in garbage piles—the dignified self-discipline needed for endurance was to be sought elsewhere. The number and kind of rejected methods of struggle for survival varies from author to author.

Like carnivalesque literature, Lenten narratives present pageants in which the borderlines between the actors and spectators are erased. The *zek* focalizer is both a spectator and a participant. After observing the common lot he or she inevitably plunges into its midst: "For the thing which I greatly feared is come upon me, and that which I was afraid of is come unto me" (Job 3:25). Buber-Neumann first hears about the Bunker prison in Ravensbrück and then is incarcerated there;[50] Ginzburg hears of punishment cells and punitive camps before being placed there; newcomers to camps first observe the frightful state of the inmates and then themselves slide down the vicious spiral toward the same condition. The process can be staved off by a separation of the person who suffers and the mind that observes: Iulia de Beausobre, for instance, personifies the alert disciplinarian part of her self as the dispassionate "Leonardo." The detachment of the intellect from affects promotes the discreteness of personality and the sense of inner freedom: "as long as you are learning, your inquisitors will not succeed in establishing between you and them the relationship they desire; they, the superior beings, and you, the degraded." Yet one's "status as a student" cannot always be maintained (Begin 1977: 21–22): at moments of passion or despair, the spectator dissolves in the participant.

Like carnivalesque literature, Lenten narratives record the intimate contact between people who under "normal" circumstances would belong to different walks of life. Here the closeness of one person to another stems not from carnivalesque exuberance but from the extreme deprivation that obliterates individual differences. Moreover, the Dionysian merging of identities in a crowd is replaced by the body language of lack: the discreteness of the body is lost not through excess feasting and the knocking down of conventional barriers but through untreated bruises, scurvy sores, frostbite, and osteomyelitis, as well as through a total absence of privacy. Nor does the mind remain whole. Prolonged chronic hunger makes inroads upon the brain, leading to loss of memory (see Shalamov's "Sententia" in *LB*), hunger neurosis (see Margolin, Marchenko), or clinical pellagric dementia (see Herling 1951). A famished *zek* finds it extremely hard to preserve the integrity of the moral self: acting "like everybody else," in contradiction to everything one may have believed in, one loses one's psychic discreteness and suffers the mental equivalent of physical disintegration.

The relationship between "physical" and "moral" survival—what it takes to stave off death, what is at stake, what price may be paid, and in what ways the physical and moral needs support each other or clash—is one of the main concerns of almost every Gulag author. Survival through sheer endurance at the general works is practically impossible, and the Lenten spirit rejects survival at the expense of others. Between these two extremes lie different shades of gray. The memoirists know that, despite the traditional belief in remorse, a conscious rejection of ethical scruples could enhance a prisoner's chances of survival. Most of them deny having taken this option, yet most of them also admit to having at some time been somewhat infected by jungle-law attitudes: the Lenten self-denial has its limits. Among the most engaging writers are those (Shalamov, Solzhenitsyn, Panin, Kopelev, Ginzburg, Marchenko, Zhigulin) who engage in a courageous self-critical probing of the problematic areas of personal experience. Considerably less interesting are the memoirists (Petrov, Gilboa, Filshtinsky) who always see themselves taking precisely the right practical or ethical stance.

Though the Lenten mode is eschatological, religious concerns hold a lateral place in Gulag memoirs. Deeply religious people were capable of the greatest fortitude in the camps: "faith takes better care of man, when things go badly with him, than man does of his faith when things are well with him" (Begin 1977: 48). Whereas some accounts of the Holocaust, in particular Elie Wiesel's *Night,* record the memoirists' break with the God who had allowed the mass murder to happen, in the Gulag, practicing Christians, Jews, and Moslems seem to have clung to their beliefs. They often treated imprisonment as a test of faith, and the sense of success in this test enhanced their endurance—John Noble's *I Found God in Soviet Russia* tells, among other things, an almost archetypal story of survival through a reawakening of religious faith in a Dresden prison under Soviet occupation.[51] The experience of people who turned away from religion in or after the Nazi camps is partly analogous to the disillusionment the idealistic Communists underwent in the Gulag; religion, as in the cases of Solzhenitsyn, Ginzburg, and Berger, could fill the void left by the breakdown of ideology. The same could also happen to people of other initial persuasions, such as the White Guard Bezsonov.

Strict religious observances amounted to an assertion of freedom through a voluntary augmentation of the suffering: one could respond to hunger by fasting, to privation by self-denial,[52] sometimes reaching ecstatic near-martyrdom. Yet, in the absence of religious faith, internalist ethics and loyalty to one's fellow sufferers could provide sufficient motives for self-discipline. In most cases, the faith in immortality is irrelevant to the concerns of the Gulag corpus: with but two or three exceptions, this corpus is secular, irrespective of the authors' beliefs. Secular attitudes are associated with the ethics of the selection of material; they are both a cause and a consequence of close attention to the semiotics of the spatial/temporal and social/ethical setting. To adapt the remark of Frederick Hoffman (1964: 4), since "that special aspect of eternity that belongs to me" is largely eclipsed by the communal element in the concerns of the Gulag veterans, "more attention is paid to time, and time achieves a spatial quality. Instants of time become spatial objects in a scheme of succession; it is their spatial quality that attracts and not their sequential nature. An age whose people are little convinced of immortality or little comforted by the hopes of it is likely to produce a literature that emphasizes the spatial qualities of life. This literature is also concerned with the density of objects, with their texture, and with the specific values residing in experiences." One of the features of spatialized time is divisibility (the "stages" topos), as well as the evaluation of its capaciousness in terms of action, pain, exhaustion, or relief.[53] The chronological narration that focuses on the details of the texture of the experience is based on a secular vision.

Indeed, there is little or no description of the physical conditions of imprisonment in memoirs suffused with religiosity, such as the book by Boris Shiriaev about the Solovetsky camps or the 1933 memoirs of the preacher Martzinkovski, who was persecuted for religious work prior to his emigration in the twenties. The exclusive concern of Martzinkovski's book—and a central one of John Noble's—is religious consciousness and religious work in prison. By contrast, Panin's text is essentially secular, despite the passionate religiosity that helped him to preserve his integrity of character and action[54] and to remain undaunted during the interrogations (cf. *GA* 5: 11);[55] religiousness is part of Panin's subject matter rather than his narrative prism. The same is true of the narrative of the Catholic priest Jean Nicolas. Likewise secular are the narratives of Ginzburg and of Solzhenitsyn, though they record their authors' turning to faith in the camps. A secular approach has a greater ethical force in the processing of Gulag experience, especially since the minutiae of prison and camp routine, including vermin and ventilation, are actually human-rights issues.[56]

Thus, in keeping with the features that Lenten literature shares with the carnivalesque, Gulag narratives combine accounts of the most lofty flights of the human spirit with the camp equivalent of slum naturalism. They also include scandal scenes, eccentric or insane behavior, explicit or implicit obscenities, jargons, national dialects and accents, and other deviations from "normative" speech and conduct. The heteroglot quality[57] of Gulag memoirs is, for obvious reasons, more pronounced in the works of Russian writers. It is particularly exuberant in Solzhenitsyn, and very rich in Solonevich, Ginzburg, and Kopelev; the language of Shalamov is, however, characterized by a combination of restrained lexical variety with a pinched, mutilated subtlety and precision that enacts, as it were, the Lenten spirit of his tales. In *If This Is a Man* Primo Levi links the heteroglossia in Auschwitz with the theme of the Babel tower, suggested by the factory tower of Buna. The symbolism of this link applies also to the Soviet camps, where heteroglossia also became a part of a counterculture that pitted itself not only against the ideology of official discourse but, more radically, against its semiotics (cf. Venclova 1979: 70–73).[58]

* * *

The lack of discreteness that characterizes the body language of both carnival and Lent finds its narrative counterpart in the lack of a watertight finish in most works of the Gulag corpus. In his preface to Weissberg's memoirs (1952: xiii), Arthur Koestler writes that even the defects of this book "seem to turn into assets in the total picture." At the time of writing the survivors are usually tired and ailing people. For them there has been no "happily ever after" either on the social or on the personal plane (though American-born and repatriated Gulag authors do follow the happy-ending convention, and so do, for other reasons, "loyalists" like Dyakov or, *distinction gardée*, Stajner). "Most of the temporary diseases or pains which at home, under ordinary circumstances, would confine one to the sickbed," writes Maria Shapiro, "pass much faster and, as it were, by themselves in prison, transport, or even camp, in this unusual condition of great nervous tension. Evidently, the concentration of the prisoners' will-power and nervous strength leads to such a cure; yet all these unhealed illnesses eventually destroy the body by causing high blood pressure, cardiac diseases and often a general shattering of the nervous system and physiology" (1983, no. 150: 243). Fatigue leaves local imprints on the memoirs written almost immediately upon regaining freedom, before the authors had sufficient time to recover. It is, therefore, not surprising that the style is sometimes imperfect, that minor details contradict the data of other sources, and that in the case of foreigners broad generalizations are made on the basis of hearsay or some Russian expressions are misunderstood. A degree of uncouthness is deliberately allowed to remain in some works by Shalamov and Solzhenitsyn. A perfect structuring of episodes (as in Ginzburg's books) can be seen as a mnemonic procedure, akin to the even groups of verses in Solzhenitsyn's poem *Prussian Nights.*

To the extent that the imperfections of the memoirs' structure or style have biographical causes, they are actually a variant of a feature shared by most documentary narratives: the seepage of the text and the context. So long as the camps exist, the memoirist's work is not finished: it attacks some aspects of the extratextual reality but does not complete the campaign. The English version of Herling's memoir reprints in appendices his 1948 and 1949 letters to periodicals concerning the Soviet denials of the atrocities of the forced labor system; Marchenko's *My Testimony* and Solzhenitsyn's *The Oak and the Calf* are likewise published together with documents that pertain to their subjects. *The Oak and the Calf* is, moreover, a literary-life sequel to the camp-life memoirs of *The Gulag Archipelago.* It has, in its turn, been followed by at least two more sequels, Solzhenitsyn's account of the people who helped him in his clandestine literary activities in the Soviet Union (1995) and his narrative of his experience after being deported abroad in 1973 (1998–99).

The main reason for the absence of a hermetic self-sufficiency in most works of the factographic narrative mode is that internal evidence does not suffice as proof either of the non-fictional nature of a text or of its veracity—other documentary texts must buttress its material. For the reader, the redundancy is to a large extent compensated by the suggestive interplay between the difference in the narratives' subjective coloration and their mutual confirmation of basic facts. Another specific reward is the reader's occasional recognition of familiar people in the narratives of authors who may or may not have been aware of each other while writing. Thus Georgii Tenno is described in *The Gulag Archipelago* and warmly remembered by Panin (1976: 298) and Dolgun; the handsome thief Valentin appears in Dolgun and Wat; the actress Carola Heinchke (or Carola Neher) passes through the narratives of Ginzburg and Buber-Neumann; the peasant grandmother Nastya, sentenced for "Trotskyism" though claiming never to have come close to "the cursed tractors," is encountered by Ginzburg (1967: 145) and Lipper (1951: 49) at the Butirki prison; Albert Loon is respectfully mentioned by Panin and lovingly described by Herman; Panin and Kopelev complement each other's and Solzhenitsyn's materials. At times, however, portraits of the same person by different writers are radically at odds with each other: Solzhenitsyn, for instance, describes Gleb Sluchenkov (from hearsay) as a heroic leader of a camp rebellion, whereas Konson remembers him as a professional criminal and an agent provocateur. Paradoxically, Konson's correction does not impoverish Solzhenitsyn's work; the two converge into testimony to the ways in which the need for heroic role models generates camp folklore. This suggests, once again, that no single work, not even Solzhenitsyn's *The Gulag Archipelago,* suffices to exempt one from the duty of attention to other memoirs; no single person's testimony is sufficient without at least a minimal context.

4 *The Gulag Archipelago*

Solzhenitsyn's seven-part *The Gulag Archipelago: An Experiment in Literary Investigation* (*GA*), first published in the years 1973–75, is a unique literary and historical document. It combines firsthand evidence with a compilation of on-record facts and hearsay; it also includes elements of reflexive essay, fictionalized narrative, pastiche, consciousness-raising pamphlet, and interpretation-cum-rebuttal of official texts. If published separately, its directly autobiographical chapters would form a rather consistent camp memoir; therefore, the book can be regarded as overlapping with the Gulag memoir genre, on whose history it had a landmark effect. Indeed, some Gulag memoirs, in particular Elinor Lipper's book, likewise include long discursive passages that attempt to systematize second- and third-hand data, with or without reference to the sources. One can, in fact, view *The Gulag Archipelago* as *including* a camp memoir, or else one can view it as *being* a camp memoir that, like most of the other, non-monumental works of this corpus, also displays goal-oriented features of other genres. In either view, *GA* shares all the main features of the camp memoir genre. The dialectical tension between the aesthetic and the ethical is immediately apparent in the collocation of *khudozhestvennoe* (artistic, literary) and *issledovanie* (investigation) in its title. The combination of the individual and the communal is manifest in its alternation of the historical and folkloristic material with long and excellently written autobiographical sections. It prominently displays the main topoi of Gulag memoirs: for instance, the first chapter is devoted to the issue of arrest; the structure of the book follows the principle of "stages" and *pulsates* between emotional appeal, neutral informativeness, and comic relief; the issue of the relationship between the "zone" and the "Larger Zone" is repeatedly addressed; the narrative energies flag toward the end. The Lenten attitude is expressed in the book's predominant valorization of self-denial, in the sense of incompleteness produced by the spiraling return to a number of issues, and in eschatological concerns, heteroglot reverberations, and an osmotic interaction with extratextual reality and precursor texts.

Solzhenitsyn's immediate contexts are the oral or written testimony of 227 survivors and sundry official Soviet publications, such as the notorious collection *The White-Sea–Baltic Canal,* Vyshinsky's and Averbakh's legal treatises, and the Stalinist penal code. Solzhenitsyn gives exemplary "between-the-lines" readings of the latter publications while also showing the gap between their explicit messages and the actual situation in the camps.[1] He also explicitly juxtaposes his narrative to directly relevant literary works—both fabrications like Pogodin's play *The Aristocrats* and genuine products of the Russian literary tradition, such as Dostoevsky's *The House of the Dead* (also variously commented on by Margolin, Ginzburg, and Herling) and Chekhov's *Journey to Sakhalin* (cf. Pervukhin 1991). Solzhenitsyn is fully aware of the potentially subversive effect of his work in respect to both Soviet literature and the classical Russian humanistic tradition. It seems, however, that, unlike Shalamov, he would have liked to minimize this subversion in the latter case.

The book's special place in the Gulag corpus is associated both with the attention it commanded because of the drama around its publication (see Scammell 1984: 813–28) and with its paradigmatic comprehensiveness, comparable to that of the periodic table before all of its blank slots were filled in. A *paradigm* is both a "model" and an "example"; it is a spatial compendium of possible variations abstracted from the flow of reality and put together by means of *specific particulars* rather than algebraic schemata. The details that structure the paradigm range from the idiosyncratic to the typical; even the typical, however, are not generalized abstractions but concrete individual cases. The principle of paradigmatic representation actually embodies the interconnection between the individual and the communal concerns.

The paradigm constructed in *The Gulag Archipelago* is multidimensional. It includes a whole spectrum of material pertaining to (a) the stages of a prisoner's ordeal: arrest, interrogation, pre-camp prison experience, and sentencing (part 1), transportation (2), life in labor camps (3, 4), *katorga* (special-hard-labor camps) (5), and exile (6); (b) the history of repressive laws and ad hoc directives (1: 2, 8–10), the history of the labor camp system (3: 1–4; 5: 1–3, 10–12; 7: 2–3), and developments in post-Stalinist times (7); (c) the geography of the Archipelago (3: 3–5, 22); (d) the sociology (3: 7–18, 20–21) and anthropology (3: 7, 19) of the Archipelago, and the ethics of camp life (4). As a result, the factual contribution of any specific witness can find a modular slot for itself in this framework.

Solzhenitsyn consciously attempts to preclude the possible side effect of the paradigmatic method, to wit, the stifling sense of authority that might make other testimony seem redundant. *The Gulag Archipelago* expressly invites emendations. Its use of unverified testimony and its insufficiency of archival documentation are undisguised. While various literary techniques compensate for the factual gaps without masking them, later sources are *expected* to complement Solzhenitsyn's data and correct his factual misprisions. Throughout *The Gulag Archipelago* Solzhenitsyn attempts to specify the time and the place of the discussed events with utmost precision, in order to enhance the historiographical value of the book yet also to challenge successor writers. Despite his theologically tinged valorization of objective truth, insistence on which is a moral imperative in one's dealing with totalitarian oppression,[2] he takes advantage of *deniability* procedures: whatever public domain evidence is not effectively denied or disproved is acceptable as true (Lang 1990: 38–41, Toker 1997b: 194–97).[3] He claims truthfulness by presenting a great amount of public-domain material, which is amenable to public verification and sufficiently specific to delimit the margin of error in the "hearsay" part of his evidence. The errors become a subpoena to fellow witnesses (Panin, Kopelev, Konson, Hershman, Dolgun, Bershadskaya). At the same time, local errors actually emphasize the over-all truthfulness of Solzhenitsyn's narrative: his emendators (Kennan 1973; Roy Medvedev 1985; S. Badash 1986: 54–58; Rozanov 1979: 8) agree that the ratio of erroneous statements to the whole volume of the narrative is surprisingly small.

Yet while striving toward the truthfulness of the factual material, Solzhenitsyn does not claim impartiality of judgment. "I am nonobjective, and I am proud of it!" says one of his characters, the painter Kondrashov-Ivanov in *The First Circle* (87, 325). Just as the gaps in Solzhenitsyn's materials are undisguised, so is his strong "ideologism," which has alienated many of his readers and which makes even his ardent admirers occasionally look up from his text in embarrassment at what strikes them as touches of insensitivity or simplification. Moments like these are seldom completely absent from any earnest conversation: though Solzhenitsyn is often accused of preaching, his works are actually always parts of a conversation, of polemics in which one sometimes overstates one's points.[4] This essentially dialogic mode takes into account the influence of other kinds of discourse on the worldview of the audience. In particular, Solzhenitsyn attacks the misrepresentations of history in official Soviet texts, but also some of the popular attitudes that they fostered; for instance, he refuses to condemn the Russian women who dated German soldiers during World War II (5: 1). Symptomatically, other people's on-record comments on Solzhenitsyn's views (discounting the invective of the official Soviet press of the sixties and seventies) often take the shape of an implicit apostrophe: they answer him and argue with him while ostensibly addressing the reading public.[5] Solzhenitsyn's mode of interaction with his audience is that of a debate rather than a sermon, a mode not unsimilar to that of the arguments between Rubin and Sologdin in *The First Circle*.

* * *

The photographs of Solzhenitsyn before his arrest, in detention, and after his release from the camps, printed at the beginning of Part I, enhance our sense of a real person speaking to us from the pages of *The Gulag Archipelago*. As noted above, expository discourse alternates with sections and chapters that narrate his own experience: his arrest in East Prussia at the end of the war (soon after the artillery unit under his command had distinguished itself in action), his transportation to Moscow, the interrogations, his new friendships in the Butyrki cells, the first camps, then the Kazakhstan camps to which he was taken after being expelled, like Nerzhin in *The First Circle*, from the *sharashka*, and his exile in Central Asia. Every "stage" in this autobiography is placed within the paradigm of the data pertaining to parallel stages in *zek* experience in general; the *sharashka* episode is elided as all too exceptional. In the nonautobiographical sections, the accumulated information is arranged on historical or thematic principles, sometimes with an element of escalation, as for instance in the listing of the methods of torture (1: 3) or the physical and moral torments endured by the prisoners during railway journeys (2: 1). The technique is here in grim harmony with the subject, since planned torture at interrogation (unlike "spontaneous" beatings) is usually escalated[6] and since on transports, one's suffering grows in proportion to the length of the journey.

The main theme of the autobiographical chapters is the growth of the author's mind. Solzhenitsyn believes that he might have been a worse person if he had escaped imprisonment (4: 1). He regrets, for instance, his behavior at the interrogations and finds consolation only in the thought that he "avoided getting anyone else arrested" (1: 3, p. 134). In the chapter dealing with stool pigeons (3: 12), he admits that he came close to being trapped into some form of collaboration with the camp police. All this is not only a matter of the confessional mode but also of diachronic paradigms: the practices of the Archipelago are stages in the history of the country and in the history of an individual conscience.

Imprisonment is presented as Solzhenitsyn's purgatory. First and foremost, it cancels the attitudes fostered by his officer's training. Solzhenitsyn is remorseful for having made a German prisoner carry his suitcase on a transport, when as a Soviet Army officer (even though under arrest), he felt entitled to such a service (1: 4). In his first camp, confident of his ability to command, he readily accepts the privileged position of foreman. Soon enough, however, he discovers that the rules of the camp are not the same as those of the army, that his officer's experience is useless,[7] and that only a profound knowledge of camp life can allow one to hold a foreman's job. He withdraws his demands on his work gang just in time to escape a murderous beating by criminal convicts. He loses his privileges one by one, and his condition is reduced to that of a common downtrodden *zek:*

> In prison too, we seemed to have grown weak, but here it went much faster. There was already a ringing in the head. That pleasant weakness, in which it is easier to give in than to fight back, kept coming closer.
>
> And in the barracks—total darkness. We lay there dressed in everything wet on everything bare, and it seemed it was warmer not to take anything off—like a poultice.
>
> Open eyes looked at the black ceiling, at the black heavens.
>
> Good Lord! Good Lord! Beneath the shells and the bombs I begged you to preserve my life. And now I beg you, please send me death. (3: 6, p. 197)

Yet Solzhenitsyn rises from his initial despair, adjusts himself to his new conditions, and accepts solidarity with his fellow inmates. His moral conversion is followed by a religious one. Here, too, Solzhenitsyn does not so much *turn* to God as *return* to the early beliefs that he had relinquished at school.

His political re-education follows a similar pattern: he rids himself of the calcinations of communist brainwashing acquired in the upper grades of high school and at the university. The first change in his political ideology takes place at the beginning of his prison life, stimulated by his Butyrki comrades ("First Cell, First Love," 1: 5). At the time of his arrest (for critical remarks on Stalin's policies in his correspondence with a friend), Solzhenitsyn was still a convinced though not fanatical Marxist. Like most intellectuals of his generation, he had, despite the muffled discourse that he may have heard at home, accepted both the academic

Marxist philosophy and the ideology of sacrifices as imperative for the construction of communism. In prison he was affected not so much by ideological counterarguments as by the new information that did not fit into the official picture of the world and had therefore been withheld from his contemporaries. Accordingly, if the first major ethical aim of *The Gulag Archipelago* is to speak for the silent victims, its second aim is to challenge the official monopoly on information[8] by supplying formerly suppressed facts. Solzhenitsyn attempts to stimulate the reader's thinking the way his Butyrki cellmates affected his own—toward a reassessment of the history of the Soviet Union. This aim is canceled as soon as his main target audience, products of Soviet education, ceases to exist. The reader who stands in no need of such "re-education" may waive Solzhenitsyn's rhetoric as obsolete or, alternatively, focus on its aesthetic aspect.

What then becomes apparent is the richness of Solzhenitsyn's techniques of persuasion and their appropriateness to the concrete subjects touched. The sheer magnitude of the bare facts is sometimes allowed to speak for itself, as when the proud construction projects accomplished by convict slave labor are enumerated (3: 22) in a dry, objective, level tone: slave labor emerges as the massive underside of history-textbook events, propaganda formulae, legal treatises, and recontextualized quotations from Lenin and Mayakovsky. Yet when the stark facts are less striking, Solzhenitsyn's individual voice lends a specific coloring to various portions of the material. In fact, Solzhenitsyn manages to turn his use of insufficiently corroborated hearsay to aesthetic advantage by making his authorial voice avowedly personal and by using the collective nature of the research for this book as a basis for heteroglossia. The inaccessibility of reliable statistics creates a need for estimates; and Solzhenitsyn makes them not so much in numbers as in image-bearing expressions. The paradigmatic approach calls for catalogues and classified lists of the aggregated material; Solzhenitsyn composes them with a vivid verbal versatility.[9] He seems to be guided by a wish to devote an individual act of attention to each entry, at the same time integrating each entry into a holistic scheme. For example, in his survey of the arrests among different religious and clerical groups in the early twenties, he avoids plain enumeration and parallel syntactic constructions; instead, he makes a point of devising a syntactically or lexically distinct clause for each category of people subjected to persecution. Unfortunately, this effect is partly effaced in translation[10]:

> Men of religion were an inevitable part of every annual "catch," and their silver locks gleamed in every cell and in every prisoner transport en route to Solovetsky Islands.

From the early twenties on, arrests were also made among groups of theosophists, mystics, spiritualists. (Count Palen's group used to keep official transcripts of its communications with the spirit world.) Also, religious societies and philosophers of the Berdyaev circle. The so-called "Eastern Catholics"—followers of Vladimir Solovyov—were arrested and destroyed in passing, as was the group of A. I. Abrikosova. And, of course, ordinary Roman Catholics—Polish Catholic priests, etc., were arrested, too, as part of the normal course of events. (1: 2, p. 37)

The original text conveys the author's awareness of the fact that each category of persecuted people consisted of individuals whom he did not know and to whom he could not pay sufficient tribute. Under these circumstances, the best he can do is avoid lexical and syntactic uniformity in listing the groups of the victims. What the English translation does not render are the different figurative synonyms of "to be arrested." In the original, men of religion "flowed as a mandatory part of every 'catch'"; groups of theosophists, mystics, and spiritualists "got caught" (or "fell in") more sporadically (*popadali*); "Eastern Catholics" were not "arrested and destroyed in passing" but "crushed in passing and jailed one by one" (*mimokhodom byli razgromleny i peresazheny*); and Polish priests "would somehow naturally proceed to jail" (*kak-to uzh sami soboi sadilis'*). The lexical and stylistic variations are, in fact, Solzhenitsyn's protest against the uniformization of the fates of so many different people. The leveling of the style of *GA* in translation is, therefore, objectionable not only on aesthetic but also on ethical grounds, though it must be conceded that most of the colloquialisms used for purposes of linguistic individualization are almost untranslatable. Indeed, when Solzhenitsyn comments on an absurd charge of treason by a phrase like *"Tak on issobachils'ia stat' predatelem,"* one can almost sympathize with the translator who settles for "And that's how he conned his way into becoming a traitor" (1: 2, p. 61).

* * *

Learning the language of the camps was an integral part of Solzhenitsyn's education. In *The Gulag Archipelago* the individual and the communal meet on the blurring borderlines between the individual style of the authorial commentary and the voices of the camp inmates, which the author recollects. These are reproduced through the use of "macrometaphors" (cf. Booth 1988: 325–32), embedding of camp jargon into the authorial discourse, indirect speech, and inset narratives. *The Gulag Archipelago* also includes hilariously debunked voices of the official Soviet press, propaganda, and legal documents. The techniques applied to the processing of the latter material are free indirect speech and mock decoding.

The most important *macrometaphor* of the book is that of the Gulag as an archipelago made up of groups of island-camps. The prisoners brought to these islands are sometimes referred to by the aquatic metaphor of the "catch" (*ulov*), the spoils of the police fishing in muddy waters. The trains that transport the prisoners are the "ships of the Archipelago" (2: 1); the transit prisons and distribution camps are "the ports of the Archipelago" (2: 2). Second in importance is the metaphor developed in *Cancer Ward:* the insular camps are the metastases of a malignant growth, swellings that, in their turn, produce further evil. To extend the latter metaphor, one could say that writing about the experience of the *zeks* is the X-ray procedure—mandatory yet only partly effective: by the time he had completed his book, Solzhenitsyn found that the cancerous cells were spreading again.

Whether these two metaphors are Solzhenitsyn's inventions or come from camp folklore, *The Gulag Archipelago* has institutionalized them as parts of contemporary culture. More idiosyncratic, perhaps, though no less apt, are such extended metaphors as the "sewage-disposal system" and the "Big Solitaire." The former metaphor is a translation of the Russian *kanalizatsiia:* underneath the surface of socialist urban construction there runs a network of sewage undercurrents decorously hidden from view. The Russian term involves a punning allusion to the White Sea–Baltic, the Moscow-Volga, and the Volga-Don *canals* constructed with forced labor.

The people arrested by categories ("wreckers," "priests," "nationalists," etc.) are referred to by the camp term of *potoki*, "streams," translated into English as "waves": prisoners are ground into the dirt and sent out of sight by sewage-disposal canals, whence they are flung onto the islands of the muddy Archipelago.

The "streams" represent the categories of citizens who are arrested at specific periods. One of them is made up of members of the outlawed socialist parties, arrested in the twenties, then released and sent into exile, and then rearrested and largely "liquidated" during the Great Terror (cf. Olitskaya 1971). This process is referred to by the metaphor *Bol'shoi pas'ians*—the Grand Solitaire, or the Great Patience Game; patience was not foreign to Stalin's cat-and-mouse strategies, nor was the reduction of people to dispensable playing cards. In view of the criminal mores in the Gulag, a card game is, indeed, a fit substitute for chess as "the great game of life."

Whereas in the memoirs of Ginzburg, Panin, Kopelev, and others, *camp jargon* occurs mainly in direct speech and is presented as part of actual dialogues, Solzhenitsyn incorporates into his authorial discourse such widespread terms as *tukhta* (or *tufta*) for "exaggerated production out-put" or *raskolotsia* for "confess (break into pieces) under interrogation." The deliberate emphasis on this type of vocabulary conveys the influence of camp life on an individual's conceptual matrix and vision of the world. This purpose is further served by the quotations of camp proverbs and sayings, which are sometimes compared with the old Russian proverbs collected by Dahl. A particularly interesting effect, also largely lost in translation, is produced by the anachronistic application of camp termi-nology to a discussion of the Decembrists' interrogations and imprison-ment in the late twenties of the previous century (1: 2, pp. 131–32). This is part of the book's intermittently pursued comparison of the penal system under the czars and in Soviet Russia.

The use of indirect discourse usually signifies the author's concur-rence in the words of the person whose messages they render. Strings of very short stories recounting the experience of individual Gulag victims supplement and intersperse Solzhenitsyn's systematic accounts of each aspect of a *zek*'s progress through the camps. These are twice-told tales, summary-type renditions of the words of others. They usually record acts of startling brutality or absurdity and are presented not as something that would *usually* happen but as something that *could,* and *did,* happen un-der the given conditions—not as *typical* but as *typifying* events and, by the same token, not as exceptions from but as logical extensions of the pre-vailing rules.

In *The Gulag Archipelago* the use of direct speech for rendering the voices of other people is generally restricted only to their particularly sig-nificant formulations in the most memorable snatches of dialogue. Long direct-speech monologues might have struck the reader as constructions rather than genuine recollections. This effect is, indeed, self-consciously exploited on the three formalized occasions when Solzhenitsyn speaks in the name of another person—twice in the voice of fictional characters, his own Ivan Denisovich (3: 7, pp. 218–21 and 223–26) and the *zek* Fan Fanych, to whom Solzhenitsyn ascribes the authorship of the satirical "ethnographical sketch" entitled "The Zeks as a Nation" (3: 19), and once in the voice of Georgii Tenno (5: 7), a "committed fugitive" of in-domitable courage whose escape plans were defeated by his humanist rejection of the "end-justifies-the-means" principle and whose dream of leaving the Soviet Union upon his release from the camps was shattered by cancer. Solzhenitsyn's telling Tenno's story for him is an act of love similar to Shalamov's writing a story for a dead friend in "The Snake Charmer" (*KR*).

The voices coming from the enemy side are rendered through pre-dominantly comic techniques. Thus *free indirect speech,* which consists of the "words of another" syntactically incorporated into the authorial discourse and uttered, as it were, with the author's sarcastic intonation, is used for official misrepresentations of reality. Propaganda officialese is sometimes joined, as an interpretive tag-clause, to authorial statement; for example: "In 1926 the Zionist society of 'Hehalutz' was [jailed] in toto—*since it had failed to respond to the all-powerful upsurge of internationalism*" (1: 2, p. 38; amended translation; italics added). The chapter "In Place of Politicals" contains paragraphs that combine neutral informative statements, direct utterances, and strings of sentences in free-indirect speech that represent the brutal responses of the police and the apologetic ones of the citizens in search of a method behind the madness of the arbitrary arrests (3: 10, pp. 299–300). In other cases, whole paragraphs parody the propagandistic self-justification of the establishment; for example:

> In other words, we never did trust the engineers—and from the very first years of the Revolution we saw to it that those lackeys and servants of former capitalist bosses were kept in line by healthy suspicion and surveillance by the workers. However, during the reconstruction period, we did permit them to work in our industries, while the whole force of the class assault was directed against the rest of the intelligentsia. But the more our economic leadership matured . . . —the more the number of plans increased, and the more those plans overlapped and conflicted with one another, the clearer became the old engineers' basic commitment to wrecking, their insincerity, slyness, venality. The Sentinel of the Revolution narrowed his eyes with even greater vigilance—and wherever it directed its narrowed gaze it immediately discovered a nest of wreckers. (1: 2, p. 44)

Here again part of the author's stylistic game is lost in the translation of the subversive image-bearing verbs *"i plany eti stalkivalis' i vyshibali drug druga"* ("and these plans clashed and knocked each other out") by the more neutral and literary "those plans overlapped and conflicted with one another." The technique used in this paragraph is the opposite of the *conventional* free indirect speech: the intonations, the statements, and the bulk of the wording are those of political indoctrination meetings and newspaper invective, yet some of the words smuggled in by the author (in particular, the mistranslated ones) debunk the official discourse and point to the crude actualities that it is meant to conceal. The paradox of the retranslation that takes place in the English version of *GA* is symptomatic: for many decades numerous translators had been investing more effort into rendering Soviet officialese than into catching up with the vigorous developments in the living "pre-Gutenbergian"[11] colloquial Russian.

Solzhenitsyn's debunking interpretation of official discourse is pitted against the regime's "expanded interpretation" of code words to the wise in legal literature or official operative instructions. A paradigm of the forms of official exegesis is presented in the survey of the different paragraphs of the capacious "political" Article 58 of Stalin's penal code. Here, it is not the letter but the spirit of the law that killeth. Thus,

> In Section 1 we learn that any action (and, according to Article 6 of the Criminal Code, any absence of action) directed toward the weakening of state power was considered to be counterrevolutionary.
>
> Broadly interpreted, this turned out to include the refusal of a prisoner in camp to work when in a state of starvation and exhaustion. This was a weakening of state power. And it was punished by execution. (The execution of *malingerers* during the war.) (1: 2, 60–61).

Another type of exegesis at work in *The Gulag Archipelago* is the "translation" of Soviet texts: even the most insipid newspapers can be read with interest if one has acquired certain interpretive skills. An opening for interpretation may be provided, for instance, by a censor's oversight. Thus, in the Preface, Solzhenitsyn refers to a journal report that frozen specimens of prehistoric fauna discovered in excavations on the Kolyma river were eaten "with relish" by those present: "The magazine no doubt astonished its small audience with the news of how successfully the flesh of fish could be kept fresh in a frozen state. But few, indeed, among its readers were able to decipher the genuine and heroic meaning of this incautious report" (p. ix).

"Those present" were, of course, famished *zeks*; only the initiated could immediately picture to themselves how "flouting the higher claims of ichthyology and elbowing each other to be first, they tore off chunks of the prehistoric flesh and hauled them over to the bonfire to thaw them out and bolt them down" (p. ix).

One of Solzhenitsyn's interpretive techniques is contextualization: for instance, Mayakovsky's verses

> Look over
> your ranks,
> watch them with care.
> Are all of them
> really
> Komsomols?
> Or are they
> only
> pretending to be?

acquire a macabre significance if one recollects that in Mayakovsky's times there was already massive repression against *ancien régime* intellectuals who had been working quite loyally for the Soviet state. Historical context likewise transforms extracts from Lenin's collected works, which thousands of Solzhenitsyn's readers had studied *sub specie aeternitatis*, from abstract theoretical discourse to instructions for terror (1: 9, 3: 1). In a brilliant extension of the same technique, Solzhenitsyn mines the memoirs of the public prosecutor Krylenko (himself eventually arrested and shot) for insights into the early public trials of the so-called wreckers and agents of imperialism, reads between the lines of the books by the prosecutor A. Vyshinsky and the jurist L. Averbach on Soviet law, and "translates" the Stalinist collection of essays on the White Sea–Baltic canal into the language of the grim reality that the essays attempted, with only partial success, to keep out.

* * *

As noted above, just as Gulag memoirs incorporate elements of diverse genres, so different parts of *The Gulag Archipelago* are written in various styles: journalistic reports, analytic commentary, feuilletons, essays, confessions, exegeses, and adventure stories. Yet the discourse with which *The Gulag Archipelago* overlaps in the most significant way is not that of any specific literary genre but that of the "literature of freedom"—to borrow a term from behaviorist psychology (Skinner 1972: 31). The widespread view of the book as Solzhenitsyn's call to Russia to repent for its sins is only partly true—at least, it is tempered by his intermittent toying with the belief that the changes that followed the 1917 October coup were imposed on Russia by the ideologies of other nations and that most of the sins to be repented are not those *of* Russia but those *against* it.[12] If there is something of which Solzhenitsyn accuses the masses of the Russian population, making no exception of himself, it is submission to aversive controls.

In behaviorist psychology, *aversive control* means subjecting a person to "negative reinforcers," such as nagging, threats, or beatings, in order to make him or her behave in a certain manner. B. F. Skinner points out the mechanics of reciprocity in aversive control: if a person submits to such a control, he or she reinforces the aversive behavior of the controller. The literature of freedom aims to induce readers to escape from or attack those who seek to control them aversively. It does not present the philosophy of freedom but "emphasizes the aversive conditions under which people live" in order to awaken the "happy slaves," and prescribes modes of action by indicating ways in which the "controlling power may be weakened or destroyed." Skinner adds that "without help or guidance people submit to aversive conditions in the most surprising way" (1972: 26–31).

At the time of the book's composition Solzhenitsyn sought to "awaken" his countrymen to their present condition by tracing it to their recent past. He was aware that his disclosures would not be entirely new: they would cause a growing sense of recognition and thus shift injustice from the periphery to the center of vision. The first pages of *The Gulag Archipelago* open a mysterious new dimension, putting us, as it were, into the shoes of a stunned Everyman who is unexpectedly arrested while treading his usual path:

> We have been happily borne—or perhaps have unhappily dragged our weary way—down the long and crooked streets of our lives, past all kinds of walls and fences made of rotting wood, rammed earth, brick, concrete, iron railings. We have never given a thought to what lies behind them. We have never tried to penetrate them with our vision or our understanding. But there is where the *Gulag* country begins, right next to us, two yards away from us. In addition, we have failed to notice an enormous number of closely fitted, well-disguised doors and gates in these fences. All those gates were prepared for us, every last one! And all of a sudden the fateful gate swings quickly open, and four white male hands, unaccustomed to physical labor but nonetheless strong and tenacious, grab us by the leg, arm, collar, cap, ear, and drag us in like a sack, and the gate behind us, the gate to our past life, is slammed shut once and for all.
>
> That's all there is to it! You are arrested!
>
> And you'll find nothing better to respond with than a lamblike bleat: "Me? What for?" (1: 1, p. 4).

At the beginning of this paragraph Solzhenitsyn writes in the first-person plural ("We have been happily borne")—to avoid a prematurely alienating accusatory tone. After the reference to the moment of the arrest, the energy of the narrative is enhanced by the shift to the second-person "you."[13] The heightened emotional pitch tends to eclipse at least three subtler stylistic touches that subliminally prepare the reader for what is to follow: (1) the oscillation between the metaphoric and the literal streets, fences, gates, and doors, which prepares us for the panorama of the world where the grimmest hyperboles, such as "to work somebody to death" or "to break every bone in one's body," become literal while actualities spill over into macrometaphors; (2) strings of homogeneous parts of the sentence (a multiple non-choice of possibilities), which prepare us for the paradigmatic method of the book (some lists are additive, e.g., "walls and fences made of rotting wood, rammed earth, brick, concrete, iron railing," while others imply alternatives, e.g., "grab us by the leg, arm, collar, cap, ear, and drag us in like a sack"; (3) the reference to "the fateful gate," a specific one destined for each of "us" (though not, as in Kafka's "Before the Law," meant for each of us alone), which prepares us for the treatment of individual life stories as versions of the common fate—indeed, while "your" response ("Me? What for?") is quite authentic, it is, though "you" may not know it, typical: multitudes have passed and will continue to pass through the same gate, saying the same things, swayed by the same feelings.

The media rhetoric ("All those gates were prepared for us, every last one!") that renounces laconicism in favor of lucidity, as if to render the narrative proof against misreadings,[14] produces the impression that this carefully crafted text is spontaneous. The touch of mysteriousness associated with the image of a gate continues the fairy-tale tone set by the opening sentences: "How do people get to this [mysterious] Archipelago? . . . at ticket windows or at travel bureaus for Soviet or foreign tourists the employees would be astounded if you were to ask for a ticket to go there. They know nothing and they've never heard of the Archipelago as a whole or of any one of its innumerable islands" (1: 1, p. 3). Prior to sounding his call for freedom, Solzhenitsyn "arrests" the reader by an implicit promise of disclosures. In a tri-partite fairy-tale structure, he enumerates the magic carpets of the Archipelago, making a bid to conciliate the *hypocrite lecteur:*

> Those who go to the Archipelago to administer it get there via the training schools of the Ministry of Internal Affairs.
> Those who go there to be guards are conscripted via the military conscription centers.
> And those who, *like you and me, dear reader,* go there to die, must get there solely and compulsorily via arrest. (1: 1, p. 3; italics added)

In addition to the classification and the anecdote-studded catalogue of types of arrest, the opening chapter voices Solzhenitsyn's first call to resist aversive control: instead of behaving submissively, the arrested person should shout, struggle, call attention to his plight, incite passersby. Friends, neighbors, acquaintances should ambush arresting officers and make the job of policemen as tough as possible.[15] Resistance may mean self-sacrifice, and, as Solzhenitsyn notes, "Every man always has handy a dozen glib little reasons why he is right not to sacrifice himself" (1: 1, 17). "The literature of freedom" sometimes restricts itself to pointing out the lack of freedom; in other cases it calls for supererogatory acts. Solzhenitsyn seems to be torn between his need to understand and explain why people did not perform heroic acts of resistance and his wish to pass judgment on "average" behavior. He earns the right to such a judgment by extending it to himself and telling us how, knowing Moscow better than did his guards, he himself actually brought them to Lubyanka, where he would be imprisoned.

Condemnation of his own submissiveness initiates the confessional strand of *The Gulag Archipelago.* The confession is moderated by the hint that had he shouted, made a scene on the escalator of the Moscow subway, or attempted to escape, his voice might have been stifled too soon:

As for me, I kept silent for one further reason: because those Muscovites thronging the steps of the escalators were too few for me, *too few!* Here my cry would be heard by 200 or twice 200, but what about 200 million? Vaguely, unclearly, I had a vision that someday I would cry out to the 200 million.

But for the time being I did not open my mouth, and the escalator dragged me implacably down into the nether world. (1: 1, pp. 17–18)

This opening for moral relativism is thus offered and then taken away by turning the physical movement of going down to the subway trains into a metaphor for moral degradation.

By contrast, the chapter ends with an example of another person's mild resistance that undermines aversive control. Solzhenitsyn moves backward to the day of his arrest, and to the following morning, when, in the company of the other inmates of his dungeon, he was taken for a toilet call in the yard:

[T]he master sergeant brusquely urged us on:

"Come on, hurry it up! With us they do it quickly!"

Not far from me squatted one of the tankmen, . . . a tall, melancholy senior lieutenant. His face was blackened by a thin film of metallic dust or smoke, but the big red scar stretching across his cheek stood out nonetheless.

"What do you mean, *with us?*" he asked quietly, indicating no intention of hurrying back to the punishment cell that still stank of kerosene.

"In SMERSH counterintelligence!" the master sergeant shot back proudly and more resonantly than was called for. . . .

"And *with us* we do it slowly," replied the senior lieutenant thoughtfully. His helmet was pulled back, uncovering his still untrimmed hair. His oaken, battle-hardened rear end was lifted toward the pleasant coolish breeze.

"Where do you mean, *with us?*" the master sergeant barked at him more loudly than he needed to.

"In the Red Army," the senior lieutenant replied very quietly from his heels, measuring with his look the cannon-tailer that never was. (1: 1, p. 23)

Thus, by quietly resisting aversive control, the prisoner manages to maintain his dignity in one of the most undignified situations to which a person may be exposed.

The anal imagery of the episode harks back to the near-mandatory naturalism of the earlier Gulag memoirs but also foreshadows the macrometaphor of the next chapter, "The History of Our Sewage Disposal System." This chapter, unlike the one on arrests, does not so much stagger the reader as offer a *systematic* view of the underside of the Soviet fairy-tale history in order to stimulate an extensive change in the reader's scheme of concepts. Accordingly, it begins by pointing out the need to correct a misconception: "When people today decry *the abuses of the cult,* they keep getting hung up on those years which are stuck in our throats, '37 and '38. And memory begins to make it seem as though arrests were never made *before* or *after,* but only in those two years" (1: 2, p. 24). Here returns the confessional tone set in the first chapter: the immense stream of peasants repressed in 1929–30 seems not to have even "scarred the Russian conscience. And yet Stalin (and you and I as well) committed no crime more heinous than this" (1: 2, p. 24). Yet if previously an expression like "you and I" referred to "our" going to the Archipelago to die, now the reader is implicated as an accomplice to the crimes: the repetition of the formula suggests the idea of the grim justice of suffering in the camps for *not* having opposed the regime.

The second section of the chapter makes a chronological survey of the "streams" of prisoners that flowed to the Archipelago before World War II; the third surveys the provisions, in letter and spirit, of Article 58; the fourth presents a synthesis of this information in terms of individual cases; and the remaining two sections continue the chronology of wartime and post-war streams. This distribution of the material creates a solid paradigm of information, a secure matrix for reconceptualizations promoted by the ensuing narrative.

Solzhenitsyn, indeed, assumes that his target audience is harboring a spectrum of wrong beliefs. He proceeds to assault these beliefs gradually, starting with the most vulnerable misprision, the underrating of arrests before and after the Great Purge. Toward the end of the book, in the third volume (Parts 5–7), he deals with two rooted "paleological" (Sommer 1976: 35–42) beliefs: (1) that the "Vlasovites" and the people who collaborated with the Germans during the occupation deserved the punishment they got (as did the Russian girlfriends of German soldiers), and (2) that the Gulag is a matter of the past.

The former belief is attacked in two stages. In the first volume the author explains the predicament of those who became German recruits in order to escape starvation in POW camps; many of them attempted to run back to the Soviet lines at the first opportunity (1: 6). Solzhenitsyn discusses the ambiguity of the phrase "the betrayal of the motherland": before the "Vlasovites" betrayed their country, it had betrayed them by Stalin's unprecedented blanket rejection of the Soviet soldiers who had been captured by the Germans (including his own son Yakov, whom he refused to have exchanged for General Paulus). The subject is resumed, and treated even more radically, in the third volume (5: 1), where Solzhenitsyn presents an entire paradigm of the attitudes that had led people to fight on the German side or hold a variety of jobs under the German occupation. His central argument rests on the sheer number of the "Vlasovites" and "collaborators": if millions of people turned against their country, it is the country, with its recent history of terror, forced collectivization, artificially induced famine, and labor camps, that must be held to blame. To this one may object by saying that Solzhenitsyn sweeps under the carpet the stories of the extreme cruelty of the "Vlaso-vites" and collaborators who hated the Communist regime; yet he seeks not so much to exonerate all the "Vlasovites" as to support his claim that, in any case, the post-war special-regime (*katorga*) camps to which they were sent and in which whole parties of new arrivals often failed to survive the first year were a disproportionate punishment for any human being.[16] Gulag authors frequently attack the self-protectiveness of those readers who wish to write off at least some of the victims of the Gulag as "actually guilty."

The penultimate chapter of the book deals with the hopeless confrontations that Solzhenitsyn, now the famous author of *One Day in the Life of Ivan Denisovich,* had with government officials and committees in his efforts to persuade them to ease the regulations of the "corrective labor colonies," as the camps were called in the sixties. Like Marchenko, he shows that at the time when *The Gulag Archipelago* was being written, the camps continued to exist, albeit in a modified form. Indeed, in the late sixties and early seventies it was the highest echelons (who must also have studied the narratives of Gulag veterans),[17] rather than the lower-grade executives, who sought to close all the loopholes of which Ivan Denisovich might have taken advantage. Solzhenitsyn made suggestions about ways to improve the prisoners' lot and was baffled when government officials countered them with glib and impenetrably callous phrases. As in the endings of most Gulag memoirs, the style of the last chapters of the book betrays fatigue; it is reinvigorated only in the story of the author's obtaining a real insight into the reasons for the toughness of the camp regulations in those years. In combination with the material of "Our Muzzled Freedom" (4: 3) these insights destroy the last traces of the impression of the camp kingdom's insular character: life in the camps is all too closely interlinked with the state of the Larger Zone that has produced them.[18] The official interpretation of the goal of imprisonment has by now shed its erstwhile lip service to "restitution" or "re-education":[19]

> suddenly, out they come—full answers to all the questions which I had carried in vain over marble floors and between mirrored walls.
>
> Raise the living standard of prisoners? *Can't be done!* Because the free people around the camp would be living *less well* than the zeks, which cannot be allowed.
>
> Receive parcels frequently, and bigger ones? *Can't be done!* Because this would have a bad effect on the warders, who get no food from Moscow shops.

Reprimand warders and teach them to behave better? *Can't be done!*
We're trying to hold on to them! Nobody wants the job, we can't pay
much, and some of the privileges have been taken away.

We deny prisoners payment for their work according to socialist
principles? Their own fault—they've cut themselves off from their
socialist society!

But don't we want to reclaim them for normal life?! . . .

Reclaim them??? The sword-bearer is astonished. "That's not what
the camps are about. A camp is a place of retribution!"

Retribution! The word fills the whole room. (7: 2, pp. 504–5)

Thus the book that seeks to change the attitudes of the reader admits,
with a degree of lassitude, the author's failure to achieve this aim as far
as the ruling strata are concerned. If the literature of the "thaw" tended
to present the Gulag as a matter of the past, the camp literature of the
seventies, dominated by *The Gulag Archipelago,* reverts to the position of
the earlier writers who maintained that the camps were an extension of
the Soviet system. Yet it places the camps not on the periphery of the
system but at its very heart.

The last chapter of *The Gulag Archipelago* is an account of the injustice
perpetrated at the very time the book was being written; most of it is made
up of information that reached the author in the letters of witnesses and
victims. There is no conclusive ending, apart from the abrupt statement
that after "the enormous state has towered over us" for half a century or
more, "there is still no law." The last chapter is followed by a short afterword and by a still shorter postscript: this lagging structure of the ending
reinforces the impression that the story is not finished and that, as time
goes by, still more might have to be said. Indeed, even *Invisible Allies,* a
sequel to a sequel to *The Gulag Archipelago,* suggests that in the early nineties, some stories are still biding their time.

* * *

I disagree with the widespread view that *The Gulag Archipelago* is not
sufficiently tightly structured. At times it deliberately simulates "an intractable and unstoppable flow of horrors escaping from Pandora's box"
(Richards 1985: 151–52): the chapters where the material escalates and
the "anecdotal" stretches where individual fates produce the beadlike
variety of the pulsation effect are practically designed to seem spontaneous. In general, the narrative manifests a considerable degree of muted
self-awareness.

The book was written clandestinely, with the completed parts hidden
in various places, which made it very difficult for the author to have the

whole work on his desk and to introduce across-the-board emendations. Yet Solzhenitsyn had foreseen these problems: hence the concentrated effort of pre-planning. Batches of new material must have been arriving in the course of the composition, but the paradigmatic matrix had been put together at the outset. There are practically no repetitions in the three volumes; and the lack of uniformity in style and mood is a merit and not a flaw since it precludes monotony and presents a range of attitudes toward the material. As noted above, Gulag writers did not seek flawlessness. Solzhenitsyn seems to have been at least partly resigned to one prominent flaw: for all the subtlety of perception and style, he allows an occasional coarseness of attitude or grossness of brushstroke, under the influence, as it were, of the heart- and spine-breaking grossness of the material itself. Solzhenitsyn suggests that sometimes one has to work with the bulldozer before space can be cleared for fine craftsmanship:

> Our Russian pens write only in large letters. We have lived through so very much, and almost none of it has been described and called by its right name. But, for Western authors, peering through a microscope at the living cells of everyday life, shaking a test tube in the beam of a strong light, this is after all a whole epic, another ten volumes of *Remembrance of Things Past:* to describe the perturbations of a human soul placed in a cell filled to twenty times its capacity and with no latrine bucket, where prisoners are taken out to the toilet only once a day! (2: 2, p. 541)

Solzhenitsyn goes on to mention the consequences of such a situation in mock-literary terms ("What a conflict! What a clash of . . . personalities! What nuances! . . . That is when the rock bottom of a human being is revealed."), all in the same long paragraph that starts with an allusion to Proust (cf. Shalamov's 1966 story "Marcel Proust" [*VL*]). This is his radicalization of the Wordsworthian stripping principle: reduce man not to essentials but to a lack of essentials and human nature is revealed in a way that puts sophistication to scorn.

Paradoxically, the evocation of this reductionist attitude, comparable to Kostoglotov's impatience with the customer who asks for a shirt by both the collar and sleeve sizes in *Cancer Ward,* expands the repertoire of contemporary human experience available to literary exploration. In a sense it also calls for sympathy for the people who, owing to the persecution or hardships they had endured under totalitarian regimes, regard a great deal of Western intellectualization as a side effect and a hidden cost of democracy.

Solzhenitsyn is well aware of the lure of reductionism. In a soul-searching moment he speaks of the adverse effects of his officer's training on his intellectual life:

> I remember very well that right after officer candidate school I experi-
> enced the *happiness of simplification,* of being a military man and *not*
> *having to think things through; the happiness of being immersed* in the life
> *everyone else lived,* that was *accepted* in our military milieu; the happiness
> of forgetting some of the spiritual subtleties inculcated since child-
> hood. (1: 4, p. 162)

This passage is an excellent example of what oft was thought but ne'er
so well expressed. It speaks of the same joy of simplification for the sake
of which people waive open-mindedness in "their own" circles, join messianic or fundamentalist movements, become radical pacifists or "got-
to-show-them" rednecks, hew their political identities with an ax, and
brand as irrelevant or noxious whatever they have no leisure to study or
whatever takes more than a one-liner to explain. Few can consistently
resist the lure of simplification: at one's worst moments one may find
that reduction of complexities is empowering; at one's better moments
one may fear that the "large letters" of intense human suffering can be
eclipsed by luxurious refinement of thought and expression.

The reason the impulse toward simplification should be treated with a
degree of sympathy when the "large letters" are involved is that it facilitates a forceful political initiative. Atrocities need to be presented sche-
matically, archetypally, at first; even sweeping generalizations can reflect
one's sense of priorities in broaching a new human-rights subject. Solzhenitsyn's combining an intense rhetoric on large issues with an abundance of fine insights and complexity of thought is one of the outstanding achievements of *The Gulag Archipelago* and, actually, of his camp
fictions as well.

Yet occasional simplification can create repercussions. Much, for instance, has already been written and argued on Solzhenitsyn's attitudes
toward Jews.[20] In a relatively recent study, A. Ben-Yakov (1988: 307–26)
shows that Solzhenitsyn displays no anti-Semitism as a socio-political phenomenon but also that, although his archetypally evil Jews are counter-
balanced by several attractive figures, his approval of the individual Jew
hinges on the latter's having shed what is regarded as typical, national
Jewish features. The issue is still sporadically debated. Solzhenitsyn's
support of the State of Israel pleases some Jewish readers but reminds
others of the British jocular response to Zionism: "You can have Palestine, provided you give us back Golder's Green." His loving portrayal of
some Jewish friends, such as Gammerov and Ingal in *The Gulag Archipelago,* proves his open-mindedness to some readers, while others maintain that all anti-Semites had their favorite Jews. In any case, Solzhenitsyn
definitely emphasizes the Jewishness of the people who shaped the Gulag
(see the page full of ugly Jewish mugs in the English version—3: 3, p. 78)
without dwelling on the disproportionate number of Jews among Stalin's

victims. He does mention that in 1953, just before Stalin's death, Jews were scheduled to become the new mass scapegoat, yet he does not seem to have noticed that since 1948 Jews had been arriving at the Archipelago in constantly growing numbers or that the camp authorities encouraged a specifically anti-Semitic hooliganism of the criminal convicts.[21]

Even the passages in which Solzhenitsyn deplores the fate of individual Jewish victims of the Gulag sometimes have offensively reductionist connotations. Thus, in the chapter devoted to the death sentence, he mentions two Jews: one convicted for possessing foreign currency and the other for having traded in steel ribbon. "Primordial commerce," comments Solzhenitsyn, "the bread and butter and pastime of the Jew, had also become worthy of the death penalty" (1: 11, p. 441). The target of Solzhenitsyn's attack here is the post-Stalinist terror against economic initiative; yet the arrow is blunted by the sweeping remark about petty commerce as "the bread and butter and pastime of the Jew." This simplification of issues (though the generic "the Jew" in English has a stronger effect of stereotyping than has its Russian equivalent) is all the more dangerous since many of Solzhenitsyn's readers, coming to the clause about the death penalty, will not bother to suppress the "serves him right" response.

In philosophy, after many centuries of debate, there is no agreement about the definition of the self. What is me: is it that which manifests itself when outer props, veneer, sublimations, or repressions are removed, or, on the contrary, is it the network of repressions and sublimations that I use to subdue the "it," or the "id," the unconscious, "the language of the other"? Is self-censorship always hypocrisy, or is it sometimes a struggle against crudeness, against the incompleteness of one's own acculturation? And is repression always anti-democratic? As a schoolboy, Solzhenitsyn was accused of anti-Semitism when he thought he was merely defending freedom of speech. He then had his first trouble with the hypocritical establishment and with a group of careerists, including vociferous young Jews (see Scammell 1984: 65–66)—ever since, to impute anti-Semitism to Solzhenitsyn is to place oneself in bad company. Yet it is clear that the young Solzhenitsyn shared the confusion of the cultural circles that did not have a viable democratic tradition to support their yearning for liberty and therefore failed to distinguish between liberalism and anarchy, between restriction on freedom of speech and restriction on instigation to violence. The smoldering anti-Jewish violence in Russia, past and present, has created a climate in which the question whether Jews should get special treatment where the disclosure of unpleasant truths is concerned must be answered in a cautious affirmative: unpleasant truths must be revealed and faced, but circumspectly, perhaps even with a balance, without the "large letters" that easily turn into slogans inspiring random hostility. Throughout his cycle *The Red Wheel,* Solzhenitsyn seeks such a balance,[22] though not without a touch of labored artificiality.

At issue here is not so much the slippery problem of anti-Semitism per se as the kind of simplification and insensitivity that may be read, or misread, as anti-Semitic. Thus, at the beginning of Book III, chapter 2 of *The Gulag Archipelago,* Solzhenitsyn promises to explain the motivation of the notorious Naphtaly Frenkel, who is supposed to have masterminded the turning of the Archipelago into an economic force at the price of a radical increase in the suffering and mortality of the prisoners. When he makes good on this promise, the explanation turns out to lie in the plain assertion that Frenkel must have hated Russia—which can be read as saying that it lay in his being a Turkish Jew. Anti-Semitism in literature consists not only in the promulgation of stereotypes but also in using Jewishness as sufficient explanation of a character's negative features or shameful acts.[23]

There may be other kinds of simplification in *The Gulag Archipelago* to which some interpretive communities may be more sensitive than others. This is one of the aspects of the book's lack of a watertight finish: it demands a continuing conversation of the kind that Wayne Booth has called "coduction" (1988: 70–75). In fact, while unregistered simplifications may be dangerous, the registered ones actually help readers to maintain their intellectual autonomy: they give rise to moments of anger and thereby release us from Solzhenitsyn's spell. It is as though the book partly canceled itself out, turning, with or without the author's intentions, into a self-consuming artifact that subverts its own authority— though not before it has caused changes in the minds it has addressed. Yet one cannot be sure *to what extent* one has been liberated from Solzhenitsyn's influence by disagreeing with his approach to a limited set of subjects. When Solzhenitsyn calls for additions to or corrections of the material of *The Gulag Archipelago,* the call should likewise be extended to the emendation of nuances of attitude, to a further elaboration of separate issues, and to an establishment of balance—in the full consciousness that the conversation is always about the Gulag, its victims, and their suffering. It is one of Solzhenitsyn's major achievements that he has provided a broad basis for a polemic that comes closest to a substitute for the Nuremberg trials. The artistic achievement of *The Gulag Archipelago* is a major factor in the creation of this effect, and the reason why the book will retain its value long after the need for this effect has passed.

5
From Factography to Fictionalization

A significant proportion of Gulag narratives published during Khrushchev's "thaw" were fictional rather than factographic; the bulk of the audience, however, read them as testimony on "what it was like in the camps." At that time camp narratives stood a better chance of publication in the Soviet Union if their claims were ostensibly artistic. In the absence of institutionalized freedom of public memory, the bi-functionality of the literary works that doubled as works of historical testimony was a helpful though not a sufficient condition of their appearance in print. In fact, both Solzhenitsyn's *One Day in the Life of Ivan Denisovich*, which was published, and Shalamov's *Kolyma Tales,* which was kept by the publishing firm Sovetskii pisatel' for several years and rejected in 1966 (see Brewer 1995b: 37), have artistic merit over and above what was needed either as a cover or as an instrument for consciousness-raising aims.

Fiction can function as historical testimony if the word "testimony" is understood not in the narrow legal sense but, more broadly, as the word of another providing a source of knowledge. Whereas in factographic works, such as memoirs, all narrative details are supposed to be referential, in fictional works referentiality is mainly restricted to the historical and cultural-semiotic aspect of the setting: the characters and the plot are understood to be representative rather than to refer to real people and actual events. In both the above cases referentiality pertains to the data that are, in principle, available for public verification: what kinds of camps existed, where they were located, how they were run, who was imprisoned in them, and like information. Indeed, historical research has made use of both memoiristic and fictional narratives to piece together such information, crediting the material of factographic witness narratives with a greater degree of probability and using the gleanings from the works of fiction mainly for expansion and corroboration. Yet both the fictional and the factographic narratives also create the conditions for another type of knowledge, the "dangerous" experiential kind that endows statistical and technical facts with a human significance and may have unpredictable effects on the attitudes of the reader.

Camp experience has been said to be "better than what one thinks but worse than anything that one can imagine" (Guthrie 1947: 10); its exact flavor cannot be described. The only aspect of camp experience that can be reenacted imaginatively at second hand is semiotic proficiency. For the prisoners themselves, the acquisition of the sign-reading skill often brought along new shocks, yet the sense of the growth of one's understanding was one of very few compensatory reprieves,[1] and such reprieves are both vicariously and directly re-enacted by the reader. Fictionalizing techniques may both enhance the direct cognitive process of the reader and bring him or her emotionally closer to those aspects of camp ordeal that are unavailable to discursive testimony.

* * *

Both memoirs and fictional narratives about Gulag experience are bifunctional; both can be legitimately read as testimony *and* as literary works. Artistic merit, usually associated with the congruence of the stance of the work and its experiential content, does not depend on the narrative's affiliation with the fictional or the factographic mode. Conversely, the amount of referential material may sometimes be greater in a novel (e.g., Solzhenitsyn's *The First Circle*) than in many a cautious memoir that suspends references to time, place, and people in order to withhold the information from the political police (e.g., Tatiana Tchernavin's *Escape from the Soviets*). Moreover, a measure of fictionalization is almost inescapable in memoiristic works.

The word "fiction" is derived from the Latin *fictio*, which can mean "making," "feigning," or "lies." In contemporary philosophy the word "fiction" is usually identified with "making": any selection from the flow of reality, whether in our memory, oral narratives, or written texts, is already a fiction, a *construct*. In traditional literary studies, "fiction" means "feigning," constructing make-believe images, events, or scenes. In media language, a "fiction" is often a euphemism for a "lie."

Whereas a memoirist can be discredited if found guilty of "fiction" in the latter sense, elements of fictionalization in the former two senses can actually enhance the impact of bona fide testimony. I shall now attempt to show that the specificities of the Gulag-memoir material occasionally demand such fictionalizing moves as a goal-oriented *selection* of material and a make-believe *staging* of memory in dramatic blow-ups.

* * *

A memoir reflects extratextual reality in an at-least-thrice-mediated way: any personal perception is selective; memory effects a further sieving; and the process of composition involves further choices between things to include and things to leave out. In bi-functional works such as Gulag memoirs the choice may sometimes be between the aesthetic coherence of the narrative and the comprehensiveness of testimony—not all the details that have to be put on record fit in with the main design of the book. The choice is not always deliberate: when a work is written in a certain heightening of the spirit, not every memory is allowed to emerge from beneath the threshold of consciousness. Hence many details are restored in later works: cf. the relationship between Primo Levi's *If This Is a Man* and *Moments of Reprieve*, or between Shalamov's *Kolyma Tales* and *The Glove or KR-2*, or even between Kravchenko's *I Chose Freedom* and *I Chose Justice*. The interactive seepage between the text of Gulag testimonies and their context may thus result from the clash of the drive toward coherence and the imperative of providing maximal evidence. The drive for coherence may shape the main body of the work, but then the pressure of the excluded material necessitates appendices and sequels.

Sieving the recollections means that the author's mind has entered a contest with the random flow of external reality. Authors who use the chronology of their camp ordeal as a basis for the sequence of materials in the memoir allow external reality a greater degree of influence over their narratives and also produce the sense of a greater fidelity to fact. This effect is not subverted by associative digressions from the main line of the narrative, though here the contingencies are those of an unruly memory rather than the uncontrollable external events. The chronological method is more typical of the narratives written before the seventies than of the belated narratives, whose authors no longer felt obliged to cover all the main points in their testimony and had reason to fear redundancy if they did so. Therefore, in the belated narratives the material is mainly controlled by the arguments that the authors wish to make or the effects they wish to produce; external contingencies in the selection of material are largely reduced to the context: the authors assess and attempt to fill in the gaps in the works of their precursors.

Yet even in those cases when the flow of events "the way they actually happened" is given the main sway over the selection of the blocks of material, the author can assert his or her control of the shape of the work through the distribution of emphases. Since Gulag memoirists usually wish to give pride of place to communal concerns, they tend to downplay the workings of a single individual's autobiographical consciousness. As a result, the use of the first-person perspective does not always suffice as an effective organizing principle of the text. As if to compensate for this inadequacy, the sense of narrative coherence is bolstered by highlighting specific aspects of the content of the testimony—the dominant concerns of a memoir thus turn into *themes*, semantic redundancies that double as constituents of aesthetic structures.[2]

Here are a few examples.

One of the main themes of the memoirs of Solonevich is *khaltura*. In modern parlance this word denotes either a counterfeit slap-dash job or else moonshining. What Solonevich means by it is an economically useless job from which the performer benefits because it promotes the interests of his direct superiors. According to Solonevich, a disproportionate percentage of the Soviet population is, knowingly or not, engaged in *khaltura*;[3] besides, hundreds of thousands of workdays are expended on guarding prisoners or setting up Potyomkin-type propaganda façades. The theme of *khaltura*, also explored for its comic potential, thus carries part of the author's message concerning the futility of all earnest endeavor in the Soviet Union.

Buber-Neumann's memoirs have two interrelated unifying themes: friendship and dignity. Alongside willpower, her version of "biological wisdom" (Des Pres 1977: 226–47) involves concentration, alertness, and an ability to form friendships.[4] In every environment she became a member of a mutually supporting group (women were not as promptly reduced to the dystrophic state that, as Shalamov repeatedly asserts, made active friendships impossible). The stages of her experience are distinguished not so much by the transports from camp to camp as by her relationships with different people, culminating in her friendship with Milena Jesenska. Buber-Neumann's final acts of friendship are her attempts to restore her fellow sufferers' dignity through her writing.

The unifying theme of Herman's *Coming Out of the Ice* is regeneration through love: love for his father induced him to accompany his parents from America to the Soviet Union; love for a surrogate father-figure, the brave and generous Finnish American Albert Loon, keeps him from irreversible degradation (at a certain juncture Loon saves Herman's life, literalizing the metaphor of salvation); in exile upon release, the love of his wife Galina saves him from insanity. The leading themes of Alexander Dolgun's story are cultural identity and self-discovery. In front of the reader's eyes torture transforms the distinctly American happy youngster into a typical cagey, cunning, hard-faced *zek*. National traits seem, however, to have been resumed by the narrating voice: Dolgun's story is the most Franklinian of Gulag memoirs insofar as he portrays his different public identities at the allotropic stages of his life.

Less intentionally, a narrative may be unified by a tension rather than a theme. Thus the aesthetic self-awareness of Kopelev the narrator of *To Be Preserved Forever* contrasts with the insufficient moral self-awareness of Kopelev the focalizer; thus also, Panin's pride in his intellectual and physical powers clashes with his Christian humility.

The demands of individual thematic patterns often interfere with the common morphological variables of Gulag memoirs. Bershadskaya's *Trampled Lives* begins not with the topos of arrest but with a brief account of her childhood and youth—to show that there had been a life before it was trampled. The book is thematically unified by stories of lives wantonly crushed by the regime: mothers are tricked into parting with their prison-born babies; a man in loud agony is left to die in a booth in the prison corridor; prisoners die of unrelieved privation in trains; an army general obtains his mother's release from the camps only to find that she has gone mad (a guard who sees him sobbing commits suicide). The metaphor of trampling is eventually literalized: a crowd of prisoners, forced to stampede, *tramples* to death those who have fallen down. The theme reaches its climax in the image of tanks moving into the Kengir camp and literally crushing hundreds of prisoners (see also *GA* 5: 12).

Olitskaya's memoir dispenses with another Gulag topos, the motif of the journey out in the ending. It closes with "Maria Ivanovna's mine"—an image not of motion but of stasis. Maria Ivanovna was a doctor who certified deaths after executions, and the mine bearing her name is a mass grave ("you cannot call it a cemetery, can you?" [1971, 2: 270]) of the type that Shalamov describes in "Lend-Lease"—camp folklore has thus linked the gold extracted from the mines of Kolyma with the real treasure wasted there. Olitskaya does not describe the end of her second prison term, her third arrest in the mass wave of 1948–49, or her return from Kolyma: "Maria Ivanovna's mine" is presented as the bottom line of the political process whose stages have been reflected in the structure of her book. The closing image of the common grave reinforces the sense of the blending of identities that her narrative suggests by the very haziness of its character portrayal, despite her desire to preserve her own political and moral self intact. The narrative breaks off at the point when it becomes particularly difficult for the protagonist to maintain the discreteness of her identity. Suggestively, among the last episodes of her book is one about a woman gang-raped by criminals in Kolyma and another about her own narrow escape from a similar fate.[5]

At times, however, the memoirist may become uneasy that the flow of random experience seems to accommodate hackneyed schemata, such as "the irony of fate," "moments of crisis," or "the play of perspectives." Ginzburg, for instance, is embarrassed when her remembered images (a policeman's boot crushing photographs of women prisoners' children; officers and their ladies dancing on the ship's deck while prisoners crouch in the stench of its holds) remind her of shopworn cinematographic symbolism. By contrast, the aesthetic patterns that stem from the mutual adjustment of the content and the stance of a memoir can be self-consciously signaled. For instance, the three epigraphs of Kopelev's *To Be Preserved Forever* (from Goethe, Pushkin, and Akhmatova) serve as thematic keynotes for the relationship between the material and the method of his confessions, enhancing the aesthetic appeal of the text without damaging its factographic pact with the reader.

When the conditions of reception allow the aesthetic function of a narrative to dominate the informational function, the thematic patterns of a text gain further resolution. If the basic data about the setting have already been assimilated, the reader is at leisure to appreciate the art of the narrative. The recurrence of themes or motifs, explicit or unstated, can now move to the foreground and begin to function not merely as a coherence-reinforcing measure but also as a path to subtler semiotic insights or, plainly, as a source of aesthetic appeal in its own right. This can happen, for instance, on a rereading of Shalamov's story "Khleb" ["Bread"].

The story is an account of a lucky break that a prisoner gets when sent to work in a bakery. Our most urgent concern on the first reading is with this reprieve from the focalizer's usual starvation. On a repeated reading we are in a better position to register the rhythmic recurrence of an unstated motif that links the main narrative details: the motif of the optimal exploration of severely limited possibilities. At the beginning we are told how the piece of herring that one gets every second day is to be eaten (slowly, with skin and bones) and how the most is made of the daily bread rations if they are savored, like candy, in the morning. The foreman of the bakery has a few seconds to choose two workers from the column of the *zeks:* he too wants to use the situation to the best advantage and get people who are not too weak to work, will not steal, will not plot intrigues. Whether because most of the workers of the bakery are sympathetic ex-prisoners or because one should not muzzle the ox that turns the mill wheel, the foreman first offers his two borrowed slaves bread and tea. But the loaf he gives them is second-rate bread. The stoker throws this loaf into the fire and brings the prisoners a loaf of the best white bread. They protest against the destruction, saying that they could have taken the other loaf to the barracks in the evening, but the stoker promises to give them other bread to take back. After long starvation one must not eat too much at once: the quality of the bread should be improved in preference to increasing its quantity. At the end of the day, the two *zeks* are, indeed, given bread to take to the barracks; the focalizer shares it with his neighbors—for once he seems to be no longer hungry. Yet, as usual with Shalamov, the thematic knot is undone at the end: at night the protagonist keeps dreaming of bread and of the mischievous face of the stoker who is throwing the loaf into the fire. The dream, a subversion of the Gospel parable of the loaves, is also a version of the more or less typical oneiric self-tantalization of the chronically starving, which, like daytime fantasies of feasts, promotes stomach secretion, further damaging the prisoner's health (in the camps it was advisable to resist the temptation of talking about food or of listening to such talk). The shape of the dream also suggests that, though done for the protagonist's sake, for optimizing his advantage, the burning of bread is a sacrilege. The person most responsible for it, however, was not the sympathetic stoker but the half-heartedly benevolent foreman, who had forfeited his chance of maximizing succor.

"Bread" is one of Shalamov stories whose status as factography or fiction is deliberately blurred. It is written in the first person and based on Shalamov's own experience during his stay in the typhoid quarantine in Magadan, yet it may be to some extent fictionalized to strengthen its thematic coherence: the theme of optimization within the story irradiates upon its narrative method. Thus the very interpenetration of the narrative modes is, as it were, nested in the material itself. Some other two prisoners would be sent to work in the bakery the next day, and still others the day later: each of the smallest of the narrative details, even if grafted for the sake of the thematic design, might actually be literally true of the experience of one of them.[6] And since the story includes few or no idiosyncratic touches, its narrative details may be perceived as representative, like the details in a piece of realistic fiction.

* * *

Whereas the selection of material implies the potentially shapeless *profusion* of recollections, the other fictionalizing move, that of "staging," is a response to the *limitations* of human memory and vision. It stands to reason that the crucial episodes of a person's life might be remembered with what physicists call "good resolution," or that a detailed spontaneous memory might visit the writer at the time of composition. Many of Shalamov's stories, many chapters of Ginzburg's memoirs, and such episodes of Solzhenitsyn's *The Gulag Archipelago* as the scene in the yard on the morning after the arrest (see Chapter 4 above) seem to be the products of such a spontaneous memory. To say this is to express one's trust in the author's adherence to the factographic pact.[7] In principle, however, it is rather difficult to distinguish the gifts of spontaneous memory from those of imagination.[8]

"Staging," or dramatic "blow-up" in a narrative, is *an area of hesitation* between the fictional and the factographic procedures. The fictional pact involves the reader's acceptance of the so-called *as if* convention,[9] according to which one suspends disbelief when recognizable actions, thoughts, or features are ascribed to non-documentable subjects or when non-documentable actions, thoughts, or features are ascribed to recognizable historical personages. The factographic pact between the author and the reader presupposes that this convention is not operative and that narrative details *refer* to actual people and events.

Minor errors of the memory do not disrupt the factographic pact. The credibility of a memoir is actually enhanced if the author discusses the limited reliability of memory: in Shalamov's "Galina Pavlovna Zybalova" (*KR-2*) the focalizer's memories of a little girl seen many years previously are corrected by the woman into whom that girl had grown. Yet these are minor matters, like the exact color of the girl's coat. If one's memory has reshuffled the timing and attribution of such details as who said what or who closed the door or dropped a pencil, no damage is done to one's referential credibility unless these details happen to be specially meaningful. On the other hand, given contradictory evidence, the factographic pact cannot survive a redistribution or reversal of morally charged actions. In his novel *The First Circle* Solzhenitsyn testifies to the workings of the prison institute but not to the individual events: though the characters of Rubin and Sologdin are based on those of the real Kopelev and Panin, the very change of the names signals the possibility of further transformations. Indeed, Sologdin's decision concerning his invention is diametrically opposite to that taken by "the real" Panin, and his love affair in the *sharashka* actually belongs (judging by an episode in Kopelev's *Ease My Sorrows*) to the person behind Rubin. Such transpositions, legitimate in a novel, would not be reducible to the ordinary margin of mnemonic error in a documentary text; a hypothetical memoir in which they could be detected would emerge either as counterfeit or as mendacious, and decidedly disrupting the factographic pact.

A memoirist's wish to avoid endangering the factographic pact might be recognized in techniques of insurance against minor imprecisions. One such technique is summarizing long stretches of conversations, with the blow-up staging used only for flashes of particularly significant scenes and direct speech only for particularly colorful utterances or particularly memorable ones—what journalists call "sound bites." Indeed, it takes special circumstances for retrospective memory to reliably retain the exact words heard many years ago:[10] utterances remembered verbatim are usually remarkable for their style, wit, wisdom, or semiotic load, or for the biographical crossroads at which they were made.

Yet some cases of staging do not really imply that concrete utterances are "quoted" verbatim. In memoirs, lengthy direct-speech monologues are sometimes employed in conventionally representative rather than referential ways. These are pseudo-scenic utterances (Sternberg 1982: 94); they "stage" a phenomenon instead of describing it in the author's own words. Thus in Olitskaya's memoir long passages of direct speech are reserved for declarations of faith: real people turn into dramatis personae as they explain their moral-political *Credo* in direct-speech exposés. This device is further explored in the memoirs of Kopelev, whose philological gusto is artistic in its own right. Kopelev's characters are portrayed through long dramatic monologues that colorfully express their beliefs, attitudes, dispositions, tastes, levels of education, and cultural or national affiliations[11] and that obviously bring together utterances culled from different occasions, *staging* the personality with the help of a basically theatrical convention.

Two of Lev Konson's narratives stage first-person outpourings of young camp guards, enlisted soldiers who do not quite understand the nature of their experience. Here the factographic pact is endangered because the first-person speakers of the two short stories are not identical with the authorial persona. However, though the text does not indicate the circumstances under which the speakers' narrative acts are supposed to take place, the reader may still resolve the hesitation in favor of the factographic pact by imagining their monologues as addressed to, or overheard by, the authorial persona. Their first-person discourse may then be read as Konson's endeavor to understand the mindset of people who wish to live untroubled by the glimpses they had caught of prisoners chained to wheelbarrows in a secret zone[12] or of the extermination of a whole settlement affected by an epidemic. Or else it can be read as staging "hearsay" evidence—or else, on the contrary, as mediating Konson's approach to *Room One-Oh-One*, as well as suggesting, with Primo Levi, that the real witnesses have not survived. Thus an avowedly fictionalizing move expands the significance and the effect of hearsay testimony and compensates for the limitations in its reliability.

* * *

A special case of "staging" is the sample convention: a memoirist may give a "deconcretized" (Sternberg 1982: 93–100) yet scenic presentation of events that took place a number of times. Thus, in order to show that his youthful intellectual curiosity could be satisfied in the library of the Solovki prior to 1936, Yury Chirkov presents the following exchange with the librarian:[13]

> Give me *Vapaus* and *Der Emes,* I would ask Rudnev.
> Can you read in Finnish and in Yiddish, the surprised Archbishop would inquire.
> I would like to see what they look like, I would say in embarrassment.
> (1991: 28)

The forms of the verbs, "would inquire" and "would say" (*sprashyval, govoril*) indicate the "iterative" (Genette 1980: 116) nature of the episode, but the reference to specific periodicals in languages that the author did not know suggests that this dialogue is a *sample,* a synecdoche for many similar events.

A sample, however, may also consist in the staging of a deconcretized scene that the memoirist did not witness, as in the following extract from Panin's *The Notebooks of Sologdin:*

> To men who have never experienced it, the fantastic power of Chekist terrorism must seem beyond credibility, and the actions that issue from it must appear without rhyme or reason. To make this statement clear, let me give an example, quite usual in the climate of those times.
> In the spring of 1942 two prisoners were desperately craving a smoke. . . . After all else failed, there was only one last resort: bolstering themselves with the criminals' principle of survival at all cost, they went off to see the camp godfather (as the security officer is known in the camp slang). They knocked and walked in. The godfather received them cordially. Have a seat, he said. On his desk was an open cigarette case with cigarettes made of real golden *makhorka.* But he didn't offer them one. He simply waited to hear what they had to say—these hand-rolled cigarettes had their price. . . .
> Chief, our tongues are hanging out. How about a smoke?
> What is all this? Did you drop in just for a smoke? he asked mockingly. Or do you have some business?
> You know we wouldn't dare walk in here just for nothing, don't you? We want to tell you about a *kontrik* who is spreading propaganda and denouncing the system.
> Who is he?
> They gave his name.
> Very good! First of all, let's write down all the details. Then we'll have a smoke.
> All the while, he blew smoke practically in their faces. A formal statement was drawn up and signed. After receiving the blood money— a hand-rolled cigarette apiece—the two nicotine addicts left the godfather's office, almost reeling as they took puffs.

The possibility of being denounced in this way kept us in a constant state of terror. (1976: 117)

Panin could not be present in the room where this scene took place, nor does he refer to his source of information. The conversation is assembled from ritualistic gestures and utterances,[14] on the basis of his knowledge of the camp codes. To departicularize the event, Panin withholds the names of the volunteer informers and of the policeman. The identity of their victim is, as it were, censored out, though actually the victim is here likewise deconcretized: many people might have been betrayed in some such manner. Thus, though the episode is presented as *one* example of in-camp relationships, it is also made to function as one *example:* the range of the applicability of the sketched behavior patterns is expanded. By eliding names Panin refrains from ascribing non-documentable actions to concrete people whose fate could be verified: he does not claim that the concrete N was betrayed in this precise fashion; in other words, he ascribes a plausible act to non-documentable characters. Yet he activates the *as if* convention at only half its force: the scene is structured as an algorithm for "selling a person for a cigarette," with a few vivid "typical" details included for reality effect. But for the scenic blow-up, the claim that a person could be betrayed for a smoke might have sounded like a conversational hyperbole. Panin takes recourse to a semi-fictionalizing technique in order to demonstrate how, during "the dark and magical night of Stalin's dictatorship" (Tertz/Sinyavsky 1965: 147), figures of speech kept actually turning into physical facts.

The deconcretization of the scene and the resulting appeal to the sample convention is one reason the episode is not perceived as breaking the factographic pact even though it infringes on the conditions of first-hand evidence. Another reason we remain here in the realm of historical testimony is that the deconcretization is only partial. There is, for instance, an indication of the time range in which an event like this would take place, spring 1942: other survivors, including Solzhenitsyn (*GA* 3: 20) and Shalamov ("Condensed Milk," *KR*), likewise testified that in the early wartime period security operatives were liable to be sent to the front lines and that in order to prove that they were needed in their soft berths in the rear, they incriminated prisoners and had them reconvicted on new charges (the cigarettes are, indeed, blood money—in 1942 the operative would really act on the deposition instead of just filing it away). The approximate date of the scene is a public-domain landmark, which renders the regularity exemplified by the episode amenable to verification.

From the sample convention it is but one step to the representative, fictional mode. In a work of fiction, the above episode might have been presented not as an iterative scene but as a concretely individualized event, with the characters and places given concrete names. This may be partly the case with Shalamov's "Bread"; more strikingly it is the case with his "The Snake Charmer" (*KR*). The latter story contains an inset narrative that the author self-consciously ghostwrites for a dead friend, weaving the setting and the action out of typical features of camp life. In both the fictional and the factographic work the scenic blow-up can thus function like the proof of a theorem: the non-self-evident phenomenon is rendered convincing through simulating the rituals that bring it about.

* * *

Factographic literature usually includes materials that belong to the *public* domain, to the *private* domain, and to the domain of *privileged access*. Public-domain materials set the action in a *concrete time and place*; they testify to the events that happened to *specific people*[15] and can, therefore, be subjected to verification. By including such data, an author challenges denials and invites confirmations; the factographic pact is reinforced if, after the passage of time, this information is *not* effectively denied by witnesses or historical research. By contrast, the material that belongs to the private domain (the author's emotional and intellectual experience) and to the domain of privileged access (the author's otherwise undocumented interviews with specific people or testimony about events or places from which there are no other survivor reports) remains in principle unverifiable. The reinforcement of the factographic pact through public-domain landmarks largely enhances the author's credibility in the other two domains as well, yet they still present areas of hesitation.

For some readers private-domain material (in which the memoiristic narrative act overlaps with the autobiographical act) is convincing if it conforms to normative ideas about human responses—hence the vast popularity of Evgenia Ginzburg's memoirs. For others, the narrative of a prisoner's inner life may appear even more keenly truthful if it diverges from what we might traditionally consider normative (cf. Roman Jakobson 1971: 40–47)—hence, for instance, the impact of Herling's and Margolin's remarks on hunger neurosis. In any case, the private domain inevitably represents an area of hesitation: the reader may doubt whether the memoirist is not describing what *should have been* felt instead of what *was* felt in the remote past. The doubt is significantly reduced when there is an element of critical detachment (or plain shame) in a memoirist's references to his or her past attitudes, or when—as in Solzhenitsyn's account of his arrest and first prison experience (*GA* 1: 1)—the past responses are analyzed from the standpoint of present attitudes. Oleg Volkov (1990: 54) likewise describes his *Pogruzhenie vo t'mu* [*Sinking into Darkness*] (1987) as a subjectively processed autobiography, which amounts to the admission of fictionalizing transformations, since, in principle, any autobiography not reducible to a collection of answers to a detailed official questionnaire is a subjective processing of experience. Though the emotional intensity of the past experience is more forcefully reproduced when the memoirist still identifies with his or her state of mind at the time of the described events, the memoirs in which the fo-calizer's actions, responses, and attitudes are presented as uniformly nor-mative sooner or later evoke the reader's distrust.

The problem of the truthfulness of the private-domain materials and even of the nature of the text-reader pact is particularly acute in the case of the "twice-told" tales, narratives whose materials have already been rendered by the same author in previous narrative acts. Anatolii Ryba-kov, the author of the famous *Children of the Arbat,* calls such a narrative "Novel as Recollection" ("Roman-vospominanie") and starts it by admit-ting that after having parceled out his experience in three tales about childhood and three novels about youth, he finds it difficult to tell the actual from the invented (1996 #7: 3). Vladimir Petrov's would-be mem-oiristic accounts of his passages from Kolyma and through the Nazi oc-cupied territories likewise seem to belong to this group. The memoirs of Evgenia Ginzburg sometimes come close to this mode since, as Ginz-burg tells us, the material of many of the chapters had once been the content of the stories she told to family and friends.[16] In the case of such twice-told tales, at a certain point one starts to listen to oneself recount-ing the events instead of attending to the spontaneous gifts of one's memory.[17] However, in the case of Ginzburg (or Dolgun, another spinner of oral yarns) testimony is the marked function of the public act of writ-ing, whereas their oral telling of camp stories to family and friends was dominated by other functions, such as amusement, consolation, self-jus-tification, or plain human contact.

The domain of privileged access is likewise generally not amenable to the test of deniability. In the cases of memoirs that present rare or un-usual information about well-known people or evidence about atrocities of which there are no confirmatory survivor accounts, the responsibility for crediting or mistrusting privileged-access information devolves on the reader: we are challenged to evaluate its consistency with available related materials or with other parts of the memoir itself. This evaluation is often based on one's literary taste, or else on a sixth-sense recognition of the genuine and the counterfeit. It would not be easy to explain, for instance, why readers are inclined to accept Konson's account of his friendship with the writer Arkady Belinkov in a shared prison cell yet to doubt Irina Odoevtseva's glibly romanesque account of Andrei Bely's confidences to her.

At times, however, the truth-value of the privileged-access material can become suspect owing to narratological features. Solonevich, for instance, occasionally slips into flamboyantly novelistic long scenes, such as the several pages of a Dostoevskian argument between the author and one of the last idealistic Bolsheviks in the camp administration. The name of the interlocutor is withheld—ostensibly in order to protect him, yet also to deconcretize the scene and preempt the test of deniability. The conversation sounds more like a theatrical staging of a clash of ideologies than a record of a spontaneous wave of memory, a reliving of an episode from the author's past. Whereas Panin's staging of the sellout for a smoke is presented as an imaginative (re)construction of an iterative event, Solonevich's morality-play dialogue is set in concrete circumstances as a singulative occasion,[18] bearing the marks of fictionalization. One may note, however, how small the distance can be between the cautious suppression of names in order not to harm real people left behind and the deliberate deconcretization that precludes verification procedures, especially since for the purposes of camouflage memoirists sometimes attribute "to one person the actions of another" (Plyushch 1979: 5). Here too, the fictionalization of part of the Gulag-memoir material stems from the very nature of the reality that the narratives continue and reflect.

In 1978 a new emigrant to Israel, Maria Ioffe, widow of the Soviet diplomat (and Trotsky's close associate, Adolf Yoffe),[19] published a book called *One Night: A Tale about the Truth*, listing its date of composition as 1958. The book is a largely autobiographical story of the Great Terror in the camps near Vorkuta, in the shadow of executions similar to the 1938 shootings of Kolyma prisoners. The first-person focal character is given the author's name and some of her biographical data; the main concern is with her prolonged confrontation with the banal and insipid NKVD officer Kashketin, who is invested with the duties of the local Angel of Death. The nature of the author-reader pact is not clear. At first, the seeming randomness of details suggests that the narrative reproduces the actual collocations of events, yet most of the details eventually interconnect in a quite novelistic way. When stories about Stalin's past or Bukharin's last hours are told during a chance pause in a grim prison transport and when "Ioffe's" vacant hours of pure suffering in the punishment cell are "filled" with notes on the history of the camps (redundant in the seventies but potentially revelatory for the readers of the fifties), the "plot" begins to look like a fictional vehicle for general testimony, whether firsthand or hearsay. This impression is reinforced by the profuse dialogic blow-up of an ideological argument between "Ioffe" and Kashketin. Lighter camp anecdotes are smuggled in by the Scheherazade motif: "Ioffe" keeps Kashketin occupied by stories of camp romances so as to reduce the working hours that he has for torturing her cellmate—and probably to stave off her own execution. At the end "Ioffe" and a few other prisoners, taken out of the camp at night, believe that they are being driven to their execution. Yet the portrait of Yezhov has recently been removed from the prison wall, and the reader might know that his replacement by Beria was followed by a halt on death sentences in the camps. The openness of the ending, however, makes one hesitate not just about the protagonist's fate but about the nature of the reader-author pact: the use of a *moriturus* as the focalizer would be possible only in a fictional narrative. Whether fictional or factual, however, Ioffe's tale offers an imaginative re-construction of the experience of the victims of shooting. Tellingly, the worst is not "staged"; the reader is not taken to the mouth of the execution pit; the focalizer does not lose her fortitude and shrewdness; she does not disintegrate, and she is spared active physical torture. Thus the imagination balks at "Room 101": a survivor cannot evoke the ultimate horror.

Yet the prominent uncertainty as to the fictional or factual status of the story reduces an emotional engagement with its content by fragmenting the reader's attention. This effect would have been avoided by an acknowledged fictionalization, as in the case of giving the focalizer a name different from the author's own. Whereas the impact of camp memoirs is enhanced by the reader's wondering about the possibility of accepting factographic narratives as works of art, it may be diminished by hesitation concerning the author-reader pact. However, this hesitation may be a variant of the pulsation method in narratives of atrocities.

Thus, fictionalizing transpositions, replacement of temporal sequences by thematic ones, competition with random reality for narrative control, experiments with imaginary perspectives, and scenic blow-ups constitute attempts to widen the field of imaginative re-enactment. They provide partial correctives to the insufficiency of verbal communication of circumstances radically different from normative experience. A recourse to undisguised fictionalization, a movement away from the specific, actual, and singulative toward the iterative, representative, or plausible is the next step in this endeavor.

* * *

This is a qualitative step insofar as it cancels the factographic pact, yet the gap it creates between referentiality and non-referentiality is not unbridgeable. Referentiality is measurably present in many a work of fiction; most literary texts, fictional as well as factographic, construct models of extratextual reality, making use of different combinations of the representative and the referential.

The models in questions can be based on the principles of replication, simulation, or formalization. Replication is an attempt to model the structure of the original by identifying its constituents; simulation consists in tracing the way things work, that is, the function of specific constituents; and formalization involves a competition with the original for philosophical or aesthetic coherence.

Shalamov's middle-period play "Anna Ivanovna"[20] displays features of all three types of modeling reality. The action takes place in the roadside diner, which, as Shalamov notes in "The Lawyers' Plot," is the most useful setting for a comprehensive representation of Kolyma life. The location sets the conditions necessary for a *replication* of Kolyma society: representatives of a hierarchical cross section, from privileged bosses to emaciated prisoners, make their passage through it. The characters and the spectrum of ethical positions that they represent form a paradigm similar to those constructed in Solzhenitsyn's narratives and plays.

The play is also a stylized *simulation* of the mechanics of the social relationships in the camps, reminiscent of Panin's iterative "sample" scene of a denunciation for a cigarette.[21] The incidents seem to be both typical and random. Horrifying events are enacted with a quotidian calm, as if it were quite natural for an average man to denounce his beautiful wife or cook up a charge and conviction for a former mistress, quite natural for an excellent doctor to be driven out of the hospital to the general works for not toadying or to lose his life for trying to send his poems to "the mainland," quite natural for a police sleuth to shoot a fugitive without warning, or for the condemned "goners" (*dokhodiagi*—people who have reached a near-irreversible, possibly lethal, stage of emaciation) to attract no attention while stopping on the way to their death in Magadan (cf. "The Lawyers' Plot"). Separate utterances touch upon characteristic aspects of Kolyma life—in the absence of Shalamov's stories and sketches, the play would require something like the "Sidelight on History" that follows Hochhuth's *The Deputy*. The plot hinges on the consequences of the criminals' refusal to work and their readiness to pay for their privileges by denouncing political prisoners. The tragedies of the doctor and the waitress are caused by the kind of contingencies that, under these conditions, such characters are likely to face.

Most fictionalized testimony, whether epic or dramatic, is, directly or indirectly, metafictional: somewhere along the line, the fictionality of the plot is signaled to us, as if to remind us of the truthfulness behind the artifice. For the benefit of the public, Shalamov makes the participants say things that in actual circumstances would remain a matter of tacit mutual understanding. The absence of literal reference is emphasized by the symbolic surname of the heroine, Rodina (Russian for "motherland" as well as the feminine form of the surname Rodin): the mother(land) is callously betrayed by her own former and present lovers; her son is destined to remain in the boarding school (in the clutches of depersonalizing official indoctrination); she herself has committed a *crime de la passion;* she makes profane compromises but appreciates goodness and retains her pride. At the end of the play, Anna Ivanovna Rodina is arrested on a political charge. Sent off on a transport, she refuses a package of food from the person who has betrayed her. As in Solzhenitsyn's *Cancer Ward,* the details of the plot oscillate between the literal and the deliberately incomplete allegorical layer of significance. This is an element of *formalization*—helping "reality" to achieve the shapeliness that is usually preempted by contingencies.

Thus it is on the moral and allegorical planes that the play refers to Gulag realities. The literal level of referentiality is further subverted by anachronisms. In the last sentences of a brief afterword, Shalamov notes that though neither penicillin nor the machine guns referred to in the play were used before World War II, "Anna Ivanovna" is "a pre-war play" (1986a: 364). Indeed, a hasty concoction of charges, the torture of prisoners, and summary executions were most typical of the years 1937–38, but the references to the "bitch war" pertain, rather, to the mid forties. By telescoping facts that belong to different periods, Shalamov suggests that the main ethical issues remained unchanged before and after the war. His concomitant cancellation of the dramatic illusion, somewhat in the spirit of Silver Age experimentation, is an essential feature of the docudrama. In the words of Rolf Hochhuth, "anyone in this day and age who . . . does not 'openly and honestly declare war on naturalism in art,' must capitulate in the face of every newsreel—if only because the latter can present 'the raw stuff of the world' far more drastically and completely than the stage. For the stage—Bertolt Brecht with his theory of alienation was not the first to discover this—remains true only if, as Schiller says in Wallenstein, 'it itself frankly destroys the illusion it creates'" (1964: 288).[22] An anachronism sometimes emphasizes the significance of issues that goes well beyond their fictional objectification, as if burning peep-holes in formal masks. Like Gulag memoirs, Gulag fictions are necessarily (and often deliberately) flawed. The formalization is never perfect; and reminders of the fictional status of their plots bring into further relief the solidity and coerciveness of the settings.

The three types of models can accommodate the analysis of the narrative methods of both factographic and fictional works. The dominant fictionalizing procedure involved in *replication* is addition: the selection and recombination of material tends to complete the time-and-space setting with the details necessary for the construction of a conceptual paradigm. *Simulation* involves subtraction: details irrelevant to the mechanics of the proceedings tend to get purged. Shalamov's and Solzhenitsyn's Gulag plays ("Anna Ivanovna" and "The Tenderfoot and the Tart")[23] contain elements of both, though Shalamov's stories have a dominant tendency toward simulation and Solzhenitsyn's novels toward replication. Both of the plays refer to the regularities of camp life and provide indirect moral testimony about it. Formalization, however, moves toward a further level of abstraction in reference. Involving self-referential touches, it creates conditions for the integration of images and motifs from camp life (and sometimes from the existing literature on camp life) into new intellectual constructs that include awareness of the camps but are not dominated by it. In terms of the literary-historical process, such a development usually takes place in the later works, written after the main task of testifying has been largely accomplished.

6 Varlam Shalamov

The blurring of the borderlines between the factographic and the fictionalized is nowhere as meaningful as in the stories of Varlam Shalamov. To the end of his days, in his notes and conversations, Shalamov maintained that everything that he wrote in the stories was literally true. The stories themselves, however, subvert the claim of precise referentiality, whether by using fictional perspectives, by pointing to the faultiness of individual memory, or by displaying self-contradictions and factual inconsistencies. An apt term for Shalamov's narrative mode is "veridical fiction": it "bespeaks the real through the production of an illusion" in order to propel the reader's mind "into recognizing a truth hidden, secreted, from view," a truth accessed through the author's firsthand traumatic experience (Rovner 1977: 8ff.). In fact, what Shalamov's verbal simulations of camp experience accomplish is a type of referentiality that is voided of the singulative component.[1] Referentiality usually implies a link between any singulative textual detail and an individual extratextual particular, event, or person. If the detail is "representative" rather than pertaining to a specific element of actuality, the factographic pact is endangered, and an element of the fictional-realistic mode is introduced (cf. Toker 1997b). Yet this type of fiction can double as testimony—if only because, as Shalamov repeatedly suggests, at a certain stage of starvation, the experiences of different individuals become near-identical (the differences having faded away along with their memory and flesh), and so any narrative detail used as a sample of a regularity may well turn out to be literally true of some of the multimillion martyrs.

The author's own qualification as a firsthand witness to the events narrated is inevitably at stake in "veridical fiction." Shalamov's biography, which an analysis of his oeuvre must therefore take into account, is, in itself, a story of the clash between the individual and the communal, the incomparably singular and the shared.

* * *

In Shalamov's 1966 short story "Riabkon" (*VL*), the quack Yampolsky,[2] who is in charge of a camp hospital, deals with the shortage of beds in a would-be benevolent manner: he precipitates the death of Peters,[3] a tall Latvian prisoner who has been stubbornly clinging to life, by giving him a hot bath in a wooden barrel. Peters's bed, the longest in the ward, is then given to another tall patient, the title character; the authorial persona (the focalizer) moves to Riabkon's bed. About forty years after the events of the story, Shalamov himself occupied a bed that the authorities wanted to vacate. On January 14, 1982, law-enforcement officers carried him away—blind, deaf, and helplessly protesting—from the nursing home to an unspecified destination. Only three days later did doctor Elena Zakharova find him in a psychiatric warehouse, dying of untreated pneumonia—he must have caught cold on the way. She says (1988) that he recognized her and stroked her hand. By a camphor injection she prolonged his life for half an hour.

According to Vladimir Nabokov, life imitates art, rather than the other way round. When the art in question is documentary prose, which forms *a sequel to and outgrowth of its own material* (cf. Eakin 1985: 9) rather than detached mimesis, the semblance of imitation reflects the recidivistic character of history. In a 1966 notebook Shalamov recycled Marx's aphorism: "History, having been tragic, returns to us as farce. But there is also a third phenomenon, a third embodiment of a historical pattern—in a senseless horror" (1995: 146). This too Shalamov knew firsthand.

Shalamov believed that a writer must be not a spectator "but a participant in the drama of life—a participant not in a writer's garb, not in the role of a writer" (1996: 429). In the story "Zhuk" ("The Bug"), written in the seventies, a vicious insect rushes at the focal character's leg, with the intent to sting; the focalizer[4] does not budge out of its way. For him, the objectivity of an ideal spectator is less important than the genuine albeit useless knowledge of pain. Detached objectivity, which Shalamov disowned, would have its own bias, one stemming from a reality outside the observed events. His own loyalties were to his own material, rooted in his own life and in the lives ruined like his own, not to the mental set of an external target audience. This choice may have limited the immediate contemporary appeal of his work while paving its way to canonicity, a status that it is now beginning to acquire.

* * *

Varlam Tikhonovich Shalamov was born in 1907, in the northern town of Vologda, which under the czar had served as one of the places of exile for revolutionary intellectuals. His father was an Orthodox priest, his mother a schoolteacher. The family had spent the years 1893–1904 in Alaska, where the father was the priest of the Kodiak parish and took an active interest in the social and economic situation of the native Aleutians (see Kline 1998: 18). The youngest of the children, born after their return, was named Varlaam, after the patron saint of the Vologda cathedral. Eventually he dropped one of the *a*s from his name: in an inner revolt against the patriarchal head of the family, he rejected his father's religion.

In the autobiographical tale "Chetvertaia Vologda" ["The Fourth Vologda"] (1985: 17–216) Shalamov mentions that since childhood he suffered from acrophobia and a chronic nose congestion; his father mistook them for lack of courage and stamina. He also discovered in himself the mysterious gift for speed-reading: while waiting in the library line to check out the allowed two books, he would finish a third one. Like most speed-readers he had a powerful memory.

Shalamov's beloved elder brother Sergei was killed in the Civil War; the father went blind after this event—his glaucoma must have been exacerbated by weeping. Though Sergei had fought for the Red Army and though the political views of Tikhon Nikolaevich had been progressive, the priest and his family soon found themselves among the persecuted.[5] Well known as a gifted scholar, young Shalamov was denied the necessary recommendation for admission to a university. His father attempted to persuade him to study in the theological academy and become a clergyman; instead, Shalamov went to a Moscow suburb to work as a literacy instructor and then, for over a year, as a tanner in a factory. His newly acquired proletarian status made him eligible for the open admission to Moscow University.[6] Many years later he would write that when he enrolled in the law department, his father "prayed on his knees the whole night. But, as usual, in vain" (1985: 181).

Shalamov's two years as a law student were also a time of a literary apprenticeship (see 1987b). In the twenties the Moscow literary life was, indeed, active and rich. Different literary schools printed periodicals and collections and held discussions, poetry readings, workshops.[7] Surveillance had not yet dampened intellectual life because its pervasiveness was not yet evident. This may have been among the reasons for the rise and fall of numerous anti-Stalinist groups (Avtorkhanov 1983: 198–210). Stalin's methods of consolidating power and his preparations for the assault on the peasants could not but give rise to opposition, and the residue of the erstwhile relative freedom of speech enhanced this opposition's naked vulnerability to the secret police. Shalamov's 1962 sketch "The Twenties," dealing with this period, ends with the recollection of the poet Musa Djalil's reading of Pushkin's "The Prisoner" ("I am sitting behind bars in a damp dungeon") and with the following pregnant remarks:

> What trials awaited anyone was, in the twenties, not possible to tell.
> Together with my friend I treaded, through many a night, along "the crooked streets of Moscow," trying to understand the time and find my own place in it. We wanted not just to read poetry. We wanted to act, to live. (1987b: 37)

Thus Shalamov disappears into "the crooked streets of Moscow."[8] On February 19, 1929, he is arrested for involvement in the dissemination of the "Letter to the Congress," the so-called Testament in which the dying Lenin pointed out the negative traits of Stalin as well as of other members of the Politbureau.

In a solitary cell in the Butyrskaia prison Shalamov would wait "impatiently for the guard to leave, so [he] could again pace the cell and think about [his] life that had such a lucky start" (1990a: 7). Traditionally, indeed, a true Russian intellectual did not quite qualify without having a taste of prison (1990a: 9). The six weeks of his pre-trial confinement helped him to forge his inner independence, which was subjected to atrocious tests when he was sentenced to three years of hard labor and sent, with a consignment of thieves, to the Vishera camps in the north of the Ural mountains. Meantime, his parents in Vologda had fallen into complete destitution. In Shalamov's 1959 story "The Cross" (*AL*) a blind priest hacks off a piece of his golden cross to sell for food. "The Monk Joseph Shmaltz" (1985: 226–28)[9] is a sequel to this all too real episode and a message of gratitude to the Aleutians and his father's successor among them for the hard-earned small sums that they had sent over to support his parents. After his release and return to Moscow in 1932, Shalamov, now a Moscow journalist, visited his parents again, and then attended their funerals.

He was married, father of a little girl, and author of a few published short stories as well as of a thick batch of unpublished ones (eventually burned by his family) when he was again arrested, on January 12, 1937. Sentenced to five years of imprisonment, he was sent to Kolyma with a special instruction: "to be employed only on hard physical labor."

Shalamov was familiar with the origins of the Kolyma camp empire. In 1931, at the start of the exploitation of that region's immense resources by means of convict labor,[10] the man placed in charge of the "Dalstroi" trust was Eduard Berzin, formerly of the Latvian Riflemen who had protected the young Soviet power in 1917. Berzin had commanded the Vishera complex of labor camps where Shalamov served his first term; there he selected his team, and they went eastward to build roads, open gold mines, conduct geological research, and establish agricultural settlements in the vast regions on both sides of the Kolyma River. This vast project exacted an enormous price in the lives of forced-labor pioneers, whose minimal welfare was of no concern to either Berzin or his subordinates (Dallin and Nikolayevsky 1947: 108–46; Conquest 1978: 49–55, 109–19, 125–76).[11] Once the initial economic groundwork was completed, the political prisoners' conditions improved: their workday was of reasonable length, the criminal convicts were not encouraged to abuse them, and there was some remuneration, so that they could even send small sums to their families. All this changed at the peak of the Great Purge. Berzin was arrested in December 1937 and shot in August 1938,[12] after the wave of terror that had swept through the whole country the year before reached the "planet," as Kolyma was called in camp folklore. Under the Dalstroi head Pavlov and his deputy Garanin, the Kolyma forced labor camps turned into camps of slow (and frequently accelerated) extermination—this is described in Shalamov's 1964 story "Kak eto nachalos'" ["How It Began"] (*AL*). As if to make room for new consignments of victims,[13] the killing of prisoners by hunger and overwork was supplemented by summary in-camp trials—the names of those executed at night were read at each morning's roll call. The most immediate victims were the "Trotskyites"; next came the depleted "goners" whose output fell below 30 percent of the quota.

Shalamov was brought to Kolyma in the autumn of 1937 and survived 1938. That year he found himself on the brink of death from exhaustion, working twelve to sixteen hours a day in the Partizan gold mine, between beatings, indignities, and punishment cells. It is believed that what saved him from being shot was his handwriting (which in his late years would become almost illegible owing to Ménière's disease). In his 1964 story "Handwriting" (*AL*), a prisoner by the name of Krist is summoned to an interrogator after work. The interrogator has trouble writing: Krist, whose handwriting is calligraphic, starts taking his dictation one evening a week. He gets neither food nor cigarettes for this service but is excused from work the following day. On one occasion the interrogator picks up one of the files, reads it, and then silently tears it up and throws it into the stove. Only retrospectively does Krist understand that the file destroyed in front of his eyes must have been his own. The interrogator himself is executed in a purge.[14]

In December 1938 Shalamov was brought to Magadan for a cooked-up trial bound to end in a death verdict. He was saved by the turning of the tide: his interrogator became a casualty of a local intrigue promoted by Beria's anti-Yezhov measures. The episode is the basis of the 1962 story "The Lawyers' Plot" (KR).

More dead than alive, Shalamov was placed in a huge Magadan barrack described in the 1959 story "Typhoid Quarantine" (KR). From there, a few months later, he was sent to the geological prospecting expedition at Chernoe Ozero, and thence to the coal mines in the Arkagala region. In 1942 his five-year sentence was extended "until the end of the war." "For systematic failure to meet the quota" he was transferred to the punitive camp of Jelgalla, where, in 1943, a new accusation was concocted against him. Paradoxically, this saved him from the vicious spiral because the lighter charge ("Anti-Soviet Propaganda," rather than his initial "Counter-revolutionary Terrorist Activity") eventually eased his way to lighter employment. Owing to advanced dystrophy, after the trial in Yagodnoe, he was sent not to the mines but to a "vitamin outpost," where dwarf-cedar needles were collected for a supposedly vitamin-rich extract. Later that year Shalamov managed to make his way to the Belichie hospital, his pellagric diarrhea being fortunately mistaken for a symptom of the "officially recognized" dysentery. This hospitalization changed his fate, but not without further ordeals and struggles.[15]

In the fall of 1945 Shalamov was sent to a lumbering camp where the workers who did not meet the quota were given no bread. He walked out of it, reached the Yagodnoe settlement, submitted a complaint, and was incarcerated; these events are reflected in the 1959 story "Kliuch Almaznyi" ["The Almaznyi Spring"] (AL). Owing to his recent ten-year conviction, however, he was not tried for escape; instead, he was sent back to Jelgalla. The 1964 story "The Artist of the Spade" (AL)[16] is based on his experience upon his return to that punitive camp, also described in the 1967 story "Gorod na gore" ["The City on the Hill"] (VL).

In the spring of 1946 Jelgalla was evacuated to make room for Soviet POWs repatriated from Italy (cf. "Major Pugachev's Last Battle" [LB, 1959] and the ending of "The Green Procurator" [AL, 1965]). From the transit camp in Susuman ("The Golden Taiga" [KR, 1961]) Shalamov managed to contact doctor A. M. Pantiukhov, who, recollecting him from Belichie, got him hospitalized and eventually saved his life by sending him to courses for paramedics; see "Dominoes" (KR, 1959) and "Kursy" ["Courses"] (AL, 1960). Shalamov was released from camp in 1951, but had to stay and work as a free paramedic in the Central Hospital, in Debin, on the left bank of the Kolyma River; later he worked in the outpost of Baragon. At that time he devoted his spare time to poetry. His first poems were written, in an unexpected burst, in 1949; a notebook containing them was sent to Boris Pasternak, who responded with a long and warmly encouraging letter.

In November 1953, eight months after Stalin's death, Shalamov obtained permission to leave Kolyma; see "Pogonia za parovoznym dymom" ["Chase of Locomotive Smoke"] and "Train" (*AL*). He came to Moscow for two days, to meet his wife and Pasternak. Released prisoners were not allowed to stay in Moscow; therefore, up to his exoneration in 1956, Shalamov had to reside in small towns in the Kalinin district. On the eve of his return to Moscow he broke with his wife—the love that had survived the parting did not survive the reunion. Galina Ignatievna Gudz had been exiled to Kazakhstan after his arrest; in order to be allowed to return to Moscow in 1947, she formally divorced Shalamov. She tried to put her life together again and brought up her daughter to love the party rather than "the enemy of the people" who was to blame, as it were, for the ten blighted years of their lives. Shalamov never found his way to his daughter's heart; nor did he agree to forget his past and turn over a new leaf, as his wife demanded. After his return from Kolyma, his life was devoted to remembering and writing.[17]

Yet Shalamov could not resume his literary career where it had been interrupted in 1937. The promising writer of the thirties had been forgotten. His new stories were too radical to be published even during the best of the "thaw"; not even Solzhenitsyn, at the height of his Soviet success, could push them into print. Yet they leaked into Samizdat, earning him the profound respect of a small circle of intellectuals. Selections of his poetry (often arbitrarily purged by the censor) did get into the press but, as Sergei Nekliudov, the son of his second wife, the writer Olga Sergeevna Nekliudova, points out, Soviet readers of the fifties and sixties tended to be more responsive to the poetry of young rising stars like Bella Akhmadullina and Andrei Voznesensky, who (along, one might add, with Evtushenko and Rozhdestvensky) were just entering the stage as representatives of the future. Mature writers, associated with what was perceived as "a still very recent gory and shameful past," were eclipsed. The public wanted poetry that would combine intimate intonations with non-official public concerns and avant-garde forms. For Shalamov avant-garde forms were an anachronism, a matter of the poetic experiments of the twenties; he explored what he considered the infinite potentialities of classical Russian verse. For poetry readers of the "thaw" years this was an untimely agenda (Nekliudov 1994: 163–64).

In Moscow Shalamov did freelance journalism and refereed submissions to *Novyi mir*. He received a small pension (which was increased only after a long struggle for the recognition of his years of labor in Kolyma). His work was impeded by hearing problems that started intensifying in 1958. In 1957, when his Kolyma friend A. Dobrovolsky was arrested for anti-Soviet propaganda, Shalamov feared a new wave of terror (Sirotinskaya 1992: 215). That year he was brought to hospital in a fit (cf. the story "A Seizure" [*AS*]), the onset of Ménière's disease, which would cause him much suffering. Nevertheless, the first ten years in Moscow were his *anni mirabili*. He revived—for a brief while—like a Kolyma twig gracing a Moscow apartment in his story "Voskreshenie listvennitsy" ["The Revival of the Larch"] (*VL*).

Some of Shalamov's stories were smuggled abroad by appreciative readers and published, somewhat unsystematically, in Russian émigré journals, and then in German and Italian. Shalamov is known to have objected to a separate publication of his stories. During the "stagnation," the rule was that whatever appeared in Tamizdat could not be published in the Soviet Union—and publication in his homeland had always been Shalamov's dearest wish. Moreover, for a good reason, he wanted his stories to appear in organized cycles, in the sequence he himself worked out (Aigi 1987: 159).

The lack of control over the fate of his works was only part of Shalamov's late-life tragedy. His physical condition kept deteriorating and his resentments growing; because of his unaccommodating temper, fastidiousness, pride, jealousy, and physical disabilities that made communication difficult, he kept losing (and rejecting) his friends one after another (Brewer 1995a). In 1966, after his estrangement from O. S. Nekliudova, Iraida Pavlovna Sirotinskaya entered his heart, having first come to solicit his manuscripts for the Central Archive of Literature and the Arts. A mother of three, Sirotinskaya could not devote her whole life to Shalamov, but she loved and cherished him in her own way. Their relationship became more distant in the mid seventies, but Sirotinskaya did not lose touch with Shalamov. He appointed her his literary heir.

The February 23, 1972, issue of *Literaturnaia gazeta* came out with a letter from Shalamov, condemning the foreign publication of his stories, denying his initiative in the matter, and stating that "the issues of Kolyma tales have long been removed by life." It is rumored that the writer Boris Polevoi, editor of the monthly *Iunost*, had prevailed on Shalamov to sign this statement; however that may be, the publication of his poetry collection *Moskovskie oblaka* [*Moscow Clouds*] seemed to hinge on it. The letter is puzzling in that it contains recognizable imprints of Shalamov's style and yet also includes features that cannot be found in any of Shalamov's other writings—for example, the repetition of the cliché *zlovonnye* ("foul-smelling"), which never occurs in Shalamov's prose but is a recurrent element of Soviet invective. According to Iulii Shreider (1989: 229), Shalamov denied having been "forced" to sign the letter (cf. Oja 1985: 62–63); Sirotinskaya (1992: 218; 1994: 137–38) explains that he insisted on his right to do so, was heartbroken afterward, but talked himself into rallying. Shalamov may have hoped that the compromise would open doors for the publication of his work—*Moskovskie oblaka* did, in fact, come out several months later. He was obviously also determined to reject conformity to the principles and practices of the Moscow dissident circles[18] just as he rejected conformity to the party-line mode of thinking. Yet he had not anticipated that he would create the effect of a toppled idol, a hero who failed, a rebel who sold out. Such a discrediting of a contemporary intellectual beacon was certainly among the goals of the authorities; in the fall of the same year the KGB would succeed in breaking the will of the dissidents Yakir and Krasin.

The letter may have helped Shalamov to obtain the benefits of membership in the Writers' Union, but it enhanced his tragic isolation.[19] One of Shalamov's recurring concerns was with the ultimate battle of books — *"kto kogo perezhivet, tot togo i perememuarit"* ("the one who survives will outmemoir the other" [1989b: 61]), a form of blackmail that he resisted by breaking off friendships and punctuating his letters and notes with harsh remarks that the present-day reader is free to interpret either as records of unrestrained bitterness or as *urbi-et-orbi* insurance against posthumous disparagement. In 1978, *Kolymskie rasskazy,* a volume containing 103 of his stories, was published by Michael Geller in London; blind and deaf, Shalamov held it in his hands and understood what it was.

Meanwhile, Shalamov's health kept deteriorating—the Kolyma twig would have but a short time before wilting in Moscow. The body of a Kolyma survivor bore witness of its own: blindness, deafness, frostbitten skin, Ménière's disease, chronic congestion, and apparently also minor strokes, angina pectoris, Parkinson's disease, and incipient dementia. Iulii Shreider found a woman to cook and clean for him, yet eventually Shalamov broke with her too. Unable to take care of himself, in 1979 he was placed in a nursing home (see Isaev 1996). According to witnesses, in this shelter for the disabled, regulation-issue pajamas made him resemble a convict. His camp habits revived: he would rip off the bedclothes and sleep on a bare mattress, roll up the blanket and lean on it, tie his towel around his neck against theft, hide bread under the mattress, hoard lumps of sugar in his pockets—E. Shklovsky believes that all this was an expression of a tacit but determined protest (1991: 61). Judging by the testimony of Elena Zakharova, Shalamov's conduct at times showed symptoms of senility. He may also have sought privacy in deafness.

Shalamov continued to compose poems and dictate them to visitors such as I. Sirotinskaya and literary scholar Aleksandr Morozov. Owing to the success of *Kolymskie rasskazy* abroad, more people would come to see him in the shelter—to the discontent of the personnel and state security. A gripping 1979 poem by Aigi[20] said that Shalamov's room in the shelter was his last prison cell. But Aigi proved wrong—there was to be one more. They came for him again, forty-five years and two days after his second arrest. This time Shalamov is said to have yelled and attempted to resist.

The transfer of Shalamov from the shelter to a psychiatric hostel[21] was tantamount to a death verdict, since patients at such institutions did not receive proper medical treatment. It was also a form of official disgrace. These were the darkest hours before *perestroika,* when the use of psychiatric institutions had the triple aim of destroying psychological identities, circumventing justice, and proclaiming that "only a madman could think that way." Shalamov's attitude of supreme disdain for contemporary ideologisms may have been more subversive of the official value system than were the energetic activities of the dissidents. This attitude was also the basis of his lasting artistic achievement.

* * *

"I too dislike it," wrote Marianne Moore in "Poetry" about the main substance of her life. "I hate literature," wrote Varlam Shalamov in 1965 (1993b: 147) to Georgii Demidov, who also wrote stories about Kolyma. Shalamov had been living his life for the sake of literature, yet camp experience had taught him to hate "belletrization" (1993b: 144). He rejected stylistic embellishments, landscape for the sake of landscape, nonfunctional non-symbolic detail (1996: 426), traditional patterns of plot and idea, conventional emotionality, anything that smacked of stereotyped mendacities. His program was an appropriately innovative testimony to things previously unknown: "I examine some psychological *regularities* that arise in a society where attempts are made to dehumanize human beings. These new regularities, new phenomena of the human spirit and soul arise under conditions that must not be forgotten, and the recording of some of these conditions is a moral imperative of every person who has been in Kolyma" (1993b: 145; italics added).

The choice of the semi-fictional form in the bulk of his work is associated with the emphasis on *regularities* rather than isolated facts in the content of his testimony. "I do not write memoirs; nor do I write short stories," Shalamov went on to explain to Demidov in 1965. "That is, I try to write not a short story (*rasskaz*) but something that would not be literature" (1993b: 145).

There is no exact Russian lexical equivalent for the concept of "fiction" as a literary mode. There is, however, the opposite term, the word *ocherk,* which does not exist in English but can be approximately translated as "a (journalistic) sketch." Discursive *ocherk*-type passages (1996: 427) often function as descriptions of the social and cultural setting of Shalamov's story plots: these descriptions are verifiably factual, whereas the details of the plots may tend toward the representative rather than the specific. In later stories Shalamov often alludes to the subject matter of the earlier ones, turning the plots of the earlier tales into parts of the setting of the later ones. Elsewhere (Toker 1994, 1997b), I describe Shalamov's main work as Documentary Prose. His own term was "new prose": in the same cycle (*KR*), side by side with the *ocherk*-type texts, such as "Through the Snow," and directly autobiographical materials, such as "Tatarskii mulla i chistyi vozdukh" ["The Tatar Mullah and the Fresh Air"], he would place narratives that are clearly fictional, for example, "Cherry-Brandy," an imaginative reconstruction of a Mandelstam-like poet's death, and "An Individual Assignment," an inside-view account of the experience of a person who dies as the curtain falls. In a number of stories Shalamov used the name-change convention[22] to signal the possibility of other fiction-alizing displacements. All of the stories, however, are dominated by the sample convention: the most clearly fictional ones are thought experiments of the "what-it-would-have-been-like" type carried out by a *semiological* method with symbolic overtones. The author of such veridical fiction implicitly claims the ability to imagine certain situations, such as the death of a poet in the camp, perhaps as not impossible extensions of his own experience.

This procedure can be illustrated by "An Individual Assignment," a story about the fate that Shalamov had escaped but thousands of others had not. At a late stage in his ordeal Shalamov was given an "individual assignment," which meant that his individual output would be measured separately in order to determine his ration category (with the view to giving him less food) and perhaps to have him tried for malingering. If this had happened in the year 1938, the outcome would have been lethal: "An Individual Assignment" is obviously set in that terrible year and presents a Gulag version of the periodical *Selektion* in Nazi *Lagers*. This is one of the cases when the reader's familiarity with one of the two camp kingdoms can shed light on what took place, though in a veiled form, in the other.

The overseer at a gold mine announces to the prisoner Dugaev, twenty-three, fresh from the university and already exhausted, that the next day he will work alone. Dugaev is glad that nobody will hustle him, but the behavior of the other people grows strange. The foreman suddenly falls silent and raises his eyes to the evening star that has, symbolically, appeared over a hill,[23] and Dugaev's partner Baranov starts mildly fussing.

After the evening meal Baranov unexpectedly offers Dugaev a self-made cigarette, which on the first reading we may fail to recognize as one of the items in the classical repertoire of last wishes.

Exerting himself the next day, Dugaev produces 25 percent of the quota. In 1938 a prisoner could be shot for "wrecking" if he did not achieve 30 percent; Dugaev does not know this. In the evening he is called to an interrogator but asked no questions except the usual data of his file. The following day he again works with Baranov; in the evening he is led away behind the fence, to the area from which the tractor is heard roaring at night. The punchline of the story is that "having understood what the matter was, Dugaev regretted that he had labored to no purpose, on that last day" (36). Thus death is treated as a known matter of fact. The prisoner emerges as so reduced emotionally and intellectually that even in his final moments he can think of and regret nothing more than having missed a chance to rest on his last day, after his fate had been sealed by the previous day's production measurements and the pro forma interrogation. Paradoxically, this is also a major insight on Dugaev's part: he seems to understand not only what is in store for him but the whole procedure, including the fact that the tractors are there to jam the sound of the shots. Having become exhausted within a year of camp life (in the worst times a few weeks could suffice [1990a: 199]), he has been no expert on camp semiotics; and by the time a key point is revealed to him, the knowledge is largely useless. Yet though Dugaev is too tired to interpret his responses, his regret of his last day may well be read as resistance to the regime's ultimate cynicism in squeezing the last pounds of gold-bearing sand out of doomed victims.

* * *

Owing to the collocation of clearly fictionalized and clearly factographic material in *Kolymskie rasskazy,* Shalamov's reader may be uncertain about the mode of the stories that do not bear pronounced structural marks of fictionality yet at the same time also lack sufficient public-domain landmarks (dates, place names, references to identifiable people) to be read as concretely referential. When the nature of the text-reader pact is thus unclear, the reader is called upon to accept the stories as factual testimony yet apply to them the kind of analytic procedures that are appropriate to fiction.[24]

Shalamov's theory of documentary prose was worked out against the background of massive work on documentary literature in the Soviet scholarship of the period,[25] yet without much consideration for that background. For all their sweeping generality, his recorded theoretical statements are commentaries on his own stories and aesthetic conclusions from them. I shall attempt to explain his poetics using his 1959 story "A Day Off" (*KR*) as a sample.

The story typifies Shalamov's method of *simulating* the way things worked in the camps.[26] It examines the relationship between moral and physical survival—a topos in the literature of atrocities in general and in concentration-camp memoirs in particular. On a day off, a rare occurrence, a "moment of reprieve," the focal character notices two squirrels on a larch; then he sees that they have been watching his fellow convict, the priest Zamiatin, enacting a Sunday service in the forest, his face shining with happiness. When Zamiatin finishes the prayer, the narrator approaches him:

> "You were saying the liturgy," I began.
>
> "No, no," said Zamiatin, smiling at my ignorance. "How can I say mass? I don't have bread and wine or a stole. This is a regulation towel."
>
> He then adjusted the dirty "waffled" rag that hung around his neck and indeed looked like a priest's stole. The frost had covered the towel with snowy crystals; the crystal glimmered rainbow-like in the sun like embroidered church vestment.
>
> "Besides, I'm ashamed—I don't know which way is east. The sun now rises for two hours and sets behind the same mountain from which it has come up. So which way is east?"
>
> "Is it that important, the east?"
>
> "No, of course not. Don't go away. I am telling you that I am not conducting a service, I cannot do so. I'm simply repeating, remembering, repeating the Sunday service. And I don't know if today is Sunday."
>
> "It's Thursday," I said. "The overseer said so in the morning."
>
> "There, you see, Thursday? No, no, this is not mass. It's just that it's easier for me this way. And I feel less hungry," Zamiatin smiled. (182–83)

Returning to the barracks when the early darkness "fill[s] the space between the trees" (183), the focalizer finds two criminal convicts tickling a large puppy in the toolshed.[27] They slaughter the puppy to cook and eat it. That evening the criminals feast on meat soup whose origins are known only to themselves and the focalizer. Some is left in the pot after they have had their fill. They offer it to the focalizer; he refuses. Then they offer it to Zamiatin, whom the puppy used to befriend. When Zamiatin returns with the clean pot, one of the criminals amuses himself by disclosing to him what he has eaten. Wordlessly Zamiatin goes outside:

> I followed him. Zamiatin was standing in the snow, beyond the door. He was vomiting. In the light of the moon his face looked leaden. Sticky gluey spittle was hanging from his blue lips. Zamiatin wiped his mouth with his sleeve and gave me an angry look.
>
> "Those bastards," I said.

"Yes indeed," said Zamiatin. "But the meat tasted good—no worse than mutton." (185)

The story can be read as factual testimony.[28] The presence of a priest among the prisoners places it before the release of Greek Orthodox priests in 1943. The focalizer still cares for poetry, which means that he has not yet slid too far down the vicious spiral; there is, however, already bad hunger in the camps. This suggests that the events must be taking place in the winter of 1937–38, at the outset of Kolyma's most terrible year. At that time Shalamov was imprisoned in the Partizan camp, probably the geographical setting of the story. Yet the story is not amenable to the test of refutation because it contains no concrete public-domain landmarks that would help locate its setting on the calendar and map.[29]

There is no causal connection between the two events of the story, the forest mass and the eating of the dog. They may have been collocated because they *actually took place* one after the other. Or else they may have happened on different days, but the intervening gold-mine drudgery might have been unconsciously deleted from the memory. According to Aristotelian aesthetics, art removes what is accidental, trivial, and contingent in reality and achieves the form whose purity nature cannot display unaided. Even if the collocation of the two events is a product of sieving the random flow of reality and not of a deliberate recombination, we must read the story as a semiotically rich account of an actual day in the camp *yet also* inquire into the moral and allegorical significance of its collocations, repetitions, elisions, and recurrences. In other words, we must read the story as testimony—yet analyze it as a work of fiction.

Were the story to be read *only* as historical testimony, the connection between its two main events would signify the likelihood of such events happening on (or only on) days off, when prisoners have spare time and energy. Yet if the aesthetic function of the story is not thus downplayed, the link between the two events emerges as a *thematic* one.

The episode in the forest explores the theme of spiritual survival:

> I know that everyone here had something that is most important for him, THE LAST THING, that which would help him to live, to cling on to the life of which we were being so insistently and stubbornly deprived. If for Zamiatin this last thing was the liturgy of John Chrysostom, then my last saving thing was verse—my favorite poems written by others, quite astonishingly retained where everything else had long since been forgotten, thrown away, driven from memory. This only had not been crushed by exhaustion, frost, hunger, and endless humiliations. (183)

The second episode deals with physical survival: in conditions of general starvation, the older of the two criminals is an expert in slaughtering dogs for meat. Professional criminals think nothing of breaking the taboo on the eating of pet animals; in that sense they seem to be better adapted for survival in the camps.

Yet each of the two episodes contains points that subvert the easy antithesis between the moral/spiritual and the purely physical survival.

In the first episode, Zamiatin notes that remembering and repeating prayers makes him "less hungry."[30] This modifies our view of prayers and verse: in addition to helping the two characters to preserve the sense of their identities, prayers and verse also, and perhaps primarily, aid their physical endurance. And what the second episode suggests is that intellectuals in the camps are likely to be *differently* adapted to the struggle for survival.

Indeed, the main theme is now modified: the second episode points to the unacceptability of certain ways of physical survival. The criminals offer the leftover meat to the narrator because he has seen them kill their prey. While all the inmates of the barracks are tormented by the smell of meat, he curtly declines. Zamiatin does not decline, since the criminals say that the meat is mutton and delimit his obligation to them: he must just wash the pot. When the criminals reveal to him what he has eaten, Zamiatin vomits "just beyond the door" of the barrack—he can barely hold it beyond the threshold. Eager as his famished body is for calories, it rejects food that, like the narrator, he would never have accepted knowingly.

Shalamov wrote that his work on a story would begin with a desire to "bring up" some dearly bought insight, to "give it a full life"; thereupon, from his vast experience, he would pick a plot appropriate to the challenge (1996: 428). He composed mostly in his mind, in solitude, which he regarded as a person's natural condition (he liked to work when alone in a room, but amid the din of a big city), starting with an onrush of sounds and metaphors, of which only the right ones would be ushered in (1989b: 59). In his notes on prose, Shalamov frequently employs terms used in photography. One's state of mind determines the angle or the material for fixation, and one's whole psyche (attitudes, feelings, memory, language) acts as the fixing agent. In photography, the fixing agent is the substance that removes the photo materials from the plate so that nothing else should appear on the developed picture. This may be an apt metaphor for artistic selection; yet phenomenologically the chemical fixing agent is perceived as indelibly codifying the image. Thus retention merges with rejection, fixation with deletion, content with form. While composing, Shalamov would talk to himself, shout, weep (1989b: 64)—no wonder some readers respond to his laconic prose as to adrenaline shots. Only the near-completed work, fermented near the threshold of consciousness, would be put down on paper.

Readers are sometimes puzzled by Shalamov's occasional repetitions and imprecisions. This feature of his prose, ostensibly reminiscent of the almost mandatory flaws of Gulag memoirs, is usually deliberate:

> They say that an advertisement is remembered better if it contains an orthographical mistake. But this is not the only reward of carelessness.
> The very authenticity, the original nature of the work, demands "mistakes" of this kind.
> Sterne's "Sentimental Journey" is discontinued in the middle of a sentence and does not arouse anybody's disapproval.
> Why then, in the story "How It Began" do all the readers complete, correct in their own hand the sentence that I left unfinished, "We went on wor . . . " (1996: 432)

Indeed, the fricative outer surface of the narrative suits its subject: glossiness would fail to deautomatize issues. A rougher terrain grips us, slows us down, induces us to ask questions.[31] Shalamov rejects "individualization through speech," the "breath" as a measure of sentence length, conclusive endings, Hemingway's choppy dialogue amidst flowing authorial sentences, landscape and portrait for their own sake: "Is there 'color of the eyes' for the heroes of Kolyma—if such exist? In Kolyma there were no people with color of the eyes, and this is not an aberration of my memory but the essence of that life" (1989b: 63). He likewise rejects the decorum of nineteenth-century belles-lettres realism that "attempted to hide a totally indecent life beneath the veil of propriety" (1989b: 62) and the adjustments to convention made in Dostoevsky's *The House of the Dead*. His laconic, emaciated style, emotionally charged though restrained and at times cryptic, is "a stenogram" (1989b: 60) of his soul. The "new prose" that he worked out is "not the prose of a document but the prose of an ordeal borne out as a document" (*"proza vystradannaia kak dokument"* [1996: 433]). This definition involves, among other things, a rejection of the therapeutic approach to memoir writing: a writer has to reopen his old wounds in conjuring up the bad old times; "one has to brace oneself for this pain, nothing good will come out without it. That is, one has to re-live, re-feel the pain" (1993b: 131).[32] Shalamov's drafts of the seventies (as well as "My First Tooth" [*AL*, 1964]) reveal his uneasiness about the grief-assuaging effect that writing may have on the author: it is not right for the author to exorcise his past. Yet the anxiety that he shared with Adorno concerning the possible aestheticization of suffering ("there may be a profound untruth in that human suffering becomes the subject-matter of art, that the living blood, torment, pain, emerge in the shape of a painting, a poem, a novel" [1989b: 3]) is resolved by deontological imperatives: Shalamov believes that his stories are slaps in the face of Stalinism (1989b: 58) and that therefore they *are* (rather than *lead to*) the overcoming of evil (1996: 431). Though most of his stories are retrospective explorations of the semiotics of camp experience, some of them constitute acts as accusation, judgment, acknowledgment, mourning, restitution.

This type of composition is not to be confused with the *roman-à-thèse* method of constructing the plot in such a way that it should illustrate a thesis (cf. Suleiman 1983). The plot brought up to the surface of memory by the constitutive idea of a story eventually *tests* rather than exemplifies the motivating insight; this insight is not entirely amenable to discursive formulation. Indeed, in a modified "irony-of-origins" method,[33] the plot of a story can belie the narrator's generalizations: Shalamov can thus both express an idea and refrain from imposing it on the reader (see also Brewer 1995a). Thus, though the narrator of "A Day Off" regards prayer and poetry as ultimate spiritual props, the outcome of the story suggests that one's identity may be sustained by something deeper than prayer or poetry. It is not because they are culture-bound that the main characters of "A Day Off" cannot eat the puppy: in "Dry Rations" (*KR*) and "Courses" (*LB*) the narrator mentions having broken the dietary laws of Leviticus in various ways, but here the case is different—this particular dog has been a friend. Whereas in the first part of the story moral survival was presented as an aid to physical survival, now it appears to obstruct the chances of deferring starvation. As shown throughout the Lenten discourse, the answer to hunger is fasting: one has to relax one's physical tenacity, reject certain foods though one is starving, restrict the desires of one's body so as not to injure one's soul.

The story dramatizes the contradiction between standard concepts and the new type of experience. Zamiatin denies that he is conducting a mass in the forest because the proper conditions for it are absent. Yet his yearning turns his recital of the liturgical text into an earnest prayer. His regulation-issue towel is not a stole, yet it is just as majestic when embroidered by the snowflakes. He is not in a church, yet the quiet silver forest is no less sublime: the two squirrels that run up a tree are like friezes on a rococo vault—quite in tune with Shalamov's formula of general laconicity combined with one or two potentially symbol-making details (1993b: 115). The day off is a Thursday, not a Sunday, yet it is, nonetheless, a Sabbath. The meat that Zamiatin has been given is not mutton, yet while he eats it and is not told otherwise, it is mutton to him. Finally, it is not clear whether or not the priest's name, which he shares with the writer Evgeny Zamyatin, is authentic. In Gulag memoirs names were often changed in order to protect the still-living people: here, however, Shalamov may have taken advantage of the name-change convention to remind his readers of the author of the novel *We*, whose concern with an individual's self-assertion in the face of a dehumanizing system is of immediate relevance to the story.[34]

Like many of Shalamov's stories, "A Day Off" ends in a subversive punchline—instead of expressing some conventional sentiment, Zamiatin informs the focalizer that "the meat tasted good—no worse than mutton." Shalamov often began composing the text of a story with its first and its last sentences (1989c: 62), though he deplored "unexpected endings" and other "fireworks" (1993a: 115). In fact, his punchlines are often self-deconstructing: Shalamov believed that artists had no right to teach their audience,[35] even though in Russia, throughout the nineteenth and much of the twentieth centuries, they were expected to do just that. At the same time, an individual writer, just like an individual reader, is entitled to his or her own opinions. One is here in a double bind: if the audience is not yet free from the tradition of turning to writers for spiritual guidance, how can one refrain from imposing one's judgment on others without relinquishing one's freedom of thought? It is out of this predicament that Shalamov bootstraps himself when he cancels his own authority by allowing his narrative comments to clash with the implications of the stories' events.

"The well-bred contradict other people," wrote Oscar Wilde; "the wise contradict themselves." It is suggestive in more ways than one that Shalamov did not allow his friends to purge his manuscripts of contradictions caused by the faulty memory of details.[36] Indeed, "A Day Off" leads up to a dialectic conclusion that the tactics of physical survival must sometimes be sacrificed for the sake of moral survival, which is, in its circular turn, a crutch for physical endurance. And yet the two men who are acting on this principle are not consciously motivated by it: they find it in themselves without seeking. They believe that prayers or poetry sustain them; actually, it is they who sustain the life of the spirit. Obviously, the responsibility for drawing this bottom line devolves on the reader. Though a careful student of Chekhov, Dostoevsky, Leskov, and Bunin, Shalamov regarded the modernist Andrei Bely as the most significant influence on his work (see 1995: 155). Like most modernist works, his texts challenge the reader not to seek a meaning but to help create it.

In view of the subject, however, this hermeneutic endeavor must be hedged in. One could, for instance, note that in the first episode of "A Day Off" Zamiatin mentions the absence of the communion bread and wine, while in the second episode, the criminals sacrilegiously betray a friendly dog and enact a burlesque travesty of the Eucharist. Yet before pursuing the implications of this chiasmus, one must take care not to lose sight of the literal level of the story. In the literature of testimony, the literal level of significance places severe restraints on allegorization: the burden of testimony must not be intellectualized out of one's field of vision.

The criminals' killing of a puppy for meat shocks the reader, but the focalizer, though pained and disgusted, perceives it as very much in the nature of things. Shalamov gave much thought to issues associated with the Shklovskian concept of "estrangement" (*ostranenie*). He repeatedly mentions the view that it is unnecessary, perhaps harmful, for a writer to be too familiar with his material: the writer should approach his subject from the position of an outsider, a position he would share with the reader. His earlier texts clearly reject this position; and if his later ones seem to endorse it, this is because they are ironic reflections on what in the seventies looked like his ill success (see 1993a: 125–26). In a more earnest mood, in 1965, he disapproves of Hemingway's having remained a tourist in Spain, no matter how long he fought in Madrid: "new prose rejects this principle of tourism. The writer is not an observer, not a spectator, but a participant in the drama of life." He is "Pluto risen from Hades, not Orpheus who has descended there" (1996: 429). The focalizer of Shalamov's stories is an involved participant in the events described rather than a guest for the night, a writer in search of copy.

Judging by Shalamov's published notes (1990b: 71), the belief that "the writer should not know his material too well" was expressed by Solzhenitsyn in 1963; but Shalamov's critique of it is not a response to Solzhenitsyn (who, incidentally, put this principle into practice in only a part of his works).[37] His remarks on the subject appear as early as in the 1960 story "Galstuk" ["The Necktie"] (*KR*):

> It has so far been a requirement of success that the writer should be a foreigner in the land about which he writes. That he should write from the point of view of the people, with their interests and horizons, among whom he has been brought up and acquired habits, tastes, views. The writer uses the language of those, whose spokesman he is. And no more. If the writer knows his material too well, those for whom he writes will not understand him. He has reneged, gone over to his material.
>
> One should not know one's material too well. This is true for all the writers of the past and of the present, but the prose of the future demands otherwise. It is not writers who will speak, but professionals who possess the gift for writing. And they will tell only what they know and have seen. Accuracy—that is the force of the literature of the future. (152)

The statement about "professionals" (that is, people of other than literary professions) "who possess the gift for writing" is eventually qualified: documentary prose should be written by people who are "experts in their work and their soul" (Shalamov's examples were Antoine de Saint

Exupéry, Che Guevara, and Benvenuto Cellini).[38] The motivation for writing need not be teleological. So far literature has failed to preempt evil: "the experience of the humanistic Russian literature has led to the twentieth-century's gory executions that I saw with my own eyes." Shalamov does not support the contemporary belief that if the story of the atrocities is told, they will not happen again: "any execution of 1937 can be repeated" (1989b: 3). If literature does have a social function, this function is best understood in terms of Heisenberg's indeterminacy principle: "the radar is an active interference in life rather than its mere reflection" (Shalamov 1989b: 62).

Like the material of Shalamov's stories, his theoretical and critical remarks contain occasional self-contradictions, which could, perhaps, be explained away with a little effort. However that may be, he was working on the problems of short-story writing until the mid seventies, and his self-doubts, associated with the search for and a skepticism about a teleological justification of his work as well as with the sense of the ethical complexities of the content and the form of his narratives, entered into a dialectical tension with the imperative to speak. But the imperative was also a desire: for all his insistence that "new prose" should be written not by professional writers, he himself was genuinely professional. Writing— about what he knew best and cared for most intensely—was for him a necessary way of living whatever life had remained at his disposal.

* * *

Shalamov's main work is usually referred to as *Kolyma Tales*. This is, judging by Sirotinskaya's publications, both the title of the first cycle of stories, written in the years 1954–63 (the cycle that Mikhail Geller entitles *The First Death*; see Shalamov 1978), and the blanket reference to five story cycles. The most famous are the first three, from 1954–65: the second to be completed was *The Artist of the Spade* (*Artist Lopaty*) and the third *The Left Bank* (see 1992b: 160). These materials form the bulk of the first book-length publication, *Kolymskie rasskazy*, brought out by Geller in London in 1978 and subsequently reprinted in Paris. The volume also includes stories that actually belong to Shalamov's later cycles. Geller wished to follow the plan that Shalamov had drawn up for the sequence of the materials, yet was in possession of only an early version of this plan,[39] containing sixty of the more than one hundred stories. As new manuscripts kept reaching him across the border, he took it upon himself to insert them in suitable places (see Geller 1989b), hardly realizing that many of them belonged to the fourth, the 1966–67 cycle, *The Revival of the Larch*.

Sirotinskaya's approach to publishing Shalamov's works was likewise not flawless. As soon as *glasnost* permitted, she published some of Shalamov's works in *Iunost'* and *Novyi mir,* but this selective publication cushioned the first impression of his work on the broad Soviet readership.[40] Her 1989 publication entitled *Levyi bereg* includes the second and the third cycle, in the order in which they appear in Geller's edition; the first cycle opens her 1991 *Kolymskie rasskazy.* In 1992 Sirotinskaya published what is now the definitive two-volume edition of Shalamov's tales, reversing the order of *The Artist of the Spade* and *The Left Bank:* apparently, in the seventies Shalamov had second thoughts about the sequence of the cycles.[41] Placing *The Artist of the Spade* at the end of the "trilogy" makes sense biographically, because the last story of this cycle, "Train," tells about the focalizer's journey from Kolyma to Moscow, in keeping with the "journey out" topos that ends many a Gulag memoir. Yet the last story of *The Left Bank, "Sententia,"* dealing with the focalizer's spiritual recuperation from total dystrophy when sent to an easier camp, is more effective in terms of reader response. It is one of the most powerful works of the corpus, and can function both as a memorable finale and as the open-ended half-promise of a sequel. For reasons beyond the author's control, like some Gulag memoirs and like Solzhenitsyn's *The First Circle,* Shalamov's masterpiece is thus destined to exist in a non-hermetic shape, forking into two variants that, in a sense, complement each other.

The fifth cycle, written in 1970–73, bears the title *The Glove, or K[olyma] T[ales]-2.* Shalamov's corpus also includes "Sketches of the Criminal World," (1998, 2: 7–100), written in the late fifties; *Vishera: An Antinovel,* written in the early seventies and dealing with his first imprisonment in 1929–32; the play *Anna Ivanovna;* a few separate stories; the autobiographical tale "The Fourth Vologda," written in 1971; a number of autobiographical, memoiristic, and epistolary fragments; and several batches of subtle and intense lyrical poetry.

The sequence of the stories within the cycles is non-thematic and non-chronological. Two main compositional principles seem to be at work: (1) each opening story is, directly or indirectly, self-referential, devoted to issues of memory and writing; each closing story contains hopeful notes; (2) in between, the stories are arranged according to the *pulsation principle* characteristic of Gulag memoirs: pictures of acute suffering alternate with stories of reprieve. The combination of these two strategies is largely accountable for the reader's impression that, despite the ruthlessness of his narratives, on closing the book one is left with a belief in honor, goodness, human dignity.[42] The aftershine of one narrative irradiates another, so that the cognitive value, emotional coloration, and intellectual problematics of each separate story are integrated into the cumulative impact. The pulse of Shalamov's narratives maintains the reader's sensitivity to evil and pain; the reader becomes habituated but not inured to them and learns to expect evil but not to take it for granted.

In addition to its rhetorical effect, the pulsation method also possesses a significant mimetic dimension. If one judges by such stories as the 1958 "Dozhd'" ["Rain"] (*KR*), emotional respite, like inner escapes in memoir literature, could come from a prisoner's own thoughts. If a prisoner is capable of thoughts that are soothing and, in view of the need for psychic thrift, not straining, mental respites enhance physical endurance. For the focalizer of "Rain" even the idea of premature death may be positive: "It was jolly to think (*Mne veselo bylo dumat'*) that I shall not live long enough for sclerosis." The respite-yielding thoughts of Shalamov's focalizers are not daydreams (a perilous pastime in the camps); rather they are musings on minor recent instances of people's kindness, on little compensations, on the stint of food and rest that one can expect. Earthly as such thoughts may be, the word *veselo* ("jolly") is a touch of grace available only to a fine self-reliant artist:[43] the tone of the narrative combines matter-of-factness, avoidance of sentimentality or pathos, with unostentatious Lenten refinement.[44] Shalamov's focalizers distinguish ethically significant matters almost by instinct, but their conscious thoughts are slow, stark and, at critical moments, pragmatically concentrated.[45] The verses that are alive in the focalizer's active memory in "A Day Off" have faded by the time he reaches the stage described in *"Sententia,"* to return at better times.

The weight-center of each of the first three cycles is closest to one of the three main stages in a survivor's progress as described by Victor Frankl (1962: 6ff.) on the basis of his experience in Nazi camps: (1) initial shock, (2) entrenchment in camp routine, and (3) release-related tribulations.

The first cycle opens with the self-reflexive sketch "Through the Snow" (see pp. 5–6 above). Many of the stories—for example, "Pervaia smert" ["The First Death"], "A Day Off," "Posylka" ["The Parcel"], "Shock Therapy," and "Seraphim"—are devoted to the protagonist's *first* experience of a particular atrocity. But the shock of initiation is mainly the reader's. The second story, the 1956 "On Tick," both thrusts the reader into the thick of "another world" and announces a break with the traditions of Russian classical fiction.[46]

As Geller was the first to point out (1978: 11), the opening sentence, "They played cards on Naumov's berth in the barracks of the horse drivers" is an allusion to the opening sentence of Pushkin's "The Queen of Spades," a tale of gambling and an existential transgression: "Once they played cards in the apartment of the cavalerist Narumov." Yet the word "once" is omitted—Shalamov's prose is sparse in general, but this elision suggests the iterative, exemplifying character of the events of the story—

they happened not "once" but many times. Cavalry officers, sons of the gentry, are replaced by horse drivers—a job that in gold-digging camps was usually given to criminal convicts and was not scorned even by the so-called blue-blood professional thieves. The criminals have their own "code of honor," involving the sacredness of debts and, paradoxically, the legitimacy of skillful card-sharping. The name of the host is reminiscent of Pushkin's Narumov but has one letter less: motifs of truncation, diminution, reduction recur throughout the volume.[47] From the story "Lida" (*LB*) we shall learn that the typist's supposedly absent-minded omission of a letter could have immense consequences for a person's future: the fatal letter T for "Trotskyism" or "Terrorism" in a survivor's release documents could mean life imprisonment in installments.

"On Tick" thwarts expectations and reinterprets heavy-duty motifs. The criminals wear crosses not as talismans or emblems of belief but as status symbols. The distinctive feature of Sevochka, Naumov's opponent, is absolute inconspicuousness, the very opposite of the memorable appearance of a traditional Romantic villain: "His face was of the kind which it was impossible to remember. You take a look at him—and forget, lose all the features—no recognition at the next meeting" (19–20). All the narrative details carry complex significance. The dirty cushion of Naumov and the plywood suitcase of Sevochka are status symbols. The playing cards have been made from a volume of Hugo—a good book, thick useful paper (in Solzhenitsyn's *The First Circle* Ehrenburg's volume is also considered a good book—just the right size to keep the window ajar): Hugo's romanticized presentation of the criminal world makes the paper recycling particularly appropriate in the context.[48] The reference to Hugo also prepares us for "An Individual Assignment," Shalamov's version of Hugo's "The Last Day of a Condemned Man." In "On Tick" one of the stakes in the card game is a cigarette box with Gogol's profile—an allusion to the picture on the tailor's cigarette box in "The Overcoat." The climax of the story is a swerve from Gogol: Garkunov, with whom, for a payment in soup, the focal character has cut firewood for the thieves, is stabbed to death by a flunky for trying to keep his red sweater with which Naumov wants to pay his card debt. The focalizer is safe because he has nothing of his own—all his clothing is regulation-issue tatters. Whereas Gogol's Akaky Akakievich dies when deprived of the overcoat that is a stand-in for his emotional and spiritual life, Garkunov is killed for refusing to part with a prop of his identity, a thing sent him by his wife. The thieves thus aid the authorities to de-individualize the political prisoners and turn them into a uniform mass of starving slaves.

A piece of clothing from home, an aid against the Siberian frosts, doubles as an emblem of resistance to de-individualization. Pieces of clothing are often allowed into Shalamov's stories: owing to lice and cold, they are an important item with, in addition, semiotic and symbolic functions. In "Condensed Milk" (1956), the focalizer notices that the prisoner Shestakov, who turns out to be an *agent provocateur,* is wearing decent checkered socks, in contrast with the habitual camp foot-rags. On the semiotic plane this is a status badge: Shestakov holds a privileged office job, does not wear out his footgear, and does not need to trade it for food. Yet given Shestakov's determination to sacrifice other people for his own welfare, the reference to his socks can read as a symbolic allusion to Dostoevsky's *Crime and Punishment:* when Razumikhin buys a set of secondhand clothes to replace Raskolnikov's dilapidated outfit, the only item he does not get for him is socks; thus, up to the Epilogue, Raskolnikov will be walking in his old socks soaked with the old woman's blood, literally stepping on blood. Shestakov still has his socks after he has caused the deaths and new sentences of a number of people: Shalamov's story is the only punishment he gets for this crime.

"On Tick" contains no evaluative comment either on Garkunov's resistance or on the thieves' killing him; the focalizer's only thought, in place of some traditional topos of grief or outrage, is "Now I had to find another partner to cut wood with." This mercilessly laconic punchline shows that in the camps murder was in the nature of things, and indifference to it part and parcel of the inner life of people on the verge of dehumanization, people whom Shalamov regarded as martyrs who "could not and did not become heroes" (1996: 428).[49]

Cumulatively, the stories of the first cycle present an experience that, if physically survived, amounts to the death of one's former self. "The Snake Charmer" refers to camp life as "our second life in the world" (119). The 1954 stories "In the Night" and "Carpenters," placed after "On Tick," show the camp versions of such conventional notions as good manners, the sacredness of graves, honesty, work ethics; "Rain," the seventh story in the cycle, attacks the cherished humanist notion of "the meaning of life." The old belief (revived in Frankl's "logotherapy") that survival depends on one's retaining a sense of the meaning of one's life finds support in much of Gulag and Holocaust literature: prisoners can endure their suffering if they cling to thoughts of their loved ones, or to the wish to tell their stories after release, or to hopes of some day working again in their professional fields.[50] Shalamov, however, rejects the very need for the concept of "the meaning of life." In "Rain," the elderly agronomist Rozovskii, forced to dig trench-like mine-sleeves amidst the "diabolical harmony" of "the gray stony riverbank, gray mountains, the gray rain, people in torn gray clothes" (45), becomes suicidal when he "realizes" that "there is no meaning of life" (45). Whether Rozovskii's conclusion is that his own life has no meaning or that traditional discourse about the "meaning of life" is invalid (the grammar of "*smysla zhizni net"* suggests the latter), the cruel awakening is both an intellectual reflection of his loss of vitality and a further blow to his life instinct. Owing to the semiotic proficiency of a veteran, the focalizer hears in Rozovskii's outcry a preface to a suicidal act: risking his own life (he is not yet overcome by camp torpor), he jumps out of his excavation just in time to stop Rozovskii from flinging himself at a guard.

The focalizer of "Rain" feels that in himself the life instinct is strong and that nothing would induce him to commit suicide. His body has instinctively thwarted a well-laid plan for self-mutilation that could have given him a respite from digging in the soaking rain: he had placed a heavy stone so that, on rolling down, it would break his leg—but then he moved his leg away at the last moment. His existential ("stellar" [44]) thoughts are intertwined with the anticipation of modest Lenten pleasures—the end of a workday, a little food, a puff from someone's cigarette butt. He knows that, like his whole body, his brain cells are getting insufficient sustenance, but he watches himself finding positive objects of thought, such as the wisdom of a gesture of solidarity made by a woman who passed by the mine face.[51] The thoughts about food and rest are spiritualized by an amalgam of childish anticipation, satisfaction about possessing a necessary implement (a tin can), and the Lenten discipline of thinking only about one's own share. It is to these days of working in the rain that the narrator traces his belief that man is stronger than animal (animals die more quickly than people in Kolyma) because he has greater stamina and can place his spirituality at the service of his physical being (43).

In the notes collected as *The Will to Power,* Nietzsche wrote: "Suppose we realize how the world may no longer be interpreted in terms of [aim, unity, being], and that the world begins to become valueless to us after this insight: then we have to ask about the sources of our faith in these three categories. Let us try if it is not possible to give up our faith in them. Once we have devaluated these three categories, the demonstration that they cannot be applied to the universe is no longer any reason for devaluating the universe" (13). The focalizer of "Rain" has reached the point where he does not need any of these categories in order to refrain from devaluating life: a biological wisdom becomes a sufficient aid to endurance. Later Shalamov would explore other ratios of moral consciousness and physical survival: in the 1962 "The Businessman" (*AL*) he would show how the former could be sacrificed to the latter without turning a person into a villain, and in the 1967 "Vecherniaia molitva" ["Evening Prayer"] (*VL*) he would offer a glimpse of the mode of living with unallayed remorse.

The penultimate story of the first cycle is "The Lawyers' Plot," set in December 1938 and based on the author's narrow escape from execution. The focalizer is struck by the lightness of the body of a goner (*dokhodiaga*) whom he helps off a truck; he himself is another goner, almost lethally depleted.[52] The other man has been condemned to death and brought to Magadan for execution; he does not seem to care. The focalizer is on his way to interrogations that are likely to end in a death sentence; but he too has reached the stage of traveling light, of indifference to his fate. Almost dead inside, he is free from anxieties, regrets, or any other emotional load, free from the fear of death, and free from the death wish. His thoughts dwell mainly on the possibilities of rest, food, and warmth. At first he is even glad of his in-camp arrest because it frees him from work; later he learns that owing to the extraordinary frost his whole brigade has been excused from work that night, so he has gained nothing. When the car transporting him stops at Serpantinnaia, the awesome prison complex that people do not leave alive, he strongly "dislikes" this, but there is no reference to terror. When he is taken to an official by the name of Smertin (derived from the Russian *smert'*, "death"), he is merely "impressed" by the name. He does not seem to feel any particular relief when the car moves on, leaving Serpantinnaia behind; nor does he feel joy when the charges against him are dropped. Escape from death is dedramatized: the focalizer is too exhausted to appreciate the hurdle that he has passed.

It is the next story, "Typhoid Quarantine," the last of the first cycle, that emphasizes the worth of surviving the initial period in the camps.[53] Half-dead from exhaustion and scurvy, the protagonist, here called Andreev, is placed in a typhoid quarantine, where he partly revives. At first he sleeps all day except when the food is brought in. When the first need for the self-engulfing rest has been satisfied, he starts delousing. Soon afterwards he realizes that he has passed through a great trial, that some wisdom, as of a stone, a tree, a dog has kept him from dying, and that this experience may turn out to be not useless. Without resorting to the anthropological discourse of "initiation," the story shows that Andreev has come a long way and is approaching a new phase of his camp life.

Slowly his body begins to heal: first the scratch sores on the skin, then the frostbite. Then the wrist of one hand, bent around the now absent handle of the spade, unbends itself, and he starts massaging the other hand with his teeth. Even some scurvy sores begin to cover up with a layer of blue skin.[54] The spiritual sores, he believes, will never heal at all.

Eventually, the overseer begins to read out lists of names, and the prisoners thus summoned are sent off to work in different camps. Andreev's only wish now is to linger in the quarantine, delaying his return to slave labor. He notices that a name is called, but the prisoner does not answer, and his file is put aside. In a burst of inspiration, Andreev decides not to respond to his own name. For several days he avoids identifying himself, until trucks carry off most of the prisoners to the gold mines, the hungriest consumer of slave labor. Andreev identifies himself only when further hiding becomes impossible.

Though the story does not have a conclusive happy ending, it orchestrates an extremely important moment in the education of a prisoner—his passage from the *primary* to the *secondary* adaptation. The primary adaptation (like that of Volodin after his arrest in Solzhenitsyn's *The First Circle*) means learning to function in camp or prison conditions, learning the rules, the logistics, the ways to take care of one's needs. The secondary adaptation begins when one learns to break the rules and get away with it. The calculated breaches of discipline are an active though non-mutinous way of refusing to acquiesce.[55]

The issue of secondary adaptation is foreshadowed by an earlier story, "Carpenters," where a prisoner gets a lifesaving respite by pretending to have a carpenter's skills. Shalamov's work is characterized by rhythmic repetitions of both general motifs and specific story plots (see Shalamov 1992b: 177 n. 22).[56] The focalizer of "Carpenters" does not make a conscious decision to cheat: he hears himself instinctively answering a call for carpenters before he knows what he is doing—the instinct of self-preservation is more alert than consciousness.[57] In "Typhoid Quarantine," however, the mind of the goner is at work without the aid of instinct, and his subversion of the rules is not merely a ruse but also an assertion of his inner freedom. Apparently, biological wisdom may be acquired; it is not just an innate gift or a set of dynamic stereotypes. Survival and secondary adjustment are creative endeavors in which personal strength and the appeal to one's subconscious go hand in hand with the knowledge gained from formative experience.

The bulk of the cycle entitled *The Artist of the Spade* pertains to the second stage of a *zek*'s experience, entrenchment in the ways of the camp. In the metafictional opening story, "The Seizure," based on Shalamov's first bout of Ménière's disease, the focalizer has a vision of Sisyphean labor in the camp (unsuccessfully dragging a log of firewood not uphill but, symbolically, downhill) when he lies unconscious in a Moscow hospital. Soon after coming to, however, he notes that he does not "fear memories." This cryptic remark may suggest that what he does fear is the return of the camps, not in memory but in reality. It may also suggest that he is fully prepared to expose his consciousness to the visions of the past for the sake of the Sisyphean labor of bearing witness.

In the stories that follow, an entrenched prisoner's expertise provides a background for occasional new surprises. The focalizer of the title story has mastered the art of handling the spade; other prisoners are also artists: having accumulated a profound knowledge of camp life, they often find truly artistic means of escaping tougher spots. And though the spade is, emphatically, a spade, the title may also allude to Kafka's "The Hunger Artist," where, in an existentialist nausea, a person voluntarily starves himself to death (see Toker 2000).

Most of Shalamov's protagonists are people in whom the instinct of individual survival has remained strong but who limit the repertoire of the acts to which they stoop in order to get extra food, or rest, or tobacco.[58] The limits vary: the camp "prominents" beat, denounce, and rob other prisoners for the advancement of their interests; some of the ordinary zeks make a sport of becoming false witnesses or informers; some others serve as compromise-type stool pigeons; still others seek "trusty" jobs. Shalamov's fictional avatars keep clear of all this and, true to the Lenten spirit, reject all thought of jobs that would entail imposing their will on others. They may humble themselves to beg for a puff or a piece of bread, crawl on the floor in search of a crumb, rummage in garbage dumps, earn morsels by odd jobs for prisoners who had subcontracted them, keep their food to themselves (too hungry to share it with others), toy with the idea of self-mutilation, simulate dysentery or appendicitis to gain admission to hospital, and dodge round-ups, yet not bribe (though there is but a thin line between bribe and barter), nor toady, nor force others to do their bidding, nor "squeal" on fellow prisoners. It stands to reason that the secret of Shalamov's physical tenacity in the camps lay in his peace with himself on having lived up to his inner commitments.

Yet *The Artist of the Spade* also includes stories about other sorts of entrenchment. "The Businessman," for instance, deals with in-camp commerce. The issue is not new: in *The House of the Dead* Dostoevsky describes multiple pecuniary transactions among the prisoners, noting that the handling of money, no matter how small and futile the sums, is their only exercise of free choice. The literature on Nazi camps usually approves of camp commerce, especially when it involves the SS in illicit trade operations. Gulag authors do not condemn plain barter for the sake of obtaining food or necessary implements; yet their assessment of transactions that involve the guards is ambivalent. The guards would profit from clever machinations with state property; the prisoners would profit from them as well: a degree of underhandedness was almost a virtue in those who wielded any power in the camps. However, exploitation of the guards' self-interest would not stop there. Whereas in their dealings with Jewish prisoners the economically corrupt SS men became less deadly than their "idealist" colleagues, the corrupt Soviet prison guards sided with the criminal convicts: the professional thieves despoiled the political prisoners and sold the loot cheaply to the guards. The tradition seems to go back to czarist times, when corrupt jailers supported the thieves against the political prisoners even when the initial bribes had come from the latter.

The novelty in Shalamov's treatment of this issue in "The Business-man" lies in his combining it with the subject of self-mutilation. Like Solzhenitsyn and Marchenko, Shalamov treats self-mutilation with un-derstanding: sometimes the only way to preserve the whole is by sacri-ficing a part. Yet camp commerce can be as damaging to one's moral self as self-inflicted wounds to one's body. The "businessman" of the story is Kolya Ruchkin—the nickname Ruchkin (from *ruka*—"hand") indicates that he has sacrificed a hand in order to be taken off the general works in the gold mines. Yet Kolya's self-mutilation has been performed in the framework of commerce: he has exchanged his bread ration for explo-sives and then taken the bread rations from two others for allowing them to have their fingers amputated by the same explosion—thus his net profit is one bread ration.

The punchline of the story is Kolya's self-righteous account of how the other two eventually asked him to break off pieces of bread for them from his two rations and how he refused, saying that this was his "commerce" (303). The characteristic feature of goods in trade is their being de-tached, abstracted from the network of human relationships in which, as things, they had participated or been produced. Goods in trade are, as Marshall McLuhan would say, auto-amputated extensions of man. In "The Businessman" auto-amputation is literal, and damage to the human body is commercialized. For payment in bread, Ruchkin aids other peo-ple to harm their bodies: he smuggles the forbidden herring to diarrhea patients to help them stay on in the hospital and finds ways to supply goners with desired though destructive tobacco.

In a sinister swerve from the Lenten response to hunger by fasting, active self-damage is the prisoners' response to the damage caused by the exhausting labor and starvation in the camps. Parts of the body become alienated and call attention to themselves by malfunctioning. Ruchkin's palms and fingers had stiffened in a bent position, as if to hold, forever, the temporarily absent extension—the handle of a spade or a pick. But Ruchkin, says the narrator, "hacked them off, blew them off to hell" ("*k chertovoi materi*"). The same expression is repeated at the end of the story. When the other two amputees ask Ruchkin for a piece of bread from his "earnings," he curses them: "You can go to hell, I said" ("*Poshli vy, govoriu, k chertovoi materi*" [303]). His "commerce" has amputated human rela-tionships, just as he has amputated his right hand, rendering himself incapable of the handshake of friendship.

Yet Ruchkin does not regret this handicap since it will save him from the general works. What worries him is that at night the amputated hand still hurts and that in his somatic imagination it has still remained stiffly bent while the remaining left palm has already straightened out. This version of the ghost-limb phenomenon may be read as symbolic: old moral scruples still rankle after being given up. Ruchkin is glad when the irritation ceases; he is likewise happier when liberated from the scruples that were obstructing his way to physical welfare. In the camps, as Shalamov writes in the 1959 "The Red Cross" (*KR*),

> Moral barriers have been pushed somewhere aside.
> One discovers that it is possible to commit base
> acts—and go on living.
> It is possible to lie—and live.
> It is possible to promise—and not to keep the
> promises and still live.
> It is possible to drink up a friend's money.
> It is possible to ask for charity—and live! To beg
> and live! (220)

Kolya finds it easier to live after the moral barriers have been pushed aside. Yet he remains a likable fellow, not villainous and not dishonest. He has amputated a part of his humanity, has commercialized a part of human relationships, yet he has retained the other parts. Neither self-mutilation nor "fair trade" are among the worst of camp sins.

Though most of the focalizers in *The Artist of the Spade* are experienced prisoners with a profound knowledge of camp life, the cycle also contains two or three stories pertaining to the period of initiation, such as the 1964 "My First Tooth."[59] The last two stories pertain to a prisoner's release; and the ending of the last story, "The Train" (1964), resumes the motif of memory introduced in "The Seizure": the protagonist vows never to forget the camps.

The cycle *The Left Bank*, if placed third (according to what must have been Shalamov's initial plan), reads as the fulfillment of this vow. Its title commemorates the hospital on the left bank of the river Kolyma and connotes distance, remove. After the Central Hospital for prisoners had been transferred to the left bank from its previous location 23 kilometers off Magadan, patients from the new consignments of prisoners had to travel 500 kilometers to reach it. By chance or by choice, the left-bank location is reminiscent of Mt. Nevo on the left bank of the Jordan River, whence the exhausted Moses looked at the promised land, which he was unable to reach: even release does not bring happiness—the promised land devours its citizens.

"The Procurator of Judea," the opening story of the cycle, deals with self-defensive forgetting. In the winter of 1947, a rebellion broke out on the steamship *Kim*, carrying prisoners to Kolyma; the guards hosed the rebels down in the icy holds. As the ship unloads, the dead are thrown onto the bank and those alive are driven to hospitals for conveyor-line amputations of frozen limbs. The chief surgeon of the Central Hospital, Dr. Kubantsev,[60] a recent arrival from the front, breaks down and turns command over to a former prisoner. The story ends with the following observation:

> Seventeen years later Kubantsev remembered the names of each of the convict orderlies, of each nurse; he remembered all about who a prisoner "lived with," that is, all the camp romances. He remembered the rank of each of the nastier bosses. Only one thing would Kubantsev not recollect—the steamship *Kim* with its three thousand frost-maimed prisoners.
>
> Anatole France has a story, "The Procurator of Judea." There, after seventeen years, Pontius Pilate cannot recollect Christ. (614)

Unlike Pontius Pilate, the narrator of *The Left Bank* does not fear memories. Nevertheless, most of the memories of this cycle pertain to the better parts of the focalizer's experience, such as the times spent in hospitals and medics' courses.

In *The Left Bank*, as well as in *The Artist of the Spade*, the focalizer of most of the stories has more distinctive features than in the bulk of the first cycle, where he is, most often, a regular, decent, but physically and emotionally exhausted prisoner, sometimes referred to as tall (which is a disadvantage because his body needs more of the unavailable calories) but devoid of such conventional constituents of identity as personal ties, profession, memories, and belongings. In some stories he is already (or again) a goner: the flesh has almost completely disappeared from his bones; his skin has scratches, insect bites, and scurvy sores (the Kolyma counterpart of "sore boils from the sole of his foot unto his crown" [Job 2:7]); his toes suppurate; his memory cells are hibernating. In a state of near-lethal exhaustion, prisoners look and feel very much alike: the incompleteness of Shalamov's character portrayal simulates this aspect of camp life; it also forms an implicit appeal to the sample convention that neutralizes the fictionalizing element of the stories and enhances their function as testimony.

By contrast, in the later cycles the particular is not dwarfed by the general, and the overtly autobiographical touches begin to dominate, especially in the stories about the times when the focalizer's general condition had improved and he could reassemble and reactivate the fragments of his identity. The story *"Sententia,"* which closes *The Left Bank*, describes the gradual spiritual recovery of a goner assigned to the relatively light work of a boilerman. The only emotion that has never left him is anger. A few other emotions reawaken as he begins to put on flesh. Fear, an expression of the renewed will to live (he fears being sent back to the gold mines) replaces his previous fatalistic indifference. Then the love

of animals returns—"the beasts of the field [are] at peace" with an emaciated sufferer (Job 5:23), and he is "in league with the stones of the
field"—stones do not seem dead to him, let alone the grass, the trees, the
river (890). The Lenten condition of a goner transcends the everyday
normal state, and his suffering seems to be partly compensated by a near
mystical insight into the life of things. He instinctively understands the
meaning of a male bird's calling the gunman's attention to itself in order
to protect the female; unmindful of the risk, he stops the gunman's hand:
the life of the brave bird is no less important than his own. Then, one day,
with a burst of happiness, he recollects a word—first the sound and only
later the meaning. The word is *"sententia."*

There is a touch of self-irony in the connotation of pretentiousness
that *sententia* conveys (cf. Brewer 1995a); in John Glad's translation it is
rendered by "Sententious" in the title. The focalizer seems to feel this
too, and so he asks a notorious informer for a little tobacco in order to
deflect the attention that he has attracted by crying out the foreign word:
as one's physical condition improves, the metaphysical insight of a goner
begins to yield to plain semiotic proficiency.[61]

Sententia is Latin for sentence, the main grammatical unit: according
to Nietzsche's contemptuous aphorism, we still believe in God if we believe in grammar. When the protagonist regains language, he regains the
freedom that consists in infinite possibilities within conventional limitations. The story is dedicated to Nadezhda Mandelstam, widow of the poet
who had written, "The word I have forgotten that I have meant to say."

Thereafter other words begin to return to the focalizer of *"Sententia."*
The story ends with the day on which the camp commander, realizing, as
it were, the metaphor of orchestration, brings a record player to the
forest, puts it on a tree stump, and plays symphonic music:

> And everyone stood around—murderers and horse thieves, toughs
> and wimps (*blatnye i fraiera*), foremen and workers. And the boss stood
> there too. And the expression on his face was such as if he had himself
> written that music for us, for our deaf-mute taiga outpost. The shel-
> lacked record spun and hissed, and so did the stump itself, impelled
> through all its three hundred circles, like a taut spring, wound up over
> the past three hundred years . . . (892)

Like the hissing disk, memory still keeps its carvings. Having regained
language, the prisoner will be able to control the various instruments of
his inner self, like the conductor of a symphony orchestra. Music, in
Schopenhauer's view, is the direct expression of the Will—here of the
triumphant will to live. The expression on the camp chief's face shows
that even he has a sense of the sublime by which, according to Longinus,
"our soul somehow is both lifted up and—taking on a kind of exultant

resemblance—filled with delight and great glory, as if our soul had created what it just heard" (1985, 7: 3).

The focalizer never manages to get the drinking water to boil in time for meals, yet nobody minds, so long as the water is hot: "We did not care about the dialectical leap of transition from quantity to quality. We were not philosophers" (886). And yet the story deals precisely with the dialectical leap from the quantity of flesh that a depleted body puts on to a qualitative change—the sudden return of verbal memory. The *zek* focalizer is not a philosopher; but the narrating voice is that of an ex-prisoner who has partly recuperated and can relate to his former camp experience with a newly accessible philosophical depth.[62]

Thus, like the other two cycles, *The Left Bank* ends on an orchestrated note of hope. So does the cycle *The Revival of the Larch*, written over the years 1965–67. Its self-reflexive first story, "The Path," describes a paramedic's trampling a path for himself near a cabin in the Kolyma woods; this symbolically self-made path is particularly "suitable" for writing poetry during the warm months, but it becomes useless as soon as the focalizer discovers on it tracks of someone else's boots: the illusion of a poetic niche away from the world of concentration camps is shattered. The last story, "The Revival of the Larch," like the final stories of the previous cycles, deals with the motif of partial recovery. It is a symbolic narrative of the revival of a Kolyma larch twig in the home of the widow of a poet who died in the camps (another allusion to Mandelstam). The motif of poetry juxtaposes the story with the opening narrative, thus creating the impression of a self-reflexive spiral-type closure.

The Revival of the Larch achieves further philosophical depths in retrospective processing of a *zek*'s experience. The 1966 story "Quiet," for instance, implicitly amends the pointed "insight" of the depleted *zek* focalizer from the more thoughtful position of the retrospective narrator. Whereas "A Day Off" invited us to resist the generalizations of the narrator, "Quiet" suggests an insufficiency of the focalizer's ideas.

A team of goners is shown having dinner before night shift in the gold mine. Their rations are unexpectedly supplemented by all the leftovers in the pots. The windfall turns out to be an experiment in incentive, a carrot offered by the new head of the educational section of the camp. Yet after the filling meal the prisoners do not work any better than before: it would take much more to restore their strength. Moreover, having reached the mine face, one of them, a fanatical sectarian who has always disturbed the others with his chanting of hymns, commits suicide by walking out into the fog, without heeding the shouts of the guard, who is then obliged, according to instructions, to shoot him.

After work the focalizer is aware that his body kept its warmth longer than usual. Extra food (which the camp commander regards as worse than wasted) has obviously bolstered the physical and moral strength of the prisoners. Then comes his insight, the *explicit* thematic gift package of the story: "And chilling at the guesses, I understood, that this night's dinner had given the sectarian the strength for suicide. It had been the stint of porridge that he had needed to decide to die. Sometimes a person must hurry in order not to lose the will to go to his death" (110).

The sectarian, a nuisance to his fellow prisoners because of his singing, is not presented in a sympathy-arousing manner. His death may therefore function as a steppingstone to lead us to the focalizer's generalizing psychological observation. Such an attitude, however, represents a temptation that the reader must overcome. The story does not end here. To compensate for his exposure to the frost and, as it were, to chase off "chilling" thoughts, the focalizer tries to warm himself at the stove in the barracks. There is no one to sing hymns. Then comes the punchline: "And I suppose I was even glad that now it was—quiet" (110).

While still under the impression of the focalizer's insight, we tend to accept this as a touch of the realistic *couleur locale*, a detail of the moral-emotional atmosphere of the setting in which there is no space for traditional emotional responses to death. Yet, on a rereading, the last sentence is more readily perceived as part of the network of motifs whose common denominator is the theme of resistance to aversive conduct (Skinner 1972: 26–31). This issue, vitally important in Solzhenitsyn's work as well, is the implicit thematic concern of "Quiet."

The clearest example of aversive control in the story is the camp commander's explanations as to why the prisoners should be underfed and sent out into the frost:

> "An extra dinner is extra strength to struggle with the frost. Only frost can extract work from them—remember, you tenderfoot—not your dinner, and not my fist, only the frost. They wave their hands in order to get warmer. And we put staves and spades into these hands—it doesn't matter what you wave with, does it?—we place wheelbarrows, boxes, carts under them, and the mine meets the quota. Gives goldy gold . . .
>
> Now these are filled up and won't work at all. Until they begin to freeze. Then they'll wave their spades. To feed them is useless." (109)[63]

The stick of aversive control is used alongside the carrot of incentive: but the carrot is only a reminder of the usual starvation. The quantity of food in the camp is insufficient, and priority is given to the workers "who have still kept their strength and still meet the quotas in 'the main production'—giving gold, gold, gold . . . " (103). The stream of gold, evoked by the repetition, flows in a direction opposite to that of human life: the manager has sent thousands of people to mass graves "under the hill." The repetition of "still" in reference to the stronger workers reminds us that the vicious spiral will soon draw them down as well.

When a person submits to aversive control, he reinforces the controller's aversive conduct. It is not the fault of the goners that the stick works and the carrot does not: one of them tries to encourage the benevolence of the new boss by a promise to work well, yet, since this promise cannot possibly be kept, the "tenderfoot" will soon have to get inured to the status quo.

The theme of resistance to aversive control emerges, unobtrusively, also in other parts of the story. One of the prisoners is a former interrogator who used to extract false confessions and now self-protectively despises his own former victim: "You were beaten? So what? You signed —hence you are an enemy, you confuse the Soviet power, hinder our work" (104). The focalizer's intervention, "I listen to you and do not know whether to laugh or to spit into your mug," de-energizes this aversive conduct instead of reinforcing it by, for instance, an ideological argument.[64] The sectarian's staunch refusal to give his name at roll calls (members of various religious sects regarded any kind of acquiescence to the demands of the Gulag authorities as collaboration with Satan) is also a form of resistance to aversive control, which the authorities are forced to accept. The sectarian submits to the control of his teammates when he allows them to move him, place him in line, lead him to the work site. In the gold mine he works, since cumulative production results and corresponding food rations are measured not individually but for the whole "brigade." Yet as he gives common fellowship its due, he sins against his conscience by compromising with Satan. Hence his need to chant hymns—significantly, he is quiet while mustering his strength for his ultimate defiance. But despite his best intentions, his chanting becomes aversive—it gets on the other prisoners' nerves and deprives them of their rest. The sectarian is in a double bind: his singing in order to placate his conscience creates a new reason for remorse.

The focalizer suffers most because he is the sectarian's partner not only in the barracks but also at work. When once he asks him to be quiet, he gets the following answer: "I would have died a long time ago but for the songs. Would have gone—out into the frost. I've no strength. If only I had some more strength. I don't ask God for death. He sees everything himself" (105).

The logic behind this seemingly self-contradictory utterance emerges on a second reading, when we know its relation to the outcome. The first sentence, "I would have died a long time ago but for the songs," indicates what it is that keeps up the sectarian's endurance. Yet the third and the fourth sentences suggest that the sectarian actually wants to die: the life he is leading (the "everything" that God sees) is not only unbearable but also ideologically unacceptable. While talking to the focalizer, the sectarian seems to realize that, since the songs that reduce his suffering sap the strength of his neighbors, going out to meet his death is preferable. If he does not go out into the frost, it is merely because he has no strength to do so. The songs turn out to be the second best way out. The sectarian relies on God to send him death without being asked to do so. As if in fulfillment of this wish, death is sent him in the shape of the extra food that comes with the new boss, aptly dubbed "the magician." The extra food literalizes the metaphor of "reinforcement": it gives the sectarian the strength to get up and walk away, "into the mist, into the sky," as if to rid his teammates of his aversive presence and defy Satan once more.

The focalizer's request that the sectarian be quiet is also a mild version of aversive control. Yet it is not owing to the absence of reinforcement that the focalizer does not repeat the request: he understands what the chanting means to the sectarian. The sectarian is not just an aversive factor, but a person with whom he is bound in a moral relationship, however minimal. His rights must be respected. And yet it is symptomatic of a goner's condition that at the end of the story the focalizer is shown not grieving for the murdered man but deriving comfort from the removal of an irritant: "I was even glad that now it was—quiet." The word "even" suggests the focalizer's understated and underprocessed moral self-awareness.

Yet we do not have to accept the focalizer's belief that the sectarian consciously intended to commit suicide rather than to just go away into the tell-tale frost-fog.[65] The impious idea of "suicide" is not the sectarian's or the narrator's so much as the focalizer's. The sectarian's walking away from the mine is an act of defiance rather than suicide, though the focalizer does not seem to have enough energy to think this through. In keeping with the principles of modernist art, the story creates the conditions *for the reader* to complete the intellectualization. The story of the origin of the focalizer's insight emphasizes its authenticity and its private relevance but does not ensure its correctness. The use of the first-person narration is here a sign not of the autobiographical character of the story but of the "irony of origins": Shalamov disowns the authority conventionally (cf. Doležel 1980) attributed to an omniscient narrator.

* * *

Most of Shalamov's works of the late sixties and seventies are, to borrow the title of Schopenhauer's *Parerga und Paralipomena,* additions and insertions. The cycles *Vishera: An Antinovel* and *The Glove, or KR-2* continue the intellectual processing of the past begun in "Kolyma Tales." At times it seems that these later works could not have been written, or given their present shape, had the author not produced the other four cycles first: the late stories are less urgent; they continue, as it were, rather than initiate a conversation. Thus Shalamov's literary biography follows the main pattern of the history of the Gulag memoir corpus: everything written after, roughly, *The Revival of the Larch* bears the marks of belatedness. Not all of Shalamov's later texts stage separate memories with an intensity equal to that of the first four cycles. He refers to parts of the *Vishera* cycle as *ocherki* ("sketches") rather than *rasskazy* ("stories"); the intensity of the passion behind them is considerably lower than even behind his "Sketches of the Criminal World," written in 1954–60. The twig that revives in *The Revival of the Larch* has been severed from the bough: its second life cannot but be brief. In the seventies, Shalamov was again in a state of accelerating physical decline. Not surprisingly, the intensity of the "emotional heightening"—his term for inspiration[66]— could seldom peak as before. Yet the later texts reveal new complexities in the issues that had already jelled into camp literature topoi[67] and were developing into a set of schemata.

Vishera: An Antinovel (1970–71) deals with Shalamov's first imprisonment, whereas the unfinished *The Glove, or KR-2*[68] mainly concentrates on his second. Of all Shalamov's story cycles, *Vishera* is the only one with a generic subtitle. This suggests a change in genre, whereas the allusion to *Kolyma Tales* in the double title of *The Glove, or KR-2* suggests a return to the author's earlier generic principles. *"An Antinovel"* means, among other things, that the material could be subjected to verification. Indeed, even the fallibility of individual memory is here counteracted by what seems to be a deliberate incompleteness of reality-effect particulars. Nor is the "antinovel" a mere string of episodes held together by time, place, and perspective: like most Gulag memoirs it has a unifying *thematic concern.* Starting with the first sketch, "Butyrskaia tiur'ma [1929]" ["The Butyrskaia Prison (1929)"], which deals with Shalamov's preparing himself to maintain his inner autonomy and suit his word to his principles and acts, *Vishera* is a replication of a spectrum of individual *attitudes* to survival in prisons and camps.

In the second *ocherk,* the survey-type "Vishera," Shalamov records having supplemented his initial resolve by an insistence on living according to his own principles, so that even his mistakes would be his own. The biographical decision to suit the word to the deed is simulated by the narrative principle of eschewing retrospective sentiments that would have been foreign to the focalizer at the time described. The starkness of

Shalamov's narrative style is associated with the Lenten discipline that he imposed on himself in the camps, even though the formation of specific subsidiary rules of conduct would be a matter of future learning.

The story "Vishera" contains an inset biography of A. Tamarin-Miretsky (see also "Khan-Girei" [*VL*]), who, according to Shalamov, survived in the camps by a constructive endeavor: he developed the agricultural know-how that helped to improve the food supplies in the northern regions.[69] By contrast, for the prisoner described in the sketch "Lazarson," survival was linked with management activities and lucre—bribes, shady deals, and the milking of state property, with imprisonment as a legitimate stake in the game. In Shalamov's books, Lazarson nevertheless stands for a good man, benevolent according to the "live-and-let-live" principle, intelligent, not vengeful or paranoid. Yet he is presented as a person who has lost his intellectual autonomy: when angry at a subordinate, Lazarson would yell and call him names, including the appellation "wrecker" (*vreditel'*) which at the time could be a lethal charge. The anecdote of the honest paramedic Shtoff losing his power of speech in the presence of the chief of the Main Camp Administration is a comic version of a similar acceptance of official values.

At the extreme of the spectrum is the camp boss Ushakov, who survives the Terror by acting on the principle "whosoever does not kill is killed himself." Off center toward the other end is the prisoner P. P. Miller, a victim of one of the most famous show trials of the "wreckers." In Shalamov's eyes, Miller, who took care only of himself, was a camp "smartass" (*khitrozhop*): "in a fix, in a stress situation, he will move to the side, let time do its job, while you are perishing at the gallows, in a cellar, or in Baby Yar" (55). The sketch "Delo Stukova" ["The Stukov Affair"] (dealing with the "source" for the story "Prosthetic Appliances" [*AL*]), presents an account of the authorial persona's first major test of fortitude. Toward the end of *The Antinovel*, Shalamov writes about receiving Berzin's offer that he sign a work contract in Kolyma. To Kolyma, he announced, he would go only under convoy. "Don't crack bad jokes," was the camp director's reply (110).

Despite their thematic common denominator, the different sketches of *Vishera* read like fragments whose edges do not form a close fit. Much is left unsaid, and perhaps not only because an individual vision of the camp universe is necessarily limited. Some of the sketches break off in the middle of dialogues, though the more typical ending is a reference to a particular person's fate. Whereas in his earlier stories Shalamov often pitted his authorial commentary against the events of the plot, in the later ones the authorial commentary occupies a larger proportion of textual space and is subverted not by "facts" but by gaps in the picture.

The author's ethical position is made explicit along with its inherent subjectivity and its limitations.

* * *

The cycle *The Glove, or KR-2* includes a significant amount of directly autobiographical material that fills in the blanks between the jigsaw-puzzle pieces of the earlier cycles. It was written when Shalamov's health was speedily deteriorating; nevertheless, it rises to several new artistic and intellectual challenges. For instance, in 1972, the year of his fateful letter to *Literaturnaia gazeta* and of the fortieth anniversary of the massive development of Kolyma, Shalamov was moved to write "Wheelbarrow I" and "Wheelbarrow II," his detailed accounts of the main "mechanism" of the gold mines. Though stimulated by the wish to adjust the historical record, the two stories are an attempt to evoke the length of time, painful, vexing, and monotonous, spent on carting the soil out of the mine-sleeves. As noted in Chapter 3 above, most of the scenically presented action in Gulag literature takes place in the after hours, during mealtimes, smoking breaks, days off, and days spent in prison or hospital: it is during such "moments of reprieve" that prisoners could think, respond, converse, develop relationships. Many of Shalamov's earlier stories pertain to hospitals where he had more strength and leisure to observe other people and events not directly related to himself and his bodily suffering.[70] The more monotonous a long stretch of time is in the present, the fewer memory cells it seems to occupy when one attempts to reconstruct it retrospectively, and the more difficult it is to render the wearisome character of the experience. Ginzburg and Margolin attempt to render long hours of work. Yet in their accounts, the main horror is associated with starvation rather than with the endless debilitating drudgery. Gulag memoirists seldom go beyond references to the kind of work they performed, the length of the workday, and the issue of the quotas. In *Ivan Denisovich*, Solzhenitsyn presents the hours when work casts a happy spell on the prisoner who can feel proud of the results of his efforts; by contrast, in the gold mines the slave laborer is totally separated from the products of his work. Shalamov's "Wheelbarrow" sketches help the reader to imagine the prolonged torture by work, with repetitive oscillations between the concentrated effort of pushing the full wheelbarrow and the brief spans of partial relaxation on having discharged its load.

* * *

Whereas Solzhenitsyn allowed for the corrupting influence of camp life on some people yet stated that in the case of others it could lead to an elevation of the soul, Shalamov believed that, in one way or another, the camp "shift of scales" (*smeshchenie masshtabov*) contaminated every soul (cf. Todorov 1996: 32–43; Iakubov 1987; Shur 1984). Nor would he have agreed with the view (Filshtinsky 1994: 10) that by creating borderline situations the camp merely revealed, like litmus paper, people's hidden qualities. Without resorting to Herling's metaphor of disease, Shalamov describes the camp value system as almost fatally contagious. "Camp experience," writes Shalamov in the 1965 "Engineer Kiselev" (*AL*), "is totally negative, down to every single minute. A person only grows worse. Nor can it be otherwise. There is much in the camps that a person should not see. But to see the lower depths is not the most terrible thing. The most terrible is when one begins—forever—to feel those lower depths in one's own life, when one's moral measurements are loaned from camp experience, when the morality of the criminals is applied in one's own life" (336–37). Shalamov would, however, agree with Solzhenitsyn that the line between good and evil passes through every human soul (*GA* 4: 1, pp. 615–16). I shall end this chapter by a discussion of a few stories that show in what ways Shalamov traces this line.

The line is at the negative pole in the portrayal of the sadistic free engineer Kiselev, who beats the prisoners and drives them to death on his own initiative. It is also at the extreme in the 1967 portrayal of criminal chieftains ("Bol'" ["Pain"] [*AL*]). It runs close to the positive pole in the stories about G. Demidov ("The Life of Engineer Kipreev" [*VL*]),[71] Dr. Umanskii ("Veismanist" ["The Weizmanist"] [*AL*]), A. Pantiukhov ("Dominoes"), or A. Gogoberidze ("Aleksandr Gogoberidze" [*KR-2*]), but in a considerable number of other stories, it crosses the gray areas lying in between.

Thus, Shalamov shows that even the people who are thoroughly enmeshed in the corrupt system of relationships have not completely knocked down the moral barriers—they have, rather, pushed them off. The metaphor of the "line" or "moral barrier" is literalized in the 1959 story "Berries" (*KR*). Where the snow has temporarily receded from the felled forest, the prisoners employed in wrenching out tree stumps can find overripe lingonberries and bilberries (whose incomparable taste is frequently mentioned in Kolyma memoirs). Using tufts of dry grass, the guard Seroshapka has marked the area within which the prisoners are allowed to move. Several rich bushes of berries are just outside the limits, and the focalizer's partner Rybakov, who is collecting berries into a can (if he fills the can the camp cook will give him some bread for it), cannot resist the temptation. Despite the focalizer's warning, he crosses the imaginary line between the grass landmarks and is shot by Seroshapka, who then fires again into the air: according to instructions, there must be two shots, the first a warning one. The can rolls close to the focalizer and he picks it up: he knows for whom it is meant and can get some bread for it.[72] The punchline is Seroshapka's angry remark to the focalizer: "I wanted you; but you kept away from there, you bastard." It thus becomes obvious that while Seroshapka has no qualms about luring a prisoner beyond the arbitrary "limit" and then shooting to kill without warning (cf. a similar episode in Maloumian 1976: 92–93), he still *cannot* shoot the prisoner who has *not* gone off limits—killing first and stage-managing an escape attempt afterwards.[73] The arbitrary invisible line between the tufts of grass is, among other things, a residual moral "line" that Seroshapka himself does not cross.

In the 1956 story "Condensed Milk" the *agent provocateur* Shestakov, who organizes a group escape attempt and then leads the fugitives into a prearranged ambush, is not presented as an arch-scoundrel; nor is the focalizer, a would-be victim who fails to warn the other victims, presented as totally blameless.[74] The first sentence of the story indicates the focalizer's physical and mental condition: "Because of hunger, envy, like all our feelings, had become dull and helpless" (98). Chronic starvation has produced personality changes: emotions are dulled, intellectual activity impeded, and the potential for active resistance curbed.[75] The experience of people who have reached an advanced stage of dystrophy is different from anything familiar to healthy organisms; hence it can hardly be explained in a discursive manner. Only the total artistic effect of the text can convey, at least in part, the quality of the moral predicament involved. The physical symptoms of this condition are the scurvy sores on the focalizer's (let us call him "Shalamov") legs: his body has already shed all its fats and has started burning its protein. The brain has been affected as well. In the course of the story, trying to persuade the narrator to flee, Shestakov spouts Dolores Ibaruri's slogan:

> "'Better to die on your feet than live on your knees,'" said Shestakov with an air of pomp. "Who said that?"
> Who indeed? It was a familiar phrase. Yet I lacked the strength to remember who and when had said those words. All that smacked of books was forgotten; one did not believe in books. (99–100)

"Shalamov's" failure to place the quotation known to every Soviet school-child[76] is a symptom that his brain has already disembarrassed itself of general memory. Yet it is still tenacious of the logistics of survival: the irreversible stage of pellagric dementia has not yet set in. Thinking is a physical effort but not yet an impossible one: "It was hard to think. For the first time the material nature of our psyche appeared to me in all its palpability. It was painful to think. But I had to" (100). "Shalamov" understands not only that the escape attempt is a provocation but also that some benefit may be reaped from it: he intimates that he will join if

Shestakov first gets him some food to help muster his strength. In accordance with the Lenten spirit, they settle on condensed milk in preference to canned meat or fish.[77]

At night "Shalamov" dreams of the treat—for once raising his eyes, as it were, beyond the grim line of the mining-site horizon, to the Milky Way. In the evening of the following day, the two cans of condensed milk give him the strength to turn the tables on Shestakov:

> "You know," I said, carefully licking the spoon, "I changed my mind. Go without me."
> Shestakov understood, and left without saying a word. (102)

"Shalamov" is left to face the ethical significance of his conduct:

> It was, of course, a worthless act of vengeance, weak like all my feelings. But what more could I do? Warn the others? I didn't know them. But they needed a warning: Shestakov managed to convince five people. They made their escape the next week; two were killed at Black Springs and the other three stood trial a month later. Shestakov's own case was handled separately, "for legal considerations"; he was taken away, and I met him again at a different mine six months later. He wasn't given any extra sentence for the escape attempt; the authorities played the game honestly with him even though they could have acted quite differently.

Then comes the punchline:

> He was working in the prospecting group, was shaved and well fed, and his checkered socks were still in one piece. He didn't greet me, though why not? Two cans of condensed milk are, after all, not such a big deal . . . (102)

Though the bulk of the story has been working up to the near-orgasmic gustatory pleasure, the punchline reminds us that the two cans are, after all, not "a big deal." "Shalamov's" minor victory is ironically deflated. The extra calories will soon be burnt up.

On being told that after the event Shestakov would not greet "Shalamov," the reader may think that Shestakov wishes to avoid the witness of his shameful act. Yet the punchline suggests that Shestakov is probably free from shame or remorse; he may just be holding a grudge against "Shalamov" for double-crossing him. All the feelings of guilt and all the need for self-justification that come into play are exclusively "Shalamov's." He has obtained something from Shestakov on false pretenses; whereas, as the penultimate paragraph tells us with a kind of melancholy sarcasm, the authorities have played fair in this case—they could have used Shestakov and then shot him to cover their tracks.[78] The ultimate ironic belittling of the two cans of condensed milk reflects "Shalamov's" residual hankering after a prima facie morality. He has, after all, broken a contract, albeit with a double-crosser. Obviously, however, the real cause of his remorse lies in his failure to prevent Shestakov's deception of five other people—though, all things considered, in his dystrophic condition he could not seek them out. According to a contemporary moral convention, failing to help someone is perceived as less bad than deliberately hurting someone (Harman 1977: 111).[79] Amidst chronic starvation, sharing a spoonful of condensed milk would require a superhuman effort, let alone the summoning of a goner's last energy to seek out the prospective victims of the provocation.

On meeting Shestakov in the epilogue, "Shalamov" is not averse to greeting him: he is not entitled to a righteous stand. Mainly, however, he does not expect the stool pigeon to try to destroy him for having deciphered him. Shestakov, it appears, is not the kind to deliberately seek to hurt another person *on his own initiative*. In ethical theory this is called the principle of the "double effect": it is bad enough to hurt someone while seeking other goals; but it is still worse to actually aim to injure the other (Harman 1977: 58). Thus the acts of both Shestakov, the instrument of the victimizers, and "Shalamov," the victim, are describable in terms of bad and worse, or bad and less bad. The two have drawn the lines across their souls at different distances from the poles of total saintliness and total evil.

A diametrically opposite situation is described in the story "Shakhmaty Doktora Kuzmenko" ["The Chess Set of Doctor Kuzmenko"] (*KR-2*). "Shalamov" and Dr. Kuzmenko, formerly a camp surgeon, are about to play chess using a unique set fashioned out of the prison-ration bread that has been chewed and brought to a moldable condition by the prisoners' saliva. This chess set, whose figures represent historical personages from the Times of Trouble, the period of political turmoil following the death of the czar Boris Godunov, was made by the sculptor Kulagin. Two pieces are missing: the black queen, now lying headless in Dr. Kuzmenko's drawer, and the white rook. Driven to the lethal stage of pellagric dementia, Kulagin started eating his chessmen. It was too late; he died after swallowing the rook and biting off the head of the queen. At this point the surgeon makes the following remark:

> "I did not give the order to get the rook out of his stomach. It could have been done at the post-mortem. Also the head of the Queen. . . . Therefore this game, this match, is two figures short. Your turn, maestro."
> "No," I said. "I somehow don't feel like it any more." (458–59)

"Shalamov's" nausea here is not a matter of tactile squeamishness: more likely, it is caused by the sudden realization that there is a moral gulf between him and the kindred intellectual with whom he has just been engaged in a highly meaningful conversation about historical documentation, unsolved mysteries, and prisoners' fates. A person is perceived as morally alien if he or she so much as *considers* certain things as *options* (Williams 1985: 185). Surgeons and pathologists are known to be hardened, and, after all, Dr. Kuzmenko did not commit the sacrilege of having the missing chess pieces extracted from the corpse. Yet the way he speaks about it suggests that he must have *considered this option,* which makes it impossible for "Shalamov" to play chess with him, at least with this particular set. Here the discovery of the qualitative difference in the moral make-up of the two men on the same side of the barricade starkly contrasts with the reluctant discovery of the quantitative nature of the difference between "Shalamov" and Shestakov, a defector to the other side.

In *The Glove, or KR-2* Shalamov's measurements of the distance between prima facie imperatives and the moral semiotics of the camps apply to the authorial persona as well as to other people. In the story "Vechnaia merzlota" ["Permafrost"] (*KR-2*) adherence to high-minded new-broom prima facie rules leads to a tragedy: the focalizer, a newly appointed medic, demands that a healthy prisoner be sent off to general works and his place as a janitor be taken by a goner who can be rescued that way; what he does not know is that the able-bodied janitor is weak in spirit and will commit suicide rather than face the work in the mines. The story ends with the words "And I suddenly understood that it was too late for me to study medicine and life" (246)—one may, apparently, fail the test of faith by clinging to the faith too tenaciously. Yet the whole issue of the test of faith is called into question by the two narratives that follow "Permafrost," namely "Ivan Bogdanov" and "Yakov Ovseevich Zavodnik" (246–52 and 253–63).

The protagonist of the latter story is a black-haired, black-bearded Jew, once a fiery Civil War commissar. No self-righteous "idealist," Zavodnik is able to preserve himself and help the prisoners who work in his small woodcutting team. He supplies the hospital with the firewood it needs and with the unregistered extra as bribe. His personal integrity (his possessions and diet are the same as those of the unprivileged prisoners) combines with a bland readiness to cook the books; his personal courage and violently passionate outbursts against oppression combine with a readiness to slave for the mildly corrupt hospital director. In terms of the *all-things-considered* morality, his conduct is right. However, the end of the story suggests that his slave-master relationship with a representative of the authorities is not just a case of outward contingencies: despite his fiery assertions of independence, Zavodnik, like Lazarson in "Vishera," seems to have lost his moral-intellectual autonomy. When the narrator visits him, safely re-installed in his pre-camp job in Moscow, they recollect a friend and benefactor who has not been allowed to return to his native Leningrad. Suddenly Zavodnik says: "The government knows better. It's in my and your cases that everything is clear, and with Iarotskii it is probably a whole different sort of thing . . . " Obviously, Zavodnik has lost the clarity of moral vision, a camp survivor's most treasured compensation for the years of suffering. In 1937, in the Lefortovo torture prison, Zavodnik, no Judas, had assaulted the interrogator who wanted him to "expose" his former boss, the veteran Bolshevik Zelenskii. His hip was broken by the ensuing beatings, leaving him with a permanent limp. After recuperation in the prison hospital, Zavodnik signed, without reading, everything that could save his life—by that time Zelenskii had been shot anyway (253–54). In the last line of the story Shalamov says: "I have never been to see Yakov Ovseevich Zavodnik again, though I remain his friend" (263). Zavodnik did not, indeed, commit any concrete act of betrayal after which one would no longer wish to be his friend; he merely became the regime's accomplice after the fact.

Zavodnik's story immediately follows that of the bookkeeper Ivan Bogdanov, who had likewise made his relatively smooth way through the camps by systematically cooking the books in the service of corrupt bosses. What strikes one on a first reading of "Ivan Bogdanov" is the lack of warmth with which the narrator describes this handsome young man who helped him twice—when he sought out and destroyed the record of the instruction that Shalamov should be kept at hard physical labor and when he appeared on the scene, like a godsend, with some stocked-up onions of which, sick and conscious of avitaminosis, Shalamov had been dreaming. At the end of the story it turns out that Bogdanov's acts of kindness are a complement of his involvement with the secret police: willing to help Shalamov make sense of an impending new frame-up, he mentions, in a matter-of-fact way, that he has "worked for them" as an informer. This is Shalamov's version of the "double agent" topos: if Judas kissed in order to betray, people like Bogdanov may have betrayed in order to kiss.

Since the early nineties, when the reputations of great numbers of people in the post-Gorbachev Russia, the Baltic states, East Germany, and elsewhere were ruined by revelations of their past relationships with the secret police, the problem of the extent of moral responsibility for such relationships has become a topical issue. The collaboration is sometimes represented as a compromise: "Yes, he did sign, he did write a pro-forma report—but in such a way as not to do anybody any actual harm." Here again, the *all-things-considered* morality is invoked to counterbalance the old prima facie rule, according to which one should not make any deals with the NKVD, the KGB, the Stasie, and such like. In Gulag literature this rule is called into question but indirectly reconfirmed in, for instance, Antoni Ekart's account of his cat-and-mouse game with the secret police, in the character of Ruska Doronin, "the double," of Solzhenit-

syn's *The First Circle,* and in Yury Dombrovsky's wearily charitable exploration of a dense network of betrayals in *The Faculty of Unnecessary Things.*
Solzhenitsyn tells the story of his having come dangerously close to some
sort of a compromise with the surveillance operative in his Kaluga-Gate
camp (*GA* 3: 12), but his general treatment of informers and stool pigeons is almost uniformly and conventionally negative. Shalamov, like
Solzhenitsyn, belonged to the majority that regarded deals with the secret police as tantamount to selling one's soul—to a notoriously devi-
ous buyer. But his was not a blanket condemnation. The intensely highlighted onion in "Ivan Bogdanov" can be taken as an allusion to the
parable presented in Dostoevsky's *The Brothers Karamazov:* for having
given an onion to a beggar, an old sinner is given her chance of salvation.
Paradoxically, while Shalamov is usually regarded as presenting the most
gloomy view of camp conditions and experience, to some extent he is
more tolerant of his fellow-sufferers than those authors who, like Solzhenitsyn, insist on the possibility of moral elevation in the camps. And
yet, while denying himself the right to judge Bogdanov, Shalamov seems
to reserve the right of withholding the kind of sympathy with which
he would write about the doctor Andrei Mikhailovich in "Dominoes" or
Andrei Platonov of "The Snake Charmer." At the end of "Perchatka"
["The Glove"], the first story of the cycle, Shalamov claims that one
should remember all the good things a hundred years, and all the bad
things two hundred. "This," he concludes, "is where I differ from all the
Russian humanists of the nineteenth and the twentieth centuries" (180).
Whereas Solzhenitsyn, Panin, and Olitskaya posited the necessity of constant political struggle with the oppressive regime while Ivanov-Razumnik
and Evgenia Ginzburg regarded such struggle as futile and opted for
preserving the cultural tradition in expectation of better times, Shalamov
insisted on the necessity of a thorough critical reassessment of this tradition, a reassessment from which not even Pushkin's conceptual blue-
prints were exempt.[80] Among the focal points of his subversion is the
insistence on *the truth* as a higher value than any one's conception of *the
good.* "When I hear talk of 'the good,'" he wrote to Iulii Shreider in 1968,
"I pick up my hat and leave" (Shreider 1989: 233).

Shalamov's main contribution to the repertoire of world literature
lies in his courageous and philosophically profound exploration of the
psychology of prolonged physical and moral suffering, of the inner life
of people whose consciousness shrank as a result of a coercive, energy-
draining heightening of the sensations of hunger, cold, and fatigue.
Verbal art has no way of rendering these states except through their results: the contraction of horizons, the reversed-telescope view of values,
the effacement of a spectrum of emotions, the acute sense of relative

priorities in the satisfaction of one's needs. In order to convey at least the cognitive value of such an experience and help the readers adjust their attitudes to the ethical reality that it represents, Shalamov devised the kind of prose that epitomizes the nature of a literary document as a multifunctional object whose form is grounded in an ethical intention so genuine that its artistic merit seems to be the natural consequence of its truth.

7 The Gulag Fiction of Aleksandr Solzhenitsyn

Whereas in reading most of Shalamov's stories one hesitates between accepting them as fictionalized or as directly referential, the pact offered by Aleksandr Solzhenitsyn's *One Day in the Life of Ivan Denisovich* and *The First Circle* is, formally, fictional. These works belong to a type of "veridical prose" that is dominated not by generalized, almost algebraic, referentiality, as in the case of Shalamov, but by the sample convention. The characters and events are not referential, yet they are felt to be typical, to present a paradigm, a *replicating* model of human attitudes and fates enmeshed in a system of regularities that obtained in the world of the camps. Essentially, the pact that the reader is invited to enter is *metafictional:* it promotes attention to the links between the texts and the reality that they point at, as well as to the nature, extent, and purpose of the fictionalization.

* * *

The life of an author of veridical fiction is the mandatory immediate context for his works. Aleksandr Isaevich Solzhenitsyn was born in 1918, in Kislovodsk, a posthumous son of an officer killed in a gun accident after his return from the World War I front lines.[1] His childhood was spent in Rostov on the Don, where his mother worked as an underpaid secretary while making every effort to conceal her upper-middle-class origins. At Rostov University he studied physics, mathematics, and history, while also taking an extra-mural course in literature at the Moscow Institute for Philosophy, Literature and Art. From his early days he dreamed of writing the history of the October Revolution, unable to foresee what a critical stance his many-volume epos *The Red Wheel* would take toward it in the seventies and eighties.

After Germany's assault on the Soviet Union in June 1941, Solzhenitsyn was mobilized, completed an officer's course, and, until 1945 served with distinction in the artillery. Toward the end of the war his unit was stationed in East Prussia, the approximate site of the defeat of General Samsonov's armies in August 1914, which Solzhenitsyn would describe in the first novel of *The Red Wheel* series. It was here that Stalin's purge of the army overtook him: ten days after leading his battery out of a German encirclement, he was arrested for remarks made in a letter to a friend. Under the influence of his cellmates in Moscow's Butyrki prison, he began to move from his Marxist convictions to a radically critical view of the Soviet ideology and society.

Solzhenitsyn served a part of his eight-year sentence in labor camps in or near Moscow (see *GA* 3: 6 and the play "The Tenderfoot and the Tart"). Later he was transferred to the Marfino in-camp research institute, the Mavrino *sharashka* of *The First Circle*. The last two years of his camp life were spent in Ekibastuz near Karaganda, the approximate setting of *One Day in the Life of Ivan Denisovich,* where, not long before his sentence was to expire, he participated in a strike. At that time he had a swelling in his abdomen, and he revealed it at a "convenient" moment, when the incipient rebellion was crushed and his visibility on the scene of action might have led to new tribulations. The tumor was surgically removed in a camp hospital; Solzhenitsyn was released soon afterward and sent into exile in Kok Terek in southwestern Kazakhstan. The lump began to grow again, causing bad pains. It was near-miraculously cured in a Tashkent hospital, where Solzhenitsyn would eventually set his novel *Cancer Ward.*

In the camp Solzhenitsyn started mentally composing a poem ("Prussian Nights") and contemplating a play and a novel. The actual writing, still secret, began after his release. In Kok Terek he became friendly with fellow exiles Elena Aleksandrovna and Nikolai Ivanovich Zubov (the Kadmins of *Cancer Ward*), who initiated him into the fine art of hiding manuscripts (1995: 3–25). In 1956 he was allowed to return to European Russia. Observations made in the village of Miltsevo, his first station, inspired his story "Matryona's Homestead." Returning to Natalya Reshetov-skaya, who had divorced him a year before his release, he moved to the town of Ryazan; there he taught high school physics and mathematics while continuing to write "in the underground," in the hope of recording all he had to say before the regime, or cancer, might catch up with him. In 1961, after the Twenty-Second Party Congress, he judged the time propitious for getting some of his camp stories into print. The story of the November 1962 *Novyi mir* publication of *One Day in the Life of Ivan Denisovich* (see Solzhenitsyn 1979: 10–49; Scammell 1984: 282–449), flanked by a convoy of loyalist works in other periodicals,[2] is well known.

* * *

The appearance of *One Day in the Life of Ivan Denisovich* dealt a crushing blow to the view of Soviet concentration camps as a marginal phenomenon. This effect was due not so much to the work's informational content as to its narrative art. The story does not present a totally reliable and comprehensive picture of labor-camp experience. It tells the truth, but not the whole truth, being set in a Kazakhstan camp, where life was better than in the lead-mining camps of the same region or in the icy Arctic camps. This is a special-regime camp: the inmates wear numbers but are spared the company of professional criminals. The construction work on which they are employed is more acceptable in human terms than mining—at bricklaying a prisoner could, possibly, whip up the work enthusiasm that facilitated the story's publication in a Soviet journal.[3] In a letter to Solzhenitsyn, Shalamov points to a number of symptomatic features that distinguish the camp in the story from the Kolyma camps he had known: there is a cat—it has not been killed and eaten; one needs spoons —the mush in the bowl is not totally liquid; the hands of Ivan Denisovich are not frostbitten (1990b: 62–89).[4] All this must have been true for the place and the time, 1951. Accordingly, in a word-to-the-wise manner, Solzhenitsyn weaves into the story allusions to the rising wave of squealer murders (see *GA* 5: 10), a prelude to the camp uprisings of the fifties.

Solzhenitsyn himself admits having "lightened" the material in order not to forfeit his opportunity to publish it (1979: 13).[5] Yet the sweeping impression of realism in the presentation of a *zek*'s life is not merely a matter of the relative ignorance of the reading public; it is produced by his *paradigmatic* technique. Though the tale seems to unfold in a straightforward, traditional, and goal-oriented way, it is a carefully crafted obliquely self-reflexive narrative.

The paradigmatic method of *Ivan Denisovich* consists in its systematic account of a largely representative day, from reveille to lights out. The narrative is punctuated with references to the position of the sun or the moon—the watchless prisoners' aids in telling the time. The story begins and ends in a darkness pierced by floodlights; in between, the prisoners work in a building whose windows are covered with roofing felt for warmth. This foul-is-fair switch of light and darkness evokes the post-Dostoevskian theme of a hard-labor jail as "a world apart," as well as the Biblical motif of "darkness in daytime" (Job 5:14).

The narrative presents the conditions of camp life and human responses to them. Samples of practical logistics of adaptation alternate with those of specific emotional states, such as the after-lunch numbness of Buinovsky—a stage in his transformation "from an eager, confident naval officer with a ringing voice into an inert, though wary, zek" (1963: 81). The cast of the characters is a social cross section, including minor paradigms of the charges on which people were imprisoned in the postwar years and of in-camp behavior patterns. The details of camp life are presented not as static features of the setting but as a paradigm of possible events, with the reader kept in suspense about the success or failure of Shukhov's consecutive tasks.

The testimonial function of the story is enhanced by its calculated inclusion of an optimal amount of data on camp life. The auxiliary character of the story's events is partly veiled: the discourse on the topography and semiotics of this minor dystopia does not become ponderous because different aspects of the setting are discussed at exactly the most relevant moments of the story time. Thus the jobs that can be done before the morning roll call are listed after Ivan Denisovich Shukhov awakes; the possible outcomes of the frisking, when that ritual begins. Information blocks are, moreover, usually provided when Shukhov is supposed to be waiting for something, for example, for his turn to be frisked—they fill, as it were, the monotonous stretches of the story time. We learn what a medic must do in the camp infirmary while Shukhov is sitting there with a thermometer, hoping that he has a sufficiently high temperature to be released from work; the procedure for getting parcels from home is explained while Shukhov is securing Tsezar's place in the parcel queue; the life of Shukhov's family in their home village is referred to while he is walking to the work site and thinking what to write his wife in the next letter. Though the narrative is largely our guidebook through the camp setting, the reader is constantly held in suspense about the successive hurdles that the protagonist has to overcome. The sequence of the situations in which Shukhov tries to minimize the misery of his hungry and sick condition de-emphasizes the dominance of replication over simulation in the referential mode of the story.

The replicating, paradigmatic method is both well served and well masked by the choice of a peasant's point of view.[6] This choice is a deliberate reminder that the peasants, rather than the Old Bolsheviks and the intelligentsia, were the most numerous victims of Stalinist repression. The focus on the peasant has, moreover, a narrative function: the character of Ivan Denisovich is perfectly suited for the exploration of the tensions between individual and communal concerns. Though Shukhov is a well-rounded personality rather than a generalized Everyman, he is free of the eccentricities that might undermine his representative status. He wholly identifies with the common lot of the prisoners, at the same time constantly seeking little individual benefits that sometimes rub off on his associates.[7] Owing to his cleverness, skills, alertness, cunning, mischief, stamina, and benevolence, this peasant-craftsman is sufficiently endearing to invite the reader's empathy. Yet Solzhenitsyn also presents Shukhov as ignorant and as earnestly holding archaic folkloristic beliefs (e.g., that God thriftily splits the old moon into stars). This distances us from Ivan Denisovich and helps us to observe him more critically, noting, for instance, that his sense of justice is not infallible, that his compassion is selective, and that there are gray areas in his conduct (e.g., when he snatches a tray from a weaker prisoner in accordance with the "might-is-right" principle). Solzhenitsyn modifies the archetype of Tolstoy's saintly Platon Karataev (Shneerson 1984: 116), judiciously avoiding sentimentality.

Though Shukhov is the focal character of the narrative, the authorial third-person voice does not always imitate his plain-folk camp idiom: not all the syntactic constructions and vocabulary are typical of an uneducated man. On at least one occasion the narrator presents information unavailable to Shukhov—the fact that the prison doctor has turned a young poet into a medic so that the latter may have the time and the privacy to write (33–34). Here Solzhenitsyn breaks the rules of focalization[8] in order to remind the reader of a generation of writers swallowed up by the Gulag. As in camp memoirs, aesthetic finish is deliberately sacrificed to ethical considerations.

In order to supply information about camp life and logistics, Solzhenitsyn employs two conventions of internally focalized narratives: (1) the presentation of what the focalizer sees or thinks at a given moment of the story time and (2) the presentation of what he knows of the situation in general. Thus the shortness of the time at the prisoners' disposal after work is conveyed through Shukhov's weighing his options on the way back to the barracks. By contrast, the possible ingredients of the prisoners' balanda (trash soup) at different seasons, catalogued while Shukhov is supposed to be eating this soup for his breakfast (28–29), reflect not his concrete thoughts of the moment but his diffuse general awareness.[9] In cases of minor decision-making, Shukhov seems to be communicating with himself: the combination of his characteristic idiom with a more literary authorial style reflects the partially verbalized nature of his deliberations; the author seems to be "translating" the non-verbal movements of his consciousness. The setting, described for the benefit of the reader, includes many things that would be too familiar for Shukhov to register. When these details are discussed in an idiom similar to Shukhov's, the narrative seems to suggest the way in which Shukhov might show the ropes to a newcomer (cf. the tour-guiding topos in utopian narratives); this impression is enhanced by the naïve mistakes made by a recent initiate, Captain Buinovsky. The social distance that separates the two men precludes Shukhov's volunteering advice; the equivalent of such advice is reserved, as it were, for the reader, who is placed in the cognitive position of a camp debutant.

The paradigmatic effect of the story hinges on the catalogue-like structure of the informational blocks. Almost each block contains a spectrum of possibilities: what can be done by the prisoners, what the guards might do to them, what they might expect should the circumstances change. The day is relatively lucky (which helps to ease the broad audience's way into the camp subject and get the material past the censor): usually the better of the potential alternatives materialize. The worse possibilities are, however, likewise evoked: Shukhov might have been sent to the punishment cell (like Buinovsky); his column might have failed to beat that of the tool shops to the camp gate after work; a parcel from home might have failed to arrive for Tsezar. What looks like a multiple-choice situation actually leaves Shukhov very few options: most often he knows the alternatives but has no way of telling which of them will emerge.

The resulting suspense about the outcome of each episode and the resulting theme-cum-variations deployment of motifs (e.g., theme: morning; variations: all the things that can be done before the first roll call) ensure the absence of monotony. Always relevant, pedagogically timed, clear, and narrated in a colloquial but not chatty manner, the blocks of information about camp conditions and the logistics of adaptation never slip into *longeur*. The handling of space in the story is likewise unobtrusively comprehensive: instead of presenting the camp topography in an "on-the-left/on-the-right" manner, Solzhenitsyn mentions the landmarks as Shukhov is walking past them. The reader's realization that the story of the fictional Ivan Denisovich may be just a vehicle for "an anthropologist's guide to the institution" (Hosking 1980: 41) is kept in abeyance.

The paradigmatic method is bolstered by frequent reminders that, despite Shukhov's picaresque feats,[10] the narrated events represent a variation on the usual state of affairs. Shukhov's lucky breaks are but *reprieves* from suffering. The last paragraph places his day into the perspective of his ten-year sentence; the words "as usual" in the first paragraph prepare us to accept the story as a sample:

> At five o'clock that morning, reveille was sounded, as usual, by the blows of a hammer on a length of rail hanging up near the staff quarters. The intermittent sound barely penetrated the windowpanes on which the frost lay two fingers thick, and they ended almost as soon as they'd begun. It was cold outside, and the campguard was reluctant to go on beating out the reveille for long. (17)

Like Gulag memoirs, the story includes the Larger Zone topos: despite the barbed wire, the camp is not encapsulated—the guards, with their paranoia and their talk about cereals, are but slightly better off than the prisoners; and Shukhov's family in the village may be as hungry as himself (cf. also Rothberg 1971: 20).

A comparison with the Nazi *Lager*s is invited through the presence of a former POW who had been tortured by the Germans and, once back in his homeland, sent to the camps instead of to sanatoria (this too was quite a revelation to many of the contemporary readers). The first-paragraph reference to the guard's reluctance to go on banging in the bitter cold creates a somewhat more relaxed atmosphere than the one known to reign in Nazi camps. A realistic detail like the *pulsating* on-and-off sound shades into symbolism: in tune with the "pulsation" method of camp memoirs, the story avowedly deals with an "off" stage in a *zek*'s ordeal, with a reprieve that, one knows, may well be followed by acute suffering. In his previous camp Shukhov nearly died of scurvy and exhaustion.

The story thus repeatedly encourages our checking of its material against our own picture of reality. It also contains an auto-descriptive hint that reminds us of the metafictional nature of the reader-author pact. In the hope of being offered some tobacco Shukhov stays to listen to the dialogue between Tsezar and another intellectual, X 123, "a stringy old man who was serving a twenty-year sentence" (83). X 123 scolds Tsezar for praising the spectacle of the dance of the *oprichniki,* the czar's terror police, in Eisenstein's film *Ivan the Terrible* and thus closing his eyes to the moral significance of that terror gang in Russian history. X 123 brands Tsezar's defense of art as technique ("Art isn't a matter of *what* but of *how*" [84]) not only as a hollow escape into aesthetics ("It's all so arty there's no art left in it. Spice and poppy-seed instead of everyday bread and butter!" [84]) but also as a support of the Lie: "And then, that vicious political idea—the justification of personal tyranny. A mockery of the memory of three generations of Russian intelligentsia" (84). When Tsezar counters that Eisenstein would not have "gotten away with" any other interpretation, X 123 explodes: "Gotten away with? Ugh! Then don't call him a genius! Call him an ass-kisser, obeying a vicious dog's orders. Geniuses don't adjust their interpretations to suit the taste of tyrants!" (84). A parenthetic remark registers Shukhov's disapproval of the insufficient attention that X 123 pays to his food: "He ate as if his lips were made of wood. The kasha would do him no good" (84). Gulag writers (e.g., Panin 1976: 161–63; Shalamov, *KR* 111–19) often comment on the way in which one's rations should be eaten, but the function of Shukhov's disapproval here is also to preempt an unqualified acceptance of the attitudes of X-123.[11] Solzhenitsyn himself had "lightened" the story so that it might pass the censorship while sensitizing the reader to the proximity of Room 101.

The strange ways of art in a totalitarian society are refracted in the account of Shukhov's thoughts about the carpet-painting, the profitable occupation described in his wife's letter:

> All you had to do was to put the stencil on and paint through the little holes with a brush. There were three sorts of carpets . . . : the "Troika," an officer of the hussars driving a beautiful troika; the "Reindeer"; and a third with a Persian-style pattern. They had no other designs, but people all over the country were glad to get these and snatch them out of the painters' hands. (50)

Whereas anyone, as Shukhov's wife writes, can produce the stenciled carpets, the three professional painters in Shukhov's camp are employed in drawing the numbers on the prisoners' clothing.[12] Thus the artists are officially reduced to living stencils; unofficially, they are engaged in painting pictures for the camp bosses, catering to their tastes.

The motif of the stencil also pertains to the relation of Gulag writing to the national literary tradition. Solzhenitsyn had once toyed with Tolstoy's suggestion that a novel could take for its subject the life of all of Europe for a century or the life of a peasant for a single day. He considered describing a day in the life of a schoolteacher. As the project would not get off the ground, he switched to the Gulag material that was urging him on and reverted to the Tolstoyan idea of concentrating on a peasant (Scammell 1984: 382). Yet despite Solzhenitsyn's well-known interest in Tolstoy (whose philosophical ideas he reluctantly rejected), his historical material and context did not allow him to stay within the framework of nineteenth-century realistic fiction. *Ivan Denisovich* describes not what is possible in a normal state of affairs but, rather, what is possible when the distorted becomes the norm. Like most of Solzhenitsyn's other work the novella is denied the watertight formal finish of the classical novel with its jealously guarded dramatic illusion. There is a two-way seepage between the fictional world and the extratextual reality—through the implicit auto-descriptive questioning of the model that the story constructs and through the occasional formal imperfections that in effect signal the author's privileging, if need be, of the "what" over the "how." The multiple-choice listing of alternative occurrences and their conditions is likewise a sign of narrative self-consciousness and of the functionality of the "plot": the paradigmatic method of *Ivan Denisovich* is Solzhenitsyn's version of the Borgesian "forking-paths" technique.

At the historical juncture when *One Day in the Life of Ivan Denisovich* was being prepared for publication, its author was in a double bind. He had to resign himself to telling only part of the truth in order to have his camp material published in the USSR, but he also had to present this incomplete truth as *typical* (rather than as individual, marginal, contingent) in order to legitimize his subject matter. The paradigmatic narrative method provided the solution (finding ad hoc solutions is thematized in the story); and it was largely this technique, as well as the force and the genuineness of the author's ethical drive behind it, that extended the sense of the representative character of Shukhov's experience to the whole subject of the Gulag. The ethics of the story's form lay in the aesthetic choices that helped to institutionalize its subject as material for literary exploration.

* * *

One of Solzhenitsyn's earliest major works was the novel *The First Circle,* completed in 1958. In 1963–64, encouraged by the success of *Ivan Denisovich* (*Novyi mir* also accepted a few more of his stories), Solzhenitsyn "lightened" the novel, toning down its politically most subversive material. A variant of this self-censored 87-chapter revision (*FC87*) made its way to Tamizdat presses in 1968.[13] Later the same year, the hopes of publication in the Soviet Union having vanished, Solzhenitsyn restored the original version of the book. This 96-chapter version (*FC96*) was amended in 1978 and came out as volume 1 of the Vermont-YMCA *Collected Works.*[14] However, until its Moscow publication of 1990, this version did not reach a public as broad as that of *FC87,* which remained an ontological event in its own right. As a result, the less subversive *FC87* graces the bookshelves of Samizdat and Tamizdat audiences, whereas the more subversive *FC96* those of the formerly more conformist *glasnost* readers.

In terms of their material, the two versions complement each other like Borgesian forking paths. In a 1978 retrospect Solzhenitsyn wrote: "Such was life during all those years, either under the constant pressure of conspiracy or in the race of an imposed struggle, that there was no time to manage everything: to give the completed works a finished form. No works printed in Soviet publications could have such a form: the vaults of censorship were always oppressive, or else someone's safety demanded concealments. There was also the natural shortcoming of the Samizdat:

the author could not control retypings—and it is in such a variant form that the books would reach the West, and be published. In those cases when I sent the work to the West myself, neither I nor the people close to me could check the galleys" (3). *FC96* is free from these shortcomings, longer, and in some ways richer, yet its artistic quality does not consistently surpass that of *FC87*. In *FC96* Innokenty Volodin is arrested for phoning the American embassy to say that a Soviet spy is about to receive the secrets of the American atomic bomb; in *FC87* his "crime" is calling the doctor who has treated him in his childhood to warn him against contacts with foreign colleagues. Here Volodin is stimulated by a purely moral impulse—the aim of his non-political humane act is to prevent the doctor's arrest; his own suffering for such an act is all the more unjust. This version of the plot is a forceful indictment of the regime that victimizes morally innocent people: Volodin's first name is "Innocent," and he emerges as a lovable, sophisticated, yet not particularly complex young man.

In *FC87* Rubin's collaboration with the police in the capture of Volodin is particularly heinous and but weakly excused by the indication that but for Rubin's narrowing down the circle of suspects, more people might have been arrested. By concentrating on the scientific aspect of his work, Rubin defers thoughts of the predicament of the potential victim, whose voice he rather likes. Always the philologist, he is more interested in the etymology of the suspects' names than in their impending fate. Moreover, not content with basic research in phonoscopy, he proposes a practical application: a phonoscopic library to supplement the fingerprint collections of the police.

In *FC96* the moral significance of Rubin's endeavors to place phonoscopy at the service of the secret police is milder. As a sincere Communist and patriot, he believes in helping to reinforce his country's defenses: one need not, indeed, be a fanatic to condemn defectors and approve of one's country's counterespionage. Here Rubin's error is presented as ideological rather than moral—he does not understand that the atomic bomb should be kept out of Stalin's reach. This version of the plot is closer to the actual event involving Lev Kopelev, the prototype for Rubin.[15] *FC96* partly exonerates Rubin in the Volodin case. The account of Rubin's surging memories of having been tricked into denouncing his own cousin (*FC87:* 412–13) presents him as a victim of the regime's manipulations, a near-tragic character whose proud virtues lead him to acts that he will have to forget in order to go on living. In *FC96*, to heighten the drama, the cousin is turned into a brother (168–69).

The two versions also differ in the portrayal of Volodin. In *FC87* he is a young "Epicurean," a member of the privilegentsia, a Soviet golden youth who, on discovering papers left by his late mother, finds out, with resentful astonishment, that Soviet education has deprived him of vast intellectual treasures. The discovery removes the scales from his eyes and awakens him to the political and moral corruption of the regime that he serves. The extent of his conversion is not defined, though it is shown that he welcomes a similar awakening in his wife's sister Klara. Yet Volodin does not undertake any really subversive action; he is punished for freedom of thought and a personal loyalty, which is a more representative experience, and a more poignant predicament, than that of his counterpart in *FC96*.

In *FC87* the sense of the tragic absurdity of Volodin's fate is tinged with tenderness and pity; in *FC96* it is partly replaced by ideological issues. Here Volodin's education is completed by his uncle Avenir, whose name, French for "the future," evokes the liberal revolutionary enthusiasm of the early years of the century. Volodin's calling the American embassy is an ideological act, and it is not "for nothing" that he is ultimately to suffer. In the broader context of Solzhenitsyn's work, this turn of the plot reflects two problematic positions.

The first issue is that Solzhenitsyn's longing for supererogation, evident in, for instance, his discussion of people's behavior on their being arrested (*GA* 1: 1); this longing can be traced throughout his writings.[16] His works stage a conflict between two views of human potentiality: the "low" view, that bases motivation on self-interest and is brilliantly applied in his analysis of the fears and interests of the society dominated by the Gulag (*GA* 3: 20, 21; 4: 3), and the "high" view, that accepts the possibility of self-denial, heroism, uncompromising honor, and spirituality (*GA* 4: 1 and 4).[17] Solzhenitsyn believes that imprisonment can lead to moral transcendence; yet he does not downplay his awareness that camp experience can have the opposite effect: in *The Gulag Archipelago* the chapters on moral elevation and degradation are juxtaposed (4: 1 and 2). He is, moreover, keenly aware that the mortality toll in prisons and camps largely voids the issue of its meaning:

> Lev Tolstoi was right when he *dreamed* of being put in prison. At a certain moment that giant began to dry up. He actually needed prison as a drought needs a shower of rain!
>
> All the writers who wrote about prison but who did not themselves serve time there considered it their duty to express sympathy for prisoners and to curse prison. I . . . have served enough time there. I nourished my soul there, and I say without hesitation:
>
> *"Bless you prison,* for having been in my life!"
>
> And from beyond the grave come replies: It is very well for you to say that—when you came out of it alive! (*GA* 4: 1, pp. 616–17).

If Shalamov, Margolin, and Herling insist that camp experience always changes people for the worse, Solzhenitsyn cherishes examples of personal heroism, stoicism, and intense spiritual life in the camps. Yet the two attitudes differ mainly in emphasis, which is largely grounded in each writer's view of himself before and after the camps. Solzhenitsyn dislikes his young self, regards his early ideology as a mistake, and regrets the corruption that the Soviet upbringing had produced in him: in prisons and camps, his second university, he was gradually disembarrassed of layers of moral-intellectual dross. In Shalamov's case, on the other hand, there were no ideological errors to regret: though the ideals of his youth were those of the revolutionary movements, he had always been immune to Stalinist propaganda. The camps wrecked his body and may have damaged his moral self, yet it seems that his Aristotelian belief that suffering is detrimental to character is related not to acts[18] but to inaction, ranging from minor inconsiderateness (e.g., for Kozlik in "Dominoes") to an incapacity for supererogation ("Condensed Milk"). Like Primo Levi (1988: 129–31), Shalamov knows that a depleted goner is physically incapable of heroism: even in "Major Pugachev's Last Battle," the uprising is organized by still-healthy prisoners only recently brought from the front. Yet this cannot completely silence the remorse of a person brought up in a cultural tradition where there is nothing between egoism and altruism, where rational individualism is almost completely identified with the former[19] while the latter spills over into supererogation. Whereas Shalamov's stories test and reject this tradition in intellectual terms, emotionally he remains its captive.

Unlike Shalamov, Solzhenitsyn does not insist on a reassessment of the traditional demand for the supererogatory; the demand is not withdrawn, though the nature of supererogation has changed. The dimension that *FC96* loses in comparison with *FC87* is that of the relativization of the supererogatory: *FC87* shows how a totalitarian society turns minimally active humaneness into heroism and conscious callousness into norm.

The other issue involved in Volodin's fate in *FC96* is that of poetic justice. Volodin's responsibility is presented as hereditary: his father participated in the Bolshevik terror. At the end of the chapter that describes Volodin's visit to his uncle, Avenir hints that the sins of the fathers may, indeed, be visited on the children. This suggestion is integrated into the broader network of the novel's motifs, but its ring on the intertextual plane is disturbing: in *The Gulag Archipelago* Solzhenitsyn confesses, for instance, that he cannot treat Latvian prisoners with the same sense of shame and compassion as he does the Lithuanian and Estonian: Latvians of the previous generation had played too active a role in the Bolshevik revolution ("My attitude to the Latvians was more complicated. There was a fatality in their plight. They had sown the seed themselves" [*GA* 5: 2, p. 44]). The honesty of this admission only partly outweighs the unfairness of the attitude or the danger of perpetuating a stigma. The most sophisticated intellectuals have their paleological moments. In Solzhenitsyn, touches like these are aesthetically flawed insofar as they *express* ready-made attitudes instead of *testing and refining* them; they liberate a part of the audience from the author's spell yet lend support to the simplifications and prejudices of another part. Still, as noted in the previous chapter, the imperfect quality of Gulag writings is a mark of their veridical authenticity.

Thus, though *FC96* is a richer text, especially with its brilliant chapters on Stalin, it is not in all respects better than *FC87*. In fact, the bifurcated existence of *The First Circle* and its interactive seepage with extratextual reality can be regarded as aspects of its metafictional pact with the reader.

* * *

The paradigmatic method of *The First Circle* involves strategies analogous to those of Hemingway's in *For Whom the Bell Tolls:* the frame of a few days in which the experience of a lifetime has to be lived; the cast of characters who exemplify different perspectives; glimpses of human reality on both sides of a conflict; the expansion of the scope through inset narratives, flashbacks, and occasional epic catalogues. The parallel techniques must have been called for by a shared need to telescope epic breadth into a claustrophobic setting.

The four days in a *sharashka,* as prison research institutes were called, compress the biographical material of a few years and project a vast view of the Gulag-dominated society, even though institutes of this kind housed but a small minority of *zeks.* The quasi-classical unity of time and place[20] enhances the intensity of the narrative, whereas the *paradigmatic method* prevents the setting of the novel from encapsulating its repertoire.[21]

The method consists of such compositional principles as the "node" structure of the plot, a cross-sectional deployment of characters, a polyphonic arrangement of scenes, and the variations-on-a-theme pattern in the use of recurrent motifs.

A *node,* or a "knot," is Solzhenitsyn's term for a point in time where different strands of action intersect (this is the structural principle of Solzhenitsyn's *The Red Wheel:* each volume is referred to as "a knot"). The historical juncture of *The First Circle* is December 1949, the eve of Stalin's new wave of terror, characterized, among other things, by an intensification of police surveillance. Against this background the novel knits together crises in the lives of different characters: Volodin's suicidal phone call (ironically synchronized with the honors awarded his father-in-law, Makarygin), Gerasimovich's refusal to seek release despite his wife's desperate plea, Nerzhin's assertion of his inner freedom at the risk of expulsion from "the first circle" of the Gulag to its deadly common camps,[22] Sologdin's morally questionable and tactically admirable bid for freedom, and Yakonov's and Roitman's discoveries of the precariousness of their tightrope perch. The drama is heightened by poignant moments in the prisoners' private lives—annual rendezvous with their wives, the beginning or end of camp romances, the arrival of long-awaited letters from home.

The intersection of different planes of action generates a seesaw pattern: as Yakonov's prospects sink, Roitman's rise, and vice versa; as Nerzhin and Gerasimovich are on their way to the grimmer circles of the Archipelago, Sologdin is on his way to release. The principle of nodes dispenses with causal links between such events; instead, the model of connection here is that of "resonance" (Eagle 1977: 52). The role of causality in the peripeteia is small in comparison with that of fatal contingencies: a Gulag inmate is seldom given a chance to make decisions; when he is, his decision may brutally reverse the course of his moral and physical life without becoming a link in a causal chain.[23] Hence the absence of paranoia on the part of veteran prisoners despite their dependent condition and awareness of secret informers; hence also the prevalence of gesture over action. As in most works of camp literature, the structural features of *The First Circle* are rooted in the mimetic content.

The absolute dominance of crisis situations in the plot is one of the major features of the carnivalesque and Lenten narrative modes. A carnival is officially limited in time; and a narrative that creates a carnivalesque atmosphere usually concentrates on a limited period when inclinations, dispositions, and resentments mount to a liminal pitch. A crisis is usually brought on by the gradual increase of the pressures that have been created and obfuscated by the previous social or biographical routine. Whereas the plots of practically all novels contain culmination points followed by dénouement, the emphatically crisis-type plots, in Solzhenitsyn as in Dostoevsky, need no single event (such as an arrival, a departure, a storm, or a discovery) to put the hidden tendencies of the characters to the test: these tendencies grow by themselves until, according to the dialectical principle that Sologdin pathetically seeks to debunk, quantity turns into quality.[24] The gradual increase in quantity is well expressed by the developments of cancerous growths, undetected at first but eventually bringing people to the hospital in *Cancer Ward*. In *The First Circle* the crises are likewise natural, though less obvious, outcomes of previous tendencies: the growth of Nerzhin's mind, the welling paranoia of Stalin and Abakumov, the progress of Research and Development work in surveillance techniques, and the increase in the characters' nervous fatigue.

The node structure of the plot lays the groundwork for an expansion of the novel's repertoire: each of the strands of the knot leads out in a different direction. It also sharpens the presentation of essentials and helps dispense with contingencies. The Aristotelian aesthetics that underlies this technique is explained by the painter Kondrashev-Ivanov in one of the auto-descriptive touches of *The First Circle:* an artist starts his work by admiring nature but then discovers that it has flaws and incongruities (*FC87,* 324); he then seeks to attain the full expression that nature itself does not provide. As Rubin points out, the method has a liability: one may end by overcondensing the colors of good and evil.[25] Yet the heightening that Solzhenitsyn achieves through the crisis-node technique is not so much an intensification of quality as an enhancement of emotional intensities, intellectual issues, and moral dilemmas.

The nodal points of the plot bring together characters who form a replicating *cross section* of different social strata: from government circles, through the scientific elite in prison, to plain-folk prisoners like the concierge Spiridon.[26] There is also a hierarchical paradigm of the system of surveillance, with Stalin at the top, the minister of state security and lesser officials lower down, and prison operatives, guards, and informers at the base. Whereas each personage represents a locus in a cross section, most characters are clearly individualized; there is something of Dickens and Dostoevsky in Solzhenitsyn's ability to convey the flavor of a person's physical presence.

Solzhenitsyn expands the repertoire of the novel through the letters that different characters receive from their families as well as through their conversations and memories. He juxtaposes accounts of the vicious "palace" life of the higher echelons with accounts of the genuine intellectual life of the prisoners, as well as with an element of "slum naturalism" (Bakhtin 1984: 116–19) transpiring through the letters of Dyrsin's wife, through accounts of the privations of the students in the hostel, and through memories of transports, transit prisons, and "real" camps.

The cross sections relate not only to social standing and education but also to ethical attitudes. The Makarygin episode,[27] for instance, presents a spectrum of ways in which the educated class can achieve a *modus vivendi* with the regime: from the thought-suppressing wholeheartedness of the prosecutor Makarygin, through the skillful casuistry of the literary critic who courts Klara, to the uncomfortable compromise of the writer Galakhov. Beyond the pale is an unusual guest, the daughter of a detainee, humiliated by an official to whom she appeals for help; on the margins is the taciturn, embittered Serbian Communist whom hospitalization has so far shielded from the purges; on his way in is the war veteran Shchagin, a Soviet variety of a fortune hunter; near the top, and ready to fall, is the enervated Volodin, hourly expecting arrest.

In a comment on his notion of polyphony, "Each person becomes the main hero as soon as action reverts to him,"[28] Solzhenitsyn understates his achievement. Polyphony is also an apt description of the auditory aspect of the paradigmatic method of *The First Circle.*

Indeed, the dramatically rendered episodes of this novel produce quasi-auditory effects, as of several simultaneous channels of sound. A stereo effect obtains in the chapters that record *the noises of a common room:* being constantly in the presence of various people is an integral part of a *zek*'s experience. Chapters like "Dante's Idea"[29] synchronize conversations; sound tracks seem to overlay and jam one another, and scraps of dialogues in one spot become audible during lulls in dialogues in other parts of the room.

In scenes that present *single conversations with many participants,* the stereo effect is produced by juxtaposing the general conversation with the silent thought track of some of the participants—for example, the tortured Muza and Nadia among their student-hostel roommates or Volodin at the Makarygin soirée. A particularly complex interplay of the outer and the inner attitudes takes place in the scene of the German Christmas celebration, where the thoughts of Rubin and those of his German friends run at cross purposes, as well as at Nerzhin's birthday party, where Rubin, Adamson, Kondrashov-Ivanov, and Sologdin likewise think their somewhat unfair mutually resentful thoughts in silence. Solzhenitsyn seems to suggest that no matter how sophisticated an individual thought process may be, subjectivity usually amounts to simplification. Fictionalization procedures such as a departure from an authorial first-person observer's stance may signify strenuous efforts to transcend the limitations of a single vision, subjecting the author's attitudes to the test of the autonomous dynamics of narrative imagination.

Stereo effects accompany even the novel's few *solo performances.* Thus *FC96* juxtaposes the officialese of prison announcements or the political jargon of the lecture on dialectical materialism with the captive listeners' thoughts or sarcastic responses. Stalin's interior monologues are played against the sycophantic text of his recently published biography, against a book of invective against Tito, and, most devastatingly, against the disembodied text of Stalin's would-be "actual" life story.[30]

Yet the dominant type of dramatic episode in *The First Circle* is that of *dialogue,* ranging from the gentle reticence in Nerzhin's rendezvous with Nadia, through the passionate quarrel of Rubin and Sologdin, to the brutality of the Shikin-Doronin confrontation. Even these episodes involve polyphonic effects, owing to the tacit presence of third parties or to the reader's awareness of voices in the thematic background. For instance, the magnetic soundtrack of Volodin's incriminating phone talk forms the backdrop of the prison-yard conversation between Rubin and Nerzhin in *FC96;* Stalin's conversation with Abakumov overshadows the clash of Yakonov and Sologdin. The meeting of the Gerasimovich couple is staged against that of the Nerzhins; both take place under the eyes of the guards.

The dialogues do not end in shared intellectual conclusions, but they enhance the characters' shared sense of the importance of the issues raised.[31] Their earnestness, in particular in the Sologdin-Rubin dispute, amounts to a resistance to the government's policy of "so treating the questioner that problems which appeared at once overwhelmingly important and utterly insoluble vanish from the questioner's consciousness like evil dreams and trouble him no more" (Berlin 1969: 23). Conceptual inconclusiveness is associated with the intellectual stance taken by Gleb Nerzhin, who treats prison as his school of life, is ready to listen to all opinions, befriends people who hold diametrically opposite views, and maintains a provisional skepticism.[32] Nerzhin secretly engages in historiographical scribbling because he is constantly in search of a pattern, a clarifying paradigm—the paradigmatic method of the novel is, as it were, metafictionally nested in this pursuit. He burns his notes before leaving the *sharashka*—both because they may lead to trouble and because they do not yet contain what he has been seeking. The harsher circles of the Gulag may give him better answers. In the symbolist painting of Kondrashev-Ivanov (*FC87:* 257–58), a knight must negotiate an abyss before he reaches the castle of the Holy Grail.

The polyphonic structure of scenes is enhanced on a rereading of the novel. Though by a demonstratively lucid style Solzhenitsyn seeks to preempt misreadings and provide a basis for a broad intellectual interchange, the full force of his dramatic irony emerges only on a repeated reading. The scene of the mock trial, for instance, gains an additional dimension when we see that Rubin is provoked to this performance by the stool pigeon Isaak Kagan, so that the latter might have something not too grave to report; a number of early scenes acquire new overtones because we know that Ruska Doronin and Lieutenant Nadelashin are likewise informers, each of his own kind. The chapter "Dante's Idea" gains a new interest when we are able to identify some of the speakers. Like the *zek*s who have already completed their initiation, on a repeated reading we are more attuned to camp semiotics and more sensitive to the cross currents of attitude and emotion broadcast from different parts of the crowded room. From subdued learners on a first reading, we turn into alert interpreters on the second.

In keeping with the "pulsation" method of Gulag literature, *The First Circle* concentrates on a period of respite in the protagonist's life, but the *theme-with-variations* handling of motifs, the fourth aspect of its paradigmatic method, provides ample reminders of the general background of suffering. The exceptional nature of the main characters' present situation, "a golden dream" (*FC87:* 579), is forcefully rendered through the efforts that some of them make to remain in "the first circle" and by the amazed responses of the newcomers (*FC87:* 5–9). Links with other circles of hell are established through allusions to the previous experience of Sologdin, the narrative of Volodin's arrest, the scene of Doronin's inter-rogation, and the expulsion of a group of prisoners from the *sharashka* at the end of the novel, completing, as it were, the circle that starts with the scene of arrival in the first chapter. "Multiple non-choice" passages, reminiscent of *Ivan Denisovich,* further expand the Gulag repertoire of the novel:

> Perhaps he will not arrive at his destination. In a cattle car he may die either of dysentery or of hunger, because the zeks will be hauled along for six days without bread. Or the guard may beat him with a hammer because someone had tried to escape. Or, at the end of the journey in an unheated car, they may toss out the frozen corpses of the zeks like logs. (*FC87:* 558)

> Yes, the taiga and the tundra awaited them, the record cold of Oy-myakon and the copper excavations of Dzezkazgan; pick and barrow, starvation rations of soggy bread; the hospital; death. The very worst.
> But there was peace in their hearts. (*FC87:* 579)

In the scenes of Volodin's arrest and his initiation into prison life, the method is slightly different. Here it is made clear that all the humiliating rituals of the prisoner's passage from the Larger Zone to the cells of Lubyanka are routine; a paradigm is implied in the hints that millions of individual victims are passing through the same demolition of identity on a regular basis. Hence the dispassionate impersonality of the veteran guards and the secretly sympathetic curiosity of the new guard who asks Volodin, "Who were you?" (*FC87:* 549).[33]

Another implicit paradigm registers the promptness of the detainees' adaptation to the prison ways. Volodin turns out to be a quick learner:

> The guard left him locked in the room, and Innokenty tried to figure out how to keep his trousers on without suspenders and without most of the buttons. Having had no chance to profit from the experience of dozens of earlier generations of prisoners, Innokenty puzzled a while and then solved the problem alone, just as millions before him had solved it. He discovered where to get a belt: he tied his trousers with his shoe laces. . . . He had not yet worked out how to keep his jacket closed. (*FC87:* 536)

Here, as in *Ivan Denisovich,* Solzhenitsyn presents a lighter case from the paradigm of suffering: Volodin has not been entirely unprepared for the arrest; nor would he be tormented by wondering about its cause. Within several hours he is shown shedding his former pleasure-loving self and acquiring the qualities of a seasoned *zek* who will combine endurance with curiosity and, like Shukhov, appreciate minor improvements. The novelist emphasizes this by recording Volodin's amusement at the picture of a cat on the mug that he is given in the isolation cell; in the next "box," the really "innocent" Shchevronok, whose name Rubin had failed to cross out on the list of suspects, is worse off: "he could not have smiled at the cat at this moment" (*FC87:* 529).

Volodin's first day in prison shows that he has the makings of a camp survivor.[34] In *FC96* this impression is overshadowed by the insistent omens of his heading for an execution (the death penalty was, indeed, legally reintroduced in January 1950).

The Lubyanka episodes are a variation on the theme of Moscow prisons. The regulations in each prison are compared when the *sharashka* inmates are awaiting the meetings with their wives, which usually take place in the prisons rather than in the institute itself: the fortress they are taken to this time is Lefortovo. A third prison, the overcrowded Butyrki, comes alive in the humorous inset "Buddha's Smile." The paradigm of prisons is supplemented by the quasi-bunker from which Stalin rules his empire.[35]

The theme of the prisons is associated with that of surveillance. In his fear of having his telephone tapped (Volodin is, appropriately, a victim of tapping), Stalin has commissioned a scrambler. A procedure for planting microphones in people's homes has been developed in another *sharashka;* there is a stool pigeon in every fifth bed in the dormitory; the secret police are trying to infiltrate students' hostels; Nerzhin and Rubin are victims of secret control in the army. Further technological projects involve devices for listening in on people's conversations in public parks and taking snapshots of whoever passes through certain doors. Visual surveillance ranges from the technology for watching people in Stalin's antechamber to the Judas-window in Lubyanka cell and latrine doors.

The characters' attitudes toward surveillance form yet another paradigm. The best flatly refuse to cooperate: though sorely tempted, Gerasimovich declines the offer to apply his engineering skills to surveillance gadgets in exchange for release. Sologdin, by contrast, gives the authorities a telephone scrambler in return for release—but then a scrambler is, strictly speaking, not an aid in surveillance but an insurance against it. Siromakha, the king of stool pigeons, spies on his colleagues with zeal; Lieutenant Nadelashin writes denunciatory reports so that he may spend the rest of the time indulging his innate kind-heartedness in his relations with the prisoners; Ruska Doronin, an intrepid adventurer, becomes a double agent, unwittingly adopting the behavior pattern that Solzhenitsyn's prelude to the Bogrov chapters in *The Red Wheel* traces to the turn-of-the-century anarchists.

The most complex among these variations is the case of Rubin, who rejects the police officer's assertion that a faithful Communist must support his country by ratting on his friends, yet who eventually, out of his enthusiasm for phonoscopy, slips into assisting the police in their manhunt. His wish to be useful and to actualize at least some of his potentialities plays an important role in the phonoscopy project. Yet the lovingly portrayed Rubin has staunchly resisted recruitment as an informer. The archetypal role of Judas is therefore transferred to Isaak Kagan, who was arrested for non-denunciation but has turned informer in prison. Apparently, the paradigm of informers would not be complete without a treacherous Jew.[36]

Surveillance is a cosmic theme. As Nabokov's John Shade tells his snooping neighbor, a totalitarian regime cannot do without the secret police, and creation of the secret police is the "end of the world" (1962: 156). The *sharashka,* which is governed through surveillance mechanisms and works to perfect them, is one of the nerve centers of a world out of joint.[37]

Finally, one of the centrally important motifs of the novel is that of meat (see Halperin 1973: 271–75; Akeley 1984: 4–6). Variations on this motif are associated with the passage from carnival to Lent. In the spirit of the carnivalesque mode, the main characters of the novel are ideologists in search of answers to ultimate questions; its setting spans palaces and slums; its action abounds in scandal scenes, oxymoronic juxtapositions, and reversals of hierarchies. The mandatory reference to the supernatural takes the ironic shape of Stalin's megalomaniac attempts to perpetuate his own cult. Prison life leads to free familiar contact between unlikely companions. The symbolism of the novel is quasi-carnivalesque: food is available, and there is a rhythmic recurrence of the motif of feasting.

Yet whereas a true carnival embraces the whole community rather than a small part of the population, the novel shows that the families of the *sharashka* inmates are living in privation and that the prisoners in regular camps are starving. The life of the establishment elite represented by the Makarygins is a feast amidst the plague; the life of the *sharashka,* like friendly conversations in Gulag memoirs, is a temporary reprieve from the common condition of suffering.

Accordingly, the festive exhilaration of the discourse presided over by Nerzhin, Rubin, and Sologdin often leaves an unpleasant aftertaste. Ideological discussions and montage performances take place in the close vicinity of informers; makeshift banquets can lead to punishment cells; and ideological debates can turn into ad hominem attacks. Therefore, despite our concern for the characters' welfare, it is aesthetically fitting that the semblance of Shrovetide should come to an end in the last chapters of the novel and that Lent should set in with Volodin's arrest and Nerzhin's preparations for the transport. Carnivalesque touches strike a jarring note in the literature of the camps.

In *The First Circle* carnivorousness is associated with the work of the security apparatus, the great "meat-grinder." The minister of state security Abakumov is described as a meaty (fleshy) person; Stalin's fingers are "greasy"[38]—a symbolic equivalent of what "all the aromas of Arabia" cannot erase (one of the main treats of Stalin's recent alcoholic binge is the collective beating to death of Bulgarian Communist Traicho Kostov, rather in the spirit of stories told of Beria). Through Stalin and Abakumov, the motif of flesh is linked with that of surveillance. The Russian word for "surveillance," *slezhka,* is etymologically related to *sled,* "footprint," "trace": the living word leaves traces and, passing through mechanisms, is turned into the deadly text of an indictment. Volodin's fatal phone call is recorded by one machine, passed through another, and eventually translated into a warrant for his arrest. The conversations of the prisoners are likewise transmitted by informers and collected in files until the meat-grinder gets around to processing them into charges.

According to the peasant wisdom of the janitor Spiridon, one can judge things by a simple criterion: "The wolfhound is right and the cannibal is wrong" (*FC87:* 401). The main characters' refusal to collaborate with the cannibalistic meat-grinder is tantamount to renouncing flesh —literally and figuratively. The last meat soup that Nerzhin has in the *sharashka* before his departure marks the end of the cakes-and-ale reprieve. Collaboration with the cannibals and the feast amidst famine are rejected. Nerzhin accepts the hardships that are in store for him as ascetic purification.[39] "He who is deprived of all material strength always achieves victory in *sacrifice,*" Solzhenitsyn will eventually write in his "Lenten Letter" to Patriarch Pimen in 1972 (Dunlop 1973b: 555).[40]

The self-sacrifice demanded by Solzhenitsyn's version of Lent in *The First Circle* involves giving up individual self-actualization. Hence, the heated eschatological debates of the characters: conversational flights of the spirit (infrequent in the democratic West, where intellectual intercourse takes other forms) are an exquisite luxury within the culture of non-self-actualization, where, for those who are unwilling to make compromises or sell out to the secret police, most avenues of intellectual activity and professional achievement are cut off. In the assertion of their ethos, the main characters have to join the communal Lent rather than opt for pseudo-carnival; by doing so, they reject the possibilities of symbiosis with the state. While totalitarianism blocks most paths to a full realization of individual potentialities, in their resistance to it overt nonconformists voluntarily give up a few of those paths still open to them.

The loss of intellectual versatility, reversible if better times come not too late, is compensated by a clear conscience, stamina, and insight.

Thus it is not merely the subject matter and the exploration of characteristic topoi but also such features as the aesthetics of ethical engagement, the absence of a hermetic finish, the dialectical tension of the individual and the communal, and the Lenten flavor of the narrative that connect *The First Circle* with the memoirs of Gulag survivors. Yet the intensity of the dramatic illusion, the unforgettable characters, and the vastness and coherence of the paradigm grant this work a place apart.

8 In the Wake of Testimony

Narratives that testify to the Gulag provide a context for works of fiction that display a vivid consciousness of the Gulag but do not have a marked testifying function. This secondary corpus clarifies, modifies, or refines the conceptual schemata initiated in the witness narratives, though without offering to revise them in radical ways.

The treatment of the Gulag in the post-testimonial fiction is associated with the types of biographical links that the authors have with the camps. The writers who have been imprisoned tend to opt for the realistic mode, whereas those who have only secondhand knowledge about the camps more commonly resort to experimental techniques. I shall survey some of the most striking examples of these tendencies, with special attention to belated residues of the testimonial function.

* * *

One of the earliest works suffused with an intense awareness of the camps yet providing no referential data about them is Solzhenitsyn's *Cancer Ward*. It seems that this novel, published abroad in 1968 after having been accepted and then rejected by *Novyi mir*, could come into being only after the greater urgencies had been dealt with in *The First Circle* and *Ivan Denisovich*. It presupposes the existence of camp testimonies, though not necessarily already published ones. It traces a new *cultural code*, a network of camp-generated assumptions and significances shared by the author and the initiated audience; it also trains non-initiated readers to recognize and decipher camp semiotics.

The action takes place outside the barbed wire, but still in its shadow. The predicament of the patients in a Tashkent hospital is placed against a "nodal" year, 1954, when hopes for better times to come had not yet been darkened by the Soviet invasion of Hungary. Circulating in the ward is the blue-cover journal *Novyi mir* with Vladimir Pomerantsev's seminal article "On Sincerity" (December 1953), the harbinger of the thaw on the literary scene. The mood of the novel is colored by the sense of an incipient recovery: symbolically, toward the end, the protagonist, Oleg Kostoglotov, is shown apparently recuperating from an acute form of cancer. But then so is the bureaucrat Rusanov, a member of "the new class" (Djilas 1965: 37–69) and a still solid cog in the meat-grinding machine.

The novel unfolds to the rhythm of the diagnostic activity: while the doctors determine the physical condition of the patients, the reader, occasionally helped by the semiotic expertise of Kostoglotov, discovers the types of the characters' connectedness with the camps: the nice-guy soldier Akhmadzhan suddenly voices the dehumanizing brutality of a brainwashed camp guard (cf. "The Kids with the Tommy Guns," *GA* 5: 9); the surgeon Lev Leonidovich betrays his camp past by the use of the camp term *raskololsia* ("split up") for "confessed" (cf. Solzhenitsyn's report on camp medical sections—*GA* 3: 7, 214–18); the ethnic German Vera Gangart and the gentle Tartar Sibgatov turn out to have been victims of Stalin's ethnic transfers (cf. *GA* 6: 2, 3, 4; Conquest 1960); the educated and unusually conscientious janitor Elizaveta Anatolievna discloses that her husband is still serving a second-round term (cf. *GA* 1: 2) behind the barbed wire.[1] Rusanov is promptly recognized as an *apparatchik* who had built his career on sending his victims to die in the camps.

In retrospect, one can turn to Solzhenitsyn's own Gulag writings and to the testimonies of other survivors for annotations on practically all the characters of *Cancer Ward*. Thus, Kostoglotov emerges as a *zloi fraier* (thieves' jargon for an experienced, confident, and tough political prisoner) described by Panin; avatars of Akhmadzhan trample the pages of Bershadskaya and Krasnov; doctors like Lev Leonidovich alleviate the suffering of Shalamov and Margolin. Comments on the rise of Rusanov can be found in Solonevich, who analyzes the social phenomenon of "activists."[2]

The metaphor of the camps as metastasized cancer, recurrent in *The Gulag Archipelago*, first crystallized in *Cancer Ward*. The novel's dice of medical fate are loaded with allegory:[3] (a) cancer of the neck overtakes Rusanov, a representative pillar of totalitarianism; (b) cancer of the heart is diagnosed in a young Ukrainian, whose nationality connects him with the main victims of the artificially induced famine of the early thirties; (c) cancer of the tongue is allotted to the forced-labor overseer Yefrem Podduev, who had lied to his women but had refused to protect the exhausted prisoners by lying to the authorities;[4] (d) advanced cancer of the colon is the lot of the intellectual Shulubin, who had ("gutlessly") given up self-actualization (cf. "Our Muzzled Freedom," *GA* 4: 3) in order to avoid arrest by remaining inconspicuous. Judiciously, however, the Dantean adjustment of punishment to crime is not extended to every patient. Moreover, the symbolism of the types of cancer in the novel shades into its cultural code since its recognition depends on the reader's familiarity with the recent history of the country.

In tune with its themes of diagnosis and cure, the novel dwells on the experience of release more extensively than that of imprisonment. Its last chapters are devoted to the *inner life* of a released prisoner and to the place of camp semiotics in his vision of the world. The majority of Gulag memoirs neglect the released prisoner's emotional and intellectual adjustment to life outside the camps. The subject is an unwieldy luxury, partly because the attitudes of camp graduates at large are colored by the neurotic clash between feelings of superiority to the new environment and of inadequacy in dealing with it. Moreover, the leveling effect of the camp on its inmates having been canceled, the vast variety of personal experience makes it impossible to imagine a "representative" case. The individual flavor of life after release is too dependent on time, place, age, gender, state of health, family ties, financial status, nationality, profession, presence or absence of friends, a clear or a troubled conscience.[5]

This is not to say that Gulag literature does not comment on the *practical* problems of release. Alexander Dolgun mentions that many released prisoners had fatal accidents because, having been escorted from place to place for too long, they no longer remembered individual safety precautions. Vladimir Petrov hints that the prisoners released from Kolyma on the eve of World War II ran the risk of being immediately rearrested even when their documents were in perfect order. The last and most successful short story in Sergei Maksimov's collection *Taiga* describes the predicament of a prisoner released in the mid thirties and, despite the shortage of labor, denied employment because no one wants the responsibility of hiring him. A similar situation pertaining to the late sixties is depicted in Marchenko's *Live Like Everyone*.[6] Treated as a pariah, forced to register at the police station every week, denied residence permits in bigger towns, forced to cling to the most unsuitable jobs, kept under constant surveillance, reduced to appealing to friends and acquaintances for loans to stave off hunger, the ex-prisoner had more urgent concerns than the subtleties of intellectual readjustment. Even though after Stalin's death things improved, homecoming remained a difficult subject.[7] In memoirs its treatment was further impeded by the fact that at the time of composition, the authors' experience of imprisonment had been encapsulated, while their readjustment to life in the Larger Zone was often still incomplete.

In *Cancer Ward* Solzhenitsyn creates a situation in which the problem of psychological readjustment is separated from practical anxieties about lodgings and jobs and can therefore be examined more closely. The novel enlists our sympathy for the seasoned *zek*, Kostoglotov, who, like Solzhenitsyn himself, has been racked by pains in the abdomen soon after the end of his camp term, who disgusts Rusanov and offends the aesthetic sense of passersby (cf. Rzhevsky 1978: 70–86). This rugged personage is presented as morally reliable yet not saintly, compassionate yet shrewd, generous yet thrifty, avid for the life that has passed him by yet ready for ascetic self-discipline, capable of suffering in silence yet determined to struggle for his rights like a loud-mouthed trouble-maker. Like Shukhov, he is not infallible: he slips into callousness (when his love-game with Zoya prevents either of them from paying more than perfunctory attention to a dying lung-cancer patient), into wholesale simplification (when he suspects his former fiancée of foul compromises because she has survived the camps), and into intellectual self-righteousness (when he talks to people just to seek confirmation of his own views).

The semiotic system constructed by Kostoglotov has provided him with value yardsticks that are sufficient for the hospital (another closed institution) but fall short on the day he is discharged. The beauty of the rosy Tashkent dawn strikes him like that of the first day of creation. This is what release from camp might have been like, had it not been marred by fatigue and uncertainty. Because he now already has a niche, his makeshift home in Ush Terek, he can afford both to engage in introspection and to immerse himself in the sensual feast.

At first his camp-generated system of concepts accommodates the profusion of new images. Kostoglotov thinks of the life that his successful cure has given him as "a makeweight addition" (*dovesok*) to the main chunk of the bread ration. The Oriental architecture, with the windows facing courtyards rather than streets, pleases him by its emphasis on the privacy of which he has long been deprived—to others it might suggest a form of imprisonment. The single shashlyk that he enjoys turns his thoughts first to the riddle of the "two-storey" incomes of the drivers who can afford five apiece, and then to the insatiability of human wishes and the relativity of the happiness that once lay in a loaf of coarse bread. The queue for deficit goods in the department store does not surprise him

—this is the order of things in "our muzzled freedom." But hearing a customer ask for a shirt by both the sleeve and the collar sizes gives Kostoglotov a shock: he has not expected such sophistication in triviality to exist in the world that also contained the camps.[8] By righteous indignation he staves off a sense of inadequacy; soon, however, he is humbled again—first by catching a glimpse of his scarecrow self in a mirror and then by his embarrassment at not knowing what gift he should get for Vega.[9]

Kostoglotov is proud of his "useless knowledge" of life and death, yet it becomes apparent that he has been handicapped by it: pain, of which he has known too much, and privation, which he is still suffering, contract one's world, limit the number of objects of consciousness, and dwarf whole spheres of experience (cf. Scarry 1985: 27–59). On recovery it takes time to reinstate these objects or admit the value of other people's interests and pursuits. A recuperating person's ability to draw distinctions can only gradually extend to the fields that prolonged suffering has pushed beyond his or her horizons; the profundity of experience in one area can be detrimental—temporarily or permanently—to the fineness and amplitude of response in other areas.

Kostoglotov regains composure when he can again rely on his camp education (in preserving order in the queue for the train) or when he does things out of plain commitments to friendship—buying a light flat-iron for the Kadmins or visiting the zoo because he had promised Demka to do so. The zoo is, of course, another form of captivity, supplementing those of the hospital and the camp. Here, with the animals evocatively framed by their cages, Kostoglotov creates a *zek* equivalent of a medieval bestiary. Each caged animal becomes a symbol of some aspect of the prison system (see also Porter 1987: 677–78 and Kern 1975). The sign that says "The porcupine leads a nocturnal life" brings to his mind the nightly interrogations—"We know: they summon him at nine-thirty p. m. and release him at four in the morning." In the badger, described as living "in deep and twisted burrows," he recognizes a cagey veteran *zek*—"That's for real! A fine young fellow, this badger, but what is left? His face is mattress-striped, he's a real inmate." The bear's cage seems too small—it is "not a cell, but a 'box,' a strict-confinement dungeon." The yellow-eyed tiger evokes his hatred: "An old political prisoner who had once been in exile in Turukhansk . . . had told him that, no, those eyes were not velvet-black, but yellow" (583–86).[10] Turukhansk is the place where Stalin spent some time in exile before the revolution (and also the place where Iuz Aleshkovsky composed what would become one of the most popular camp songs, "Tovarishch Stalin byl bol'shoi uchennyi"[11]).

The tiger is, however, a literal tiger even if it does remind Kostoglotov of Stalin. "Thus did Oleg find a distorted significance in everything he observed" (583): the novel trains the reader to recognize the system of significances produced by the Gulag world yet also to move away from it. Kostoglotov's mind is presented as "so addled that he [can] no longer consider anything naively and with detachment" (548). Yet on his one day in Tashkent he begins to feel the limitations of his vision. The image of the spring bloom of the apricot tree, blending with the novel's mood of partial improvement, suggests that some day his handicap may be overcome. The skills of camp life can stand him in good stead, yet the concepts formed there are not comprehensive: the profuseness and complexity of both nature and society escape their bounds. Kostoglotov's sexual impotence becomes an emblem of intellectual inadequacy. Both may be temporary, yet in the meantime he shrinks back into his nooks—the luggage-rack bunk on the train and the arid Central Asian village at the end of the trip. In the closing lines of the novel his face is buried in his knapsack—he has seen enough for a day. His booted legs stick out into the corridor, the toes dangling like "a dead man's"—an allusion to the prisoners who died in the trains and ships during the long transports, or else to Kostoglotov's being partly deadened inside.

When the former overseer Podduev is discharged so that the hospital should not have his death on its records, he thinks that he must still get dressed and, overcoming his feebleness, trudge through the streets to the railway station. His imagination does not reach further than that; later it is at the station that he is found dead. On parting with Podduev, Kostoglotov shakes his hand with a fellow-soldier's sympathy: it is you now, I may be next. It is not clear whether Kostoglotov is supposed to die on the train: rather, he is dismissed in a covertly metafictional move.

Indeed, Kostoglotov is a fictional character endowed with many of the author's own features but not with a writer's vocation. On his aborted visit to Vega, he is repelled by the sight of the bedding left to dry by the tenants of the house where she lives. Solzhenitsyn fashions Kostoglotov as a soldierly light traveler with a scorn for the bulky paraphernalia of rooted life. Yet the scorn for the bedding—tinged, perhaps, with anxiety over his possible sexual impotence—is also associated with the fear of the lack of privacy in communal apartments. Here the author's extratextual reality seeps through into the fictional world: during his post-release exile, Solzhenitsyn would not get married because—until he returned to his former wife—he could not trust any woman with the secret of his "underground" writing (see 1979, ch. 1). Kostoglotov's visit to Vega's house contains a detail that evokes such wariness: the hostile, suspicious neighbor who turns him away from Vega's communal apartment is exactly the kind of person whose prying would be considerably more oppressive to Solzhenitsyn than to his protagonist.

Moreover, Kostoglotov's insistent demands that his doctors tell him how much time he has left to live likewise make better sense in the light of the author's worries whether, upon leaving the hospital, he would have enough time to commit to paper all that he had in his mind. Kostoglotov does not seem to have any specific mission: whereas Podduev fails to plan his actions beyond reaching the railway station, Kostoglotov does not quite seem to know what to do with that diminished thing, his life. This is another metafictional touch: ever since *The House of the Dead* fictional transpositions of prison experience have tended to raise problems of consistency (Morand 1976: 20–24)—Dostoevsky's protagonist has been imprisoned for a *crime de la passion*, yet his fellow convicts treat him as the political prisoner that Dostoevsky himself actually was. A similar inconsistency in *Cancer Ward* suggests that though the novel does not present testimony to specific people or events, it conveys the flavor of a first-hand post-camp experience and explores the cultural semiotics that lies at its base.

* * *

Whereas for Solzhenitsyn the decentering of the camp subject in *Cancer Ward* was associated with the need to explore the lingering effect of camp experience, the novels of another camp survivor, Yury Dombrovsky (1909–78),[12] skirt the subject of the camps as unmanageable. Dombrovsky's *The Keeper of Antiquities* (1964) and *The Faculty of Unnecessary Things* (1978) are, like *Cancer Ward*, set on the perimeter of the whirlpool, but these two novels deal not with the return from the Archipelago but with the roads that lead to it. They thus link up with the older literary tradition of concentrating on the reasons for the incarceration and eliding the daily ordeals and humiliations of prison routine. *The Keeper of Antiquities*, whose 1964 publication in *Novyi mir* was the compensation that Tvardovsky demanded for the banning of Aleksandr Bek's *The New Appointment*, deals with the period shortly preceding the protagonist's 1937 arrest:[13] it is permeated with a sense of suppressed anxiety. The protagonist attempts to close himself up in the "ivory tower" (Senfeld 1979: 370) of his office in the attic of the Alma-Ata museum, where he works as a curator, yet his contributions to the local newspaper lay him open to wanton accusations by people with personal grudges. *The Faculty of Unnecessary Things*, completed about eleven years later, is a somewhat loosely fitting sequel: if in *The Keeper* the conflicts are provoked by a misguided newspaper rumor of a python in *kolkhoz* fields, here, at approximately the same period, the NKVD strikes because of the theft of an archeological find. Switching from first- to third-person narrative, *The Faculty* also covers the protagonist's arrest, interrogations, and near-miraculous release. The camps are dealt with only in the inset stories of the people the curator Zybin meets in prison. Presented at this remove, the camp emerges as a setting where intellectuals lose their poise: hunger and confusion reduce them to acts that shame would press into oblivion. According to Miletich (1986: 1163–64), it was on Dombrovsky that Shalamov modeled his Shelgunov, the protagonist of "Pain," an intellectual who is fascinated and fatally fooled by the criminal chieftain. In a poem about his hope that the unbearable may blaze up in the form of art (see Shtokman 1989: 108–9), Dombrovsky makes a reference to a sphere of experience that he cannot bear writing about, his own "Room 101."

Both the novels contain loving descriptions of Kazakhstan's capital Alma-Ata, of the regions around it, of its forgotten historian Castagnier and its ingenious architect Zenkov, of an archeologist's work in the museum, and of the blissful days of his vacation in a little seaside town. Some of the passages are reminiscent of Konstantin Paustovsky's romanticism, but whereas Paustovsky's spiritualized heroes lived in a universe almost as untouched by Stalinist repression as the settings of Alexander Grin's romantic yarns, in Dombrovsky's world the repression slowly but inexorably grows into a major factor (see Woodward 1992b: 897–99; Turkov 1989: 226).

One of Shalamov's objections to the genre of the novel was that it required a connecting tissue useless for the work of testimony. Dombrovsky's *Faculty* is a celebration of the useless. Indeed, the law department from which most of the characters have graduated has become a faculty of desuetude: now the main qualification of a Soviet jurist is the ability to formulate the politically correct lip service to legality and to cover up a brutal disdain for traditional law and justice. Historical knowledge is likewise officially useless in a society where the rewriting and forgetting of history are the order of the day, where archeological gold turns into bullion and antique coins end up in an interrogator's private collection. "Unnecessary" in this society are "reason, respect for truth, . . . and the most basic human values" (Woodward 1992b: 897); useless, by definition, are the protagonist's moments of aesthetic bliss. Unlike Shalamov, whose moments of aesthetic experience were possible only (or mainly) when reminders of the camps were blotted out, Dombrovsky demonstrates the coexistence, side by side, of the grim social realities and the sensual opulence of the Central Asian scenery, a treasure-house for "useless" aesthetic reveling. The NKVD *memento mori* actually enhances the carnivalesque enjoyment of the tenuous sensual and intellectual feast.

The Faculty of Unnecessary Things places a romantic fascination with the region's past[14] and its mysterious luxury of the senses into the matrix of a *roman policier*. Yet rather than a traditional "whodunnit," this is a postmodernist narrative, where the process of detection tends to lead one further away from rather than closer to the solution of a case. The novel's method of modeling reality is closer to Shalamov's simulation of the dynamics of processes than to Solzhenitsyn's attempts to replicate the given conditions: it is shown how "higher" politics impinges on the ways in which the Alma-Ata NKVD plies its trade of concocting false charges. Zybin is released because he does not incriminate himself but also, and mainly, because the NKVD officials' ambitious project of staging a show trial in Alma-Ata, emulating the Moscow Grand Charades, is condemned by the central authorities as politically incorrect: why should Russian wreckers choose the "provincial" Alma-Ata rather than great Moscow? If there is to be a political show trial in Alma-Ata, the accused should be Kazakh nationalists.

Whatever is lost by Dombrovsky's opting for fiction rather than documentary prose is compensated by the dramatization of the realms of experience not available as the firsthand evidence of a *zek*, that is, by the imaginative inclusion of the perspectives of others. Yet Dombrovsky's narrative does not emphasize the element of testimony to the times of trouble; it concentrates on exploring the incremental encroachments of the totalitarian regime on a scholar's dreamy blend of aesthetic and existentialist commitments.

At the end of the novel we see the protagonist conversing with the recently recruited informer Kornilov and the recently sacked interrogator Neiman, now a candidate for arrest. The scene is an epiphany, a modern version of Christ between a reluctant Judas and a failed Pontius Pilate.[15] If Shalamov was fastidiously impatient with the confessions of former interrogators, it is easy to imagine Dombrovsky lending them a curious ear.[16] His novels probe the combination of humaneness and brutality not only in the NKVD interrogators but also, albeit in a different proportion, in most of the characters—none can cast the first stone. Treacherousness is endemic: this is, perhaps, the main unsolved mystery of the novel. In a response, as it were, to Bulgakov, the novel presents its own version of Christ's Passion. The story, an inset development of the novel's recurrent themes, is offered by a former priest. In a Dostoyevskian dialogue with Kornilov, the priest explains, among other things, that in addition to the open treachery of Judas, there must also have been a secret denunciation by one more of the apostles—no one knows which one, or why. Eventually, Kornilov informs on the priest, only to find out that the priest has already written a denunciation of Kornilov.

At the same time the inset story lays emphasis on Christ's decision to suffer a terrible death rather than recant and thus erase the work of his life. This decision is partly re-enacted by the protagonist's staunch resistance to the interrogators. Unlike Christ, however, Zybin (whose name is reminiscent of the ripples on the surface of the water), remains as slippery as his interrogator considers him to be.[17] He is self-indulgent, erudite, pensive and hard-drinking, warm, and humanly responsive, yet also prone to out-of-sight/out-of-mind callousness, a far cry from the traditionally pure Christ-like heroics. In tune with Zybin's elusiveness, the text enacts a para-detective game of arousing and thwarting the readers' expectations through a play of recurrent images, motifs, and allusions: our anticipations fail to be realized just as, in a society governed by an arbitrary capricious ruler, people's calculations come to naught. In the episode where Stalin is deciding the fate of Georgii Kalandarashvili, up to the last moment neither the reader nor Stalin's assistant can foresee the outcome of the dictator's musings.

Zybin succeeds in resisting his interrogators because he is lucky and also because he puts the whole of his physical and spiritual energy into his confrontations with them; quite naturally, he is shown collapsing after his exertions. But the author does not always sustain the level of spiritual upsurge the character exemplifies. Dombrovsky's text only occasionally rises to peaks of emotional intensity comparable to Shalamov's. Even so, its emotional plateau is higher than that of most Soviet novels officially published during the "stagnation" period.

While working on his novel in his room in a Moscow communal apartment, Dombrovsky kept on responding to life and its vicissitudes with personal warmth and desperate courage. He was usually surrounded by admirers, apprentices, and spies; his fortunes fluctuated, and a great deal of liquor flowed. Beginning in 1969, his life was brightened by his marriage to the daughter of the woman on whom he had modeled Klara Faizulayevna in *The Keeper* and *The Faculty* (Senfeld 1979: 374).

This changed in 1977 when the émigré journal *Vestnik RKhD* published Dombrovsky's story "From Zybin's Notes," a kind of epilogue to *The Keeper* (see Tsvetkov 1978: 116) or perhaps to the still-unpublished *Faculty*, complete with a few powerful sketches of camp life. The main subject of this story is the conversion of a Communist true believer in the camps, a widespread though non-ubiquitous topos of Gulag literature, especially Gulag fiction. A former high-ranking official who thinks nothing of antagonizing a roomful of fellow prisoners by justifying the repression of which they and himself are the victims sheds his ideology when shocked by a love scene between a camp boss and a female NKVD operative in the sordid dressing room of the prisoners' bathhouse. The *inamorati* are exchanging coyly banal yet quite earnest courtship formulae as if they were in a health resort for the *apparatchiks*, while all the emaciated ugliness, misery, and humiliation of the prisoners is staring them in the face; in the middle of his lyricisms the man actually kicks back the prisoners who have been pushed onto the floor in proximity to his boots. This spectacle eventually brings the stubborn old "true believer" to a religious conversion. In a sense, this fictional analysis of the mechanics of a Communist's disillusionment is a comment on sundry similar conversion narratives, including the memoirs of Ginzburg, Kopelev, and perhaps even Solzhenitsyn. A fanatical Communist's ideology is a closed system[18] unassailable by rational argument alone. By contrast to people with less fervent commitments, the true believer will not be persuaded by personal suffering, even his own, since the teleology of the system justifies its "cost" in individual suffering. What can induce such a person to give up the dogma is an unobstructed view of an abnormality—not suffering, but abnormality—resulting from the conditions created by his utopia-in-the-making. The conversion of Zybin's fellow prisoner is the product of a sudden "enlightenment" of this sort. In more impressionable people, similar about-faces can, apparently, also come gradually, through a succession of minor grim epiphanies: in the autobiographical chapters of *The Gulag Archipelago* as well as in the memoirs of Ginzburg and Kopelev, the authorial personae are shaken by a *series* of minor shocks from a *series* of revolting encounters with the perverse, the depraved, and the absurd in the system of relationships established by the regime that they had faithfully served.[19] The waving, pulsating structure of camp memoirs may be associated not only with the monitoring of the reader's emotional response but also with the biographical pattern of successive steps toward a conversion in a memoirist's past. This is one of the examples of the way fictional works enhance the intellectual constructs that are also present, in a lower relief, in memoir literature.

The final part of "From Zybin's Notes" is set in the post-1956 Alma-Ata. Here Dombrovsky brings back another character from *The Keeper* and *The Faculty*, the director of the museum, formerly an army officer who had fallen into disgrace. Next to Solzhenitsyn's Rusanov, Dombrovsky's Director is one of the most fascinating portrayals of a Stalinist official who interprets the logic of the state terror and identifies with it. Unlike Rusanov, however, the Director is a gifted and kind person, who would rather protect than victimize his associates and whose timely behind-the-scene activities in *The Faculty* eventually help to turn the tide for Zybin. The story presents further insights into this rather charismatic person, a mixture of talent, warmth, insight, and superficiality of commitment. His very superficiality—an ambiguous flaw—is what has kept him reasonably humane in the times of the terror and what comfortably cushioned his anti-Stalinist about-face of 1956.

Strange things started happening in Dombrovsky's life after this profoundly subversive story came out. This was one of the gloomiest of "stagnation" years. Dombrovsky did not conceal the fact that preparations were being made for Tamizdat publication of *The Faculty of Unnecessary Things*. Obviously, as far at the KGB was concerned, this was going beyond the tolerable eccentricities of an expansive bohemian ex-*zek*. In November 1977, not long after another troublesome ex-*zek*, the poet and translator Konstantin Bogatyrev, was murdered by agents of the KGB, Dombrovsky, now almost seventy, was beaten in the street by well-trained attackers. There were also threatening phone-calls and suspicious repeated falls (Vulfovich 1997: 147). Within a year Dombrovsky was dead. Like Bogatyrev, he was a convenient victim—well known to the intellectuals of the capital yet still insufficiently famous abroad. For a politically passive writer with dissident sensibilities, the so-called "wide popularity in narrow circles" could be even more fatal than a lack of publicity to a political protester.

The story "From Zybin's Notes" produces an impression of the tip of an iceberg. Despite Dombrovsky's reluctance to write about the camps, it is likely that by now, the year 2000, not all of his Gulag materials have been published: one wonders, for instance, about the content of the pages excised from *The Keeper* by an editor at *Novyi mir* in 1964 (see Tsvetkov 1978: 116). Dombrovsky is reported to have said: "In camp prose, Shalamov is number one, I am number two, and Solzhenitsyn number three" (Sirotinskaya 1994: 122). This might suggest that the total volume of his camp prose must have been vaster than is now known: unfortunately, Bulgakov's assertion that manuscripts do not burn is truer in the metaphysical than in the literal sense.

* * *

When the heroine of Pasternak's *Doctor Zhivago* is arrested in the closing pages,[20] the novel does not follow her to the camps—this is another story to be told in other ways. By contrast, in Vasilii Grossman's *Life and Fate*, completed in 1961, confiscated by the KGB, and published posthumously during *glasnost*, the ex-husband of one of the heroines is shown perishing in a camp at the hand of a criminal convict to whom he had refused to kowtow. Though the story is fairly typical, Grossman's camp episode remains schematic: a writer who has not seen the camps from the inside remains powerless to capture their atmosphere. Paradoxically, the quality of Grossman's imagination here falls below that of his imaginative reconstructions of the ultimate horror of the Nazi gas chamber in the same book.

Literary traditions seem to have provided novelists with flexible matrixes for evoking the experience of victims of executions; yet a purely imaginative construction of an individual's daily existence in a concentration camp, unsupported by firsthand memory, is a near-impossible artistic challenge.[21] Russian writers who were not in the camps tend to avoid realistic presentations of life behind the barbed wire, tacitly admitting their inability to do justice to the routinized misery of this nadir of human condition or to the apparent sordidness of the ways of adjusting to it. The most they can offer is second-degree witnessing, that is, testimony, explicit or implicit, to their responses to the testimony or the silence of others.[22]

On the other hand, the rich corpus of literature on the Gulag has eventually created the sense that a literary model of Soviet life cannot be complete if it ignores that subject completely. Artistic responses to this challenge seem to have taken three main forms: *Room 101 taboo, dystopian satire,* and *the grotesque.*

In the majority of narratives by non-witnesses, the camps are *Room 101,* where imagination fears to tread; their partial contours signal gaps in the narrative models of reality. The action of the narratives is set on the threshold of imprisonment, in the liminal spaces familiar to the authors. Thus Lidia Chukovskaya's *The Deserted House* and *Going Under* focus on the experience of women whose loved ones have been arrested.[23] Anatoly Rybakov's saga (*Children of the Arbat* and its sequels) deals with the arrest and exile of the protagonist (the author too had managed to avoid the camps), refers to the arrests of others, gives us an external view of a column of camp inmates, but does not lead us inside the camps.

In Yury Trifonov's *The House on the Embankment* and *Disappearance* people are arrested, vanish from the stage, and are not followed. The protagonist-narrator of Mikhail Kuraev's "Nochnoi dozor" ["The Night Patrol"] (1990: 45–112) tells the story of his work as an arresting officer and assistant interrogator; in spite of his sympathy for his victims, he never tries to imagine their further fate in the prisons and camps. The finely sketched protagonist of Kuraev's "Kapitan Dikshtein" ["Captain Dikshtein"] (1990: 113–254) is shown to be obsessed by a turning point that took place in his life during the Kronstadt rebellion, but the narrative omits his three spans in the camps, two in the Gulag and one in a German POW camp—even though some features of his character suggest indelible traces of this experience. In Leonid Borodin's "Povest' strannogo vremeni" ["A Tale of Strange Times"] the main weight of the tragedy is shifted from the fate of the arrested person to that of his miseducated and callously manipulated son. In Aksyonov's fantasy *The Burn* [*Ozhog*], though part of the action is set in the Stalinist Kolyma and the protagonist's mother is arrested, we cannot follow her into the camps; but one traumatic glimpse through a door of the interrogation room where the protagonist's friend is maimed by a sadistic henchman suffices to make us sympathize with the protagonist's oneiric revenge.

The Faithful Ruslan (1975) by Georgy Vladimov is a bridge between the realistic treatment of the threshold of *Room 101* and the refraction of the camps in experimental narratives. Its main theme is failure to adapt to life after the 1956 exodus from the camps. The ex-prisoner Solzhenitsyn was in a position to treat this subject realistically in *Cancer Ward;* Vladimov, a second-degree second-generation witness (his mother had been imprisoned in 1952), distances the camp realities by means of focalization: the center of consciousness in his narrative is the guard dog Ruslan. Thus, the flashback scene of, for instance, the guards' hosing down a barracks full of prisoners who refuse to work in terrible frost is framed into the dog's "investigations" of the conduct of its pack of canines. Yet if the atrocity is thus de-emphasized, its details gain a symbolic significance when another dog, the "pensive" Ingus, angrily attacks the serpent-like hose.[24] The choice of the focus also produces a great number of local felicities and pregnantly defamiliarizing touches.

The 1956 evacuation of the camps after the mass release of the prisoners is a tragedy for Ruslan. His training has rendered him unfit for other duties. He cannot adapt to new conditions, is deeply hurt on realizing that his adored Master (*khoziain*—Stalin was sometimes colloquially referred to by this word) does not love him, and starts following a released prisoner who is living in the nearby settlement with a woman named Stiura. The ex-prisoner thinks that he has adopted the dog, but Ruslan's idea is to watch that the man should not run away. Ruslan feels that, even after boarding the train to his hometown, his new ward is not up to departure; he therefore refrains from pulling him out of the car. And indeed, at the last moment the man jumps off the train, into the arms of the understanding Stiura: he does not have the courage to rejoin the family who may no longer want him.

Wryly debunking the "female succor" topos, Vladimov presents the practical, tolerant, and kind-hearted Stiura, whose capacity for adaptation makes life bearable for herself and others, not as a saintly long-suffering chaste feminine figure but as a "fallen" woman, who, in the bad times, had opportunistically adjusted to the prevailing treacherousness and has much to regret and puzzle out in her past. Given a different Pavlovian conditioning, Ruslan, the quite admirable and essentially kind-hearted animal, would have made an efficient aid to a sportsman or a loyal and merry companion of country children. The same seems to be true of the human characters of the tale.

Whereas Solzhenitsyn's *Cancer Ward* trains the reader to decipher the cultural code of the Gulag, *The Faithful Ruslan* presupposes the reader's familiarity with the semiotics of the camps. Thus when a released prisoner addresses Ruslan's Master as "*vologodskii,*" we are supposed to recognize the reference to the particularly tough convoy guards recruited from the Vologda region. We are expected to understand that a prisoner's breaking the ranks at the entrance to the camp is a suicide attempt and to identify a sneaky, pathetic prisoner ("please, think of my predicament" —*voidite v moe polozhenie*) as an informer. By contrast, the narrative incorporates explanations of a less well known subject—the logistics of a guard dog's training—also uniquely symptomatic of the system of relationships established in the camps.

Like the best of Gulag prose, *The Faithful Ruslan* is almost entirely free of leisurely descriptions or digressions: every detail is either functional or symbolic. For instance, a sentence such as "Thus a dog's service would always end in death at the hands of the Master" (1975: 13) functions on both the literal and the allegorical planes, reminding the reader of Stalin's shooting thousands of his own faithful servants, whom the newspapers of the purge years called "mad dogs." Such games of *double entendre* were among the (wrong) reasons for the novel's underground popularity in the sixties and seventies, when the reading public was prone to confuse the genuine aesthetic achievements of a story or a poem with the Aesopian possibility of reading it "between the lines." The hints must have been too clearly subversive for the novel to be published in the Soviet Union even before the massive "squeeze" (*zazhim*) of 1966. In 1975, having circulated in Samizdat for ten years, it was published by Possev in Germany. In Russia it came out only during *glasnost*.

* * *

The Faithful Ruslan stands apart as a Gulag recycling of the genre of "the story of a dog" (cf. Chekhov's "Kashtanka," Jack London's *White Fang*, and Kafka's "Investigations of a Dog"), which translates the eschatological problems of a specific space-time into the human/canine body language. Another experimental genre more widely represented in post-Stalinist Russian literature and peculiarly adapted to refractions of the Gulag is the genre of *dystopia*.[25]

This genre combined a response to the awareness of the world of concentration camps with a charge against standard Soviet fiction. While official Soviet philosophy rejected affiliations to either "ideology" or "utopia" (Mannheim 1955) and claimed a scientific view of the world,[26] Gulag narratives, and the dystopian narratives that came in their wake, highlighted its utopian aspects. Moreover, the disclosure of the forced-labor underside of Soviet society suggested that the novels that presented the achieved socialism as a basis for potentially universal happiness did not really model the existing society but *projected* one in which the absence of private ownership of the means of production had, indeed, brought justice for all.[27] It showed that the completion of the instrumental program of socialism, the foundational idea of its utopia, was not—and perhaps could not be—accompanied by the implementation of its humanistic moral program.[28] The dystopian fiction of the post-Stalinist years was a satirical exploration of this discovery.

The first major dystopia of the twentieth century, Evgeny Zamyatin's *We*, was written in 1920–21, before the Gulag had filtered into the consciousness of the post-revolutionary Russian intellectuals: it was the terror-fraught political structure as a whole rather than its forced-labor aspect that inspired dystopian imagination. However, subsequent Russian dystopian works include Gulag-related codes, their outré political satire finding, as it were, a storehouse of ready-made motifs in the barbed-wire enclosures that reproduced the general liabilities of the Soviet society in a condensed and heightened manner.

If the term *dystopia* is understood to refer to any cruel setting, rather than, narrowly, to an experimentally invented inhumane society, then one can distinguish two kinds of dystopian literature published even in the pre-*glasnost* Soviet Union: (1) the "Aesopian" (see Loseff 1984)—ostensibly realistic works set in foreign countries with brutal regimes (e.g., Dombrovsky's novel *Obeziana prikhodit za svoim cherepom* [*The Ape Comes for Its Skull*], ostensibly dealing with Nazi Germany but hinting at Stalinist Russia), and (2) science fiction novels, such as *The Snail on the Slope* by the Strugatsky brothers, where the atmosphere of grim secrecy and dehumanization promotes the reading of numerous narrative details as connoting the Gulag realia, so that sensitized readers perceive the nightmarish forest setting of the novel as a version of the Archipelago. Several works by the Strugatskys both catered to the popular demand for oneiric science fiction and used the attributes of this genre as a camouflage for vignettes of state-promoted terror.

Yet up until the nineties the main venues for dystopian fiction were Samizdat and Tamizdat. Vladimir Voinovich, the celebrated author of *The Adventures of Chonkin,* also used a science fiction framework in his *Moscow 2042,* where the time-machine plot is a functional vehicle (in the direct sense of the word) for a dystopian satire. A time traveler, a fictional extension of Voinovich himself, flies from West Germany to a Gulag-type dystopia of central Moscow in the year 2042. Communism, it seems, has been built there; at least one finds the principle of communist distribution—"from everyone according to capacity, to everyone according to need"—grimly implemented: the inmates (the whole population seems to be living in a Zone) are forced to collect the "secondary product," their excrement (which is then exported through pipelines to the West as raw material), as a condition for being allowed to receive the "primary" product—the horrible synthetic food of Orwellian public canteens—as well as the right to self-serve sex in hygienic establishments. Thus the foundational principle of the Moscow dystopia is the reversal of the "secondary" and the "primary," a Swiftean somatic parody on the Marxist reversal of the traditional valorization of the material and the spiritual. In keeping with the history of Stalin's times, the protagonist, a known opponent of the Communist system, is received with cautious honors, whereas another time traveler, an ardent supporter of the system, is subjected to horrifying tortures. Minor details of the setting echo narratives of Stalinist practices—for example, the intractable protagonist narrator is eventually thrust from a position of privilege to one of total privation. The person who eventually overthrows the dictatorship (to establish not a democratic state but a theocracy with archaic paraphernalia) is the emigrant writer Carnavalov, who travels to the future Moscow out of his seventies' estate in—Vermont (after having practiced his re-entry on a white horse). The second Russian revolution and the actual acts and attitudes of Aleksandr Solzhenitsyn, who returned to Russia in a quite different way in 1994, have disproved the caricaturesque prophesies of Voinovich. However, they left intact the novel's value as a satirical protest against any ideology's claims to possessing the key to absolute social good. The genre of dystopia is particularly convenient for this protest because it reveals the corruption of initially benevolent ideologies by absolute power.

A critique of a political idealism that refuses to recognize its own contingencies is also undertaken in Vasily Aksyonov's 1980 fantastic novel *Ostrov Krym* [*The Island of Crimea*]. The novel is a dystopia in reverse, an imaginative exploration of the processes that lead to a murderous Soviet invasion of the flourishing island into which the Crimean Peninsula is "miraculously" turned in the novel. The narrative is not haunted by Gulag motifs, but its vocabulary includes camp terms, used either in their direct sense, as in the case of the thieves' jargon *kaif* for "enjoyment," or in the figurative sense, as in the case of *balanda,* in-camp trash soup, for ideological eclecticism. The reader is thus recurrently reminded of the camps and implicitly invited to test the issues raised in the novel against that mental yardstick.

The island-state of Crimea, a kind of capitalist Russian Taiwan, founded by the White Guard officers who had retreated there during the Civil War, is also inhabited by the native Crimean Tatars (who are thus presented as having escaped their forced resettlement decreed by Stalin after World War II), by the offspring of the English sailors who had decided to stay in the Crimea in the early twenties, and by a whole variety of other nationalities. This prosperous society is destabilized by nationalistic ideologies pursued with a suicidal earnestness. The protagonist, Andrei Luchnikov, a larger-than-life figure with vast talents and a heroic upbringing, conducts an ultimately winning yet self-immolating struggle for the reunification of the Crimea with the USSR, sacrificing both himself, his loved ones, and numerous other people on the altar of a naive version of "the Russian idea."[29]

At the background of *The Island of Crimea* one can feel the Soviet dissident intellectuals' fears that Western democracies may be led—by their own intellectual elite—to a suicidal capitulation to totalitarian monsters. The novel also stages a tension between a critique of active political utopianism and the recognition of a popular thirst for inspiring, or rather self-empowering, ideologies. The multi-culturalist paradise of the independent island of Crimea is not based on any consciously chosen foundational idea, but various groups of its inhabitants pursue their own ideas with passionate intensity: all except the protagonist's son Anton lack the self-irony to realize that pluralism can be a sufficient basis for a healthy social life. The KGB "curator" of Crimea, who is obsessed with the Marxist "Foundational Idea," eventually literalizes the metaphor of the fatal attraction of ideological self-engulfment by leaping to his death in the raging Black Sea.

One of the conclusions that great numbers of Russian intellectuals have drawn from the history of the Soviet state is that forcing a whole population into the Procrustean bed of any specific view of prescribed general contentment produces a catastrophic ratio of suffering to happiness. The almost mandatory presence of Gulag motifs in modern Russian dystopian literature reflects the influence of Gulag testimonies on the origins of this conclusion.

* * *

Another textual imprint of the Gulag cultural code on the tissue of Russian fiction is the recurrent *realization of somatic metaphors*.

In Shalamov's story "Prosthetic Appliances" (*AL*) a group of prisoners is sent to solitary confinement. As they are registered, they have to hand in their outer clothing as well as their prosthetic appliances—a metal corset, an artificial limb, a hearing aid, or an eye. The protagonist narrator has no such appliances; his body is still whole. "So what will you hand in," he is asked by the guard, "your soul?" The punchline of the story, functional in the immediate context and symbolic in the broader one, is "'No,'" I said, 'My soul I shall not hand in'" (1978: 532). If the testimonial function of this story is seen as marked, then the prisoners' docile relinquishing of the extensions of their bodies reads as symptomatic of their proneness to humiliate themselves by accepting the precautions of the prison authorities at face value. If the artistic function is seen as the marked one, then the same detail reads as a literalized metaphor for trustfully giving away parts of their identities, or else as a symbol of the alienation of the slave's body, with its amputated ersatz parts only quantitatively differing from the parts that the slave is, in the meantime, allowed to keep.

As Andrei Sinyavsky has observed, the realization of metaphors was a characteristic feature of the Stalinist civilization. Indeed, with Stalin's demand for "criticism and self-criticism" even if no more than 5 to 10 percent of it were true, from 1934 through 1953 arrests were often based on anonymous denunciations by jealous colleagues or greedy neighbors. It seemed as if an average person's thought could suddenly become omnipotent: there was little distance between (step 1) the wish to have a certain person out of one's way, (step 2) the verbal hint of a denunciation, or a written report, and (step 3) the person's disappearance: it was not as if one were really performing a messy murder. If one wished to eliminate a person from one's own world, put an end to a friendship, cancel an offending influence, one could translate one's mental state into an action that did not greatly differ from a mental event: a few words, a phone call, a few jotted lines. The Archipelago inmates' return to the "mainland" in the mid fifties led to a wave of suicides and real or affected mental diseases among high-ranking KGB officials and collaborators: the reappearance of their victims must have meant (in addition to the ironically unjustified fear of revenge)[30] a return of the repressed, a version of the Freudian "uncanny."

The despotism that thus translated the atavistic sense of the thought's omnipotence into reality also turned metaphoric invectives into literal accusations. Sinyavsky notes that whereas Lenin "was speaking metaphorically when he used the term 'agents of the bourgeoisie' to describe Mensheviks or Western Social Democrats; or when he accused them of 'selling' the interests of the working class," Stalin "took everything literally": on his orders "investigators began torturing people arrested as agents of the bourgeoisie so that they would confess to spying for the Japanese, the Germans, or the English. The metaphor was taken to its real-life conclusion" (1990: 88).

While Stalinist media rhetoric realized metaphors in dead earnest, dissident writers foregrounded this device and laid it bare, disclosing its mechanics to the reader. The specific contribution of Gulag motifs to the process seems to consist in grotesque *somatic* metaphors. In Gulag narratives, expressions like "stabbing one in the back," "an eye for an eye," or "whoever does not work, does not eat" are all too often used not in their customary figurative but in their atavistically literal sense. Somatic imagery has been a versatile vehicle for political satire at least since *Gulliver's Travels;* yet Gulag narratives have endowed it with a particular significance: a slave has to answer for everything with his or her *body*—the relationship between production quotas and the size of the rations is but one expression of this regularity. It is from camp narratives that the technique of somatic literalization spills over to such works as Sasha Sokolov's post-modernist novel *Mezhdu sobakoi i volkom [Between Dog and Wolf]*,[31] with its setting of a grotesque shelter for the handicapped, symbolizing the damage sustained by the citizens of a totalitarian state, and with its sudden explosion into an oneiric carnival of swapping artificial teeth or limbs, suggestive of exchanging parts of individual personalities. In Yuly Daniel's "This Is Moscow Speaking" (1991: 71–99) citizens are offered a unique opportunity of murdering undesirables—not metaphorically, by betraying or denouncing them, but literally, and with impunity (at least one perfectly nice woman is quite willing to avail herself of the chance to get rid of her husband, provided her lover does the actual "messy" job). Literalizing a dead metaphor, Vladimov's dog Ruslan will not "eat out of a prisoner's hand." And in Sinyavsky's "Pkhentz" (1986: 215–45) the drying out of the E.T.-like protagonist's bandaged limbs and the blinding of his hidden eyes likewise signify the "atrophy" of individual talent in the standardizing xenophobic society.[32]

* * *

The literary career of Andrei Sinyavsky (1925–97) began in the shadow of his father's imprisonment in the last years of Stalin's rule (and of his own brush with the KGB that attempted to use him to entrap his friend Hélène Peltier). Sinyavsky lost the Communist beliefs of his generation earlier than most of his coevals. Having opted for an unfettered creative freedom, he started writing in a way that, as he knew in advance, was unpublishable in his homeland. With the help of Peltier he smuggled his and Yuly Daniel's early writings abroad, where they came out under the pseudonyms of Abram Tertz and Nikolai Arzhak. The identity of these two writers was discovered, and in September 1965 they were arrested. In February 1966 Sinyavsky was given a seven-year camp sentence. Released shortly before the expiration of the term, he emigrated to France.

Sinyavsky's literary production of the pre-camp days is different from his more mature, post-arrest writings, but there are thematic and modal continuities between them. In both his early and his late work Sinyavsky chose to engage not in bearing witness to social phenomena but in a philosophical processing and artistic transformation of experience. Nevertheless, his experimental pre-camp fiction is linked to Gulag semiotics, if only through dystopian motifs and literalized somatic metaphors, and his post-camp writings move closer to memoir literature, as though in response to consciously rejected but subconsciously powerful urgencies of testimony.

One of the earliest of Tertz/Sinyavsky's Tamizdat works, written in the late fifties, is the pamphlet *On Socialist Realism*, which ends by suggesting that to break out of the Procrustean bed into which Soviet literature has been forced one needs "a phantasmagoric art" in which "the grotesque" would replace "realistic descriptions of ordinary life" (1965: 218). The literary program thus outlined was put into effect in his *Fantastic Tales*, as well as in his carnivalesque dystopian novel *The Makepeace Experiment* (*Liubimov* in the original, 1964), which deals with the failure of a utopian experiment undertaken by a well-meaning but poorly educated young man named Lenia Tikhomirov. The experiment is limited to his beloved (*liubimyi*) native town, whose name may also be an allusion to Saltykov-Shchedrin's Glupov, the polis of fools, while the idea of geographical restriction is a parody on Lenin's emendation of Marxist theory: one can, according to Lenin and Stalin (though not according to Marx and Trotsky), build socialism in only one country rather than worldwide. The foundational principle of Lenia's utopia is that of *happy slaves* who will be made to *believe* that they are happy and that their needs and desires are fully satisfied. Lenia discovers in himself a hypnotic power to jam people's senses and make them misperceive reality in ways that he deems expedient.

The novel thus literalizes the macrometaphor of "the dark and magical night of Stalin's dictatorship," with which Tertz/Sinyavsky opens *On Socialist Realism* (1965: 147). Whereas Bolshevik utopianism demands suffering in the present for the sake of happiness in the future, Lenia's priority is *immediate* happiness for the citizens of his polis. It is first stimulated by his attempt to impress a woman, that is, by his search for his own individual happiness. On discovering hypnosis, Lenia, who wishes to act according to the "love-thy-neighbor-as-thyself" maxim, induces his townsmen to take the available mineral water for vodka and the canned red peppers for meat.[33] Eventually, hypnotic power, like all power, corrupts: Lenia begins to enjoy making people love, work, or die at his command. The town turns into a version of a parapsychologically guarded concentration camp, with the inmates working themselves to death. Like most dystopias, this magic kingdom is both exclusive (intruders are unwelcome) and imperialistic (the long-term plan is to export its brand of happiness). Yet on winning his girl, Lenia becomes impotent—an allegory on the ultimate powerlessness of any dictator. He loses control over himself: his thoughts run berserk, and the people around him behave accordingly. The women undrape; the men exchange blows; a young fellow dies when Lenia swears at him—uncontrolled fantasies are thus fulfilled and expletives turn into voodoo curses.[34] As in thermodynamics, the fate of a closed system is to lose energy. Entropy grows almost from day one, with only temporary intermissions; in the end the experiment of turning involuntary Lent into a fake carnival leads to grotesque carnage.

Lenia's principles conflict with one of the main ethical lessons of Gulag literature: one should not impose one's will on others, even for their own good. The hypnotic rule of the once gentle Tikhomirov, reminiscent of the snake-like spellbinding powers of many historical tyrants, literalizes the idea of turning people into robots. Sinyavsky was, as noted above, a theorist of the literalization of metaphors as well as a writer who deliberately foregrounded this rhetorical device. The metaphors realized in the plots of his fiction often shade into allegories or symbols. In *Liubimov*, for instance, the idea of the incompleteness of identity without faith is graphically embodied in a character who has helped to dismantle a monastery and winds up with a paralyzed arm. In "Pkhentz," one of the most memorable of Tertz's "fantastic tales," different aspects of the somatic predicament of an extraterrestrial "alien" symbolize the spiritual handicap of an artist in the Soviet society (Nepomnyashchy 1995: 64–76). Ordinary life is often rendered in schematic flashes that invite figurative readings, whereas the reality-effect of separate details at times dramatizes the ways in which "everyday life" distracts us from transcendent signification. For example, if the prurient remark of a character in "At the Circus"—"Real women acrobats ought to be seen without any clothes on. And not in a circus, but in an apartment, on a tablecloth, in the middle of pineapples" (1986: 150)—strikes us as characterizing some decadent enclave, we may overlook its functionality in the broader context: its hint at the transfer of "the performing body out of the world of performance" (Nepomnyashchy 1995: 76) and at the blurring of the borderline between carnivalesque art and ordinary life. Sinyavsky's early texts implicitly blame the reader for a tendency to privilege the literal at the expense of the figurative, for letting the body distract one from the spirit. Even the sympathy that one tends to develop for the trials of the protagonist of "Pkhentz" is eventually perceived as competing with the figurative significance of his body language for the reader's attention. The religious vision behind this narrative technique reduces its accessibility for people raised on the diet of socialist realism. Yet if our sympathy for the characters occasionally interferes with our detached construction of the significance of their conduct, our response may also be understood as modeling the function of sympathy in the cultural climate that precluded a variant of the Nuremberg trials. The polysemous yet inwardly consistent suggestiveness of figurative constructions is one of Sinyavsky's ways of being "truthful with the aid of the absurd and the fantastic" (1965: 219).

Sinyavsky's later narratives, written in the aftermath of his own camp experience, give more weight to the mimetic and the referential material: one hardly needs fantastic inventions since camp reality is, in itself, sufficiently grotesque. Tertz/Sinyavsky's main "Gulag" works, *A Voice from the Chorus* and *Goodnight!*, present formerly unrecorded nuances of camp life, even though the emphasis is on the relationship of the individual with his conscience rather than on testimony to socio-political abuse. Yet the concern with conscience brings the books close to the Gulag memoir corpus: they share, for instance, the *Bildung* topos of Gulag literature— the "liberating prison" (Levitt 1991: 51) leads to, or at least enhances and refines, one's intellectual maturity. In the inset story "Glasses" in *Goodnight!*, the authorial persona, just released from the camp after a span of incarceration between four particularly blind walls, discovers that he needs reading glasses: in the camps and prisons they had not been necessary. The episode endows a somatic image with a figurative meaning: Sinyavsky actually becomes "far-sighted" during his "internship" (*stazh,* Tertz/Sinyavsky 1992: 266) behind bars, yet when the metaphoric intellectual liberation is literalized in the actual release, the changed vision comes to be perceived as a handicap.

Tertz/Sinyavsky's literary-critical works, *Strolls with Pushkin* and *V teni Gogolia* [*In the Shadow of Gogol*]—the former written in the camp and the latter begun there and completed after release—reflect a vision affected by the camp experience. In a quest for expressiveness, the "hyperbolic prose" (*utrirovannaia proza,* 1990: 61) of these works is occasionally spiced with typical camp language. What Tertz/Sinyavsky emphasizes, however, is that though the "internship" is a communal experience, the content of the education one receives is individual. This is also borne out by the continuity of his concerns and attitudes in the works written before and after his imprisonment.

The thematic continuity of his corpus is maintained by the development of the theme of self-elimination (Holmgren 1991: 969; Levitt 1991: 51–61; Nepomnyashchy 1995: 97–108, 149–96). In "Graphomaniacs" (1986: 169–214), one of Tertz/Sinyavsky's early grotesques, a character maintains that a writer should empty out his obtrusive idiosyncratic self and become a mere channel for the flow of his materials. This Keatsian idea is given an earnest theological development in "Unguarded Thoughts," a collection of aphorisms composed shortly before Sinyavsky's arrest. Here the theme of the onion-like peeling of one's identity enters into a dialectic tension with the theme of accumulation as expressed in covetousness, the loading and stuffing of the self, the snowballing of experience.

The Lenten consequences of the same theme are explored in Tertz/Sinyavsky's post-camp *A Voice from the Chorus,* a collection of sketches, notes, and aphorisms culled from the letters he had written to his wife from the camp. As the outer social layers of one's exhausted self are stripped off, one can rise to the challenge of *kenosis,* a self-overcoming for the sake of turning into a conduit for "inspiration" in a near-literal sense of this word: "why not just be contrary and go on living when it's no longer possible, when thought itself is almost extinguished by fatigue and apathy? Here, at rock bottom, is where you get to your feet and begin!" (1976a: 5).

Sinyavsky's Lenten reduction of the self amidst the hunger and privation of the camps is not based on the same model as Shalamov's secular ascesis. Shalamov's depleted focalizers refuse to entrust their "soul" to anyone's keep and strive to maintain a sense of themselves, if only through inner resistance to oppression. Their suffering is an ethical version of the test of faith, and their Lenten near-mystical merger with the natural environment ("in league with the stones of the field") is caused by the porousness of the outer envelope of their selves. On the "rock bottom" they *endure*, rather than "begin." Nor is their feat less admirable than the new start of the "voice" in *A Voice from the Chorus:* from their standpoint, Sinyavsky may never have even touched rock bottom. However that may be, his Lent is a kenotic rather than an ascetic experience, and his texts allude not to Job but to Abbakum in the pit and Jonah in the belly of the fish—a prophet hollowing himself out of rationality to pour forth the vision that has entered his being as it might enter a funnel or a pit (32).

In "Strolls with Pushkin" Tertz/Sinyavsky presents his controversial view of Pushkin's genius as associated with a form of inner emptiness that allowed for an unobstructed transformation of life into art. *A Voice from the Chorus* continues to explore this theme, yet with a difference. Whereas in "Unguarded Thoughts" the stripping of the personality is a way to kenosis, *A Voice from the Chorus* takes kenosis as its starting point and goes on to test the ways in which the self-voiding admits a partial blending with *the other,* in an interplay of the individual and the communal. The book strings together records of in-camp discourse, thematically resonant (*"'Even dying is useful to a writer'"* [44]; *"'He's so brainy it's enough to scare you!'*...[on the] inadmissibility of being too intelligent" [183]), culturally symptomatic ("A comment on Lensky's aria 'Oh, whither, whither have you gone'...'*Will he be singing long, this Maupassant?*'" [210]), or just profoundly moving ("From a letter: '... *And Dad cries too, because of you. Whenever he sits down to eat he cries and says: here we are, eating—but our Slavka isn't with us'*" [18]). The author is a part of the chorus. Out of a melancholy solidarity, he records the remarks of his fellow prisoners with which he can sympathize alongside those that are morally repellent and culturally alien to him; the latter often present oxymoronic collocations that express so far unexplored adventures of human souls, for example, *"To disentangle a vicious circle"* (30; cf. Pomerantz 1993: 181). The author's own voice is also given a few solo performances, musings on the psychological effects of incarceration-as-ascesis or on literary representations of dystopian captivity: the gradual divestment to which Swift subjects his Gulliver and a divestment followed by reaccumulation in Defoe's *Robinson Crusoe* (21–24). Whereas Dombrovsky gives Stalinist terror a ramifying place in a poetic cosmos that also includes extensions of Golgotha, the Last Supper, and cultural feasts in times of the plague, Sinyavsky places the Gulag in a context of cultural history tinged with a theological vision.

In *Goodnight!*, a semi-confessional autobiographical novel, religious concerns recede. Of all Sinyavsky's works, this book comes closest to documentary prose. It contains a strong element of testimony about the "dark and magical night" of Stalin's terror and the mists of stagnation-era repression. By contrast with the grotesque gusto of his pre-camp narratives, where fantastic images whisk the reader's attention from the literal to the figurative plane, in *Goodnight!* the texture of the narrative details is dense and the themes submerged. The novel continues to pursue Tertz/Sinyavsky's concern with self-divestment, yet this thematic strand provides not so much a unifying principle as a semantic field for the novel's multiple self-contradictions. Nor does it accommodate all the separate issues to which, despite his denial of the obligation to testify, Tertz/Sinyavsky nevertheless bears witness. Thus, whereas in memoir literature recurrent themes help to control the pressures of testimony, in Sinyavsky's novel these pressures partly disrupt the thematic coherence and align the novel that disavows testimony with factographic witness narratives.

The stripping down of the authorial persona's identity is enacted through the confessional structure of *Goodnight!*. Paradoxically, it proceeds through the accumulation of material in the five chapters of the text, the five stages in his unwrapping, down to that secret point in his personality where he bifurcated into Sinyavsky and Tertz. The first chapter, "The Turncoat," deals with the removal of Sinyavsky's conventional social status through his arrest, interrogations, trial, and imprisonment. The respected university lecturer is first reduced to the confused butt of the interrogators' mockery, then to a helpless undernourished *zek* ("Hands behind your back!" . . . "A step to your right or left, and I'll shoot without further warning"), and eventually to a worn-out aging man in camp rags. The last, however, accumulates more than he has been deprived of and eventually comes to feel an enormous experiential superiority to the slick engineers in his railway carriage on the way back to Moscow upon release.

The narrative goes on to "unwind"[35] the earlier layers of his self. Chapter two, "The House of Assignations," deals with his communal camp self, here presented through the prism of a *zek*'s annual conjugal meetings. In dealing with the most intimate matters, the emphasis shifts from the referentiality of "The Turncoat" to representativeness: the arrival of Maria Rozanova-Sinyavsky is treated not only as a highly individual experience but also as a sample of the desperate attempts of the Russian women ("Why just Russian? Lithuanian, Ukrainian, Armenian, Jewish, Kirgizian, Laplandian wenches—from every which way they travel to the House of Assignations" 1992b 2: 402) to encourage their imprisoned husbands, feed them, reach out to them, make love with them—not just for the shared pleasure but so that (use-it-or-lose-it) the husbands might not take to drinking upon release (1992b 2: 403). Sinyavsky finds it expedient to have the jailers think about his meeting with his wife in terms of sex alone; but she is telling him, in hastily scribbled notes—to keep it secret from the mouse-like hidden tape recorders—about the public responses to his trial, about the Samizdat White Book put together by Aleksandr Ginzburg (published abroad in 1967) and including Shalamov's then anonymous "Letter to an Old Friend" (see 1986b), about Solzhenitsyn's refusal to actively join his and Daniel's defense, and other matters:

> Maria clips ciphers like grass and throws fingerfulls of paper macaronies into the sauce-pan: Aragon, Tvardovsky . . . One hell of a soup. Ehrenburg . . . Your pencil—keep the rustling down! . . . Shalamov. To an old friend. Ginzburg . . . Solzhenitsyn . . . Should not have turned to him. He's got other things on his mind. But the motivation! A writer must earn his glory in his own country . . . Signatures collected . . . Vigorelli . . . Who is Meniker? Vika Schweitzer was fired because of you . . . They make deductions from Golomshtok's salary for refusal to give evidence . . . (1992b 2: 408)

Thus public matters are turned into a private exchange, whereas physical intimacy is turned both into their cover and into a bridge between the Sinyavsky couple and multitudes of other couples similarly reunited for a brief while in the gatehouse of the camp. At the end of the chapter, the end of the lovers' night together, the wealth of their shared world is translated into the naked language of sex. Yet this self-divestment before parting ("I am finished. Crashed and slandered" [1992b 2: 455]) links the couple not only with their closest community but also with the wider community of ecstatically, self-immolatingly mating animals. The text becomes deliberately ambiguous: "In the furor of the consciousness of your end, you express yourself already not with your face, not with a member of society, but with an appendix of yourself, possessed by reason and continuing the eloquence in the same thundering verbs: 'Believe me! Understand me! Remember and remain!' In a high-flown tone, almost tragically, yet, I assure you, with total plainness" (1992b 2: 456). The words "not with a member of society" may be taken as referring to the face (as opposed to the sexual "appendix"), yet also to the common-denominator genital, which is then opposed to something like the soul, the reason-possessed and mutely eloquent appendix of the commonplace self.

The themes of divestment and the reversal of the private and the public continue in the particularly moving third chapter of the novel, "Father," where, however, the emphasis is on ascesis rather than on kenosis.

The author's father, a member of the gentry and heir to the family estate, had, before the revolution, donated his property to the cause of the revolution. In Stalin's days, barely surviving outside prison due to his Left SR past, he instills in his son a valorization of stoical poverty, a point in which Marxist revolutionary principles converge with Christian idealism. One of the greatest blows to Sinyavsky's young life is his father's arrest in 1951. Probably as a consequence of the electrical shocks given him during the interrogations, upon his release his father believes that wires have been implanted in his brain so that the police might eavesdrop on his conversations and thoughts. To protect the people around him from the prying of the police, he gives up one of the greatest pleasures of private life in a totalitarian state—frank conversations with the select few trustworthy beloved people. Thus the metaphor of the incursion of the totalitarian state into one's private life is cruelly literalized as an imagined somatic implant.

In the fourth chapter, "Dangerous Liaisons," the theme of the divestment of the self is replaced by the theme of the criminal divestment of another. The chapter begins with fairy-tale episodes concerning the actress A., who has spiritualistic powers and is believed to allow the spirits of the departed to use her as a medium. At a certain point she repulses an obnoxious spirit that attempts, as it were, to empty her out and use her as a conduit for its provocations: the ideal of self-elimination is here held in check by the imperative of self-assertion, the same imperative that has made Sinyavsky (like El Campesino before him) keep his beard despite the threats of the interrogator. Sinyavsky's favorite fairy tale is the one in which Stalin's spirit visits A. in her exile shortly after his death and, using the names of his victims the way one might use the names of towns to convey the spelling of a word on the phone, asks her to forgive him his sins. By reducing the dead "to letters on an ouija board" (Nepomnyashchy 1995: 292), Stalin's ghost attempts to empty people of their individualities. The actress A., probably chosen by Stalin's ghost as the first letter of the alphabet, tells him that she absolves him of what he has done to her but not of what he has done to others: he should visit each victim personally and ask for forgiveness.

Composing the novel in the eighties, Sinyavsky was no doubt familiar with the memoirs of Evgenia Ginzburg, who tells us that in 1949 ex-prisoners living in Kolyma were re-arrested, literally, in alphabetical order, realizing a metaphor for sweeping, undiscriminating persecution. In "The House of Assignations" he recollects his wife's comparing their reunion to making love "in a morgue," thus restoring to the figurative plane a metaphor that was, quite in earnest, literalized in the "magical night" of Stalinism: Elinor Lipper's book, for instance, contains an inset story in which the trysts of hospital janitors take place in the morgue, with a corpse literally standing guard at the door.[36] Alternatively, like Shal-amov, in *Goodnight!* Tertz/Sinyavsky occasionally turns his actual experi-ence into a ramifying metaphor: his briefcase, heavy with books, prevents him from joining the stream of people flowing to Stalin's funeral, which is about to turn into a huge stampede with hundreds of victims—thus, his life is both literally and figuratively saved by the books.

But books, a physical burden and a life-saving amenity, are not the building blocks of an ivory tower. While Stalin is dying, Sinyavsky is spending his days in the library studying foreigners' accounts of the early seventeenth-century Times of Trouble that followed the appearance of Demetrius the Pretender.[37] The irrationality and the horrifying blood-shed that followed the murder of the legitimate heir to the throne, the infant Prince Demetrius,[38] emerge as a typological foreshadowing of the no less gory contemporary experience. Of all the inventive tortures and executions of the period, Sinyavsky chooses to dwell on the cutting off of the witnesses' tongues so that they might not bear testimony: literaliza-tion of somatic metaphors is not new under the sun. At the end of the chapter, the gleanings from historical accounts are transformed into a parable on means and ends: according to this apocryphal *Gedankenex-periment,* the near-surreal atrocities of the Times of Trouble are caused by the Virgin Mary's compassion for her namesake, the Tsarina Maria, mother of the murdered prince. As if atoning for his erstwhile rejection of his private life, atoning for his sacrifice of his filial commitment on the altar of public good, Christ now takes pity on his mother and promises to return Demetrius to her protégée, at least for a time, no matter at what cost. He thus reverses the time-honored tradition of East European revolutionaries and sacrifices the public for the sake of the private, with similarly dire results.

The last chapter of the book tells the story of the informer S., who has been maneuvered into providing a cover for the author's attempts to evade collaboration with the secret police. The authorial persona has been fascinated by S., a talented poet and artist, whom he has regarded as a budding genius. Contrary to Pushkin's unwillingness to believe that genius and villainy could coexist in the same person, Sinyavsky finds that such a coexistence is quite in the nature of things. Though he paints the portrait of S. as a cross between a Dostoevskian Stavrogin and a Kierke-gaardian aesthete who lives totally outside the system of moral concepts, he interprets him as a case of the hollow man, whose soullessness can be, in accordance with the theory of the artist's self-elimination, an equally streamlined conduit for both artistic inspiration and villainous drives. Yet the genius of S. does not attain fruition: apparently, true artistic cre-ation is a matter of tormented self-divestment rather than ready-made inner void.

The "real person" behind the portrait of S., Sergei Khmelnitsky, eventually struck back at Sinyavsky for disclosing their intimate conversations, for creating fictionalizations reinterpretable as lies, and for reshuffling some facts of the past and attributing to one of them what was true of the other. In Tertz/Sinyavsky's reference to S. as dead, Khmelnitsky saw a hypocritically insufficient camouflage of the clues to his identity. Actually, however, this distortion of the facts well known to Sinyavsky's Moscow entourage was a deliberate signal of fictionalization: by denying a referential foothold to separate details, *Goodnight!* compels the reader to hesitate between referentiality and representativeness—as do, in fact, Shalamov's documentary fictions, as well as those memoirs that change names of people and places to protect those left behind.

Goodnight! is offered to the reader as "a novel": it is thus supposed to subordinate the referential to the representative and to allow fictional recombinations that would not be legitimate in a bona fide memoir. Khmelnitsky reads the book referentially, protests against its treatment of his image, suggests that back in the sixties, by openly blowing his cover, Mrs. Sinyavsky's defamation of his character actually helped him to free himself from the KGB, and claims that Sinyavsky was, for a while, as much a police informer as he himself was.[39] Both were, he claims, victims of the times. Khmelnitsky is obviously offended by the passage in which Sinyavsky renders the complaints of S. about the historical injustice of his being ostracized for having denounced two people in the past:[40]

> he has found the culprits of his misery. And they are those—no kidding—on whom he had informed, whom he had buried, sunk. You shouldn't, he says, have messed up my biography, guys, you shouldn't have spoiled my reputation. OK, so you've sat five out of your ten years in the camps. Big loss—five years! With me, it's my whole life going down the drain because of you. My career is ruined. I cannot show my face in decent society. People whisper. Edge off. Avoid frank conversations, confessions. So compare, who has the worst of it—you or I? Isn't there any justice in the world? (1992b 2: 574–75)

Despite the tone of grotesque satire that offended Khmelnitsky, the passage suggests that in the "magical night" of Stalinism the question who would become the victim and who the informer was rather a matter of statistical chance, of a Borgesian Lottery in Babylon, and that the fate of the informer could be harder than that of the victim.[41] The argument is not totally absurd if one bears in mind that the secret police must have had quotas of secret recruits as well as of arrests. Nevertheless, the psychological and moral makeup of each individual had much sway in the matter, the "lucky lottery tickets," to adapt Ehrenburg's notorious metaphor, being reserved only for those who would manage to avoid the test.

The self-contradictions of *Goodnight!* (Khmelnitsky's article actually an-notates some of its *aporiae*) and the oscillations between Sinyavsky's admiration for S., shamefaced empathy with him, and liberating disgust invite the readers to turn upon themselves: on which side of the blurry divide would each of us find him- or herself under similar conditions? One of the connotations of the title[42] is that we can sleep quietly only so long as we are not *actually* subjected to such a test.

On losing sight of their "tails" in a Moscow street (a dangerous state of uncertainty), Hélène Peltier says to Sinyavsky, "Let us get out of here, Andriushka." In a narrative move from the literal to the metaphorical, her words reverberate outside their context: Sinyavsky realizes that he needs an exit and that his exit will be into writing. The incident signifies the birth of the writer wearing the mask of Abram Tertz, the Odessa bandit who, in a popular doggerel, invites guests but gets drunk before they arrive. Art is a matter of breaking away from convention, of asserting one's freedom—not only from the lies of the totalitarian regime with its socialist realism but also from subservience to the social order coming from the counter-establishment. For Sinyavsky, that also means relin-quishing claims to "the truth," especially the absolute truth. In the 1974 article "The Literary Process in Russia" Sinyavsky writes: "Having exor-cised ourselves from the lie, we have no right to succumb to the tempta-tion of the truth, which will lead us back to socialist realism inside out. . . . A young man once appeared in my apartment and said: 'I am an anti-communist! I am for the truth'! At the time it sounded splendid: here was someone who was not afraid to speak out. Later, however, doubts and analogies came to mind. Suppose someone were to go around repeating: 'I am an anti-fascist!" Very nice . . . except that it is somehow too common-place, unconvincing, cheap. Why take as the yardstick of your own value something that you consider worthless? . . . I am, I must confess, rather suspicious of realism; I have a feeling that a new lie might develop from it" (1976b: 98).

Yet Abram Tertz's books are more complex than the programmatic statements made in his articles: they test rather than apply on-record ideas. Despite his rejection of Solzhenitsyn's imperative to testify, in *A Voice from the Chorus* and *Goodnight!* Sinyavsky's self-divestment has turned him into a witness both to the actual imprisonment that added depth to his perspective and to the prison-like constraints of the totalitarian state, from which he broke out, as from a womb, to become a writer. His literary imagination, however, would keep returning to "the dark and magical night" of his own gestation.

A determined non-joiner, Sinyavsky could well afford to reject the conventions of Gulag testimony: the main work of testimony had already been done by others. It is as if the protagonist of Camus's *The Fall* could have gone on living peacefully with himself if somebody else had given evidence about the suicide to which he failed to bear witness. Unlike the writers who would regret their belatedness, Sinyavsky had good reason to exult in it, since it granted him greater freedom to transform his materials. In-camp experience itself is excluded from *Goodnight!* because Sinyavsky had already dealt with it in *A Voice from the Chorus*—significantly, the one aspect of the camp that is described in *Goodnight!*, the conjugal reunion in "The House of Assignations," is the one that he had had no need to describe in his letters to his wife. Yet the story of the protagonist-narrator's arrest, his remarks on prisons and camps, and the account of the ways in which totalitarian terror impinged on the lives of two generations tallies with what the reader, at least the Russian reader, knows from other sources, producing an almost inevitable hesitation between the fictional and the factographic pact.[43]

Like camp memoirs, *Goodnight!* starts with the author's arrest and ends with a train journey, a journey toward creative, if not political, freedom. And though both the terms of the ethical/aesthetic dichotomy had limited acceptability to Sinyavsky, the investigation carried out in *Goodnight!* is both aesthetic, insofar as it deals with the metaphors of self-liberation, and ethical, insofar as it is devoted to the issues of self-divestment and interaction with others. As in the camp memoirs written by ardently religious authors, the exclusion of concrete information about the conditions of daily life reflects a religious vision, while also pointing to the *belatedness* of Sinyavsky's work. Moreover, the camp conditions that he knew were milder than those in the days of Stalin; the day-to-day suffering of the victims was no longer so excruciating as to claim urgent first-priority consciousness-raising efforts from every survivor-witness. Sinyavsky could *afford* not to give concrete testimony, yet his choice of the genre option does not necessarily have to be applauded (as it often has been) as an escape from a slavery to fact.

"It is Solzhenitsyn's constricting *imperative* that Sinyavsky rejects," writes Donald Fanger (1986: 123). Indeed, the imperative to testify to abuses can, like dissident culture in general, be as constricting as the demands (for *narodnost', ideinost', partiinost';* see Hosking 1980: 3) of the official socialist realism; nevertheless, Sinyavsky's ability to claim an exemption from it was a matter of propitious timing rather than of artistic courage. Recognition of this state of affairs is embedded in *Goodnight!*, where, on being sent from prison to the train station on the way to the camps, the authorial persona recognizes his experience as perfectly conforming to what he has read about similar "transports": what is belated in not just Sinyavsky's post-camp text but also his camp experience itself. His familiarity with precursor accounts of imprisonment enriches his own ordeal with a sense of recognition and then sanctions his imaginative transformation and formalization of the biographical material—somewhat along the lines of his pre-camp grotesques.

Yet an arbiter called to rank Sinyavsky's *Goodnight!*, Shalamov's *Kolyma Tales,* and Solzhenitsyn's *The Gulag Archipelago* according to artistic merit would hardly offer precedence to *Goodnight!* Opting for or against testimony need not mean either forfeiting or privileging artistic endeavor. As most readers of documentary works well know, we turn to memoirs in quest of facts, but, having done so, in the process of reading we are often struck by their literary excellence. We then question whether to regard them as art or as well-penned testimony. In that sense, multi-functional works of documentary prose share a major feature of modernist art—the fact that the hesitation about the extent to which they are works of art is an integral part of their aesthetic effect. In the case of modernist art, this hesitation takes the shape of a "suspicion of fraudulence"—perhaps the artist is pulling our legs; is this, anyway, art at all?[44] In the case of documentary prose it turns into caution: can one grant life-writing—that is, a direct account of personal experience—the status of art? What is commonly called art is certainly not the only source of aesthetic experience. Major Gulag works end up creating conditions for this experience through the interconnection of the structure and rhetoric with the shared but subjectively perceived material. Just as ethical engagement and aesthetic drive converge in the production of these works, so the responses in the reception terminus combine the search for knowledge with ethical compulsion and with the exposure of one's mental and emotional self to unforeseeable change.

* * *

This book should not end with an aesthetic point, not even one with abundant ethical ramifications. Moreover, an account of the literary processing of the Gulag experience would not approximate even a porous comprehensiveness should it elide the sympathetic view from the other side of the barbed wire. Perhaps the most artistically significant fictional transformation of a jailer's perception (not counting Vladimov's tour-de-force guard-dog novella) is the 1982 semi-autobiographical novel by Sergei Dovlatov, *The Zone.* An enfant-terrible intellectual expelled from the philological faculty of Leningrad State University in 1962, Dovlatov was conscripted into the army and spent his service in the armed-guard units posted in camps for criminal convicts. The experience turned him into a writer, and also caused the alcoholic addiction that is believed to account for his early death. Dovlatov's stories were first published after his 1978 emigration.

In *The Zone* Dovlatov puts together separate sketches of camp life from the viewpoint of a guard, interspersing them with italicized comments addressed, as it were, to his Russian-American publisher and explaining, among other things, that the manuscript contains approximately 30 percent of the material of his original work, which was smuggled out of the country in little batches "by courageous Frenchwomen" and got scattered on the way (an allusion to the smuggling of Sinyavsky's and Kuznetsov's manuscripts out of the USSR). Dovlatov thus gives a new twist to the uncodified tradition according to which an authentic camp narrative necessarily lacks artistic finish.

Whereas Sinyavsky's novels may, to some extent, be read as subversive responses to Solzhenitsyn, *The Zone* looks back, with a touch of anxiety, to the work of Shalamov. In one of the messages to the publisher, the narrator of *The Zone* quotes the sarcastic remark of the critic A. Genis: "You keep worrying that it will come out like in Shalamov. Don't worry. It won't" (110). Dovlatov's stories do not, indeed, attain the passion and the philosophical depth of Shalamov's, but a number of Shalamov's concerns and techniques undergo a new metafictional processing in Dovlatov's chiseled spare fragments. The stance of a guard, however reluctant and humane, yields a view different from that of a political prisoner. The narrator of Dovlatov's story "Nashi" ["Ours"] once thought that his experience as a camp guard was not all that different from that of his cousin who had been imprisoned in a camp; he recants after his own brief incarceration: for all the similarity of landscape and physical hardship, the world does not look the same from the inside and from the outside of the "zone" (1991: 47).

Like Shalamov, Dovlatov takes recourse to the technique of a "lyrical hero" in whom the reader can recognize some of the author's features, such as height (Dovlatov too was very tall) and education, yet whose different name signals the fictionalization. Dovlatov's focalizer is Boris Alikhanov, a former student with a Tatar-sounding name that half-alludes to Dovlatov's non-Russian (Armenian and Jewish) origins. Unlike Shalamov's avatars, Alikhanov does not manage to translate his cultural detachment from his environment into a moral detachment. On New Year's night he attempts to prevent his fellow guards from taking turns having sex with a drunken woman from a neighboring forced settlement. When they leave, however, he cannot take his mind off the sordid details of the scene, involving, it seems, the use of the single available condom. After his mates return silently to their living quarters, Alikhanov gives in to the temptation: he goes to the woman and has sex with her, brusquely and brutally, without thinking about the venereal disease she is likely to carry.[45] An intellectual's squeamish superiority to his psychologically stunted associates is no insurance against moral contagion.[46]

Taking the relativist position, the narrator of *The Zone* maintains that good and evil are functions of contingencies, that they are arbitrary (*proizvol'nyi* [67]) rather than intrinsic to individuals. Yet *proizvol* in the adjective *proizvol'nyi* means "tyranny," and the connotations of arbitrary power subvert the narrator's relativistic generalizations. Dovlatov also lays bare Shalamov's device of having the events of a story contradict the narrator's commentary: he gives a sympathetic presentation of Captain Yegorov's courtship and conjugal life, stating that this "dull and malicious animal" comes through as quite likable owing to the "metamorphosis of the creative process" (74). In point of fact, the story activates Yegorov's attractive and repulsive features in an alternating manner, suggesting (as Ginzburg does in her account of the security officers taking her classes after her release from the camp) that a quite admirable human potential has been perverted by Yegorov's type of service.

To his consternation, the focalizer discovers that the criminal convict Kuptsov, his open antagonist, is actually his alter ego, a man who inwardly thrives on alienation. Kuptsov is a "hereditary" thief who still lives by the "honest thieves'" code and therefore refuses to work, even at the cost of the steady depletion of his body in the punishment cells. His adherence to the code is not motivated by the fear of his fellow "blue-bloods"—as the focalizer tells him; he is the last of his gang, the only one left:[47]

> "Listen, you are alone! The thieves' code no longer exists. You are just one."
>
> "Right," Kuptsov smiled wryly. "Solo. I perform without a chorus."
>
> "So you'll kick the bucket. You are one against all. And hence in the wrong . . . "
>
> Kuptsov uttered slowly, clearly, and sternly:
>
> "*One* is always in the right . . . " (55)

But Kuptsov is not the only distorted mirror image of the focalizer. Another one is the illiterate and corrupt guard ironically nicknamed Fidel, who repeatedly protests, "We don't dig politics" (*Politiku ne khavaem*), picks fights, oppresses convicts, stars in devil-may-care drunken debauches, but breaks down and cries when torn between his friendship with the focalizer and his prescribed duty to shoot him for insubordination. As in Shalamov's stories, there is an individual moral barrier that even the worst of the camp guards will not cross. And yet this is the same Fidel who demands that Kuptsov's wife sleep with him as a condition for allowing her a conjugal tryst with her husband. And it is the same brave Kuptsov who on that occasion implores the woman to comply.

Toward the end of the book, when put under further pressure to undertake any sort of work, in order to avoid punishment cells for refusal, Kuptsov mutilates his left hand with an ax that the focalizer lets him have, the ax with which he expects Kuptsov to attack him. As testimony the episode is not necessary—Gulag literature is replete with stories of characters' self-mutilation. Its function in the narrative is obviously symbolic: if one's sense of identity is totally bound up with an adherence to a code, this may be at the cost of the identity's wholeness and discreteness. In camp conditions, such regularities have direct somatic expressions.

Yet Dovlatov's main emphasis is still, and always, on the absurdity and the perverseness of the conditions that lead to this reduction and misshaping of human beings. Reversing the tendency to move away from the imperative to testify, the self-referential techniques of *The Zone* actually enhance its consciousness-raising function. As an Aksyonov character has put it, the camps are still "places undeserving of habitation" (*mesta nedostoinye prozhivania* [1983: 153]). In the late nineties, though there does not seem to be any more political imprisonment in Russia, the topicality of the issue is still not a matter of the past. Dovlatov clearly suggests that not even a recidivistic criminal convict should be warehoused under conditions dehumanizing to everyone involved. One might add that there still is a need for international struggle against the concentration or "re-education" camps and forced labor that still exist in other parts of the world.

* * *

Unless these calls are voiced and find response, the lessons of the Gulag, as processed by its first- and second-degree witnesses, will not have been assimilated.

Twentieth-century European atrocities have made it clear that post-Enlightenment canons of philosophy, poetry, and fiction have left their public vulnerably unprepared (cf. Milosz 1953: 111–34). In a bend-sinister development of progressive intellectual ideals, the October Revolution, which had held out the promise of future universal justice at the price of an unspecified amount of present sacrifice, led up to events that consumed more human lives than any previous historical upheaval. In the wake of these events writers as different as Shalamov, Nabokov (in *The Gift*), and Solzhenitsyn (in *The Red Wheel*) have offered a reassessment of different elements of their cultural tradition—in particular its "love of humanity" at the expense of a clarity of vision and honesty about the past. This reassessment went hand in hand with the late-twentieth-century shift from the discourse of "love" to the less demanding discourse of "respect" as a basis for ethical theory and practice.

In *Was Stalin Really Necessary?* Alec Nove writes that Stalin's major policies, such as the drive to industrialize an agrarian country at top speed and the concomitant drive toward the forced collectivization of agriculture, were a matter of objective economic and political necessity for a Communist government; these measures led, with a similar necessity, to mass terror. When economic revolutions of such a huge scale are forced upon a population, "excesses" become statistically inevitable. Though the dynamics of the revolution created conditions for people like Stalin to establish a dictatorship, Stalin's personal qualities may have been responsible only for the "excesses of excesses" (1964: 17–39).

This theory, whose validity I am in no position to judge,[48] would help to explain why, partly aware of the liabilities of Stalin's character, his future victims in the Bolshevik Old Guard supported him, even against each other—believing, perhaps, in the need for his ruthlessness. Yet Nove's model should be supplemented by cultural considerations: owing not least to their own version of honor and to their dedication to the common cause rather than to personal power (cf. Avtorkhanov 1983: 216–46), intellectuals like Bukharin stood no chance in their resistance to Stalin's unscrupulous maneuvering, could not foresee its extent, and failed to imagine its practical consequences. Their inherited cultural tradition could not provide such foresight. Nor could the victims of Stalin's expedient terror draw on their early reading in order to understand what mixture of power-struggle regularities they were up against. In literature evil took the forms of vanquishable local and personal aberrations, of atavistic counterparts of natural disasters, of Romantic temptations, of Dostoevskian nightmares or Kafkaesque traps; eventually it was identified with the exploitative social structure. The large-scale twentieth-century evil—routine, banal, shoddy, and massive—had no precedent in either the imaginative or the documentary literature of the past: the inmates of the Archipelago had to study it firsthand and without a suitable ready-made conceptual grid. No wonder they felt obliged to report the results, if they survived their discoveries.

In other words, Gulag literature fills a gap in the literary representation of human experience of evil. In doing so it only partly overlaps with Holocaust literature, because in works of the Holocaust corpus (with a few exceptions, such as Primo Levi's memoirs, which are, in spirit, akin to the literature of the Gulag) the Nazi *Lagers*, with their chimneys, gas chambers, and inventive wanton sadism, have a flavor of the diabolical and the apocalyptic.[49] By contrast, the horror of the Gulag lay not so much in diabolical cruelty as in its very matter-of-factness. And it is precisely the callous matter-of-factness of most proceedings and the outward innocuousness of their regular-guy perpetrators that make them practically impossible to imagine without aid.

In their different ways, most Gulag narratives implicate their readers in the same sorts of callousness, past and present, that can align them with the perpetrators of mass repression. Most contemporaries of Soviet totalitarianism are more ready to condemn the identifiable agents of terror

(Gulag legislators, officials and guards, informers, purge activists, executioners) than to recognize the radical flaws in their own past attitudes: from the righteous "mercilessness" of the "revolutionary morality" and a reluctance to foresee its consequences ("who could have thought?"), through popular defense mechanisms ("most of them deserved this"), to accomplice reticence ("the less said the better") and head-in-the-sand blindness ("we did not know"). The title that Shalamov gave one of the sketches in his "Vishera" is "V lagere net vinovatykh" ["There Are No Guilty Ones in the Camp"]—yet one of the reasons why Nuremberg trials were impossible in Russia is that in the Larger Zone few were innocent.[50] Reversing the attribution of the guilt, Anatoly Zhigulin's poem "Zabytyi sluchai" ["A Forgotten Case"] (1989: 217) tells of the strangling of an informer in a prison cell, with all twelve of his cellmates holding the rope, so that everyone should be implicated; after a passage of years, the reasons for the vengeance fade from memory, but the twelfth part of the murder still lies on the speaker's conscience. The poem invites an allegorical reading: few contemporaries escaped the touch of the rope that went around the necks of the victims of terror—victims, some of whom had also been cogs in the "meat-grinder" itself. The blanket accusation can eventually elicit a blanket amnesty: whereas according to the erstwhile Russian tradition, the criminal was the "unfortunate one" who had brought into the open those tendencies that we may all have felt and suppressed—if only just—in ourselves, the later Gulag literature, such as Zhigulin's poem, Sinyavsky's *Goodnight!*, and even some of Shalamov's stories of the seventies or Dombrovsky's *Faculty*, admits the traitors and the informers within the pale of the shared humanity as the unhappy exponents of impulses known to all and mastered by most.

Mainly, however, camp narratives show us ways of turning our awareness into sympathetic imagination. A death in the camp may be thought of as just another death; even when one knows the main principle of the Gulag economy, to wit, maximizing production output while minimizing expenses on dispensable workforce, one is still reluctant to imagine the precise consequences of this principle in terms of the conduct of the camp officials and the state of the victims' bodies and souls. Camp narratives force us to visualize the mechanics of a disgusting, lingering, unquiet, dehumanizing death. The revelation is uncanny—new and horrifying but somehow recognizable in the logic with which it follows from the things one has known all along. Even if one does recognize the potential harm of principles like "no omelet without breaking eggs" or "that is moral which promotes the interests of the party," even if one knows that, according to the laws of nature, penal facilities do not automatically expand when the dictator decides on a new wave of arrests and that the guards and police operatives are not free from vested interests, one still does not wish to follow these premises through to their logical conclusions, especially since their consequences involve not only conventional gore or poised asceticism but also very literal lice, bedbugs, mosquitoes, rats, stuffiness, stench, pellagra, scurvy, sores, frostbite, gangrene, puss, dementia, a spectrum of humiliations, and a ubiquitously lurking threat of sudden death.[51]

After the immediate topical significance of Gulag narratives is canceled, the best of these works retain a broader cultural significance, not by virtue of an autonomous aesthetic function but owing to their residual bi-functionality: their *artistic achievement* is bound up with their exploration of callousness and their creation of conditions for counteracting it, whether through a discharge of emotion or through an intellectual simulation of the process of refining moral sensitivity. Callousness, the ability to abstract oneself from the suffering of another (strikingly contrasting with, and often held in check by, the proverbial Russian kind-heartedness) is, unlike the apocalyptic cruelties of the Holocaust, an understandable human feature that cannot be reduced to the effects of a species of utilitarianism artificially fostered by political indoctrination and the practical administrative pressures of a totalitarian mass society. All of us can find its germs in ourselves. When Gulag literature cries out against callousness, it targets a phenomenon of universal significance.

"If only it were so simple!" writes Solzhenitsyn. "If only there were evil people somewhere insidiously committing evil deeds, and it were necessary only to separate them from the rest of us and destroy them. But the line dividing good from evil cuts through the heart of every human being" (*GA* 1: 4, p. 168). Gulag literature addresses both sides of the individual heart. Its admonitory voice addresses us not only as potential victims but also as potential accomplices to the crimes.

In his attempt to explain his generation's early enthusiasm for Communist ideals, Milan Kundera (1981: 8) wrote:

> Yes, say what you will—the Communists were more intelligent. They had a grandiose program, and plan for a brand-new world in which everyone would find his place. The Communists' opponents had no great dream; all they had was a few moral principles, stale and lifeless, to patch up the tattered trousers of the established order. So of course the grandiose enthusiasts won out over the cautious compromisers and lost no time turning their dream into reality: the creation of an idyll of justice for all.[52]

Gulag literature demonstrates the underside of the known approximation of such an idyll, while it also attempts to breathe new life into the "few moral principles," shake them out of their lethargy or staleness. The best of Gulag works also attempt to dispense with the rhetoric of the previous century's sentimental humanism, which, in view of the atrocities that it did not manage to prevent and may have been partly responsible for, ended by giving morality a bad name.

Other literary lore may have forestalled some of the more general ethical discoveries of Gulag literature. Thus, the idea that one may respond to hunger by fasting and resist oppression by asceticism goes back all the way at least to the Sermon on the Mount ("And whosoever shall compel thee to go a mile, go with him twain" [Matthew 5: 41]).[53] Yet known truths produce novel effects in new contexts. Gulag authors had ethical missions based on various concepts of the educational effect of literature. In view of the recidivistic tendencies in historical development, many of them hoped that by writing about the atrocities they had witnessed they would make such atrocities less likely to recur. Others sought rather to pay tribute to the dead, fulfill their requests, grant meaning to their lives, or else to show what was hidden by official discourse, affect beliefs, test and refine attitudes—and, against a keen awareness of the crash of the utopian dreams and sentimental illusions of the past, to reassert hopes of progress, freedom, justice, and moral growth. Ultimately, in retrospect, the teleological explanations for the need of Gulag memoirs and other testimony to atrocities do not suffice. The need for revealing the truth and struggling against lies and oblivion is a deontological value in its own right. Some old beliefs wear better than others, and not without reason: the element of subjective ideological agenda is usually weaker in one's idea of what is "true" than in one's idea of what is "good," especially what is "good for society" or "good for future generations." The history of the rise and fall of the Soviet regime and its culture suggests, among other things, that the ancient principle of valuing the truth for its own sake cannot be sacrificed with impunity.

Notes

INTRODUCTION

1. This is Langer's reading (1975: 2) of Theodore Adorno's early anxieties (1965: 125) that it may be barbarous to write lyrical poetry after Auschwitz. Adorno eventually modified his radical position.

2. The fact that not only self-sacrificial heroism but also individual survival can claim intrinsic moral credit has been recognized only rather recently. Terrence Des Pres (1973: 45) regards this shift in the history of ideas as one of the reasons for the revival of interest in camp literature in the early seventies.

3. GULag is an acronym for the Chief Camp Administration, *Glavnoe upravlenie lageriami,* in the Soviet Union in the heyday of Stalin's rule. The word came to denote Soviet concentration camps in general because of its use in Solzhenitsyn's *The Gulag Archipelago.*

4. The estimates made by survivors were frequently even higher. Robert Conquest, however, cautiously inclines to the figure of 7 to 8 million for another peak year, 1938, and to 40 million as the total number of the repressed, including the victims of the artificial famine, up to 1953 (1990: 486). Cf. also Rosefielde 1987.

5. The census of 1937, whose results were suppressed, must have been more accurate, since Stalin had the members of the Census Board shot (see Conquest 1990: 487).

6. For a discussion of the rhetoric that pushes Soviet labor camps out of the focus of Merleau-Ponty and Sartre's "Les Jours de notre vie" see Lefort 1976: 15–19. Elaine Scarry (1985: 60–81) shows how the language of the classics of military science, such as Liddel Hart and Mankiewich, conceals from view the pain, the maiming, and the destruction of human beings. The works of Gulag revisionist historians would amply reward a similar scrutiny.

7. See *GA* 3: 5; Razgon 1994: 13–14. Various kinds of record falsification form a recurrent theme of Shalamov's stories.

8. Following the suggestion of Antonov-Ovseenko (1991: 3), one should,

for instance, ask whether the documents on the numbers of prisoners that have been processed by Bacon (1994), or Getty et al. (1993) include the prisoners subcontracted from the NKVD by large industrial and road-building projects.

9. Cf. Bukovskii 1996: 50, on the selective release of KGB archive documents as a form of disinformation.

10. In the brochure published by the Lower Kolyma Museum of History and Culture, G. V. Samoilova (1996: 6) notes that her requests for files pertaining to concentration camps were frequently answered by the claim that the files had been destroyed because their term of preservation had expired.

11. "All the tragedies of literature seem to me ridiculous by comparison with what we are living through," says a prisoner's wife in Solzhenitsyn's *Cancer Ward.* "School children write compositions about Anna Karenina's unhappy, tragic, doomed and who-knows-what-else life. But was Anna unhappy? She chose passion and paid for passion; that's happiness! She was free and proud! . . . Where can I read about *us*?" (1968: 554–55). Cf. Muchnic 1973: 291–92.

12. Shalamov, "O proze" ["On Prose"] (1989a: 544).

13. On knowledge as amenity and "dangerous knowledge" see Harrison 1991: 1–8.

14. A sad paradox: in the Prague University of the fifties Mukařovský was shunned by students as a notorious Stalinist (Wolf Schmid, in conversation).

15. As recently as 1989 the number of prisoners in Chinese forced-labor camps is believed to have been 16–20 million; see Wu 1992: 15.

16. A notable exception is *Diaries* and *Mordovskii marafon* [*The Mordovian Marathon*] by Eduard Kuznetsov, smuggled out of a Brezhnev-era camp with the help, it is rumored, of Sakharov's wife, Elena Bonner.

17. This monumental epic is discussed separately owing to its great historical and literary value. In no way, however, can it be regarded as a sufficient literary source on the Gulag experience for any individual reader. Solzhenitsyn himself would hardly view it as an alternative to the corpus as a whole; indeed, he was always intent on eliciting further testimonies of the Stalin era—see, for instance, P. Grigorenko (1982: 378–82) on Solzhenitsyn's attempts to persuade him to record his firsthand observations concerning the Soviet disregard of the imminence of the German onslaught in 1941.

1. SOVIET LABOR CAMPS

1. The insufficiency of the public exposure of the Spanish concentration camps in Cuba and the British ones in the Boer War was among the reasons why no odium was attached to the term "concentration camps." At the time it referred merely to enclosed and guarded areas where suspects were temporarily "concentrated" for purposes of incapacitating potential resistance (see also Bacon 1994: 43).

2. Cf. Berel Lang's argument (1990) that the idea of genocide can be traced back to certain aspects of the Kantian moral system and Geoffrey

Hartman's opposite view: "it is impossible to see either fascism or anti-Semitism as belonging simply to the history of ideas: they belong to the history of murder" (1991: 131). Both the Holocaust and the Gulag belong to both; the theories behind the latter, such as the gradual disappearance of prisons under socialism, the re-education through labor, and the economic self-sufficiency of the camps proved unfeasible, "yet the GULAG Archipelago emerged anyway" (M. Jakobson 1993: 5).

3. Though such sentences, basically amounting to fines, were often difficult to enforce, they helped to reduce government subsidies to prisons and camps.

4. Shalamov (*KR-2:* 35–36) believes that this was the first Soviet concentration camp.

5. In the years 1934–54 the secret police would be subsumed by the People's Commissariat for Internal Affairs, the NKVD, and then transferred to the KGB (Committee of State Security).

6. For coordinated information on the Solovetsky camps see *GA* 3: 3 and the three-part study by a "second-wave" émigré writer Mikhail Rozanov (1979, 1980, 1987) who had earlier written a narrative of his own camp experience (1951); see also Boris Sapir's narrative (Dallin and Nikolaevsky 1947: 170–88) as well as the memoirs of Olitskaya, Shiriaev, Volkov, Likhachev, and Chirkov. The September 1990 issue of the journal *Sever* (see Klinger 1990) is completely devoted to selected materials on this first giant camp complex.

7. By the early thirties most of the Mensheviks and the SR had served prison sentences and were living in exile in the eastern regions. During the Great Terror they were rounded up and sent to the camps. By then all real and imaginary political offenses were subsumed under different paragraphs of the capacious 58th article of the criminal code, and their bearers were assigned the worst regime in the camps, the polar opposite of their erstwhile privilege.

8. Survivors' opinions are divided on the question of whether the prisoners' slave labor was cheap and hence profitable to the state (Stajner, Marchenko) or whether, on the contrary, it was overly expensive due to its inefficiency and waste of human resources (Solonevich, V. Tchernavin, Solzhenitsyn, Ekart). The issue is discussed in a historical perspective in Dallin and Nikolaevsky 1947: 88–107. The short-term gain from slave labor proved to have disastrous long-term effects.

9. Pogodin's infamous play *The Aristocrats* was part of this build-up. See its discussions in Geller 1974: 151–57 and Gliksman 1948: 165–71. As a tourist, Gliksman had seen the play performed in Moscow; he would ironically recollect that experience behind barbed wire after his escape to Russia from the German onslaught in 1939.

10. Some of the contributors went on cooperating with the regime: Vera Inber demanded the death penalty for her cousin Trotsky (see Dovlatov 1991: 31) and Kataev denounced fellow writers (see Volkov 1987: 80–81). As to Gorky, whose death may have been medically speeded up (see Orlov 1953: 261–76), the darkest episode in his biography was his 1929 visit to the

Solovki: he is believed to have seen through its Potyomkin-village front, yet to have chosen not to protest. "Stalin killed him for no reason, out of excessive caution," Solzhenitsyn remarked. "Gorky would have sung hymns of praise to 1937 too" (*GA* 3: 2, p. 63 n. 29).

11. Lengyel's spokesman (1973: 42) believes that the number of dossiers opened by the secret police may have reached 60 million.

12. These are tendencies rather than rules. In some of the more central camps reasonable survival was possible in the worst times; and in the best times there also existed some deadly *dokhodilovki* (Bardach 1989: 133), or "death oases" (Petrus 1953: 87).

13. For comprehensive research on the German POWs see Bärens 1965; special attention to Austrian POWs is given in Karner 1995.

14. At the time rumors were also judiciously spread that the government intended to dismantle the abhorred collective farms.

15. Wallenberg himself apparently never reached the camps: it seems likely that he was secretly executed in 1947, after a failed recruitment effort (see Sudoplatov 1994: 265–76).

16. "Kharbinians" are mentioned in almost every camp memoir dealing with the post-war years. The best known Gulag narratives by Kharbin intellectuals are "Zhenskii kontslager" ["The Women's Concentration Camp"] by Maria Shapiro and *Lagernyi vrach* [*A Camp Doctor*] by A. Kaufman, a leader of the Jewish community of Kharbin who found himself in the same concentration camp with a Kharbinian fascist, his former enemy (see Stephan 1978: 89, 364–65).

17. The charge was "suspicion of espionage"—in the prison parlance, "for an Okay" (Maevskaia 1993: 9).

18. Some of these prisoners had, indeed, participated in the Nazi atrocities. After the dissolution of the Soviet Union, in the Baltic republics the exoneration was as indiscriminate as the arrests of the forties, with the real war criminals benefiting from the erstwhile injustice to the innocent victims.

19. Since in pre-1940 Lithuania, teachers in government schools usually belonged to the Riflemen's Union, there was a very large percentage of teachers among the deported Lithuanians. In his Introduction to the 1989 collection *Leiskit į tėvynę: Tremtinių atstiminimai* [*Let Me Go to My Homeland: Memoirs of Exiles*], Kęstutis Pūkelis describes this as the intellectual decapitation of the nation, similar to the Babylonian policy in occupied Judea. On the same policy in Western Ukraine see Anders 1949: 69.

20. The term is problematic not only because it was officially no longer in use but also because most of the purge victims had not been engaged in any political activity (see *GA* 3: 10). Some were known to feel flattered by such an "intellectual" charge as "Trotskyism." It was precisely the insufficiency of perceptible logic behind the arrests that crushed the people's spirit.

21. Solzhenitsyn's film script "Znaiut istinu tanki" ["Tanks Know the Truth"] (1981b) is based on such events in Kengir.

22. Crossing the railway bridge in Vilnius in February 1953, one could see that the rails were crowded with (still empty) cattle cars—the usual means of transportation of deportees.

23. The firsthand account of the affair by Dr. Ia. Rapoport was published the same year (1988) as his daughter Natalya's reminiscences of her life under the shadow of the "doctor's plot."

24. The years 1955–56 also saw reforms in the country as a whole: a minimum wage, improved pensions, elimination of tuition fees, repeal of the law that fixed workers to their places of employment, etc. (see Nove 1989: 6).

25. In the seventies, as head of the KGB, Yury Andropov gave the term "prophylactics" a new meaning: attempts to intimidate beginning dissidents without actually arresting them (Bukovskii 1996: 93–94).

26. The hunger was also associated with the food shortages in the whole country. In the years 1956–61 peasants would say that in the camps they ate better than in their collective farms (Murzhenko 1985: 127).

27. The 1961 reform that introduced four different camp regimes (general, reinforced, strict, and special) also separated first-time criminal offenders from repeat offenders. Abramkin et al. suggest (1992: 102) that this liberated young first offenders from the moderating influence of elderly inmates, weakened the sway of the criminal "code" that had maintained some sort of *modus vivendi,* and promoted an unrestrained power struggle among them, as well as the so-called *bespredel* phenomenon, the rule of force and fraud unlimited by any rules.

28. Among the victims of special "press-hut" cells there were not only political prisoners but also criminals whom the authorities wished to pressure into cooperation. "Press-hut" thugs are most often a "lower caste" of criminal convicts (Abramkin 1992: 117–18), that is, a type of collaborators, or "bitches," who have good reason to fear the company of their "incorrupt" criminal brethren and will enter into any conspiracy with the authorities in order to be kept in separate cells.

29. Cf. Bukovskii's argument (1996: 197–233) that Gorbachev's *glasnost* and *perestroika* was a "Chekist" ploy well calculated to elicit financial assistance from the West.

30. Later some of the camp facilities were used for alcoholics: the wisdom of the proverb "a holy place never stands empty" was appreciated in the camps.

31. The fanaticism with which such principles were put into practice suggests that the appeal of Communist ideals was associated with their kinship with millenarian fantasies (see Losskii 1957: 112–16) and converged with "a distortion of the Russian messianic idea" (Berdiaev 1962: 250) of the Divine Kingdom on earth.

2. THE LITERARY CORPUS

1. When Gulag narratives are studied as merely *historical evidence* (as in Rozanov 1979: 13–31), the chronology of the authors' arrests provides a more convenient principle of periodization.

2. Zorin's bibliography of Soviet prison and camp literature refers to 67 books and articles on Soviet prisons and concentration camps published

abroad before 1939 (and to over 500 items in all). The history and the cover-up codes of official Soviet literature on the Bolshevik terror and the labor camps has been extensively discussed by Dariusz Tolszyk in *See No Evil* (1999), a recent thoughtful study that reached me only when the present volume was in the proof stage.

3. Some of the secret "desk-drawer" memoirs written at the time have recently been moving from their hiding places to the press; many have, no doubt, been lost, destroyed, or confiscated.

4. Before the Great Terror, political prisoners sometimes still obtained such releases when disabled.

5. The second of Zaitsev's two books, *Chetyre goda v strane smerti* [*Four Years in the Land of Death*], was published two years after his 1934 suicide in Shanghai. In general, however, the rate of suicides among former Gulag prisoners seems to be lower than that of Holocaust survivors.

6. Unlike Klinger and Bezsonov, Malsagoff presents not a personal narrative of his experience but a static description of the Solovetsky camps and of the atrocities perpetrated in them.

7. Stalin must have wished to forestall the foreseeable food shortages of the collectivization period by boosting the output of fisheries.

8. The names and the structure of the Soviet security organs changed, but its headquarters (on Lubianskaia Square), and hence its nickname, remained the same.

9. *The Russian Enigma* is the title of the London, 1979, reprint of Ciliga's memoirs; his writings were first published in 1938. Zorin's entry on this writer (1980: 26) is inexact.

10. See Rozanov (1979: 138–44) for an explanation of the backlash effect of the exaggerations. The memoirists Malsagoff (1926), Essad-Bey (Leo Nussbaum, 1933), and Kiselev-Gromov (1936) come in for particularly sharp criticism (1979: 14–21). Zaitsev (1931: 3) also notes that a copy of Malsagoff's book was sent to the prisoners of Solovki for public refutation.

11. Primo Levi's suggestion that Holocaust survivors may be false witnesses since the "true" witnesses are dead (1988: 63–64) is less true in application to the Gulag. Many Gulag survivors had been on the threshold of death from exhaustion, pellagra, or infectious diseases. In the Nazi camps, prior to liberation, there was generally no recovery for people who had reached the stage of total dystrophy; in the Gulag, such a recovery was sometimes possible, because of the help of kind-hearted individuals among the medical personnel and the absence of institutionalized *Selektion*.

12. The lack of such insight is compensated by the force of the author's emotions and the vividness of his narration. Among the particularly poignant moments in the story are his near-hysteria at the sight of a hungry child to whom he can offer but minimal succor and his helping an illiterate peasant conduct his correspondence with his wife in a famine-struck region. The latter episode prefigures the Nerzhin-Spiridon relationship in Solzhenitsyn's *The First Circle*.

13. The Sudoplatovs (1994: 277) give the number as 21,857, adding that the total of nearly 26,000 Polish prisoners had been systematically executed

and that this "was followed by the deportation of 1.2 million Polish civilians to Siberia and Central Asia."

14. See Remnick 1994: 3–9 on the exhumation of corpses in 1991.

15. The majority of imprisoned Polish Jews were left to die in the Gulag, while their families in Poland were being massacred by the Nazis (the fate of Margolin's mother, Gliksman's wife and child, and the families of Bardach and Fisher, whose memoirs likewise describe the 1939 flight of Jews from Poland to Russia and their subsequent experience in the Gulag). Herling-Hrudzinski blames the Soviet authorities for the exclusion of Jews from the Sikorski amnesty; Margolin, however, believed that it was the Polish army that did not want them (1952: 198)—both are right in part. Begin and Gilboa were rejected by the recruiting post of Anders's army, allegedly for health reasons, which Gilboa identifies as circumcision; Begin demanded a meeting with the commander, and the rejection was reconsidered.

The painter Joseph Czapski, who has described his experience in a POW camp, his frustrated search for those who had perished in Katyn, and his evacuation to Persia with Anders's army, mentions the Polish officers' reluctance to accept Jews as "morally indifferent to the Polish cause" and interested only in refuge and a chance of leaving the Soviet territory. Czapski does not deny that traditional anti-Semitism likewise played its role here, despite what he regarded as an opportunity of "acting with humanity and justice" and winning the good will of the people "who had never been assimilated into the body politic of the nation, and who, in some cases, were hostile to Polish aspirations" (1952: 29).

16. Later developments (1949–55) in Yertsevo are described in the memoir of Filshtinsky 1994.

17. Chapter 11 of *A World Apart* tells of prisoners who derived solace from *The House of the Dead*. By contrast, Solzhenitsyn, Shalamov, and Margolin refer to Dostoevsky's book mainly to show that in the Gulag prisoners fared worse than in the czarist *katorga*.

18. During wartime, pellagra, caused by lack of niacin yet perceived as "the disease of despair," was more widespread than the pre-war scurvy.

19. Some readers believe that Herling's *A World Apart* is largely fictional. If that is true, then one may sense a touch of anti-Semitism in his selection of the details in this episode.

20. Though, once targeted, the four Germans would hardly have escaped execution and though for some prisoners a speedy death was preferable to the "general works" (see Shalamov's "Permafrost" [1990a: 242–46]), actually the man's choice was between the swift and *certain* death of the four and his own *probable* slower dying.

21. Kravchenko committed suicide in February 1966, probably owing to debts and depression. He was believed to have been hunted by the KGB in South America as late as 1956.

22. The English translation is entitled "The Other Kingdom." The original title has become an idiom, as has also the title of Rousset's next book.

23. See Rousset 1951a and 1951b and Margolin 1970 (reprinted in 1975: 275–302). Rousset won the suit but was awarded only symbolic damages.

24. In her 1948 preface to the memoirs of de Beausobre, Rebecca West wrote: "To write of Russia today is dangerous. I do not allude to the obvious material danger that, as has occurred more than once in the United States and on the Continent of Europe, one may afterwards be found dead in a hotel bedroom, having, apparently, committed suicide. That is a danger which the courageous must face as part of this very disagreeable day's work. I allude to the danger that what one says, if it is not condonation of all Russian practices, may be taken as propaganda for the idea of declaring war on Russia. But one may regard the Government of Russia as given to trafficking with evil without wishing to kill Russians or devastate Russian land" (7).

25. The word "z/k" (often pronounced *zek* rather than *ze-ka*) used in the original title is, according to the prevailing opinion, an abbreviation of "convict" (*zakliuchennyi*); according to the minority opinion, it is an acronym of *zakliuchennyi kanalarmeets* ("convict canal-army man"), dating from the days of the White Sea–Baltic Canal.

26. Cf. Gilboa (1968: 60): "I began my career in the North at 'heavy hard labor,' quickly passed to 'medium hard labor,' and then proceeded to 'light hard labor.' In all these categories, the variations are still small and you go out to 'production,' which means you work outside the camp and not on service jobs inside. Later I was assigned to 'weak units' numbers one, two, and three. Shortly after that, I was transferred to a sort of small hospital, then to a 'recovery center,' and finally back to the top again quickly to descend the whole gamut once more." This could be regarded as a story of comparative luck, since the author was not plainly left to die of exhaustion. The first extensive comment on Margolin's book (Dubrovskii 1954) is suggestively entitled *The Machine of Mass Murder.*

27. Like Shalamov and Lipper, Margolin views camp hospitals as a humane institution that impeded the process of the extermination of the prisoners; Solzhenitsyn, on the other hand, emphasizes routine medical malpractice in camps and prisons.

28. From the late thirties on, the policy of the Gulag administration was to separate the members of a family, thus undercutting the prisoners' vitality and speeding up the leveling of their identities. Friendships made in the camps were also under attack; see, in particular, the memoir of Hella Frisher in Vilenskii 1988: 356–439.

29. His self-respect had to withstand the pressure of disproportionately hard work in the company of powerful shock-workers. Yet the latter would inevitably weaken after a few months of overexertion—as Solzhenitsyn also points out, making efforts to meet the quota and get the best rations was more lethal than resigning oneself to less food and less work.

30. The number of calories added to the food did not compensate for the energy expended on the struggle for a place at the stove or for privacy while eating. In retrospect, however, Margolin's insistence on taking over the ritual of cooking can be interpreted as an attempt to stave off what is now called the Stockholm syndrome—captives' lapse into a filial attitude toward their food-providing captors.

31. Her first husband was Martin Buber's son Raphael; see her brief biography in Koestler 1966: 9–11.

32. Neumann was the author of the slogan "Hit the Fascists wherever you meet them." Stalin, however, held a different opinion at the time, for whatever reason. Cf. Alexander Wat: "it was absolutely clear to Stalin what would happen if a great powerful nation with a great future went communist. Stalin knew that communism had to be kept within boundaries controlled by the NKVD and the army, primarily the Chekists. . . . If it spread further, not in little countries like Poland but in countries like Germany with its eighty million people, then Moscow's role would have fallen immediately and become secondary" (1990: 31–32).

33. A similar terrible predicament of a woman whose husband has been purged and who is soon to follow him emerges most clearly from the diary of Iuliia Piatnitskaia, *Dnevnik zheny bol'shevika*. The author of the diary entries is losing her sanity in front of the reader's eyes—to regain it, according to her son's testimony, after her own arrest and deportation to a Karaganda camp.

34. Among them were Franz Korichoner, founder of the Austrian Communist Party, and physicist Alex Weissberg, an Austrian-born communist, who had come to the Soviet Union in order to participate in the industrial expansion of the thirties and was arrested during the Great Terror. Weissberg's memoir *The Conspiracy of Silence* describes the years 1937–39 in Soviet prisons. The recent debate about the numbers of purge victims renews the historical relevance of Weissberg's exploration of the semiotics of pre-trial imprisonment, his exemplary processing of the trickle of available information to make assessments of the fluctuations during the Great Purge. His book also offers insights into the psychological mechanisms that underlie a spectrum of attitudes to false confessions under torture. Weissberg was spared camp experience: upon extradition he was released from a Gestapo prison to a ghetto, escaped, and joined the forces of the Resistance.

35. Thus, *Kriegsschauplätze der Weltrevolution* deals with the activities of the Comintern between 1919 and 1943; *Von Potsdam nach Moskau: Stationen eines Irrweges* is its more personal sequel; *Die erloschene Flamme* is a story of the disillusionment of a generation.

36. Margolin studied Lipper's experience in the courtroom and found the right strategy for delivering his 45-minute speech uncurtailed (see 1975: 275–95).

37. Cf. Kornblith 1993: 90 on the "Law of Small Numbers": "vivid information is just as effective in creating beliefs as it is in reinforcing them, and the effect of statistical information pales by comparison."

38. Whereas the majority of ordinary prisoners were treated callously—although seldom with "useless" cruelty for its own sake—Stalin's henchmen took a pointedly sadistic pleasure in grinding to dust distinguished personalities, starting with Zinoviev, Kamenev, and Pyatakov and ending with people like the theater director Meyerhold (see Shentalinsky 1996: 25–26).

39. Foreigners may have been more sensitive than Russians to tendencies in monitoring the camp demography. For example, one of the reports

received by General Anders from his recruits stated that in 1940, in Chukotka lead mines, the Poles were assigned the worst galleries, and when most of them died, chiefly of lead poisoning, they were replaced by Georgians and Kazakhs (Anders 1949: 73). That was the background against which the Katyn massacre should be seen.

40. Their appeal was resisted. *La trahison de clercs* in matters of the Nazi tyranny pertains also to the issue of the Gulag. Up to the sixties the response of Western democracies was muted, for reasons such as *Realpolitik* expedience, the intellectual elite's anxiety about the future of left-wing movements, the common fear of a new war, or the governments' wish to preempt hostage situations. Thus, the French government seemed apprehensive that, if the conditions of the prisoners in the USSR were exposed, the Soviets would retaliate by, for instance, delaying the repatriation of the Alsace-Lorrainian prisoners of war (see Rigoulot 1984: 171–212). The resulting policy of appeasement had all the marks of at best a double standard and at worst a surrender to terrorist blackmail; see O'Neill (1982) for the responses of American left-wing intellectuals to the data on Stalinist repression—from disillusionment, through entrenched incredulity or deliberate "it-is-true-but-better-not-talk-about-it" self-censorship, to downright justification. For a critique and a history of the French public's attitude toward Soviet labor camps see Lefort 1976: 9–43 and Rigoulot 1991. Pierre Rigoulot's *Les Paupières lourdes* (1991) is also an invaluable history of the publication of Gulag materials in France, including a number of important books that have remained inaccessible to me.

41. For a more detailed discussion of *Taiga*, as well as of Shiriaev's and Boris Filippov's camp stories, see Agenosov 1998: 396–409.

42. See Amalrik (1982: 45–47) on the continuing relevance of NTS in the sixties and Bukovskii (1996: 169–73) on its exploitation by the KGB in the seventies and eighties.

43. The title alludes to nightly interrogations as well as to Koestler's *Darkness at Noon.*

44. A number of secondary sources survey the experience and writings of Gulag prisoners from different countries; see Vihavainen on Finnish prisoners (with special attention to the narrative of Boris Björkelund, of the "Leino's captives" group to which Parvilahti also belonged); Rigoulot (1984) on the French, and Fautré and De Latte (1980) on Belgian prisoners.

45. Cf. the story of General Putna's conduct in Shalamov's "The Necklace of Princess Gagarin." By contrast, in the memoirs of Suren Gazarian (1989, 1: 37–42) a prisoner makes false denunciations of high officials in the naïve hope of thereby exposing the absurdity of the charges.

46. Krasnov writes that unlike the Soviet-educated "Vlasovite" officers, Peter Krasnov was treated with respect, even though his fate was sealed; all the Cossack generals were sentenced to death by hanging.

47. Dimitri Panin disapproves of Krasnov's horrifying sketch of the routines in the special-regime Ozerlag camp complex (1976: 307), yet it stands to reason that as a "Vlasovite" Krasnov would have been exposed to a harsher treatment than even the "counterrevolutionary" Panin.

48. Nicholas Tolstoy (1977: 187) believes that Krasnov was poisoned by Soviet agents.

49. "Khrushchev made it seem as if the Party was more to be pitied for what it had endured than condemned for what it had permitted and supported" (Rubenstein 1980: 7).

50. The Glavlit censorship went hand in hand with the editorial self-censorship. The publication of Solzhenitsyn's *Ivan Denisovich* precluded the publication of Lidia Chukovskaia's *The Deserted House* (in 1962 the novella was entitled "Sophia Petrovna") in *Novyi mir* because the journal could not afford to exhibit a "tendency."

51. Portions of Dyakov's narrative came out earlier in the journals *Zvezda* and *Oktiabr'*.

52. As Larisa Naidich shows through a linguistic analysis (1995: 20–91), an experienced reader would recognize the signs pointing to the absence of truth value in much of Soviet official discourse.

53. Dyakov signs away a month's pay (which has recently been reintroduced; he evidently does not need it for extra food) and makes a round of the hospital wards to sign up bed-ridden patients. Not one of those who have money refuses, except, of course, the "Banderovites," the "Vlasovites," and the *"polizei."* Judging by the memoirs of Marchenko, the *polizei*, people who had served in the police under the German occupation, would, on the contrary, be the more likely to sign up, out of opportunistic sycophancy; other prisoners would sign mostly out of fear of denunciation.

54. See Chirkov 1991: 271–73 for sober and sad memories of Todorsky in the camps, at an earlier period.

55. This is the reason why Solzhenitsyn suspects that Dyakov, "the biggest loud-mouth of all the loyalists," was an informer. He adds that Dyakov "was not merely a trusty but an aggressive trusty": in the first version of his story, published in *Zvezda* no. 3 (1963), before he was shamed for it by Lakshin in *Novyi mir* no. 1 (1964), Dyakov "elegantly explained why an intelligent person ought to avoid the crude lot of the common prisoners ('a chess tactic,' 'castling'—i.e., setting someone else in the forefront of the battle)" (*GA* 3: 11, pp. 345–46).

56. This narrative alibi literalizes the "why-always-look-at-the-bad-things" metaphor, with which the Soviet literary bureaucrats chided the authors who were getting out of line.

57. The Soviet training of not generalizing upon "separate abuses" is probably responsible for Dyakov's blindness to the tendencies represented by the individual events that he mentions. His narrative "betrays" rather than records symptoms of the anti-Semitic campaign (the dismissal of the camp commander Rabinovich), of Stalin's strike against the second generation (the imprisonment of young Arutiunian, son of a prominent Bolshevik purged in the late thirties), and of the stoolie killings of the fifties (the threats received by the "loyalists").

58. In another case of rhetorical subversion, Dyakov complains about his hard lot while actually recording an extraordinary piece of luck. Soon after the appearance of his fistula, he is summoned to the head doctor, who, he

says, has a reputation for toughness: "From his kind one could not expect allowances." The doctor notes that the fistula will not heal fast and then adds: "But you have no business sticking to the bunk. One has to work!" (40). Dyakov is then appointed librarian and medical statistician. Instead of admitting that this is the best thing that could happen to any prisoner, Dyakov insinuates that the hard-hearted doctor did not allow him to recuperate. He also hints that the quotas for physical work were not impossible—one day (only one) he was sent to saw firewood and, despite his bleeding, produced the quota a quarter of an hour ahead of time.

59. This is practically a reductio ad absurdum of the phenomenon of *podmen*, the method of substitution and counterfeiting through which traditional notions like "good and evil," "humanism," and "objectivity" were taken over by Soviet discourse but endowed with a different meaning.

60. Avtorkhanov ascribes the "impersonal, 'collective' style with the same vocabulary and standard sentences and without oratorical devices, lofty phrases, lyrical deviations, or even a personal pronoun" that swept through the Soviet periodicals from the mid fifties on to Khrushchev's influence (1959: 376).

61. "If de-Stalinization was taken to its logical conclusion it would indicate that most of the top leaders, including Khrushchev himself, were responsible for the crimes of Stalinism. Even more was this true of the upper levels of the bureaucracy in every sphere of Soviet life, ranging from the armed forces to the economic ministries, from the police to the administration of the arts. . . . Only a Nuremberg-style trial could deal with the enormity of the crimes committed against the innocent Soviet population" (Scammell 1984: 467). The first major writer to fall into disgrace after the policy twist of 1964 was Ehrenburg, whose memoirs claimed that in the thirties *everyone had known* about Stalinist crimes.

62. Prior to 1964 about the only materials that circulated in Samizdat were collections of unpublished poems by yet unknown authors and, in the republics such the Ukraine, early dissident political statements. Lyudmila Alekseeva (1984: 242–49) writes that the groups of young poets who issued handwritten collections were numerous but unlinked and usually unaware of each other; hence members of separate groups are often convinced that the credit for starting Samizdat belonged to them. Actually, Samizdat arose spontaneously in many places at the same time, in response to the same cultural-political conditions. Among its harbingers were also student literary wall-newspapers and handwritten collections put together in different colleges and for a while semi-tolerated by the authorities.

63. English translation published in G. Saunders 1974: 61–188.

64. Vol. 1 was published by Possev of Frankfurt in 1967. The second volume was first published in Russian in 1979 by Arnoldo Mondadori.

65. Ginzburg's husband, Pavel Vasilyevich Aksyonov, was eventually also arrested, tortured, and given a death sentence, later commuted to fifteen years of hard labor. An article based on an interview with him at the age of ninety was published by K. Smirnov in 1991. For glimpses of Ginzburg in her last years see Orlova and Kopelev 1990: 340–47, 352–58, 367–72.

66. This brief text is printed as the Epilogue to Stevenson and Hayward's translation.

67. Not every reader: Aleksandr Tvardovsky preferred to retain his view of Ginzburg's position as party-elitist. Shalamov was critical of her; and Lesniak referred to her as a privileged party fanatic (1993: 176), both unfairly extrapolating from the impressions gathered during a relatively fortunate period of her camp life. Lesniak, moreover, must have been offended by her ambivalent portrayal of his wife, Nina Savoeva.

68. "Kazhdyi mig, svobodnyi ot stradanii" ["Every Moment That Was Free from Suffering"], in Ginzburg 1985, 1: 1–5.

69. Cf. the title of *Out of the Whirlwind: A Reader of Holocaust Literature*, ed. Albert H. Friedlander. The English titles of Ginzburg's two volumes, *Journey into the Whirlwind* and *Within the Whirlwind*, are well chosen: the loss of the marching fricative iambus of *Krutoj marshrut* is compensated by the connotations of an irrational power whose energy must ultimately exhaust itself. English-speaking readers are reminded of Poe's "A Descent into the Maelstrom," where the narrator is drawn into a lethal whirlpool but finds himself watching its action with curiosity and without loss of reason or common sense.

70. Ginzburg also implicitly traces her growing realization that the old world may not have been as totally decadent as she had been taught to believe. In this respect she was somewhat ahead of her time. See Davies 1989: 11–26 on the "rehabilitation" of pre-Revolutionary Russia during the *glasnost* period.

71. Here too Solzhenitsyn was rather ahead of his time; see *GA* 1: 2. However, separate intellectuals, such as the physicist Lev Landau, had secretly anticipated this ideological development as early as the thirties (see Gorelik 1997).

72. The page with the story of their final parting at the train station was missing from the Samizdat manuscript that reached the Possev publishing house (II: 86).

73. Nicholas Berdiaev notes that the Russian populist movement (*narodnichestvo*) had psychological roots: "As a rule the *narodnik* who is member of the Intelligentsia does not feel himself an organic part of the whole mass of the people or that he fulfilled a function in the life of the people. He was conscious that his position was not normal, not what it ought to be, and even sinful. Not only truth was hidden in the people but there was also hidden a mystery, which it was necessary to unravel" (1962: 102). In his 1908 paper "The People and the Intelligentsia," Aleksandr Blok spoke about the "vital force" of the people and the "line of no access" between the people and the intelligentsia (1955 2: 85–91). Marchenko's books, especially *Zhivi kak vse*, deny the existence of such a line; according to the sage Varsonofiev in Solzhenitsyn's *August 1914*, it is wrong to identify "the people" only with peasants and blue-collar workers. For a useful recent discussion of the problem see E. A. Shklovsky 1991: 9–13.

74. Merle Fainsod (1970: 429) mentions that for Soviet second-wave emigrants the mid twenties seemed like "the golden age": while the OGPU

was consolidating its power, "its direct impact on the mass of Soviet citizens who had no connections with the 'former people' or with the pre-revolution-ary parties of the left was still slight. The OGPU no doubt inspired fear even among those who were not caught in its toils, but the limited character of the categories against which its punitive actions were directed created a wide-spread illusion of safety and security." Osip Mandelstam's "Do you think that everything is fine because the trams are running?" pertains to this period. Shalamov recollects it as the time when "everyone considered it his duty to join one more public struggle for the future of which people had dreamed for centuries in the *katorga* and exile" (1993: 115).

75. Olitskaya's sense of failure strikes a contrast with the poet Anna Akhmatova's conviction that in the most difficult times she was "with her peo-ple." This may seem paradoxical, because Akhmatova was an elite poet whose late work became rather esoteric. Ill adapted to the chores of daily life, Akhmatova nevertheless was, and felt, part of her people as she stood in the queues at the windows of prison offices, waiting for news of her arrested son, trying to send him parcels, keeping her poetry and thoughts underground so that she might not endanger him further. Nadezhda Mandelstam speaks about Akhmatova's inner freedom and unwavering hostility to the regime, yet Shalamov believes that even she lost part of her autonomy by internal-izing some of the Soviet limitations on individual freedom (see "O moei proze," 1989c: 67). Multitudes of people, including the great poet, interi-orized the yoke at least to some degree; those who had retained their auton-omy were conscious of standing apart.

76. Gorbanevskaya also compiled *The Red Square at Noon,* a book of docu-ments and narratives about the August 25, 1968, demonstration against the suppression of the Prague Spring by Soviet tanks. Soon afterward she was arrested and placed into a psychiatric hospital for almost two years.

77. The 1957–64 period is frequently referred to as the "second thaw," the first having been refrozen by the Soviet invasion of Hungary in 1956. The literary events of the first thaw were Ilya Ehrenburg's novel *The Thaw* and his articles, Olga Bergolts's defense of poetry, Vladimir Pomerantsev's arti-cle "On Sincerity" in the journal *Novyi mir,* and Dudintsev's representation of Soviet bureaucracy in the novel *Not by Bread Alone* (see Rubenstein 1980: 1–10).

78. Alexandr Ginzburg, founding editor of the first Samizdat journal, *Syntaxis,* put together a *White Book* on various aspects of the trial. Prominent among these materials was the article entitled "A Letter to an Old Friend," comparing and contrasting this trial to the show trials of the thirties. Its author was Varlam Shalamov, whose short stories had already been in Sam-izdat.

79. One of the first dissidents to foster fruitful contacts with Western journalists and promote the traffic of the dissidents' works to the West was Andrei Amalrik, author of *Will the Soviet Union Exist until 1984?* Amalrik was imprisoned and exiled to Siberia twice before being forced to emigrate; his experience and his keen insights into Soviet realities and the dynamics of the

struggle against the KGB are presented in *Involuntary Journey to Siberia* and *Notes of a Revolutionary*.

80. An inset dialogue in Kuznetsov 1979: 146–59 gives a closer look at the mentality of the former *Polizei* members.

81. "'So, author,' I said to Tolya once. 'I hear you are ready to receive your royalties.' 'not really,' [Marchenko] said. 'I will be paid in years, not rubles'" (Alexeeva 1993: 161).

82. See the postscript by Larisa Bogoraz to *Zhivi kak vse*, 202–11. Bogoraz, whom many consider "the mother of the second Russian Revolution," participated in the Red Square demonstration of 1968 (see note 76), was arrested along with Pavel Litvinov, Vadim Delone, Vladimir Dremliuga, and Konstantin Babitsky, tried, and sentenced to three years of exile. At the time she was married to Yuly Daniel, imprisoned since 1965; eventually she became the wife of Anatoly Marchenko. Her experience of pre-trial imprisonment and the prolonged prison transport to Chuna is described in her 1986 memoir.

83. The foreign media also had a deterring effect on the potential witnesses for the prosecution of dissidents (see Etkind 1978: 31).

84. Elizaveta Voronyanskaya, who was forced to reveal its location, was found dead in her apartment; possibly a suicide, though Solzhenitsyn thinks otherwise (see 1995: 81–84).

85. On Bukovsky's struggle against the psychiatric confinement of dissidents, see also Bloch and Reddaway 1977: 76–84ff.

86. The historian Mikhail Kheifetz (now living in Israel) was imprisoned for his Introduction to Vladimir Maramzin's Samizdat edition of Joseph Brodsky's collected poems. His 1985 book is a consciousness-raising tale about Paruir Airikian and other Armenian independence fighters whom he met in the camps.

87. This is also true of the fiction of the period. Mikhail Dyomin's sentimentalized first-person story about a rebel turned thief uses allusions in lieu of a description of prison transports: "It was business as usual. The closeness, the stench, the thirst destroyed us. Hunger tore at our bowels . . . I could give you painful details, lots of them. . . . But the main things have been dealt with before and clearly at that. A multitude of books have been written on the brutality that reigned in Soviet torture chambers. Besides Solzhenitsyn, the theme has been dealt with by Ginzburg, by Marchenko, and scores of other men of letters, Russian and foreign. On that level I couldn't add a thing" (1981: 301). Oleg Volkov's largely autobiographical *Sinking into Darkness*, a polar opposite of Dyomin's novel on almost every count, deals with prison trains, and with its own belatedness, in a similar way (1987: 21).

88. Cf. White 1992 on the aptness of the style of modernist fiction for writing on genocide.

89. Victor Nekrasov (1984) compares Konson's method here with the short "impressionistic" stories of the Austrian writer Peter Altenberg. For a detailed discussion of Konson's book see Toker 1996.

90. Solzhenitsyn had endowed his Sologdin with Panin's good looks,

religiousness, purist vocabulary, strong will, courage, and intellect, yet he needed an individualism ("solo") stronger than Panin's to complete the paradigm of attitudes towards the NKVD.

91. Panin's philosophical credo is expressed in his pamphlet *Teoriia gustot* [*Theory of Densities*] (1982). His socio-political articles are reviewed in Issa Panin's preface to *Lubianka-Ekibastuz* (5–8).

92. It was to Kopelev that Solzhenitsyn turned for help with publishing his first camp narrative; Kopelev's second wife, the critic Raissa Orlova, took the manuscript of what would become *One Day in the Life of Ivan Denisovich* to the right person in the offices of *Novyi mir,* the editor Anna Berzer.

93. It was published in Tamizdat in 1975, five years before Kopelev's emigration from the USSR. After emigration, up to his death in 1997, Kopelev directed the Wuppertal project devoted to the study of the interaction of Russian and German cultures.

94. Kopelev's later life as a dissident is reflected in *My zhili v Moskve* [*We Lived in Moscow*] (1990), written jointly with Raissa Orlova.

95. Words have a life of their own, even when used hypocritically: "Hypocrisy is very different from cynicism or blindness. Even the censors of opinion and the enemies of the truth felt compelled to pay formal homage to the vital importance of obtaining true answers to the great problems by the best available means. If their practice belied this, at least there was something to be belied: traitors and heretics often keep alive the memory—and the authority—of the beliefs which they are intent on betraying" (Berlin 1969: 36). According to this view, Stalinist terror was less vicious than the Nazi terror because it paid lip service to humanistic values; according to a minority view represented by Margolin, it was the more vicious for the same reason, since lip service to humanism camouflaged inhuman practice (see also Rubenstein 1996: 140).

96. Cf. Kravchenko's powerful scenes of the famine (1946: 91–131). For the treatment of famine in post-1986 Russian literature see Davies 1989: 47–58; Nove 1989: 74–80; and Marsh 1995: 74–83.

97. Voinovich (1993: 45) also names the poet-translator Konstantin Bogatyrev as a person who withstood the tortures in Sukhanovka.

98. A considerable number of Americans had come to Russia at the time, attracted by communist ideals or driven by depression-time unemployment; those who did not leave until 1937 were trapped.

99. Buber-Neumann points out that though the Gestapo used no less brutal methods than the NKVD, it sought to learn the facts rather than force the prisoners to make false confessions. On the other hand, in the Gestapo prisons the "useless" humiliation of prisoners, humiliation for its own sake rather than for extracting confessions, was practiced more extensively than in the Soviet prisons.

100. The title alludes to the icy dugout in a Siberian forest where, following the ten-year camp term, Herman was forced to live after having refused to coach the team of the NKVD "Dynamo" sports club. Upon his exoneration he worked as a schoolteacher; in the mid seventies he managed to take advantage of the détente to repatriate and bring his family over to the USA.

101. A pilot and parachutist, Herman recollects having been called "the Lindbergh of Russia" (1979: 77).

102. Nikolai Krasnov (1957: 100) was likewise subjected to a mock execution but had been warned about it by his cellmates. By the mid forties this technique of intimidation had become more widely known and therefore probably less effective.

103. Volkov (1987) complements the history of political imprisonment traced by Olitskaya in a more leisurely, more conventionally literary, yet also more comprehensive way.

104. It was partly owing to the traumatic early experience described in Pyotr Yakir's *Childhood in Prison* (1972) that the KGB was able to break his spirit in 1970, dealing a painful blow to the dissident movement.

105. Roy Medvedev is the author of *Let History Judge,* a history of Stalinism in the spirit of "socialism-with-a-human-face." At present this book seems rather tame, but when it first circulated in Russia, its effect on many a reader was overwhelming. The brief psychiatric imprisonment of Zhores Medvedev turned into a landmark in the struggle against Soviet abuses of psychiatry; see the account in *A Question of Madness,* written by both brothers.

106. For many, glasnost came too late: Kamil Ikramov, for instance, did not live to see the publication of his memoirs. Fact collecting, however, had started before glasnost—see Remnick 1994: 30–35, 46–47, on young Dimitri Yurasov's single-handed attempts to systematize information about the victims of repression.

107. By his first marriage Razgon was related to Gleb Boky, the high-ranking Cheka official who had visited the Solovetsky islands in 1920 and laid the groundwork for turning the monastery into a concentration camp. He too was executed during the Great Purge, as was Razgon's father-in-law, I. Moskvin, whom Razgon believes to have nurtured Yezhov, the perpetrator of the Purge at its climax and its victim when succeeded by L. Beria.

108. Some of the authors had hoped that Solzhenitsyn would help them publish their memoirs, which he was in no position to do.

109. In some of the details, however, these explanations supplement the material of their precursors; see, for instance, Filshtinsky (1994: 49, 136–450).

110. G. Gorchakov, who had been in Butugychag yet not in its uranium industry (1995: 254–69, 310), likewise missed the import of Zhigulin's hints. His 1989 critique of *Black Stones,* M. Korallov's immediate defense of the book, and Zhigulin's own later appendices exemplify the mandatory seepage of Gulag narratives and their contexts.

111. Cf. Saunders (1996: 40–43) on names of tortures in Chinese prisons.

3. GULAG MEMOIRS AS A GENRE

1. By the same token, *The Captive of Time* by Olga Ivinskaia (1978) and *Tainy Potapovskogo pereulka* [*Mysteries of the Potapov Alley*] by her daughter Irina Emelyanova, do not belong to the genre though they include brief accounts

of their camp experience: their central concern is with the poet Boris Pasternak. Nor is Anna Larina's book a camp narrative, its main concern being with the exoneration of Nikolai Bukharin.

2. Oskar Gruenewald uses the term "camp literature" as "literature that originates from, or is likely to lead to, prisons and camps" (1987: 514). This definition, geared to the purposes of political science, is unrelated to the question of literary genre; cf. Oja 1989: 272–74.

3. Cf. Eakin: the autobiographical act is "a mode of self-invention" that is "always practiced first in living and only eventually—sometimes—formalized in writing" (1985: 9).

4. Cf. Booth 1988: 292–373 on the ethics of mixed metaphors.

5. Many of the repatriated foreign Gulag veterans were too intimidated by the KGB to talk about their experience; some stipulated that their stories be published only posthumously (see Rigoulot 1984: 206).

6. Non-disclosure of survival and escape techniques is, in general, a topos in the narratives of continuing atrocities; cf., for instance, Douglass 1987: 315–16.

7. Psychiatric imprisonment is dealt with extensively in the memoirs of Grigorenko and Bukovsky, the essays of Gluzman, and the novel *Palata Nomer 7* [*Ward Nr. 7*] by Valery Tarsis (1966). The idea of placing dissidents (including unruly daughters like Milena Jesenska) into mental facilities can also be traced to the turn-of-the-century residual belief that rejection of convention or authority is a symptom of insanity. In 1922 Lenin may have truly believed that G. V. Chicherin was insane if he could "suggest a minor change in the Soviet constitution to please the Americans and coax them to come up with a generous loan" (Pipes 1996: 8). In the Soviet Union, psychiatric incarceration began under Stalin, but then prisoners regarded it as preferable to the deadly labor camps.

8. Gulag memoirs often record their own genesis as part of camp experience. While still in Karaganda, Buber-Neumann decides to write about the truth of the camps if given a chance; many of her Comintern colleagues disapprove, believing that for the ultimate good of humanity some truths had better not be told.

9. Cf. Des Pres 1976: 27–54; Adamova-Sliozberg 1988: 49; Levi 1989: 47; Frankl 1962: 73–79.

10. This is not to deny that in some cases there might have been ulterior motives, such as capitalizing on a marketable subject or gaining a position of influence in a particular community. Such motives, however, were seldom exclusive; nor are they illegitimate unless leading to a dishonest exploitation of the subject.

11. Here and below I make use of Genette's (1980: 186–89) distinction between the "focus" (or "focalizer"), through whose eyes the narrated events are presented, and the "voice" who is supposed to be performing the narrative act.

12. On the etymology of this slang term for "prisoner" see Note 25 to Chapter 2.

13. In *Kolyma Tales,* though "utterly self-effacing, [Shalamov] is everywhere visible" (Howe 1980: 36).

14. This is why Nerzhin of Solzhenitsyn's *The First Circle* formally protests against being *personally* deprived of a few grams of food when the issue is the systematic theft from communal rations.

15. "To withstand and counteract the deadening impact of mass society, a man's work must be permeated by his personality" so that the results of this work "besides being objectively purposeful, should also reflect his own purposes in life" (Bettelheim 1960: 4).

16. Cf. Levi's first sight of the prisoners in Auschwitz: "strange individuals . . walked in squads, in rows of three, with an odd, embarrassed step, head hanging in front, arms rigid. On their heads they wore comic berets and were all dressed in long striped overcoats, which even by night and from a distance looked filthy and in rags . . This was the metamorphosis that awaited us. Tomorrow we would be like them" (1990: 26–27). Roeder opens his description of the Soviet hard labor camps of 1950–55 with his first impression of the "katorga" convicts' faces (17–19); his perplexity is soon replaced by the sense of the tragic. Cf. also Koestler's reaction to the first sight of internees in Le Vernet (1941: 88).

17. "After a fortnight of such work I again experienced that strange sensation of weightlessness in my body and that constant mist before my eyes which, I had known for some time, could be signs of approaching death" (Ginzburg 1967: 57).

18. The story is told in a separate book, *Escape from the Soviets* (1933), by his wife Tatiana.

19. At a social get-together of Rousset's witnesses, Margolin remarked that Lipper (38 at the time) only *seemed* fragile. The remark was promptly confirmed: "Elinor came up to me, bent down, took me under the knees with one hand, lifted all the 75 kilos of my weight like a candle, and so walked along the room" (1970: 8).

20. Cf. Buber-Neumann (1978: 11): "Deep friendship is always a great gift. But if such good fortune is experienced in the desolation of a concentration camp, it can become the content of a life." Ginzburg presents romantic love as one of the many kinds of love that she has known, along with love for her mother, her children, her friends. Love is emphasized in the 1989 collection of women prisoners' letters edited by Yulya Voznesenskaya.

21. Joseph Berger had been the founder of the Palestinian Communist party under the British mandate. His heroic and benevolent conduct in Soviet camps is described in Stajner's memoir. His book is a clear example of the literature of disillusionment. Toward the end of his life, back in Israel, Berger turned to religion.

22. Whereas Berger's concern is with the persecution and suffering endured by prominent personalities, Vaneev (1988) seems to claim distinction for himself owing to his privileged glimpses of distinguished people; in his narrative the background of dull daily misery, slave labor, and starvation is barely evident.

23. Cf. Wat 1990: 77 on "prison charisma." According to Margolin, one learned the inner worth of a person by sleeping next to him on overcrowded bunks.

24. El Campesino presents the roles of Lister, Modesto, and especially Dolores Ibaruri in Russia as tantamount to callously abandoning their less distinguished fellow refugees and to spying on the more prominent ones.

25. The only memoir comparable in the forcefulness of its presentation of the ordinary citizens' quotidian plight is that of Andrée Sentaurens (1963).

26. Only a few Gulag memoirs begin with an account of the author's family, childhood, and youth. Most often their authors are people who regard themselves either as public figures (Panin, El Campesino) or as unusual cases (Herman, Sentaurens, and other foreigners who have to explain what brought them to Russia) and who believe that they were arrested not for something they had done but for what they were.

27. Prisoners in transit would not be counted as belonging to any camp, even if they worked for several days in a transit camp. Masses of people would thus fall out of statistics. The prison train journey from Moscow to Vladivostok could last as long as forty-five days, upon which the prisoners would spend some time in a transit camp and about five days on board a ship on the way to Kolyma, where their first destination would be another transit camp. Thus, for over two months the Kolyma-bound prisoners would not appear in the camp workforce accounts.

28. During the "stagnation" period, while the segregation of the political prisoners from the common-law ones was practiced, the former had compartments all to themselves and were therefore spared much suffering. The conditions under which the other prisoners were transported were still very hard. The desperate devil-may-care provocativeness of the criminals on the transports of the fifties and the sixties is presented, respectively, in two novels: Vardi's *Podkonvoinyi mir* (1971) and Sinyavsky's *Goodnight!*

29. Cf. the way in which Vladek in Spiegelman's *MAUS* brushes away an interruption of his chronology: "We are now here in the prison" (1991, 1: 156)—he is obviously reliving the experience in his memory.

30. In Stalin's view, however, not even escape from the Germans and return to one's own lines redeemed a Soviet POW from the stigma; returning POWs were imprisoned on charges of espionage.

31. A recent memoir (Lie 1990: 130–32) explains the circumstances under which Norwegian prisoners of the Nazis did not consider escaping unless expressly ordered by the Resistance headquarters in London.

32. Abram Shifrin's 1973 *Chetvertoe izmerenie* [*The Fourth Dimension*] is structured largely as a narrative of a sequence of failed escape attempts; toward the end the authorial persona seems to breathe a sigh of relief when the last attempts do not materialize.

33. See Zholkovsky 1988 for a discussion of this episode in Ginzburg's book in terms of a traditional pattern.

34. Whereas Kosinski arranges his episodes in an imagined sequence based on the principle of escalation, Dolgun is reproducing the escalating

process of torture. Even so, he grants the reader moments of reprieve by explaining his methods of keeping a hold on his self between the torture sessions.

35. I am grateful to Nancy K. Miller for raising the issue in our joint seminar and to Adam Rovner for an explanation of this hypothesis. The discussion was aroused by critical comments on the possible presence of an erotic undersong in the whipping scenes in the memoirs of Frederick Douglass (see, for instance, McDowell 1991: 48–56 and Slote 1996: 30–32). I believe that this undersong is mainly the result of Douglass's Victorian indirections; Gulag literature is too frank on matters of sexual behavior to produce a similar effect.

36. "Let's go back to the cell. . . . If I keep launching into digressions and often needless rationalizations, it's not only the result of my bad habits or my literary failings, but also because it's not easy in the least to return to prison voluntarily. To return to prison after twenty-five years by the faithful exercise of memory involves my entire being and is almost a physical act; it requires the greatest concentration I am capable of, and I'm already so much older now, so much more devastated" (Wat 1990: 200–201).

37. Cf. Gilboa on a difference between the narratives of survivors of the Nazi and the Soviet camps: "The latter, even when relating horror stories, always injected an amusing comical tone into their accounts. The terrors seemed to be brushed aside, obliterated, and were replaced by the piquant aspect of their experiences. People recall what they went through in the Soviet world of prisoners with a faint smile, and their memories from there may serve as the subject of conversations at social parties. You will not encounter even one of these marks in the memory world of survivors of the Nazi atrocities: not even the trace of a pause in the blackness of their nightmares, not even a single incipient smile. A heavy burden of memory rests on both, yet how mighty the small difference is!" (1968: 302). Some Gulag survivors, however, cannot opt for funny incidents in their bouts of recollection.

38. Short intensities are more amenable to literary exploration: in an attempt to convey the sense of hard work at Buna, Primo Levi chooses the day when he has to carry heavy beams, which make his whole body ache and which, when thrown off the shoulder, produce the "ephemeral and negative ecstasy of the cessation of pain" (1990: 73).

39. Cf. Tadek's turning away from a man who is waiting for his turn to be killed in Borowski's "A Day in Harmenez"; his own reluctant involvement in the murder is one of the dead-end ethical ambivalences that run through *This Way for the Gas, Ladies and Gentlemen* (1967). Czeslaw Milosz (1953: 111–34) commends Borowski's courage in presenting his Auschwitz experience from the point of view of a "prominent" (that is, a prisoner placed into a command position over other prisoners) and notes that Borowski's actual behavior in camp was much better than Tadek's. Yet Borowski's technique maneuvers the reader in such a way that a share of the automatic sympathy for the victim, the usual focus of camp stories, is transferred to the collaborator.

40. After the initial nursing period, mothers were usually not allowed to visit their children in such shelters. Volovich managed to make her way in, but her daughter nevertheless soon sickened and died. In a story about the solitary funeral of a newborn camp baby, Georgii Demidov (1990: 12) explains that children's shelters were a financial burden on regional camp-administration units; therefore the authorities tried to prevent sexual contacts among prisoners and were indifferent to the death toll among infants.

41. "Every year, so my neighbor told me, a large batch of more than a thousand *platnois* [*sic!*] is shipped off to the camps on the island of Novaya Zemlya in the Arctic Ocean. . . . From these camps there is no return" (Scholmer 1954: 82).

42. At the interrogations, one could maintain that the informer had slandered one out of personal animosity.

43. I have heard stories of Lithuanian prisoners who gave their bread rations to those who, they hoped, would eventually still serve the cause of their motherland.

44. Since Homer, homecoming has been a subject in its own right. Primo Levi and Elie Wiesel wrote separate works about their experiences after liberation from Nazi camps. In Gulag memoirs the issue of homecoming is treated more or less extensively only when it involves problems of re-adaptation. Release from the camps is not tantamount to homecoming—this is especially obvious in the cases of the American-born Herman and Dolgun. Vladimir Petrov's wanderings prior to his immigration to the United States were originally described in a separate book, *My Retreat from Russia,* which followed his *Soviet Gold.* The later version, *It Happens in Russia* (1951), includes both parts.

45. The discussion of the features of the carnivalesque and the Lenten narrative modes in the remaining part of this chapter is based on Bakhtin (1984: 108–47) and on Ruth Ginsburg's groundbreaking 1989 essay on Lent as the second self of the carnival.

46. Evgenia Ginzburg recounts her constant attempts to domesticate prison and camp conditions, to move from crisis-pitch points to some semblance of normal life: each stage in her "steep route" is marked by relationships with people who helped her build up the sense of a family life with surrogate sisters, mothers, children—yet her card houses are always under threat, and her narrative pulsates in sequences of making a home, having it shattered, and making, and losing, a new one. If in carnivalesque literature safe biographical spaces are given up, in Lenten literature they are illusory.

47. The history of the hunger strikes of the political prisoners from the early twenties to the late thirties is traced in the memoirs of Olitskaya. On the hunger strikes of the dissident period, when cracks had appeared in the iron curtain, see, for instance, Sharansky 1988: 334–63 and Marchenko's *Ot Tarusy do Chuny.*

48. Menachem Begin fasted on the Day of Atonement despite the chronic hunger in the Lukishki prison in Vilnius. Gilboa, who had met Begin in the camps, "had heard him praised by non-Jews for his noble comportment in a

prison cell and in the prisoners' society (that's how it was: at the time that was our principal criterion for measuring a man's worth)" (1968: 47).

49. A more pragmatic kind of self-discipline was veteran prisoners' attempts to avoid thinking of food: thoughts about food would enhance digestive secretion and thus damage the stomach.

50. Cf. Primo Levi: "Here then, before our very eyes, under our very feet, was one of those notorious transport trains, those which never return, and of which, shuddering and always a little incredulous, we had so often heard speak" (1990: 22).

51. John Noble was an American of German origin whose family ran a camera plant in Dresden; he became a born-again Christian in a post-war prison, whence he was deported to camps in the Vorkuta region. The title of his book, *I Found God in Soviet Russia* (1959), refers not only to his own conversion but to his having found a growing interest in religion among the Soviet citizens in the camps. Among other points of interest is Noble's testimony that after the fall of Nazi Germany Buchenwald was run by the Soviets as their own concentration camp, with a very high mortality from starvation and disease.

52. Cf. Gilboa (1968: 87) on a Jewish ex-communist's explanation of his fasting on the Day of Atonement: "I can go hungry when the NKVD wants me to so why can't I go hungry when I want to?"

53. As the length of prison sentences in the Stalin period was practically void of meaning, imprisonment combined the limitation of space and the indefiniteness of time. This is also a recurrent theme in Joseph Brodsky's prison-inspired works.

54. A similar story of stamina rooted in firm ideological principles is told in Sharansky's *Fear No Evil* (1988).

55. Panin sometimes seems to have clung to Christianity almost out of principle, as his way of withholding consent. His ethics is internalist, and the idea of afterlife is a matter of tactics: he disarms his interrogators with his assertion that a few additional years of imprisonment are nothing in comparison with eternity.

56. Dr. A. Kaufman (1973: 21) recollects obtaining permission to get, and use, a special anti-bedbug powder in the Kharbin prison, which suggests that the prisoners' condition could have been improved if anyone cared to do so. On the other hand, the constantly recurring stories of thirst in the trains suggest that the scanty water supply was a means of keeping the prisoners subdued; and even fresh air was deliberately denied to the prisoners when new instructions required a tightening of the prison regime (the window of Ginzburg's cell was then nailed fast). In either case there would be an ethical imperative in describing such details.

57. "Heteroglossia" is "stylistic three-dimensionality, which is linked with the multi-language consciousness" of the text (Bakhtin 1981: 11). Cf. Dovlatov (1982: 78–80) on the artistic value of camp language.

58. At least three dictionaries of camp language, by B. Ben-Yakov (1982), Rossi (1987), and Galler (1994) have been published outside Russia.

4. *THE GULAG ARCHIPELAGO*

1. This technique is foreshadowed in Lipper 1951: in addition to mocking the adages of Big Brother ("you can't make an omelet without breaking eggs," "better to liquidate ten innocent persons than to let a single guilty one get away," "revolutionary alertness is essential" [45–56]) and camp slogans ("At the entrance to the small settlement of Elgen we are greeted by a wooden, green-painted arch, a kind of arch of triumph, on which in huge red letters is the inscription: 'Long live the great Stalin.' That makes us feel at home immediately. We may be ragged, hungry, lousy and frozen, but the great Stalin is with us wherever we go" [125]), Lipper performs an exegetical exercise on the writings of Owen Lattimore (1944) and Henry Wallace (1945), who visited Kolyma but chose to see nothing beyond the Potyomkin villages erected for their benefit. An interesting fictionalized view of Wallace's visit is given in Shalamov's story "Ivan Fyodorovich" (*LB*: 283–86); see also O'Neill 1982: 142–60 and 266–82.

2. See Assmann 1994 on the different significance of the search for objective truth in totalitarian and in democratic societies. Solzhenitsyn's influential essay on non-violent resistance to totalitarianism, "Zhit' ne po lzhi!" ["Live Not by Lies!"], transfers the notion of truth from the epistemological to the moral plane.

3. Solzhenitsyn justified his fictionalization of Stalin in *The First Circle* by suggesting that this was a fair consequence of Stalin's having shrouded his life in mystery. The burden of disproving the novelist's interpretation of Stalin would be on those in possession of contradictory facts.

4. In her discussion of *August 1914* Mary McCarthy (1973: 337) notes that courage is one of the highest values in this novel and that the author, appropriately, "exemplifies it in his own person to an almost alarming degree. He takes no protective measures whatever against the criticism he must have foreseen from Soviet literary officialdom and from many independent leftist writers in the outside world." A courageous dispensing with the malpractice-insurance overhead is, indeed, a prominent feature of Solzhenitsyn's dialogic mode. This is not to say that he "fixes" the test to which he subjects his views: McCarthy further demonstrates the ways in which the novel "disagrees" with the novelist (349–50).

5. Elements of dialogue transpire, for instance, through the style of Pontuso 1990, and even Shturman's extensive 1988 defense of Solzhenitsyn's views repeatedly slides into an implicit dialogue with him.

6. See Tregubov's comments (1957: 16) on the four stages of the NKVD interrogations: (1) the preliminary hearing, when the interrogator establishes how important the prisoner is and what methods are to be used in his or her case; (2) the main hearing, with the pressure upon the prisoner constantly increasing; (3) goal-oriented interrogation, during which all possible and impossible methods can be used; and (4) "special processing," used in the "important" cases if the previous stages have failed to produce results, often leading to insanity or death. Tregubov went through the first three

stages; Dolgun apparently endured all four. In some cases the first stage would be skipped, so that the prisoner should be stunned by an immediate assault; moreover, the basic pattern of escalating what is euphemistically called "pressure" would sometimes be cunningly combined with periods of reprieve.

7. Shalamov frequently maintained that one of the central rules of camp ethics is not to impose one's will on others.

8. Cf. Richards 1985: 149. Richards goes on to observe (153) that *The Gulag Archipelago* "is a history of those who are victims not only of physical suppression, but particularly of the suppression of information, and Solzhenitsyn makes it clear that his special concern is with those who have had no redress against their elimination from history."

9. On Solzhenitsyn's linguistic innovations see Carpovich 1973 and 1976.

10. As is well known, the quality of the English version of the third volume of *The Gulag Archipelago* (Parts 5–7), translated by Harry Willetts, is higher than that of the first two.

11. The characterization of the Soviet totalitarian decades as "a pre-Gutenberg Age" is Anna Akhmatova's (N. Mandelstam 1974: 8). Akhmatova's and Osip Mandelstam's later poems were for a long time preserved by memorizing, with even the handwritten backup limited or absent.

12. The view that the Bolshevik movement had a basically foreign character is discernible in Solzhenitsyn's complex attitude toward Latvians and his emphasis on the number of Jews among the heads of the Gulag.

13. See Richards 1985: 148 on Solzhenitsyn's direct engagement with the reader.

14. The principle of a foolproof style is laid bare when Solzhenitsyn italicizes a morally symptomatic clause in the writings of a loyalist and adds in a footnote, *"Kursiv na vsyakii sluchai moi"*—"The italics, to [make] sure, are mine" (3: 11, 324 n): by a self-descriptive hint at Solzhenitsyn's valorization of clarity.

15. In 1940 M. Begin declined an "invitation" to the Vilnius municipality: "If the Soviet Government . . . wants to arrest me, let its agents put themselves out and come to my house" (1977: 13). Some of the doomed people who would not confess under torture during the Great Purge drew strength from the thought that their stubbornness was a refusal to lighten the job of the police.

16. Shalamov likewise writes, with a deliberate hyperbole, that there were "no guilty ones in the camps" (1990a: 111–21).

17. In 1965 Shalamov wrote to G. Demidov that a special department to control the massive flow of camp narratives had been set up by the Central Committee (1993b: 147).

18. A further artistic commentary on this point is given in Felix Kandel's *Zona otdykha ili piatnadzat' sutok na razmyshlenie* [*The Rest Zone, or Fifteen Days for Reflection*], a tragi-comic tale based on the authorial persona's fifteen days' incarceration and focussing on the plight of a fellow inmate, an endearing though unrestrained hard-drinking worker.

19. Cf. Sommer 1976: 20–34 on the goals of imprisonment (deterrence,

rehabilitation, reform, retribution, restitution, incapacitation, re-education, integration) in the USA.

20. See a review of the subject in Scammell 1984: 958–63.

21. Tchernavin, Herling, Stajner, Scholmer, Margolin, and Vardi show a variety of ways in which the suffering of Jews in the camps was exacerbated by anti-Semitism. Parvilahti recollects that the number of arrested Jews increased noticeably as early as the end of 1945.

22. For a discussion of the balance between positive and negative Jewish characters in Solzhenitsyn's works see, for instance, Frankel 1975. Frankel also argues that Solzhenitsyn's sharing some of the Slavophile ideas need not be taken to mean that he also espoused anti-Semitic attitudes.

23. Cf., for instance, Daleski's discussion (1977: 122) of Conrad's presentation of Señor Hirsch in *Nostromo*. The ethical flaws of Conrad's text are reproduced in Gustav Herling's stereotypical presentation of Jews in the camp, the touches of mockery in his account of their plight on the western bank of the river Bug after that river became the border between German- and Soviet-occupied Poland (1987: 166–68), and in the naturalness with which he passes from the latter issue to the portrait of a Polish Jew who had turned informer. The tone in which these details are presented smacks of the traditional Polish anti-Semitic sense of superiority akin to that of Tadeusz Borowski's Auschwitz stories.

5. FROM FACTOGRAPHY TO FICTIONALIZATION

1. This triumphant command of the prison culture, rather than the nausea at prison experience repeating itself, characterizes Razgon's and Gagen-Torn's accounts of their second arrests.

2. Indeed, fragmentariness caused by the absence of specific thematic lines reduces the impact of such narratives as Grigorii Aronson's factographic *Na zare krasnogo terrora* [*At the Dawn of the Red Terror*] or even Maksimov's fictionalized *Taiga*.

3. Later Gulag narratives use the word *tufta*, or *tukhta*, which means falsifying the production results to make it seem that the prisoners have met their quotas as well as inventing useless or non-existent work. This word has crept out from behind the barbed wire and penetrated contemporary colloquial Russian, where it stands for all kinds of non-serious employment.

4. "When people ask me how I managed to survive seven years of concentration camp in Russia and Germany I can only say that, apart from the fact that my physical condition was always good and my nerves well-balanced, I never let myself slide into a state where I lost my self-respect, and, above all, because I always found people who needed me" (Buber-Neumann 1950: 230).

5. Suggestively, the criminal slang term for being gang-raped was "to fall under a tram." One of the glaring faults of the 1992 novel *Zharennyi petukh* by E. Fedorov is his presentation of "the tram" not as rape but as a pleasant reprieve initiated by the woman herself and abruptly discontinued by her at

a point that she herself determines. Even if such episodes were possible among the multi-million population of the camps, Fedorov's treatment of it is reminiscent of Dyakov's diffusions of thaw-period topical issues.

6. See Toker 1997b: 201–207 on the recombination of material in documentary prose.

7. The concept of the "factographic pact" is associated with Philippe Lejeune's view that a text's affiliation with the genre of autobiography is solely a matter of an "autobiographical pact" with the reader. According to Lejeune, a work is to be treated as an autobiography if (a) it is a retrospective prose narrative, (b) it is written by a real person (the author and the narrator are identical), and (c) it focuses on the narrator's own existence, his individual life (1989: 4). In the case of memoirs, Lejeune's (c) clause must be modified: a memoir focuses on the memoirist's actual firsthand experience and knowledge but not necessarily on his personality.

8. In *The Fictive and the Imaginary* (1993) Wolfgang Iser argues that the imaginary cannot be articulated without the fictive. The spontaneously remembered is practically indistinguishable from the imaginary and can hardly be conveyed without the help of the fictive.

9. According to Iser (1993: 4–10), the *fictional* is the selection and recombination of material under the aegis of the *as if* convention.

10. "I obviously cannot recollect the dialogue precisely. I only attempt to render the nature of the arguments on both sides" (Plyushch 1979: 109).

11. Cf. the speeches of Saul Fitelberg in ch. 37 of Thomas Mann's *Doctor Faustus.*

12. A hearsay reference to prisoners chained to wheelbarrows in an underground plant in Votkinsk also appears in Leonard Gendlin's memoir (1980: 174–75), which is, however, marred by imprecisions.

13. "There is life in boiling geysers, and there are libraries in Hell" (Mäkinen 1993: 117). The library of Solovki contained particularly rare and valuable volumes, left behind by or confiscated from the upper-class prisoners of the twenties.

14. For similar iterative scenes see, for instance, Bukovsky 1979: 67–69, Petrus 1953: 94–98.

15. The people who function as public domain landmarks are sometimes celebrities (Esenin's son, among others, for Berger, Berger for Stajner, Begin for Gilboa, Yuly Daniel for Marchenko) and sometimes persons who had become prominent in the camps. The charismatic criminal chieftain Valentin, a committed fugitive, plays an important role in Alexander Dolgun's narrative and eventually appears also in Mrs. Wat's Appendix to Alexander Wat's *My Century;* Albert Loon is respectfully mentioned by Panin and lovingly described by Victor Herman. Yet the impulse behind references to celebrated prison acquaintances (e.g., Nina Gagen-Torn's story of meeting Trotsky's first wife in 1936) can also be predominantly antiquarian.

16. There is, for instance, a significant discrepancy in Ginzburg's and Olitskaya's memories of the onions that could be obtained from the women who came up to the prison transport train at one of the stations. The two memoirists were in the same railway carriage on the way to Vladivostok, but

Ginzburg recollects the episode as the women's thrusting the onions to the prisoners, while Olitskaya recollects it as an episode of purchase and distribution, where she played the central role and was attacked by the Communist prisoners for her SR egalitarianism (she gave some onions to all prisoners, including those who had no money to pay for them). Each version of the events is geared to the concerns of the first-person protagonist-narrators.

17. When Sima Veksler and I visited the writer Lev Konson, after telling us about some of his experience in the camps, he remarked, "See, now that I have *given* you this story, I shall not be able to *write* it."

18. Following Genette (1980: 116), the term "singulative" is used to refer to events that happened once and are presented once, as opposed to "iterative" events that happened many times but are presented once.

19. Another voice from "the left opposition" is the 1995 memoir of A. Ioffe's daughter Nadezhda.

20. The play is dedicated to G. Demidov, author of "Dubar," the real person behind Shalamov's protagonist of "The Life of Engineer Kipreev" (see Iakovich 1990 and Shalamov 1993b: 142–50). The two met again in the sixties due to Demidov's friend accidentally noticing the play and its dedication.

21. A. Vardi's 1971 novel *Podkonvoinyi mir*, dealing with the camps of 1952–53, likewise seems to be structured on the principle of showing the logical mechanics of camp relationships that cannot but lead to atrocities.

22. In the story "Boris Iuzhanin" (*VL*) Shalamov discusses the Blue Blouse movement in post-revolutionary Russia as the precursor of Brecht. Cf. Groys's 1987 argument that Russian avant-garde artists were direct precursors of the Stalinist aesthetics.

23. This is Michael Scammell's suggestion (1984: 217 n) for translating the title of "Olen' i shalashovka" published in English as "The Lovegirl and the Innocent."

6. VARLAM SHALAMOV

1. Laura Kline presents a detailed discussion of the tension between the singulative and the iterative events in Shalamov's narratives, showing how the discursive references to regularities tend to subvert the singulative events and to represent them as samples (1998: 126–34).

2. "In my stories all the murderers are given their real names" (Shalamov 1995: 159).

3. Peters's prototype was, evidently, an Estonian by the name of Janis (Shalamov 1993a: 159).

4. On the distinction between focus and voice see note 11 to Chapter 3. In Shalamov's camp stories the first- or third-person focalizer is usually a prisoner, while the voice belongs to the retrospective narrator rethinking his past experience. In "The Bug," which is set after the release from the camps, the focalizer and the narrator are practically identical.

5. At this point in the autobiography, Shalamov's treatment of his father changes from critical to sympathetic.

6. With the "romantic dogmatism" of the times, he had believed in the near-mystical influence of working-class experience, yet soon discovered that it gave him nothing but physical fatigue (1993a: 116–18).

7. The power struggle within the Communist Party was reflected, in a covert way, in the struggle for influence in the publishing realm—this aspect of Moscow's cultural life does not seem to have been quite clear to Shalamov at the time, but a tacit awareness of it underlies his retrospective sketch "The Twenties" (1987b).

8. An allusion to a poem by Sergei Esenin.

9. Also printed as the last section of "Chetvertaia Vologda" in 1994: 172–74.

10. The main output was gold (eventually including gold from the teeth of the dead prisoners; see "Graphite" [*VL*]); next in importance were coal, timber, and later uranium.

11. The horrible Serpantinnaia prison was established under Berzin's rule.

12. See Chirkov 1991: 241–42 on the parallel fate of the founder of the mining-camp complexes and urban center in the Ukhta region.

13. Stalin had ambiguously suggested that the number of prisoners should be reduced (see *GA* 3: 4).

14. For a more detailed analysis of the story see Volkova 1998: 9. Volkova's book cogently demonstrates the pervasiveness of paradox in Shalamov's narrative method and makes illuminating comments on a number of stories, such as "Berdy Onzhe" (121), "The First Chekist" (123–26), "Berries" (118), and others.

15. According to the reminiscences of Boris Lesniak (1994: March 29), a former convict paramedic in the Belichie surgical ward, Shalamov spent two and a half years in Belichie (and just a little over two years in the gold mines throughout his camp ordeal). Shalamov's own memoirs written in the seventies present a more complicated story. After a fortnight of partial recuperation and a month of work as a medical orderly he was sent back to the "vitamin" camp, whence, later the same year, he managed to make his way back to the hospital (1990a: 177); the 1964 story "To the Hospital" (*AL*) is based on this experience. He made friends with the head doctor, Nina Savoeva, who was in love with Lesniak (Lesniak himself had, apparently, singled out Shalamov and started bringing him bread and tobacco during his first hospitalization). This time Shalamov stayed in the hospital longer, as a patient and an orderly. In the summer of 1944 he was sent to the brand new gold mine, Spokoinyi. There, after a brief time in the sick ward (cf. "Ryabkon" [*VL*]), he found himself in the construction brigade led by his former cellmate (cf. "Lesha Chekanov, ili odnodel'tsy na Kolyme" [*KR-2*]), who persecuted him with a renegade's vindictiveness. Eventually, Savoeva and Lesniak saved Shalamov's life by demanding that he should be sent back to the hospital. In the summer of 1945, Shalamov returned to Belichie; this time he was employed as a cultural worker, who read newspapers to the patients, until the autumn of that year.

In the seventies the friendship between Lesniak and Shalamov broke off, partly as a result of Lesniak's having been questioned about Shalamov by the Magadan KGB and not appraising Shalamov sufficiently promptly (cf. 1995: 158 and "Vstavnaia novella" ["Inset Story"] in Esipov 1994: 10–14).

16. For an English translation of this story (by N. Strazhas) see Barabtarlo 2000: 293–303.

17. Kline 1998: 58–105 presents a well-researched account of Shalamov's post-camp years. Kline believes that Shalamov's dark vision was caused not only by his camp experience but also by the disappointments of his later life.

18. The dissident counterculture could sometimes be as tyrannical as the official culture that it opposed. As a power structure, it was also somewhat superciliously exclusive. L. Alekseeva admits, for instance, that the dissidents welcomed only people whom they felt to be akin to themselves (1984: 247 and 326–27).

19. Sirotinskaya denies that he was ostracized (1994: 138), adding that he would sometimes himself turn away visitors who wished to offer moral support.

20. The Russian-Chuvashian modernist poet Gennady Aigi had, like Sergei Grigoriants and Natalia Stoliarova, helped to smuggle some of Shalamov's writings abroad. His poem "I: posledniaia kamera" ["And: the last cell"] was first published in *Vestnik russkogo studencheskogo khristianskogo dvizheniia* #136 (1982): 144.

21. A denunciation may have prefaced the move, but even without one, the human wreck, helpless yet intractable and attracting outside attention, would have been perceived as a nuisance. Lesniak (1994: March 22) writes that the last straw or pretext for the transfer was his having left a tap open in the bathroom, causing a minor flood.

22. The third-person focalizers Krist, Andreev, and Golubev are obviously avatars of the authorial persona and of each other; but the reader is made even more clearly aware of the name change when the same brutal commander appears as Kovalenko in one text and Shtemenko in another or the same interrogator as Stolbov and Rebrov.

23. "Landscape is not acceptable at all. The reader has no leisure to think of the psychological significance of landscape detours. . . . Should landscape be used, however, then extremely sparingly. Any detail of description becomes a symbol, a sign, and only then retains its meaning, vitality, inevitability" (Shalamov 1996: 426). On Shalamov's treatment of the Siberian nature see Toker 1993a.

24. As Mansell 1976 suggests, the same agenda may, in principle, obtain for the symbolic code of factographic narratives.

25. The most important statements in this theoretical debate are discussed in Harris 1990: 18–26. Kline (1998: 4) suggests that a partial background for Shalamov's method may also be sought in the poetics of "the literature of fact" promoted in the twenties by N. Chuzhak, S. Tretiakov, and O. Brik.

26. Replication and formalization methods are less frequent in Shalamov's work. An example of the former is the 1954 self-referential story "The Snake Charmer" (*KR*), in which the attempt to imagine an intellectual's predica-

ment among criminals involves a cross section of "typical" criminal characters and modes of conduct (see Toker 1994); an example of the latter is the 1963 story "Utka" ["The Duck"] (*AL*).

27. The tickling may be a means of stimulating the puppy's blood circulation in order to tenderize the meat, but the semblance of a game makes the dog's trustfully licking "the human hand" particularly poignant.

28. In a letter to Pasternak, Shalamov mentions having seen a religious service performed in a forest (1988: 59–60).

29. One's memory is seldom complete with date tags: the closest one comes to dating incidents (with the exception of such prominent events as, for instance, one's arrest or trial) is by collocating them with landmark events; thus Shalamov dates his third hospitalization by noting that he met the end of the war with Germany in the Spokoiny mine, but Hiroshima and the end of the war with Japan in Belichie (1993a: 160).

30. Reciting poetry once helped Shalamov to resist fatigue during a night in an icy punishment cell, where falling asleep would have been lethal.

31. Cf. Harrison (1993/94: 168) on "hermeneutic stumbling blocks." Cf. also Mikhailik 1996: 109–11 on grammatical ruptures in Shalamov's texts.

32. Cf. Rosenfeld on Primo Levi (1995: 124).

33. The "irony of origins" is Morson's term (1981: 129) for undermining the authoritativeness of a perspective by attributing it to an individual character rather than an "omniscient" narrator.

34. It seems that Shalamov names his other characters Merzlyakov ("Shock Therapy") and Shelgunov ("Bol" ["Pain"], *VL*) likewise as allusions to writers of the eighteenth and nineteenth centuries, respectively, whose ideas are tested in the two stories.

35. This position is most clearly expressed in the story "Galina Pavlovna Zybalova" (*KR-2*), but it is also restated in Shalamov's notes and letters. However, Shalamov's friendship with Demidov came to an end because of Demidov's taking offense at the tone of literary mentorship that he sensed in Shalamov's letters to him (see 1993a: 144–50): Shalamov did not always manage to obey his own "eleventh commandment": "Thou shalt not teach" (Sirotinskaya 1996: 449).

36. Contradictions between different stories sometimes have local rhetorical functions. For instance, the death of Dr. Umanskii (a "real person" also lovingly described by Ginzburg) is dated March 4, 1953 in "Veitsmanist" ["The Weizmanist"] but, more correctly, 1952 in "Kursy" ["Courses"]. The wrong date, however, carries a symbolic weight: the man who had set his hopes on surviving Stalin dies *a day before* the dictator's death is announced. Moreover, the discrepancy concerning the dates of Dr. Umanskii's death is, among other things, implicitly autodescriptive: it delimits the phase-shift that takes place when actual materials are transmuted into fiction. ("Courses" is an autobiographical narrative, whereas "The Weizmanist" is a fictionalized recycling of some of its material.) One way or the other, Dr. Umanskii dies *shortly* before Stalin. His demise on the eve of Stalin's "official" death brings the irony of fate into bolder relief. On the other hand, the interval between the end of 1952 and March 4, 1953, was long enough for the deaths of

thousands of other people who had hoped to survive Stalin: no matter how extraordinary a person Dr. Umanskii may have been, his experience was a version of a shared lot.

37. Cf. Solzhenitsyn's own 1999 account of this contact with Shalamov.

38. Like Cellini, Shalamov was fascinated by fellow "professionals" in various branches of arts, crafts, and sciences. He had insisted, for instance, on keeping the technical language of lace-making in his 1937 story "Pava i drevo" (1994b).

39. Shalamov paid close attention to the composition of the cycles. He insisted (1996: 430) that though the location of a few of his stories could be shifted around, the central ones must hold their allotted places.

40. "Thinking about Shalamov with respect and love, we transfer our respect also to those whom the author has named executors of his literary estate. Their moral and financial rights are unquestionable. . . . But disposing of the text of a writer of genius is an impossibly difficult task for one person. It must be the job of qualified specialists to prepare a scholarly publication of 'Kolyma Tales'—in accordance with V. T. Shalamov's creative principles so clearly presented in his recently published (for which we bow gratefully to I. P. Sirotinskaya) letters and notes" (Timofeev #3873: 11). Sirotinskaya replied with a reference to the complex publishing situation at the time—and with a hint that Timofeev did not understand the predicament (see her preface to Shalamov 1991b: 170). The history of the Soviet publishing world in the first years of *glasnost* is, indeed, a complex issue, but Timofeev is justified in believing that the manner in which Shalamov's prose started appearing in the Soviet press also reflected the tendency of assimilating his work into the conventions of the Russian humanist tradition in literature.

41. This is the opinion of Michael Brewer, to whose master's thesis (1995b) I am indebted for coordinating the information about the dating and distribution of Shalamov's stories.

42. See Frida Vigdorova's letter in Shalamov 1978: 13. Solzhenitsyn also notes that Shalamov's own stories refute his statements that camp experience was uniformly detrimental to character. In 1972 he adds, however, that Shalamov's notorious letter to *Literaturnaia gazeta* may signify his decision not to refute it after all (*GA* 4: 2, p. 623).

43. The combination of the adverb "veselo" with the verb "dumat'" [to think] is very unusual, and may be read as a sarcastic comment on Stalin's much quoted 1935 statement, "Zhit' stalo luchshe, tovarishchi, zhit' stalo veselee" ["Life has become better, comrades; it has become more jolly"]. Probably owing to its erstwhile abuses, the adverb "veselo" is rarely used in modern colloquial Russian.

44. Cf. Howe (1986: 31–32) on Holocaust memoirs: "we respond not just to their accounts of what happened; we respond also to qualities of being, tremors of sensibility, as these emerge even from the bloodiest pages. We respond to the modesty or boastfulness, the candor or evasiveness, the self-effacement or self-promotion of the writers. We respond, most of all, to a quality that might be called moral poise, by which I mean a readiness to engage in a complete reckoning with the past, insofar as there can be one—a

strength of remembrance that leads the writer into despair and then perhaps a little beyond it, so that he does not flinch from anything, neither shame nor degradation, yet refuses to indulge in those outbursts of self-pity, sometimes sliding into self-aggrandizement, that understandably mar a fair number of Holocaust memoirs."

45. In her post-camp years, Irina Karsavina, the eldest daughter of the philosopher Lev Karsavin, who died in the camps, would say that at hard physical labor one must learn to work using only half of one's strength; only a mental effort must always be unreserved.

46. "I write so that someone, on reading my prose which is so far removed from all lies, could tell his life in a similar way on any plane" (Shalamov 1989c: 3). Shalamov's reassessment of conventional topos-treatment relationships evidently belonged to this pursuit of the liberating effect on other potential witnesses.

47. Timofeev (#3870: 10) notes that the allusion draws a contrast between the unbounded spaces, the leisurely passage of time, and the freedom of motion in Pushkin's tale and Shalamov's closed spaces and the sense of time about to stop.

48. In "On a Misprision in Literary Works," (1989a: 446–50) Shalamov surveys the misleading presentations of the criminal world in European literature. In Shalamov's early days, Hugo was one of his favorite writers.

49. Unlike Isaiah Berlin, Shalamov did not believe in lip service to traditional moral attitudes. "Sympathy unsupported by action is the worst form of hypocrisy," he wrote in "The Fourth Vologda" (1985: 72).

50. Though Lawrence Langer's criticism (1982: 15–53) of Frankl's and Bettelheim's view of inner autonomy as instrumental for survival in the Nazi camps is largely just, it underplays the two psychologists' concern with situations when survival was a matter of endurance under extreme but not terminal conditions and the challenge was that of neither succumbing to torpid despair nor fighting with one's brother for a crust of bread. Shalamov's stories deal with precisely such situations. The majority of the victims of the Holocaust were killed summarily and never given the chance to test their endurance; by contrast, the Gulag, where the slaughter mainly took the shape of a gradual squeezing out of the prisoners' lives at the general works, usually did stage such a test, albeit a rigged one.

51. This is Shalamov's version of the topos of "the male prisoner being succored by an attractive female from the imprisoning camp" (McLean 1982: 257). The woman is a convict but works in the office.

52. "The lightness of the future corpse has not been described in literature. Everything is new in this story: the return to life is hopeless and does not differ from death" (Shalamov 1989b: 62).

53. The still-healthy new arrivals in Kolyma were usually sent to the gold mines; those who survived their first one or two "seasons" stood a slightly better chance of lighter jobs; most never reach this stage, cf. "An Epitaph" (*AL*).

54. In later life such trophic ulcers could reopen, with dire consequences. This happened to E. Ginzburg's husband: "Within two days of his death, at

the end of December 1959, lying in the Moscow Institute of Therapy, Anton was to say with a wry smile: 'The inmates of Auschwitz and Dachau are known by the numbers branded on their wrists. The inmates of Kolyma can be recognized by this mark, tattooed on them by starvation'" (1981: 248).

55. Secondary adjustment—pursuing unauthorized goals or employing unauthorized procedures (see Des Pres 1977: 114–32 and Goffman 1961: 188–93)—stands between primary adjustment and the subversive activity or rebellion; see the chapter "The Last One" in Levi's *If This Is a Man* (1990).

56. Shalamov would not allow his friend to edit out repetitions and contradictions in his stories (see Aigi 1987: 161). In addition to creating the impression of memory scabs in authentic survivor narratives, repetitions also produce the sense that, with but slight differences, the same things happen to different people. This is Shalamov's version of the dialectics of the common lot and individual fate: at a signal, the same accusations are brought against a sequence of prisoners, in the same order, with similar interrogators, similar perjuries, and similar prescribed sentences.

57. Cf. the story's background theme of knowing without being told, of estimation without measuring, of orientation without landmarks.

58. B. F. Skinner defines the self as "a repertoire of behavior appropriate to a given set of contingencies" (1972: 119).

59. For a detailed analysis of this story, as well as of the 1965 "Captain Tolly's Love," see Toker 1994: 179–93.

60. The real-life prototype was Dr. Rubantsev; see "The Descendant of a Decembrist" (*LB*) and 1993b: 137, 144.

61. See also Toker 1995 and 1997a.

62. Cf. Irving Howe (1980: 36) on Shalamov's "subdued philosophical temperament."

63. Of the aversive conditions in the camps, frost was the worst. Cf. Gilboa 1968: 45: "There is a scale of preferences in distress. To me it seems that the first place in our feeling of anguish went to the cold. A bit of warmth, a moment of thawing out, became an ideal superseding all other desires and taking precedence over longing for one's family, the horrors of lice, and a tortured stomach. In physics at school I had learned that heat causes bodies to expand and cold to contract. This applies not only to inanimate bodies but to living beings as well. It also works this way in the mental sphere. The world of feeling and desires also withers. It seems as if all the desires become concentrated in an exhalation of breath on blue hands." Shalamov's "Carpenters" supports these observations. The prisoners' moving in order to keep warm meant burning up their flesh much more quickly in winter than in summer.

64. Nor does the focalizer defend the torture victim who has signed a false confession. By yielding, torture victims reinforce the hand of the torturers. This is a behaviorist regularity, rather than a matter of old-fashioned codes of honor. Shalamov knew that people who broke under torture could not be either defended or blamed. For a reassessment of conventional notions concerning torture see Scarry 1985: 27–59.

65. "Old timers would measure the cold precisely even without a ther-

mometer: if there was frosty mist, that meant the temperature outside was forty degrees below zero; if one's breath came out noisily but still without difficulty, it was forty-five degrees; if the breathing was noisy and one panted, it was fifty degrees. At over 55 degrees spit froze in midair." Shalamov, "Carpenters" (1978: 28).

66. "Extraordinarily important to keep the first version. Correction inadmissible. It is better to wait for a new heightening of emotion and write the story anew, with all the right of the first variant" (1996: 432).

67. Actually (Shalamov would say "*vprochem*"—a Gogolian word that allows one to get away with a contradiction between a generalization that precedes it and a separate case that follows it), the element of response to paleological notions is anticipated in "Sketches of the Criminal World," which refute the obsolete romanticizing mythology surrounding the criminal world and offer iconoclastic pregnant testimony about it. Almost every sketch begins with an incident, a mini-story, a stimulus for hermeneutic perplexity, followed by an explanation of the behavior codes and historical developments that it exemplifies.

68. Page references are given to the text of these two cycles in Shalamov 1990a; "Vishera" has been reprinted in Shalamov 1998 (vol. 4), and *KR-2* in Shalamov 1991a, 1992a, and 1998 (vol. 2).

69. After the Revolution Tamarin had also learned what could be a life-saving manual skill, that of a hairdresser. Shalamov did not know that all this would fail him in 1938.

70. In Begin's *White Nights* the life stories of a number of fellow prisoners are likewise told in the chapters devoted to the author's recuperation in a hospital. In general, the size of the portrait gallery in Gulag works tends to be in inverse proportion to the acuteness of the physical suffering the author endured at each stage.

71. In the Russian title the word for "life" is "zhitie," as in titles of hagiographies.

72. This is a distinctive Shalamovian touch: as in "Quiet" or "On Tick," there are no expressions of mourning or grief for the dead companion. Instead, the protagonist is shown taking an immediate practical advantage of his partner's death (a version of the "inheritance" and, by implication, the "wake" topoi). For a more detailed discussion of the story see Toker 1997b: 211–14.

73. Judging by the testimonies of other survivors, such as N. Krasnov, some guards had no qualms about shooting specially selected prisoners anywhere, pretending that the prisoners had tried to escape.

74. The availability of American lend-lease tins of meat and fruit preserves in the camp store sets the story in the early forties, when the Soviet Union was at war with Nazi Germany: security officers had large stakes in an enhanced activity that would prove the need for their continued stay in the camps. Shestakov serves their vested interest, at the expense of his fellow prisoners. Yet it is the first-person focalizer who is the main target of the ethical inquiry of the narrative.

75. Todorov (1996: 38–39) refuses to deal with the moral condition of

people who have already crossed a certain threshold of suffering; Shalamov leads us beyond that threshold.

76. In view of El Campesino's criticism of La Passionaria's conduct in the USSR, one may read this passage as doubly ironic. Cf. Gibian (1980: 17): "Shalamov is a relentlessly honest observer who resorts only occasionally to a muted irony."

77. In his later years Shalamov was a vegetarian.

78. Shestakov is the namesake of the scholar involved in a large-scale rewriting of history in a series of Soviet textbooks of the late thirties. His name may have been chosen in order to evoke the covering up of the past and the falsification of records—but for all we know the name may also be authentic.

79. Obviously, this principle clashes with the spirit of supererogation fostered by generations of Russian intelligentsia: one may recall that in Dostoevsky's *Crime and Punishment* the conscientious doctor Zosimov, who never fails to come to the sick Raskolnikov and treat him gratis, is, from Razumikhin's point of view, a comfort-loving swine—because he would not give up his last shirt to a friend, only the last but one.

80. In a 1993 article on the moral lessons of Gulag prose, Iu. Sokhriakov places Solonevich side by side with Shalamov as rebels against this tradition, downplaying the fact that Solonevich emphasized mainly character typology. Sokhriakov mentions that Hitler, according to Solonevich, won the war against Russia because his experts had formed their idea of the Russian character on the basis of the Karamazovs and Platon Karataev. The literary mutiny of Shalamov involved a subversion of classical topoi and techniques and a critique of the demands for supererogation. This literary issue is, however, dwarfed by the moral/political inappropriateness of drawing an analogy between Shalamov, who consistently rejected ethnic discrimination, and Solonevich, who developed a spectrum of pro-fascist commitments.

7. THE GULAG FICTION OF ALEKSANDR SOLZHENITSYN

1. My brief survey of Solzhenitsyn's early life is based mainly on Scammell's valuable 1984 scholarly biography. The more recent (1998) and more exoteric biography by D. M. Thomas continues the story of Solzhenitsyn's life up to his return to Russia in 1994.

2. On the eve of the story's publication in *Novyi mir,* the daily *Izvestiia* hastened to publish "Samorodok" ("The Nugget"), by G. Shelest, a story of the ideologically pure behavior of Communists in the camps; Shelest's "Kolyma Notes" were later printed in *Znamia* in 1964. In 1963–1964, the journal *Iunost* printed Iu. Piliar's novel that reflects a prisoner's experience first in Nazi captivity and then in the Gulag. On these and other camp narratives officially published in the Soviet Union in the last years of the "thaw" see Geller 1974: 261–71 and Tolczyk 184–252.

3. But see Epstein 1992 on "labor of lust." Ironically, in Ekibastuz Solzhenitsyn himself was engaged in building not a power station, as in the story, but an in-camp jail.

4. Cf. Nadezhda Mandelstam (1974: 612): "for all my questioning . . . I could not form a visual image of the camps—this only came when I read *Ivan Denisovich*. Shalamov was annoyed at me over this: the camp described here, he said, was one in which you could quite happily spend a lifetime. It was an improved post-war camp, nothing like the Hell of Kolyma."

5. See Murzhenko (1985: 99–101) on the discussions of camp inmates of the sixties concerning the good and the harm done by the mutedness of the story's exposure of camp realities.

6. The presentation of camp life "through the eyes" of a peasant appealed to the poet Aleksandr Tvardovsky, the village-born editor of *Novyi mir*, and eventually even to Khrushchev.

7. Shukhov's name may be associated with the jargon word *shukhovat'*, meaning "pick up small secret advantages to oneself" (Ruttner 1975: 106).

8. Luplow discusses this passage as exemplifying a change of voice within the framework of a "third-person *skaz* technique" (1971: 406); according to Pike, the point of view (or "voice") here is that of the omniscient narrator, though the scene is "legitimized" by the presence of the protagonist (1977: 196–97). Yet the most convenient structural tool for the analysis of this text is Genette's notion of "paralepsis" (1980: 195), i.e., a temporary departure from the dominant focalization, which consists in presenting more information than is available to the focal character.

9. Such information may, in fact, represent the prisoners' communal lore; cf. Pike 1977: 202 on the collective application of the *skaz* style.

10. Shukhov is "a picaresque hero in the Russian folk tradition," a "brother of Vasily Tyorkin" (Scammell 1984: 383).

11. Indeed, X-123 oversimplifies the issues concerning Eisenstein's film, the second part of which was banned as suggesting a critique of the tyrant's rule (see Marsh 1989: 33).

12. For firsthand descriptions of the employment of an artist in the camps, including non-stenciled carpet-painting, see Nicolas 1958.

13. Parts of the book were broadcast to the Soviet Union by the BBC. In the early seventies an anonymous memoir, *Tupolevskaia sharaga* (Kerber 1996), dealing with a similar institute where the leading Soviet aviation designer Andrei Tupolev was imprisoned in 1938–41, appeared in Samizdat.

14. For a comparative analysis of the two versions see Nivat 1980: 211–28.

15. Judging by *Ease My Sorrows*, the people whose voices Kopelev had to identify were nothing like Volodin, Solzhenitsyn's lovable invention. The problems involved in Rubin's technical help to the secret police and a similar episode in Kopelev's life are discussed in Scammell 1984: 262–63.

16. Solzhenitsyn was critical of Sakharov's wasting his health and influence on the active defense of individual dissidents: dissidents, as freedom fighters, should be prepared to suffer for a good cause (see 1979: 373).

17. On the "high" and the "low" views of human possibility see Krook 1959: 1–18.

18. The only story in which Shalamov expresses regret for an action is "Permafrost," where he deplores his failure to understand a particular case, an exception to the general rule.

19. On the lack of a middle way in the Russian cultural tradition see Losskii 1957: 26–48 and 117–42, and Lotman and Uspensky 1984: 3–35.

20. The novel is a Gulag version of restricted-setting narratives ranging from Conrad's shipboard stories through Thomas Mann's *The Magic Mountain* to Aharon Appelfeld's *Badenheim, 1939:* the characters are taken out of their usual niches and placed in a closed environment, where their potentialities and liabilities are revealed (cf. Lukacs 1969: 35–46).

21. A novel's repertoire is its range of references to extratextual reality, including material culture, social and historical norms, earlier works, and moral and intellectual issues (see Iser, 1980: 69).

22. Marchenko's *My Testimony* shows that having any kind of choice was of great importance to the prisoners, even if the only choice they had would lead to still worse conditions (see also *GA* 3: 14, "Changing One's Fate"). Cf. also Eagle on the "resonance" (1977: 52) of the moments of existential choice in *The First Circle.*

23. With the amount of pragmatic improvisation practiced by concentration camp authorities and the multiplicity of untamed forces within the "zone," a prisoner's best-laid plans could be upset and the worst mistakes corrected by obscure contingencies; cf. Frankl's "Death-in-Teheran" parable (1962: 54–56) and Shalamov's "Kusok miasa" ["A Piece of Meat"] (*LB*).

24. In Dostoevsky's *Crime and Punishment,* Raskolnikov's decision to murder the old woman is not caused by any particular event: it is an almost inevitable outcome of the tendencies of his mind. Though certain circumstances trigger the fatal act (e.g., Raskolnikov's overhearing a conversation in the Hay Market), it is made clear that if the coincidence had not taken place, something else would have performed its function: Raskolnikov's plan seems to be ruined when he cannot take an ax from his landlady's kitchen, but as soon as he walks downstairs he is given an opportunity to purloin one from the caretaker's room.

25. See Fanger 1986 on other literary discussions held by the characters of Solzhenitsyn's novels.

26. In a letter to Solzhenitsyn, Shalamov praised *The First Circle* for "giving a geological cross-section of Soviet society from top to bottom—from Stalin to the janitor Spiridon" and for describing actual events: "The reader who has experienced Hiroshima, the gas chambers of Auschwitz, concentration camps, who has seen the war, will be insulted by invented plots" (1990b: 87).

27. Curtis (1984: 49–52) views the Makarygin party as a counterpart of the Rostov family party in *War and Peace.*

28. Quoted after Vladislav Krasnov (1980: 3)—Krasnov discusses the Bakhtinian concept of polyphony in application to Solzhenitsyn's work (1–12). Bakhtin's *polyphony* is the complexity of the ideological perspectives, the presence of a "plurality of independent and unmerged voices and consciousness" (1984: 6), each expressing a specific flow of psychic energies and a specific political, religious, or moral creed. However, the notion has been variously modified in modern criticism (see, for instance, Morand's discussion of the "polyphony" as a recurrent feature of writings by political prisoners [1976: 17–43]).

29. On the significance of the reference to Dante see Liapunov 1973: 231–40. The metaphor of the Dantean circles of hell for degrees of degradation and suffering on the vicious spiral was not uncommon among the intellectuals in the Gulag (cf. Margolin 1952: 17; Tregubov 1957: 131).

30. Cf. Iuz Aleshkovsky's grotesque Stalin in the novel *Kangaroo:* one cannot imagine Stalin quarreling with his conscience, so one imagines him quarreling with, and failing to control, his own left leg.

31. The eschatological dialogue peculiar to the carnivalesque mode occurs in a number of Gulag memoirs, especially those of Kopelev and Solonevich.

32. On Nerzhin's ideological quest see Dunlop 1973: 241–59 and Barker 1977: 14–18, 25.

33. While Volodin is being transformed from an affluent diplomat to a defenseless prisoner, the young guard is being transformed from a marine to a jailer (*FC87:* 549–50). The still uncorrupted guard's friendliness is another camp-literature topos.

34. In a Moscow prison Margarete Buber-Neumann received "the highest compliment in her life": a veteran prisoner told her that she was not the kind to go under in the camps. Shalamov records having received a similar compliment from A. G. Andreev, formerly the general secretary of the society of political prisoners (the society was dismantled during Stalin's move against veteran revolutionaries); see "Luchshaia pokhvala" ["The Best Praise"] (*LB*).

35. "Plato had argued long ago in his *Republic* that the despot was not a free man but at heart a slave, and he had argued elsewhere that Socrates was a free man even in prison. Solzhenitsyn has developed both points at length and has lent substance to the claim about the despot" (Kaufmann 1976: 159). On the relationship between Solzhenitsyn's image of Stalin and historical information see Marsh 1989: 135–73; on the psychological consistency of this image see Rancour-Laferriere 1985.

36. It might be incorrect to say that Isaac Kagan's Jewishness is used as a sufficient cause for his turning informer, but his motivation is presented as lying in petty greed—another stereotypical feature traditionally imputed to the Jew. A reader inclined to anti-Semitism would have prejudices confirmed by a text that distributes the threatening or disgusting features of an archetypal Jewish bogeyman among a number of characters (including the security officer Roitman and the orthodox Trotskyite Adamson, who becomes Abramson in *FC96*), though each of these characters may also be endowed with neutral or even positive features.

37. The morbidity of the novel's world is here, as in *Ivan Denisovich*, emphasized by the "night-is-day" theme: the nocturnal hours kept by Stalin and therefore by all government offices, the disruption of the diurnal round in the Lubyanka, and Rubin's sleeplessness at night and inability to rise in the morning.

38. Nadezhda Mandelstam (1970: 26) tells the story of Demian Bedny's falling into disfavor when Stalin was appraised of his diary entry about greasy finger marks in the books that Stalin had borrowed from him.

39. Cf. Primo Levi on the possibility of discerning "a crude form of asceticism" in hard labor (1988: 108).

40. Fasting, self-denial, self-sacrifice are the recurrent motifs of Solzhenitsyn's later fiction: the patients in *Cancer Ward* are underfed (though the carnivorous Rusanov, who has made his career on denunciations, is well supplied with dainties); the self-sacrificing Doctor Dontsova develops cancer of the intestine; the puritanical Vera Gangart gives away her sandwich to a surgeon; Kostoglotov can afford one shashlyk to celebrate the end of a fast—but will soon revert to his habitual ascetic self-discipline. *August 1914* starts with the period of the old-fashioned fast that precedes Assumption (and with the self-sacrifice of Sania Lazhenitsyn, who volunteers for the front); soldiers are poorly supplied with food; a pseudo-carnival breaks out in the episode of looting; and, in the revised version of this novel (the first "knot" of *The Red Wheel*), Bogrov and the Czar are linked in their aversion to self-denial.

8. IN THE WAKE OF TESTIMONY

1. The hint that innocent people were still kept behind the barbed wire was one of the most subversive touches of the novel and a sufficient reason for the novel's failure to pass the censorship.

2. The rise of activists is vividly described by Solonevich 1938: 87–125 and their further career by Avtorkhanov 1959: 55–57. Ambitious young people who lacked the intelligence, assiduity, or endurance for academic or professional training often chose to place themselves in the limelight by party-line oratory. They would complete their rise if they passed the test of "revolutionary vigilance" (i.e., collaboration with the NKVD witch hunts).

3. Cf. Wilson 1989: 175–79 on the problem of symbolism in *Cancer Ward*.

4. In the camps, the all-things-considered ethics was more appropriate than traditional moral squeamishness: practices like catering to the vested interests of officials, doing creative bookkeeping, falsifying output statistics, and stealing government property helped to keep the inmates in food; they were therefore regarded as less immoral than the prima facie "honesty" of overseers and jailers.

5. In *Cancer Ward* the life of former prisoners in their exile in remote provinces (see *GA* 6: 1 and 5–7) is mainly presented through the metonymic lucky-case method, similar to that of *Ivan Denisovich:* the Kadmin couple are in many ways more fortunate than thousands of their fellow survivors.

6. The same tale is also told by Nadezhda Mandelstam in *Hope against Hope* in relation to the period between her husband's two arrests.

7. A few true notes on the issue ring even in the "stagnation"-period fiction. Thus, V. Shukshin's *Snow-Ball Berry Red* (*Kalina krasnaia*) presents, sympathetically, and with a degree of romanticization, the Siberian experience of a recently released criminal convict who decides to break with the thieves; he eventually turns out to be a victim not only of the criminal underworld's vindictiveness but also, initially, of Stalin's strikes against the peasantry.

8. In Konson's *Brief Tales* a similar response is aroused by the presence of a magazine stand in the apartment of a friend who had never been arrested. Cf. also Shalamov's "Train" (*AL*): a released prisoner is bound to make mistakes such as buying wrong-size underwear.

9. For a discussion of Kostoglotov's feelings for Vega and Zoya, see Halperin 1985: 271.

10. The motif of yellow eyes, associated with Stalin, helps Lidia Chukovskaya keep the reader wary of the character of Bilibin in *Going Under* even when Bilibin casts a romantic spell over the protagonist-narrator.

11. "Comrade Stalin was a great scholar / Who made sense of linguistics / And I am a regular Soviet prisoner / And my fit comrade is the gray Briansk wolf." This lengthy satirical song was probably second in popularity to the grimly pathetic song about boarding the ships to Kolyma, "Mne pomnitsia Vaninskii port" ["I recollect the port of Vanino"]; in the "stagnation" years both were sung by people who had and who had not been in the camps.

12. Dombrovsky was first arrested in 1932 and exiled for three years to Alma-Ata; arrested again in 1937, he had a stroke of luck, evidently like the protagonist of *The Faculty of Unnecessary Things:* because of an NKVD change of guard he obtained a pre-trial release. In 1939 he was arrested again and spent four years in Kolyma. In 1949 he was arrested for the fourth time and sent to Ozerlag in Taishet; he was released in 1955 (see Shtokman 1989).

13. Shalamov is reported to have considered *The Keeper of Antiquities* "the best book about 1937" (Sirotinskaya 1994: 122).

14. See Woodward 1992b: 899–906 for a useful discussion of the place of the past in the novel and of the location of the present within its "cosmic" vision.

15. The name "Neiman" connects with Dombrovsky's interpretation of Pontius Pilate as an upstart, a *homo novus*.

16. When Dombrovsky was imprisoned for the third time in 1939, there were already considerable numbers of former interrogators behind barbed wire. Many of them had fallen in 1937, having (if one judges by Gazarian's memoir) been slow to understand the spirit of Yezhov's shift to a streamlined manufacture of false indictments.

17. See Turkov 1989: 226–27 for a detailed discussion of the meaningfulness of Zybin's name.

18. "[T]he mentality of a person who lives inside a closed system of thought, Communist or other, can be summed up in a single formula: He can prove everything he believes, and he believes everything he can prove. The closed system sharpens the faculties of the mind, like an over-efficient grindstone, to a brittle edge; it produces a scholastic, Talmudic, hair-splitting brand of cleverness which affords no protection against committing the crudest imbecilities. People with this mentality are found particularly often among the intelligentsia. I like to call them the 'clever imbeciles'—an expression which I don't consider offensive, as I was one of them." Koestler 1952a: 288.

19. In E. Fedorov's novel *Zharennyi petukh* [*The Fried Cock*—a reference to a camp synonym for a particularly trying experience—"the fried cock peck-

ing at one's ass"] a utopian loyalist who has been justifying the existence of the camps changes his whole outlook on seeing a fellow prisoner mutilating his hand to avoid the murderous general works. It is suggestive that this novel, which is hardly more than a self-indulgently extensive semi-parodic exercise in camp slang, takes advantage of the master topos of the literature of disillusionment as its unifying plot line. On the other hand, the Gulag episode in Vasily Aksyonov's *Generations of Winter* also centers on a religious conversion.

20. Pasternak gave the plot this final turn in the latest stage of his work on the novel in 1955, apparently under the influence of his conversations with Shalamov (see Shalamov 1988).

21. Cf. also Rosenfeld's critique of the imaginative misappropriations of the Holocaust 1980: 154–82.

22. A special group of such second-degree witnesses are writers whose parents have been imprisoned in the camps—Trifonov, Vladimov, Aksyonov, as well as Bulat Okudzhava, who deals with the parents' arrest in *Uprazdnennyi teatr* and with the mother's return and second arrest in, respectively, "Devushka moei mechty" ["The Girl of My Dreams"] and "Nechaiannaia radost'" ["Unforeseen Joy"] (1993: 238–49 and 250–59).

23. The latter novel suggests that images from the camps, camouflaged beyond recognition, may be scattered in the works of Soviet fiction even of the Stalin period: Chukovskaya paints an interesting portrait of an opportunistic writer who has distributed separate features of his camp associates among the characters of his made-to-order "industrial" novel. The shadows of people driven to death at forced labor may thus haunt the text that extols the Communist dedication of factory workers, giving it a reality-effect that it does not deserve.

24. Sinyavsky suggests that Ingus represents a doomed courageous intellectual caught up in the "service" (Tertz/Sinyavsky 1990: 76–77). In his brilliant analysis of the novella, Sinyavsky proposes to place it within the tradition of Russian literary exploration of the spiritual life of characters who are not merely miserable but also corrupted, usually by self-subjection to various types of "service."

25. *Dystopia* means a "bad place," one in which things have gone awry; it contrasts not only with *utopia*, i.e., a place that is nowhere, but also with *eutopia*, a "good place."

26. See Clowes (1993: 8). Clowes notes that in the heyday of both Soviet and Nazi totalitarianism, "ideology and utopia lost their fruitful, adversarial relationship and became one and the same in a fusion of the traditional characteristics of each." The fiction here discussed as *dystopian* she refers to by the term *meta-utopian*, because it is "positioned on the borders of the utopian tradition and yet mediates between a variety of utopian modes" (4).

27. Cf. Dovlatov 1982: 101 on the element of sympathetic magic as a common denominator of socialist realism and cave drawings: "You draw a bison on a rock—and get a roast in the evening."

28. See Malia 1994: 224. The aberrations abounding in the camps could suggest a most radical view of the discrepancy, namely that "the instrumental

program of socialism leads quite logically to the perversion of its moral program. In other words, the failure of integral socialism stems not from its having been tried out first in the wrong place, Russia, but from the socialist idea per se.... For the suppression of private property, profit, and the market is tantamount to the suppression of civil society and all individual autonomy. And although this can be approximated for a time, it requires an inordinate application of force that cannot be sustained indefinitely" (225).

29. Luchnikov's *credo* can be interpreted as a misguided literalization of Berdiaev's ideas of the future spiritual role of Russia, or else as Aksyonov's critical revision of Saharov's theory of the convergence of the capitalist and the socialist systems; see Matich 1988. It can also be interpreted as an idealized version of the Russian expansionism for which, judging by such camp memoirists as Razgon (1994: 129–67) and Chirkov (1991: 277), some of the former czarist officers among the prisoners actually praised Stalin.

30. The rate of post-1956 suicides (the most famous being the suicide of writer K. Fadeev) among the "average people" who had thus sent their neighbors to jail was, however, not high. Former prisoners have been known to show mercy to and even help their former persecutors (Ginzburg), whereas the erstwhile authors of denunciations would placate their consciences by placing all the blame on the "old times" and by receiving their surviving victims with cordiality (Delone 1984: 112).

31. The novel does not deal with the camps or Stalinism, yet its male-Cinderella motif (young provincials are, one after another, happily singled out by a *femme fatale,* after which they disappear) reminds one of the Great Purge, when people in high posts would be destroyed one after another.

32. See Nepomnyashchy 1995: 40–109 on the realization of metaphors in Tertz/Sinyavsky's *Fantastic Stories.*

33. A possible allusion to Christ's transforming water into wine at Cana (cf. Lourie 1975: 168; Nepomnyashchy 1995: 133).

34. Lenia's rise to power "tellingly begins with a struggle over language" (Nepomnyashchy 1995: 132): he first silences the leading town official during the May Day celebration; later he turns his townsmen into his own mouthpieces.

35. "To unwind" (like a spool of thread: *razmotat'*) is a camp term for getting the prisoner to talk about himself; it is also used by Sinyavsky (*poka vsego ne razmotali* [1992b: 561]).

36. A similar situation is also described, with the conventional trappings of disgust, in one of the stories of Maksimov's *Taiga.*

37. The criminal underground that kept perpetuating itself until the "bitch war" in the camps is believed to have been born during the Times of Trouble.

38. The image of this murdered child-prince, whose death cleared Boris Godunov's way to the throne, is often associated with more directly kenoticist Russian princes (see Fedotov 1966, 1: 109).

39. Grigorii Pomerantz believes that anecdotes about Sinyavsky's service as a KGB informer are thinkable, even though not true; they "stick" to him the way they would not "stick" to Solzhenitsyn, though Solzhenitsyn has also

told the story of the police attempts to recruit him. Pomerantz accounts for this by the nature of Sinyavsky's "inspiration"—"evasive, hiding, lapsing into the sordid, and then soaring upwards," and proceeding with "impudence, challenge, almost sacrilege" (1993: 179). For Peltier-Zamoyska's, Etkind's, Daniel's, and Bogoraz's responses to Khmelnitsky's article in the journal *Dvadsat' dva* (22) see *Vremia i my* #91 (1986): 222–23 and 230–36 and #93 (1986): 205–14. Etkind suggests that Khmelnitsky owed his well-being in West Berlin to the KGB and that his article in *Dvadsat' dva* must have been a result of the KGB assignment to discredit Sinyavsky.

40. The hunted protagonist-narrator of Yuly Daniel's short story "Iskuplenie" ["The Expiation"] (1991: 100–137) in *Govorit Moskva* is modeled on Khmelnitsky but written while Daniel still half believed that the man was innocent. Khmelnitsky claims to have "given" Daniel the idea of the "Day of Open Murders."

41. The reply of the victims was that but for Stalin's death they would not have been released after five years and would probably have perished in the camps, while the informer would have gone on living in contentment.

42. See Holmgren 1991: 976 on other meanings of the title.

43. A similar hesitation is also produced by the first-person narratives of Kandel and Guberman.

44. On the suspicion of fraudulence as an integral part of response to modern art see Cavell 1976: 188–89.

45. Alikhanov's main memory of the episode is that of the woman's brooch sticking in his face. In another fragment, recycling a Shalamov motif, the focalizer is tricked by criminal convicts into eating soup made out of his officer's pet dog. The dog's name, Broshka ("Brooch"), connects the two episodes through the sense of shame involved in both. The sense of shame is one of the characteristic features of Dovlatov's narrative (see 1991: 203).

46. Genis (1994: 197) would write that in his description of the flawed world Dovlatov looks at it with the eyes of "a flawed protagonist. Too weak to stand out from the reality that surrounds him, he slides on its surface, ingeniously eschewing metaphysical depth. Accepting life as a datum, he does not seek its hidden meaning. Dovlatov wins the reader over by not being loftier or better than others. (Here one can recollect the Chinese saying that the sea overcomes rivers by lying lower than they)."

47. By the seventies the sociology of the criminal underworld described by Shalamov was, indeed, a matter of the past; the criminal "code" was partly replaced by the *bespredel* phenomenon, a total absence of scruple. According to Abramkin et al. (1992: 97) only a few hundred "honest thieves" remained in the former Soviet Union by the early nineties.

48. In a later book (1989: 15–36) Nove surveys *glasnost*-period discussions of this and related issues.

49. I do not propose to takes sides with, say, Goldhagen's 1996 view of the enthusiasm of the perpetrators of the Nazi "final solution" against Hannah Arendt's and Tzvetan Todorov's (1996) comments on the banality of the phenomena that they represented: the scholars in question base their generalizations on different empirical data. When in dismissing Arendt's thesis on

the "banality of evil," Jean Améry explains that she knew Eichmann "only from hearsay, saw him only through the glass cage," he is thinking about the sadism of the Gestapo torturers and his discovery "how plain, ordinary faces finally become Gestapo faces after all, and how evil overlays and exceeds banality" (1980: 25). The paradox of the Gulag is that the prevailing majority of the people who served that "meat-grinder" were guilty not of downright sadism but of an obtuse and banal callousness; it stands to reason that those who added insult to the injury of the victims by loud-mouthed ideological condemnations were doing so in a sort of self-protective mechanism meant to thicken their insulation from the suffering of the so-called enemies of the people.

50. Many of Stalin's victims, even the grandest, like Bukharin or Tukhachevsky, had a great deal of blood on their consciences as well, and so, quite as often, had their own victims.

51. *"All of a sudden he was mortal"* (Tertz/Sinyavsky 1976a: 250).

52. Cf. also Koestler 1965: 15–25.

53. Cf. Joseph Brodsky's (1986: 384–92) comments on this verse in relation to his own experience of imprisonment.

Works Cited

The list includes, wherever possible, information on English translations of the entries. When page references are given to the original texts (owing to my interpretive disagreement with the published translations or, more often, to the problem of access to the books), the original is listed at the head of the bibliographical entry. When page references are given according to the published translations, these translations are listed first.

Because of the various systems available for transliterating Russian, there are some differences in the spellings of names, both between the text and the bibliography and occasionally within the bibliography itself. Whereas popular spellings, which more closely approximate the pronunciation of the names in English, have often been used in the body of the text, the formal Library of Congress system has been used here. For example, Russian names ending in -y in the text discussions will most likely be listed here as ending in -ii. Similarly, names beginning or ending with ya or yu in the text will probably be found here with ia and iu. Thus Yury Dombrovsky in the text becomes Iurii Dombrovskii in the corresponding bibliography entry. In the case of names for which the popular spelling differs significantly from the LOC spelling—as with Aksyonov/Aksenov—cross-references have been inserted.

TEXTS

(Memoirs and fiction wholly or partly dealing with Soviet prisons and camps)

Adamova-Sliozberg, Ol'ga.1988. "Put'" ["The Way"]. In Vilenskii 1988: 6–123. In book form: Moscow: Vozvrashchenie, 1992.

Aleshkovskii, Iuz. 1981. *Kenguru: Roman*. Ann Arbor: Ardis. English translation by Tamara Glenny: *Kangaroo* (New York: Farrar, Straus, and Giroux, 1986).

Amalrik, Andrei. 1970. *Involuntary Journey to Siberia*. Trans. Manya Harari and Max Hayward. New York: Harcourt Brace Jovanovich. Original: *Nezhelannoe puteshestvie v Sibir'* (New York: Harcourt, Brace, Jovanovich, 1970).

————. 1982. *Zapiski dissidenta*. Ann Arbor: Ardis. English translation by Guy Daniels: *Notes of a Revolutionary* (New York: Knopf, 1982).

Anders, Wladyslaw. 1949. *An Army in Exile: The Story of the Second Polish Corps*. London: Macmillan.

Anon (Mrs. Zajdlerova). 1946. *The Dark Side of the Moon*. Preface by T. S. Eliot. London: Faber and Faber.

Anon. 1974. "Memoirs of a Bolshevik-Leninist." In Saunders 1974: 61–188.

Antonov-Ovseenko, Anton. 1981. *The Time of Stalin: Portrait of a Tyranny*. Trans. George Saunders. New York: Harper and Row. Original: *Portret tirana* (Moscow: Grigorii Peidzh, 1994).

Aronson, Grigorii. 1929. *Na zare krasnogo terrora* [*At the Dawn of the Red Terror*]. Berlin: Hirschbaum.

Avtorkhanov, Abdurakhman. 1983. *Memuary* [*Memoirs*]. Frankfurt: Possev.

Badash, Semen. 1986. *Kolyma ty moia, Kolyma* [*Kolyma, My Kolyma*]. New York: Effect.

Bardach, Janusz, with Kathleen Gleeson. 1998. *Man Is Wolf to Man: Surviving the Gulag*. Berkeley: University of California Press.

Beausobre, Iulia de. 1948. *The Woman Who Could Not Die*. London: Victor Gollancz. First edition published by Chatto and Windus in 1938.

Begin, Menachem. 1977 [1957]. *White Nights: The Story of a Prisoner in Russia*. Trans. Katie Kaplan. Tel Aviv: Steimatzky.

Berger, Joseph. 1971. *Shipwreck of a Generation*. London: Harvil.

Bershadskaia, Liubov'. 1975. *Rastoptannye zhizni: Rasskaz byvshei politzakliuchennoi* [*Trampled Lives: The Story of a Former Political Prisoner*]. Paris: Librairie de Cinq Continents.

Bezsonov, Iu. D. 1928. *Dvadtsat' shest' tiurem i pobeg s Solovkov*. Paris: Imprimerie de Navarre. English translation: *My Twenty-Six Prisons and My Escape from Solovki* (London: Jonathan Cape, 1929).

Björkelund, Boris. 1966. *Stalinille menetetyt voeteni* [*The Years I Lost for Stalin*]. Porvoo: WSOY.

Bogoraz, L. I. 1986. "Iz vospominanii" ["From Recollections"]. *Minuvshee* 2: 81–143.

Brodsky, Joseph. 1986. "A Commencement Address." In *Less Than One: Selected Essays* (New York: Farrar, Straus, Giroux).

Buber-Neumann, Margarete. 1950. *Under Two Dictators*. Trans. Edward Fitzgerald. London: Victor Gollancz. Original: *Als Gefangene bei Stalin und Hitler* (Stuttgart: Seewald, 1968). The first part was first published in 1945.

Bukovsky, Vladimir. 1979. *To Build a Castle*. Trans. Michael Scammell. New York: Viking. Original: *I vozvrashchaetsia veter* [*Back to Its Circlings the Wind Is Returning*] (New York: Khronika, 1979).

Butman, Hilel. 1990. *From Leningrad to Jerusalem the Gulag Way*. Trans. Stefani Hoffman. Berkeley: Benmir Books. The original was published in two volumes by the Aliya Library, Jerusalem: *Leningrad—Ierusalim—s dolgoi peresadkoi* [*Leningrad—Jerusalem with a Long Stopover*] (1981) and *Vremia molchat' i vremia govorit'* [*A Time to Speak and a Time to Keep Silent*] (1984).

Chirkov, Iu. I. 1991. *A bylo vse tak . . .* [*This Is How It Was*]. Moscow: Izdatel'stvo politicheskoi literatury.

Ciliga, Ante. 1979. *The Russian Enigma*. Trans. Fernand G. Fernier and Anne Cliff (part 1) and Margaret and Hugh Dewar (part 2). London: Ink Links. First published as *Au pays du grand mensonge*, 1938 (part 1), and *Sibérie, terre de l'exile et de l'industrialisation*, 1950 (part 2).

Corneli, Dante. 1979. *Le Russuscité de Tivoli*. Paris: Fayard.

Czapski, Joseph. 1952. *The Inhuman Land*. Trans. Gerald Hopkins. New York: Sheed and Ward.

Delone, Vadim. 1984. *Portrety v koliuchei rame* [*Portraits in a Barbed Frame*]. London: Overseas Publications Interchange.

Demidov, Georgii. 1990. "Dubar" ["The Stiff"]. *Ogonek* 51 (December): 10–14.

Demin, Mikhail. 1981. *Blatnoi* [*Thief*]. New York: Russica. English translation by Tony Kahn: *The Day Is Born in Darkness* (New York: Knopf, 1976).

———. 1983. *Perekrestki sudeb* [*The Crossroads of Destiny*]. New York: Russica.

Diakov, Boris. 1966. *Povest' o perezhitom* [*Tale of Past Experience*]. Moscow: Sovetskaia Rossiia.

Dolgun, Alexander, with Patrick Watson. 1976. *Alexander Dolgun's Story: An American in the Gulag*. New York: Ballantine Books. First published by A. A. Knopf in 1975.

Dombrovskii, Iurii. 1977. "Iz zapisok Zybina" ["From Zybin's Notes"]. *Vestnik russkogo studencheskogo khristianskogo dvizheniia* 177: 104–25.

———. 1989a. *Fakul'tet nenuzhnykh veshchei* [*The Faculty of Unnecessary Things*]. Moscow: Khudozhestvennaia literatura. First published by YMCA Press (Paris) in 1978. English translation by Alan Meyers: *The Faculty of Useless Knowledge* (London: Harvill, 1996).

———. 1989b. *Khranitel' drevnostei*. Alma-Ata: Zasushy. First published in *Novyi mir* in 1964; reprinted in book form by the publishing house Sovetskaia Rossiia in 1966. English translation by Michael Glenny: *The Keeper of Antiquities* (London: Harlow, Longmans, 1968).

Doubassoff, Irene. 1926. *Ten Months in Bolshevik Prisons*. Edinburgh and London: William Blackwood and Sons.

Dovlatov, Sergei. 1982. *Zona: Zapiski nadziratelia*. Ann Arbor: Ermitazh. English translation by Anne Frydman: *The Zone: A Prison Camp Guard's Story* (New York: Knopf, 1985).

Dyakov. *See* Diakov.

Dyomin. *See* Demin.

Ekart, Antoni. 1954. *Vanished without Trace: The Story of Seven Years in Soviet Russia*. Trans. Egerton Sykes and E. S. Virpsha. London: Max Parrish.

Emelianova, Irina. 1997. *Legendy Potapovskogo pereulka: B. Pasternak, A. Efron, V. Shalamov. Vospominaniia i pis'ma* [*Legends of Potapov Alley: B. Pasternak, A. Efron, V. Shalamov. Reminiscences and Letters*]. Moscow: Ellis Lak.

Essad-Bey (Leo Nussbaum). 1933. *OGPU: The Plot against the World*. Trans. from German by Huntley Patterson. New York: Viking.

Fedorov, E. 1992. *Zharennyi petukh* [*The Fried Cock*]. Moscow: Itlar.

Filshtinskii, Isaak. 1994. *My shagaem pod konvoem* [*We Are Marching under Guard*]. Moscow: Vozvrashchenie.

Fisher, Lipa. 1977. *Parikmakher v Gulage* [*A Hairdresser in the Gulag*]. Trans. from Yiddish Zelda Beiralas. Tel Aviv: Derbi.

Gagen-Torn, Nina. 1994. *Memoriia*. Moscow: Vozvrashchenie.

Gazarian, Suren. 1989. "Eto ne dolzhno povtorit'sia" ["This Should Not Happen Again"]. *Znamia*, no. 1: 3–80; no. 2: 7–77.

Gendlin, Leonard. 1980. *Rasstreliannoe pokolenie* [*The Executed Generation*]. Tel Aviv: Effect.

Gilboa, Joshua. 1968. *Confess! Confess!: Eight Years in Soviet Prisons*. Trans. Dov Ben Aba Boston: Little Brown.

Ginzburg, E. 1967. *Journey into the Whirlwind*. Vol. 1 of *Krutoi marshrut*. Trans. Paul Stevenson and Max Hayward. San Diego: Harcourt Brace Jovanovich.

———. 1981. *Within the Whirlwind*. Vol. 2 of *Krutoi marshrut*. Trans. Ian Boland. San Diego: Harcourt, Brace, Jovanovich.

———. 1985. *Krutoi marshrut* [*Steep Route*]. New York: Possev-USA. Vol. 1 first published by Possev-Verlag in 1967. Vol. 2 first published in Milan: Arnoldo Mondadori, 1979.

Gliksman, Jerzy. 1948. *Tell the West*. New York: Gresham.

Gonzalez, Valentin, and Julian Gorkin. 1952. *El Campesino: Life and Death in Soviet Russia*. Trans. Ilsa Barea. New York: G. P. Putnam's Sons.

Gonzalez, Valentin, with Maurice Padiou. 1978. *El Campesino: Jusqu'à la mort*. Paris: Albin Michel.

Gorbatov, A. V. 1965. *Years Off My Life: The Memoirs of General of the Soviet Army*. Trans. Gordon Clough and Anthony Cash. London: Constable; New York: Norton. The original was first published in *Novyi mir*, nos. 3–5 (1964).

Gorchakov, Genrikh. 1995. *L-I-105*. Jerusalem: Jerusalem Publishing Center.

Grankina, Nadezhda. 1988. "Zapiski vashei sovremennitsy" ["Notes of Your Contemporary Woman"]. In Vilenskii 1988: 149–74.

Grigorenko, Petro G. 1982. *Memoirs*. Trans. Thomas P. Whitney. New York: Norton. Original: *V podpol'e mozhno vstretit' tol'ko krys* [*One Can Meet Only Rats in the Underground*] (Long Island: Detinets, 1981).

Guberman, Igor. 1990. *Progulki vokrug baraka* [*Strolls around the Barrack*]. Jerusalem: Tarbut.

Herling (Herling Hrudzinski), Gustav. 1987 [1951]. *A World Apart*. Trans. Joseph Marek. Oxford: Oxford University Press. Russian translation by Natal'ia Gorbanevskaia: *Inoi mir: Sovetskie zapiski* (London: Overseas Publications Interchange, 1989).

Herman, Victor. 1979. *Coming out of the Ice: An Unexpected Life by Victor Herman*. Oklahoma City: Freedom Press.

Hershman, Morris. 1995. *Prikliucheniia amerikantsa v Rossii 1931–1990* [*An American's Adventures in Russia 1931–1990*]. New York: Effect.

Ioffe, Mariia. 1978. *Odna noch'* [*One Night*]. New York: Khronika.

Ioffe, Nadezhda A. 1995. *Back in Time: My Life, My Fate, My Epoch*. Trans. Frederick S. Choate. (Oak Park, Mich.: Labor Publications).

Iurii Galanskov. Frankfurt: Possev, 1980.

Ivanov-Razumnik, R. V. 1953. *Tiur'my i ssylki* [*Prisons and Exile*]. New York: Chekhov Publishing House.

Ivinskaia, Ol'ga. 1978. *A Captive of Time*. Trans. Max Hayward. Garden City, N.Y.: Doubleday. Russian original: *V plenu u vremeni* (Paris: Fayard).

Juciutė, Elena. 1974. *Pėdos mirties zonoje* [*Footprints in the Death Zone*]. Brooklyn: Simo Kudirkos Kuopas. (In Lithuanian.)

Kandel, Feliks. 1979. *Zona otdykha ili piatnadzat' sutok na razmyshlenie* [*The Rest Zone; or, Fifteen Days for Reflection*]. Jerusalem: Olshanski.

Kaufman, A. 1973. *Lagernyi vrach* [*A Camp Doctor*]. Jerusalem: Am Oved.

Kerber, L. L. 1996. *Stalin's Aviation Gulag: A Memoir of Andrei Tupolev and the Purge Era*. Ed. Von Hardesty. Washington, D.C.: Smithsonian Institution Press. Translation of the expanded version of *Tupolevskaia sharaga*, first published by Cudina and Masic, Belgrade, in 1971 under the ad hoc pseudonym A. Sharagin; the second edition (Frankfurt: Posev, 1973) contained a note mistakenly attributing the authorship to the recently deceased G. A. Ozerov.

Kheifets, Mikhail. 1985. *Voenoplennyi sekretar': Povest' o Paruire Airikyane* [*A POW Secretary: A Tale about Paruir Airikyan*]. London: Overseas Publications Interchange.

Kiselev-Gromov, N. I. 1936. *Lageri smerti v SSSR* [*Death Camps in the USSR*]. Shanghai: N. P. Malinovskii.

Klinger, A. 1990 [1928]. "Solovetskaia Katorga" ["The Solovetskaia Hard-Labor Prison"]. *Sever*, no. 9 (1990): 108–12. First published in *Arkhiv russkoi revoliutsii* 19 (1928, Berlin).

Koestler, Arthur. 1941. *Darkness at Noon*. Trans. Daphne Hardy. New York: Macmillan.

Konson, Lev. 1983. *Kratkie povesti* [*Brief Tales*]. Paris: La Presse Libre.

Kopelev, Lev. 1975. *Khranit' vechno*. Ann Arbor: Ardis. Abridged English translation by Anthony Austin: *To Be Preserved Forever* (Philadelphia: J. B. Lippincott, 1977) and *No Jail for Thought* (London: Secker and Warburg, 1977).

———. 1981. *Utoli moi pechali*. Ann Arbor: Ardis. English translation by Antonina W. Bois: *Ease My Sorrows: A Memoir* (New York: Random House, 1983).

Krasnov, N. N., Jr. 1957. *Nezabyvaemoe: 1945–1956* [*The Unforgettable: 1945–1956*]. San Francisco: Russian Life. English translation: *The Hidden Russia: My Ten Years as a Slave Laborer* (New York: Henry Holt and Company, 1960).

Kuusinen, Aino. 1974. *Before and after Stalin: A Personal Account of Soviet Russia from 1926 to the 1960s*. Trans. from German by Paul Stevenson. London: Michael Joseph. First published as *Der Gott stürzt seine Engel* (Vienna: Molden, 1971).

Kuznetsov, Eduard. 1973. *Prison Diaries*. Trans. Howard Spie. New York: Stein and Day. Russian original: *Dnevniki* [*Diaries*] (Paris: Les Éditeurs réunis, 1973).

———. 1979. *Mordovskii marafon* [*The Mordovian Marathon*]. Ramat Gan: Moscow-Jerusalem.

Larina (Bukharina), Anna. 1989. *Nezabyvaemoe* [*The Unforgettable*]. Moscow: APN. English translation: *This I Cannot Forget: The Memoirs of Nikolai Bukharin's Widow* (New York: W. W. Norton, 1993).

Lengyel, József. 1973. *Confrontation*. Trans. Anna Novotny. Secaucus, N.J.: Citadel Press.

Leonhard, Susanne. 1959. *Gestohlenes Leben: Schicksal einer politischen Emigrantin in der Sowjetunion*. Stuttgart: Steingrüben.

Lesniak, Boris. 1993. "Pis'ma Varlama Shalamova" ["Varlam Shalamov's Letters"]. *Kontinent* 74: 159–79.

———. 1994. "Varlam Shalamov, kakim ia ego znal" ["Varlam Shalamov as I Knew Him"]. *Rabochaia tribuna* (March 12, 15, 16, 22, and 29).

Likhachev, Dimitri. 1991. "Solovetskie zapisi" ["Solovetsky Notes"]. In *Ia vspominaiu* [*I Recollect*]. Moscow: Progress.

Lipper, Elinor. 1951. *Eleven Years in Soviet Prison Camps*. Trans. Richard and Clara Winston. Chicago: Henry Regnery. Original: *Elf Jahre in sowjetischen Gefängnissen und Lagern* (Zurich: Oprecht, 1950).

Maevskaia, Irina. 1993. *Vol'noe poselenie* [*Free Settlement*]. Moscow: Vozvrashchenie.

Maksimov, Sergei. 1952. *Taiga*. New York: Chekhov Publishing House.

Maloumian, Armand. 1976. *Les fils du Goulag*. Paris: Presses de la Citée.

Malsagoff, S. A. 1926. *An Island Hell: A Soviet Prison in the Far North*. Trans. F. H. Lyon. London: A. M. Philpot.

Marchenko, Anatolii. 1969. *Moi pokazaniia*. Frankfurt: Possev. English translation by Michael Scammell: *My Testimony* (London: Pall Mall Press).

———. 1976. *Ot Tarusy do Chuny*. New York: Khronika. English translation by Joshua Rubenstein: *From Tarusa to Siberia* (Royal Oak, Mich.: Strathcona, 1980).

———. 1987. *Zhivi kak vse* [*Live Like Everyone*]. New York: Problems of Eastern Europe.

Margolin, Julius. 1952. *Puteshestvie v stranu ze/ka* [*Journey into the Country of Z/K*]. New York: Chekhov Publishing House. Reprinted by the Society for the Preservation of the Memory of Dr. Julius Margolin, Tel Aviv, 1976. First published in the French translation by Nina Berberova and Mina Journot: *La condition inhumaine: Cinq ans dans les camps de concentration soviétiques* (Paris: Calmann-Lévy, 1949).

———. 1960–62. "Intelligentsiia v lagere." *Novyi zhurnal:* 246–61.

Markman, Vladimir. 1978. *Na kraiu geografii* [*At the Edge of Geography*]. Ramat Gan: Moscow-Jerusalem.

Martzinkovski, Vladimir Ph. 1933. *With Christ in Soviet Russia: A Russian Christian's Personal Experiences of the Power of the Gospel in Freedom and in Prison in Connection with the Religious Movements in the U.S.S.R.* Rearranged, abridged, and translated from Russian by the Rev. Hoyt E. Porter, Hazard, Ky. Edited and published by the author (Haifa).

Medvedev, Zhores, and Roi Medvedev. 1971. *Kto sumasshedshii?* London: Macmillan. English translation by Ellen de Kadt: *A Question of Madness* (London: Macmillan, 1971).

Melgunova-Stepanova, P. E. 1928. *Gde ne slyshno smekha: Otryvki iz vospominanii* [*Where One Hears no Laughter: Fragments of a Memoir*]. (Paris: Rapid-Imprimerie).

Moroz, Valentin. 1968. "Reportazh iz zapovednika imeni Beriia" ["Report from the Beria Nature Reserve"]. *Novyi zhurnal* 93. English translation in *Voices of Human Courage* (New York: Association for Free Ukraine, 1968).

Murzhenko, A. 1985. *Obraz schastlivogo cheloveka, ili pis'ma iz lageria osobogo rezhima* [*The Image of a Happy Man; or, Letters from a Special-Regime Camp*]. Ed. Mikhail Kheifets. London: Overseas Publications Interchange.

Nicolas, Jean. 1958. *Onze ans au paradis*. Paris: Fayard.

Noble, John. 1956. *I Was a Slave in Russia: An American Tells His Story*. New York: Devin-Adair.

———. 1959. *I Found God in Soviet Russia*. New York: St. Martin's Press.

Olitskaiia, Ekaterina. 1971. *Moi vospominaniia* [*My Recollections*]. 2 vols. Frankfurt: Possev.

Panin, D. 1976. *The Notebooks of Sologdin*. Trans. John Moore. New York: Harcourt, Brace, Jovanovich. Russian original: *Zapiski Sologdina* (Frankfurt: Possev, 1973). Recent Soviet edition: *Lubianka-Ekibastuz: Lagernye zapiski* (Moscow: Skify, 1991).

Parvilahti, Unto. 1959. *Beria's Gardens: Ten Years' Captivity in Russia and Siberia*. Trans. Alan Blair. London: Hutchinson.

Petrov, Vladimir. 1951. *It Happens in Russia: Seven Years Forced Labour in the Siberian Goldfields*. London: Eyre and Spottiswoode. Also published as *Escape from the Future: The Incredible Adventures of a Young Russian* (Bloomington: Indiana University Press, 1973). Parts of the book were published under the titles *Soviet Gold* and *My Retreat from Russia*, trans. David Chavchavadze (New Haven: Yale University Press, 1950).

Petrus, K. 1953. *Uzniki kommunizma* [*Prisoners of Communism*]. New York: Chekhov Publishing House.

Piatnitskaia, Iuliia. 1987. *Dnevnik zheny bol'shevika* [*Diary of a Bolshevik's Wife*]. Benson, Vt.: Chalidze Publications.

Piliar, Iu. 1963/64. "Liudi ostaiutsia liud'mi" ["Staying Human"]. *Iunost'* 6, 7, 8/ 3, 4, 5.

Prychodko, Nicholas. 1952. *One of the Fifteen Million*. Boston: Little, Brown.

Pūkelis, Kęstutis, ed. 1989. *Leiskit į tėvynę: Tremtinių atsiminimai* [*Let Us Go to Our Motherland: Memoirs of Exiles*]. Kaunas: Shviesa. (In Lithuanian.)

Rapoport, Ia. 1988. "Vospominaniia o 'dele vrachei'" ["Recollections on 'The Doctors' Affair'"]. *Sputnik* (Israel), June 6: 10–11; June 13: 10–11; June 20: 10–11; June 27: 10–11. Reprinted from *Druzhba narodov*.

Razgon, Lev. 1994. *Plen v svoem otechestve* [*Captivity in One's Motherland*]. Moscow: Knizhnyi sad. Part of the material was published as *Nepridumannoe: Povest' v rasskazakh* (Moscow: Kniga, 1989). Published in English as *True Stories* (London: Souvenir, 1997).

Roeder, Bernhard. 1956. *Der Katorgan*. Cologne: Kiepenheuer and Witsch. English translation by L. Kochan: *Katorga* (London: Heinemann, 1958).

Rozanov, Mikhail. 1951. *Zavoevateli belykh piaten* [*Conquerors of Blank Spots*]. Frankfurt: Possev.

———. 1979, 1980, 1987. *Solovetskii kontslager' v monastyre* [*The Solovetski Concentration Camp in the Monastery*]. Vols. 1–3. (Publication of the author.)

Rukienė, Stefanija. 1967–70. *Vergijos kryžkelėse: Sibiro tremties užrašai* [*On the Crossroads of Slavery: Notes of a Siberian Exile*]. Cleveland: Viltis. (In Lithuanian.)

Rybakov, Anatolii. 1988. *Deti Arbata*. Moscow: Sovetskii Pisatel'. English translation by Harold Shukman: *Children of the Arbat* (Boston: Little, Brown, 1988).

———. 1990. *Strakh: Tridtsat' piatyi i drugie gody* [*Fear: The Thirty-Fifth and Other*

Years]. Moscow: Sovetskii Pisatel'. English translation by Antonina W. Bouis: *Fear* (Boston: Dell, 1993).

―――. 1997. *Roman-vospominanie* [*A Novel as Recollection*]. Moscow: Vagrius.

Scholmer, J. 1954. *Vorkuta.* Trans. Robert Kee. New York: Henry Holt.

Sentaurens, Andrée. 1963. *Dix-sept ans dans les camps soviétiques.* Paris: Gallimard.

Serge, Victor. 1963. *Memoirs of a Revolutionary, 1901–1941.* Trans. Peter Sedgwick. London: Oxford University Press. Original: *Memoires d'un revolutionnaire, 1901–1941* (Paris: Seuil, 1951).

Shalamov, Varlam. 1978. *Kolymskie rasskazy.* Ed. Mikhail Geller. London: Overseas Publications Interchange. 2nd and 3rd editions: Paris: YMCA Press, 1982 and 1985. Partial translations into English by John Glad: *Kolyma Tales* (New York: Norton, 1980) and *Graphite* (New York: Norton, 1981); the material of both was reprinted in *Kolyma Tales* (Harmondsworth: Penguin, 1994). French translations by Catherine Fournier: *Kolyma I, Kolyma II,* and *Kolyma III* (Paris: F. Maspero, 1980, 1981, 1982) and *Récits de Kolyma* (Paris: La Découverte/Fayard, 1986). Also published after 1987, in a revised order, in several Moscow editions prepared by I. P. Sirotinskaia, most recently as part of a four-volume collection of Shalamov's works (Shalamov 1998).

―――. 1985. *Voskreshenie listvennitsy* [*The Revival of the Larch*]. Ed. Mikhail Geller. Paris: YMCA Press. Does not reproduce the structure of the fourth cycle of Shalamov's stories, but includes some of them, along with "Chetvertaia Vologda" ["The Fourth Vologda"] and the stories "The Monk Joseph Schmaltz," "Berdanka," and "Vorigosfer."

―――. 1986a. "Anna Ivanovna." *Russian Literature Triquarterly* 19: 327–64. Also published in *Teatr* 1 (1989) and in Shalamov 1998/82: 457–501.

―――. 1987a. "Literaturnaia nit' moei sud'by" ["The Literary Thread of My Destiny"]. *Literaturnaia gazeta* (July 8): 6.

―――. 1988. Correspondence with B. L. Pasternak. *Iunost'*, no. 10: 54–67.

―――. 1989a. *Levyi bereg* [*The Left Bank*], ed. I. Sirotinskaia. Moscow: Sovremennik.

―――. 1989b. *Voskreshenie listvennitsy* [*The Revival of the Larch*]. Ed. I. Sirotinskaia. Moscow: Khudozhestvennaia literatura.

―――. 1990a. *Perchatka ili KR-2* [*The Glove or KR-2*]. Moscow: Orbita. Includes "Vishera: Antiroman" ["Vishera: An Antinovel"].

―――. 1990b. "Pis'ma A. Solzhenitsynu" ["Letters to A. Solzhenitsyn"]. Ed. I. Sirotinskaia. *Znamia*, no. 7: 62–89 (b). Reprinted in Esipov 1994: 63–103.

―――. 1991a *Kolymskie rasskazy* [*Kolyma Tales*]. Ed. I. P. Sirotinskaia. Moscow: Sovremennik.

―――. 1991b. "Kriticheskie zametki. Esse. Vospominaniia" ["Critical Notes. Essays. Memoirs"]. *Oktiabr'*, no. 7: 170–85.

―――. 1992a. *Kolymskie rasskazy v dvukh tomakh* [*Kolyma Tales in Two Volumes*]. Ed. I. Sirotinskaia. Moscow: Nashe nasledie.

―――. 1993a. "Vospominaniia" ["Memoirs"]. *Znamia*, no. 4: 114–70.

―――. 1996. *Neskol'ko moikh zhiznei: Proza, poeziia, esse* [*A Few of My Lives: Prose, Poetry, Essays*]. Ed. I. Sirotinskaia. Moscow: Respublika. Includes the full text of "O proze" ["On Prose"], 425–33, previously published, with elisions, in 1989a: 544–54.

————. 1998. *Sobranie sochinenii v chetyrekh tomakh* [*Collected Works in Four Volumes*]. Moscow: Khudozhestvennaia literatura/Vagrius.

Shapiro, Mariia. 1983–85. "Zhenskii Kontslager'" ["The Women's Concentration Camp"]. *Novyi zhurnal*, 150–53, 156–57, 158–60.

Sharansky, Natan. 1988. *Fear No Evil*. Trans. Stephani Hoffman. New York: Random House.

Shelest, G. 1964. "Kolymskie zapisi" ["Kolyma Notes"]. *Znamia*, no. 9.

Shifrin, Abram. 1973. *Chetvertoe izmerenie* [*The Fourth Dimension*]. Frankfurt: Possev.

Shiriaev, Boris. 1953. *Neugasimaia lampada* [*The Unfading Light*]. New York: Chekhov Publishing House.

Shukshin, V. 1992. "Kalina Krasnaia" ["Snow-Ball Berry Red"]. In *Sobranie sochinenii v piati tomakh* [*Collected Works in Five Volumes*], vol. 3. Ekaterinburg: Ural'skii rabochii.

Solomon, Michael. 1971. *Magadan*. Princeton: Auerbach.

Solonevich, Ivan. 1938. *Rossiia v kontslagere*. 3rd ed. Sofia: Golos Rossii. First serialized in the Paris *Poslednie novosti* in 1936. English translation: *Russia in Chains* (London: Williams and Norgate). Also published as *Soviet Paradise Lost* (New York: Paisley Press, 1938).

————. 1968. *Dve sily: Roman iz sovetskoi zhizni* [*Two Forces: A Novel of Soviet Life*]. Newark: Free Press.

Solzhenitsyn, Aleksandr. 1963. *One Day in the Life of Ivan Denisovich*. Trans. Ralph Parker. New York: New American Library. Original: *Odin den' Ivana Denisovicha*, first published in *Novyi mir* 11 (1962): 8–74.

————. 1968. *The Cancer Ward*. Trans. Rebecca Frank. New York: Dial Press. Original: *Rakovyi korpus* (Paris: YMCA Press).

————. 1978a. *The Gulag Archipelago: An Experiment in Literary Investigation*. Trans. Thomas P. Whitney (Parts 1–4) and Harry Willetts (Parts 5–7). New York: Harper and Row. Original: *Arkhipelag Gulag: Opyt khudozhestvennogo issledovaniia* (Paris: YMCA Press, 1973–75).

————. 1978b. *V kruge pervom*. In *Sobranie sochinenii* [*Collected Works*]. Vermont/Paris: YMCA Press: vol. 1 (the 96-chapter version). Soviet edition: Moscow: Knizhnaia palata, 1990. The 87-chapter version: *The First Circle*, trans. Thomas P. Whitney (New York: Harper and Row, 1968).

————. 1981a. "Znaiut istinu tanki" ["Tanks Know the Truth"]. In *P'esy i kinostsenarii* [*Plays and Film Scripts*]. Vermont/ Paris: YMCA Press.

Stajner, Karlo. 1988. *Seven Thousand Days in Siberia*. Trans. Joel Agee. New York: Farrar, Straus, Giroux. First published in 1971.

Surovtseva, Nadezhda. 1988. "Kolymskie vospominaniia" ["Kolyma Memoirs"]. In Vilenskii 1988: 252–62.

Swianiewicz, Stanislaw. 1989. *V teni Katyni* [*In the Shadow of Katyn*]. Trans. Vitaly Abramkin. London: Overseas Publications Interchange. Original: *W cieniu Katynia* (Paris: Kultura, 1976).

Tarsis, Valerii. 1966. *Palata Nomer 7* [*Ward No. 7*]. Frankfurt: Possev. First published in *Grani* 57. English Translation: *Ward 7: An Autobiographical Novel* (New York: E. P. Dutton, 1965).

Tchernavin, Tatiana. 1933. *Escape from the Soviets*. Trans. N. Alexander. London: Hamish Hamilton. Reprinted, New York: E. P. Dutton, 1934.

Tchernavin, Vladimir. 1935. *I Speak for the Silent: Prisoners of the Soviets*. Trans. Nicholas M. Oushakoff. London: Hamish Hamilton.

Tertz, Abram/Andrey Sinyavsky. 1976a. *A Voice from the Chorus*. Trans. Kyril FitzLyon and Max Hayward. London: Collins and Harvill. Original: *Golos iz khora* (Tertz/Sinyavsky 1992a, 1: 437–669; first published by Stenvalley Press, London, 1973).

———. 1992a. *Sobranie sochinenii v dvukh tomakh* [*Collected Works in Two Volumes*]. Moscow: Start.

———. 1992b. *Spokoinoi nochi*. In Tertz/Sinyavsky 1992a, 2: 337–654. First published by Sintaksis (Paris), in 1984. English translation by Richard Lourie: *Goodnight!* New York: Viking, 1989.

Tregubov, Georgii. 1957. *Vosem' let vo vlasti Lubianki* [*Eight Years in the Power of Lubianka*]. Frankfurt: Possev.

Vaneev, A. 1988. "Dva goda v Abezi" ["Two Years in Abez"]. *Minuvshee* 6: 54–203.

Vardi, Aleksandr. 1971. *Podkonvoinyi mir* [*A World under Guard*]. Frankfurt: Possev.

Veselaia, Zaiara. 1988. "7–35." In Vilenskii 1988: 359–88.

Vesyolaya. *See* Veselaia.

Vilenskii, Semen, ed. 1988. *Dodnes' tiagoteet: Zapiski vashei sovremennitsy* [*It Still Weighs Heavy: Notes of Your Contemporary Woman*]. Moscow: Sovetskii pisatel'. English translation: *Till My Tale Is Told: Women's Memoirs of the Gulag* (Bloomington: Indiana University Press, 1999).

———. 1992. *Soprotivlenie v Gulage* [*Resistance in the Gulag*]. Moscow: Vozvrashchenie.

Vinitski, David. 1984. *Sheleg kham: Misipurei Gulag* [*Hot Snow: Gulag Stories*]. Tel Aviv: Gvilim (in Hebrew).

Voinovich, Vladimir. 1993. "Delo 34840" ["File # 4840"]. *Znamia*, no. 12: 44–120.

Volkov, Oleg. 1987. *Pogruzhenie vo t'mu* [*Sinking into Darkness*]. Paris: Atheneum.

Volovich, Khava. 1988. "O proshlom" ["About the Past"]. In Vilenskii 1988: 461–94.

Voznesenskaya, Julia, ed. 1989. *Letters of Love: Women Political Prisoners in Exile and the Camps*. Trans. Roger and Angela Keyes. London: Quartet Books.

Wallach, Erica. 1967. *Light at Midnight*. New York: Doubleday.

Wat, Alexander. 1990. *My Century: The Odyssey of a Polish Intellectual*. Foreword by Czeslaw Milosz. Trans. Richard Lourie. New York: Norton. Original: *Mój Wiek* (London: Book Fund, 1977); English translation first published in 1987 by the University of California Press.

Weissberg, Alex. 1952. *The Conspiracy of Silence*. Trans. Edward Fitzgerald. London: Hamish Hamilton. Also published in the U.S. under the title *The Accused*.

Yakir, Pyotr. 1972. *A Childhood in Prison*. Ed. Robert Conquest. London: Macmillan.

Zaitsev, I. M. 1931. *Kommunisticheskaia katorga ili mesto pytok i smerti* [*The Communist Hard-Labor Prison or the Place of Torture and Death*]. Shanghai: Slovo.

———. 1936. *Chetyre goda v strane smerti* [*Four Years in the Land of Death*]. Shanghai: Far-East Division of the Russian Nationalist Party.

Zernova, Ruf. 1990. "Vremia nadezhd" ["The Time of Hopes"]. In *Izrail' i okrestnosti* [*Israel and Its Surroundings*]. Jerusalem: Aliya. First published in *Eto bylo pri nas* [*It Was in Our Time*] (Jerusalem: Lexicon, 1988).

Zhigulin, Anatolii. 1989. *Chernye kamni* [*Black Stones*]. Moscow: Knizhnaia palata.

CONTEXTS

Abramkin, V. F., Iu. V. Chizhov, M. N. Rodman, V. I. Rudnev, Z. F. Svetova, V. F. Chesnokova, F. L. Svetov, M. P. Kazachkov, and V. V. Salomatov. 1992. *Kak vyzhit' v sovetskoi tiur'me: V pomoshch' uzniku* [*How to Survive in a Soviet Prison: A Prisoner's Guide*]. Krasnoiarsk: Vostok.

Adorno, T. W. 1965. *Noten zur Literatur III*. Frankfurt: Suhrkamp.

Agenosov. V. V. 1998. *Literatura russkogo zarubezh'ia* [*Russian Literature Abroad*]. Moscow: Terra Sport.

Aigi, Gennadii. 1982. "I: posledniaia kamera" ["And: The Last Cell"]. *Vestnik russkogo studencheskogo khristianskogo dvizheniia* 136: 144.

———. 1987. "Odin vecher s Shalamovym" ["One Evening with Shalamov"]. *Vestnik russkogo khristianskogo dvizheniia* 137: 156–61.

Akeley, Ann-Ellen P. 1984. "Patterns of Imagery in *The First Circle*." In *Russian Literature and American Critics: In Honor of Deming B. Brown*. Ann Arbor: University of Michigan.

Aksenov, Vasilii. 1980. *Ozhog*. Ann Arbor: Ardis. English translation by Michael Glenny: *The Burn* (New York: Random House, Boston: Houghton, Mifflin, 1984).

———. 1981. *Ostrov Krym*. Ann Arbor: Ardis. English translation by Michael Henry Heim: *The Island of Crimea* (New York: Random House, 1983).

———. 1983. *Bumazhnyi peizazh* [*The Paper Landscape*]. Ann Arbor: Ardis.

———. 1993. *Moskovskaia saga* [*The Moscow Saga*]. Moscow: Tekst. English translation by John Glad and Christopher Morris: *Generations of Winter* (New York: Random House, 1994).

Aksyonov. *See* Aksenov.

Alekseeva, Liudmila. 1984. *Istoriia inakomysliia*. Benson, Vt.: Khronika Press. English translation by Carol Pearce and John Glad: *Soviet Dissent: Contemporary Movements for National, Religious, and Human Rights* (Middletown, Conn.: Wesleyan University Press, 1985).

Alexeeva, Ludmilla, and Paul Goldberg. 1993. *The Thaw Generation: Coming of Age in the Post-Stalin Era*. Pittsburgh: University of Pittsburgh Press. First Published by Little, Brown in 1990.

Amalrik, Andrei. 1970. *Will the Soviet Union Survive until 1984?* New York: Allen Lane. Original: *Dozhivet li Sovetskii Soiuz do 1984?* (Amsterdam: Fond imeni Gertzena, 1969).

Améry, Jean. 1980. *At the Mind's Limits: Contemplations by a Survivor on Auschwitz and Its Realities*. Trans. Sidney Rosenfeld and Stella P. Rosenfeld. Bloomington: Indiana University Press, 1980. Original: *Jenseits von Schuld und Sühne* (1966).

Antonov-Ovseenko, Anton. 1991. "Protivostoianie" ["Confrontation"]. *Literaturnaia gazeta* 5339 (April 3): 3.

Assmann, Aleida. 1994. "The Sun at Midnight: The Concept of Counter-Memory and Its Changes." In Toker 1994: 223–44.

Avtorkhanov, Abdurakhman. 1959. *Tekhnologiia vlasti: Protsess obrazovaniia KPSS* [*The Technology of Power: The Development of the CPSU*]. Munich: ZOPE.

———. 1976. *Zagadka smerti Stalina* [*The Riddle of Stalin's Death*]. Frankfurt: Possev.

Bacon, Edwin. 1994. *The Gulag at War: Stalin's Forced Labor System in the Light of the Archives*. Basingstoke: Macmillan.

Bakhtin, Mikhail. 1981. *The Dialogic Imagination*. Ed. Michael Holquist. Trans. Caryl Emerson and Michael Holquist. Austin: University of Texas Press.

———. 1984. *Problems of Dostoevsky's Poetics*. Ed. and trans. Caryl Emerson. Minneapolis: University of Minnesota Press.

Balina, Marina. 1992. "The Autobiographies of *Glasnost:* The Question of Genre in Russian Autobiographical Memoirs of the 1980s." *a/b: Autobiography Studies* 7: 13–26.

Barabtarlo, Gennadii, ed. 2000. *Cold Fusion: Aspects of the German Cultural Presence in Russia*. New York: Berghahn Books.

Bärens, Kurt. 1965. *Deutsche in Straflagern und Gefängnissen der Sowjetunion*. Munich: Gieseking.

Barker, Francis. 1977. *Solzhenitsyn: Politics and Form*. London: Macmillan.

Ben-Yakov, Avraham. 1988. "Two Currents of the Russian Nationalist Ideology from the 19th Century to the Contemporary Dissidents." Doctoral thesis, The Hebrew University. (In Hebrew.)

Ben-Yakov, Bronia. 1982. *Slovar' argo GULAGa* [*Dictionary of the Gulag Slang*]. Frankfurt: Possev.

Berberova, Nina. 1990. *L'affaire Kravtchenko*. Trans. Iréne and André Markowicz. Paris: Actes Sud.

Berdiaev, Nicholas. 1962 [1947]. *The Russian Idea*. Trans. R. M. French. Boston: Beacon.

Bergson, Henri. 1948. *Essai sur les données immédiates de la conscience*. Paris: Presses Universitaires de France.

Berlin, Isaiah. 1969. *Four Essays on Liberty*. Oxford: Oxford University Press.

Bethell, Nicholas. 1974. *The Last Secret: The Delivery to Stalin of Over Two Million Russians by Britain and the US*. New York: Basic Books.

Bettelheim, Bruno. 1960. *The Informed Heart: Autonomy in a Mass Age*. Toronto: Free Press.

Bloch, Sidney, and Peter Reddaway. 1977. *Russia's Political Hospitals: The Abuse of Psychiatry in the Soviet Union*. London: Victor Gollancz.

Blok, Aleksandr. 1955. "*Narod i intelligentsiia*" ["The People and the Intelligentsia"]. In *Sobranie sochinenii v dvukh tomakh* [*Collected Works in Two Volumes*], vol. 2. Moscow: GIKhL.

Bogoraz, Larisa. 1986. "Dushevnye muki seksota." *Vremia i my* 93: 210–14.

Böll, Heinrich. 1973. "The Imprisoned World of Solzhenitsyn's *The First Circle*." In Dunlop 1973: 219–30.

Booth, Wayne. 1988. *The Company We Keep: An Ethics of Fiction*. Berkeley: University of California Press.

Borges, Jorge Luis. 1964. *Labyrinths: Selected Stories and Other Writings*. New York: New Directions.

Borodin, Leonid. 1978. *Povest' strannogo vremeni: Rasskazy*. Frankfurt: Possev: 1978. English translation by Frank Williams: *The Story of Strange Times* (London: Collins Harvill, 1990).

Borowski, Tadeusz. 1967. *This Way for the Gas, Ladies and Gentlemen, and Other Stories*. Trans. Barbara Veder. New York: Viking.

Brewer, Michael. 1995a. "Authorial, Lyric, and Narrative Voices: A Close Reading of Shalamov's 'Sentenciia.'" Paper presented at the 1995 AATSEEL conference.

———. 1995b. "Varlam Šalamov's *Kolymskie Rasskazy:* The Problem of Ordering." Master's thesis, Department of Slavic Languages and Literatures, University of Arizona.

Brown, Deming. 1993. *The Last Years of Soviet Russian Literature: Prose Fiction 1975–1991*. Cambridge: Cambridge University Press.

Bruss, Elizabeth. 1976. *Autobiographical Acts: The Changing Situation of a Literary Genre*. Baltimore: Johns Hopkins University Press.

Buber-Neumann, Margarete. 1966. *Mistress to Kafka: The Life and Death of Milena*. With an introduction by Arthur Koestler. London: Secker and Warburg. Also published as *Milena: The Story of a Remarkable Friendship,* trans. Ralph Manheim (New York: Schocken, 1978). Original: *Milena, Kafkas Freundin* (Munich: Langen-Müller, 1977).

———. 1967. *Kriegsschauplätze der Weltrevolution: Ein Bericht aus der Praxis der Komintern 1919–1943*. Stuttgart: Seewald.

———. 1978. *Die erloschene Flamme*. Munich: Langen-Müller.

———. 1981. *Von Potsdam nach Moskau: Stationen eines Irrweges*. Cologne: Hohenheim.

Bukovskii, Vladimir. 1996. *Moskovskii protsess* [*The Moscow Trial*]. Paris-Moscow: Russkaia Mysl'–MIK. First published in French translation (Paris: Robert Laffont).

Carpovich, Vera. 1973. "Lexical Peculiarities of Solzhenitsyn's Language." In Dunlop 1973: 188–94.

———. 1976. *Solzhenitsyn's Peculiar Vocabulary: Russian-English Glossary*. New York: Technical Dictionaries.

Cavell, Stanley. 1976. *Must We Mean What We Say? A Book of Essays*. Cambridge: Cambridge University Press.

Chukovskaia, Lidia. 1965. *Opustelyi dom*. Paris: Librairie des Cinq Continents. Originally entitled "Sof'ia Petrovna." English translation by Aline B. Werth: *The Deserted House* (London: Barrie and Rockliff, 1967).

———. 1972. *Spusk pod vodu*. New York: Chekhov Publishing House. English translation by Peter M. Weston: *Going Under* (London: Barrie and Jenkins, 1972).

Clardy, Jesse V., and Betty Clardy. 1978. "Alexander Solzhenitsyn's Ideas of the Ultimate Reality and Meaning." *The Ultimate Reality and Meaning* 1: 202–22.

Clowes, Edith W. 1993. *Russian Experimental Fiction: Resisting Ideology after Utopia.* Princeton: Princeton University Press.

Cohn, Norman. 1957. *The Pursuit of the Millennium.* London: Secker and Warburg.

Conquest, Robert. 1960. *The Nation Killers: The Soviet Deportation of Nationalities.* London: Macmillan.

———. 1978. *Kolyma: The Arctic Death Camps.* London: Macmillan.

———. 1986. *The Harvest of Sorrow: Soviet Collectivization and the Terror-Famine.* New York: Oxford University Press.

———. 1990. *The Great Terror: A Reassessment.* Oxford: Oxford University Press.

Crossman, Richard, ed. 1949. *The God That Failed.* New York: Harper and Brothers.

Curtis, James M. 1984. *Solzhenitsyn's Traditional Imagination.* Athens: University of Georgia Press.

Daleski, H. M. 1977. *Joseph Conrad: The Way of Dispossession.* London: Faber and Faber.

Dallin, David J., and Boris I. Nikolaevsky. 1947. *Forced Labor in Soviet Russia.* New Haven: Yale University Press.

Daniel, Iulii. 1986. "Eksgumatsiia predatelia" ["Exhumation of a Traitor"]. *Vremia i my* 93: 205–209.

———1991. *Govorit Moskva.* Moscow: Moskovskii rabochii. First published by Filipoff (Washington, D.C., 1962) under the pseudonym Nikolai Arzhak. English Translation by Harold Shukman and John Richardson: *This Is Moscow Speaking, and Other Stories* (London: Collins, Harvill, 1968).

Davies, R. W. 1989. *Soviet History in the Gorbachev Revolution.* Bloomington: Indiana University Press.

Delbo, Charlotte. 1995. *Auschwitz and After.* Trans. Rosette C. Lamont. New Haven: Yale University Press.

Des Pres, Terrence. 1973. "The Heroism of Survival." In Dunlop 1973: 45–62. Selected and reprinted from "The Survivor: On the Ethos of Survival in Extremity," *Encounter* 37 (1971): 10–19.

———. 1977. *The Survivor: An Anatomy of Life in the Death Camps.* New York: Pocket Books. First published by Oxford University Press in 1976.

Diamond, Cora. 1991. *The Realistic Spirit: Wittgenstein, Philosophy, and the Mind.* Cambridge, Mass.: MIT Press.

———. 1994. "Truth: Defenders, Debunkers, Despisers." In Toker 1994: 195–221.

Djilas, Milovan. 1965. *The New Class: An Analysis of the Communist System.* New York: Frederick A. Praeger. First published in 1957.

Doležel, Lubomír. 1980. "Truth and Authenticity in Narrative." *Poetics Today* 1: 7–25.

Dombrovskii, Iurii. 1959. *Obez'iana prikhodit za svoim cherepom* [*The Ape Comes for Its Skull*]. Moscow: Sovetskii pisatel'.

Dostoevskii, Fedor. 1956. "Zapiski iz mertvogo doma" ["Notes from the House of the Dead"]. In *Sobranie sochinenii v desiati tomakh* [*Collected Works in Ten*

Volumes], vol. 3. Moscow: Gosudarstvennoe izdatel'stvo khudozhestvennoi literatury.

Douglass, Frederick. 1987. "Narrative of the Life of Frederick Douglass." In *The Classic Slave Narratives,* ed. Henry Louis Gates, Jr. New York: Mentor.

Dovlatov, Sergei. 1991. *Chemodan.* Moscow: Moskovskii rabochii. English translation by Antonina W. Bouis: *The Suitcase* (New York: Grove Weidenfeld, 1990).

Dubrovskii, V. 1954. *Mashina massovogo ubiivstva* [*Machine of Slaughter*]. Munich: "Ukrainian Peasant," Ukrainian Free Academy of Sciences.

Dunlop, John B., Richard Haugh, and Alexis Klimoff, eds. 1973. *Aleksandr Solzhenitsyn: Critical Essays and Documentary Materials.* New York: Macmillan-Collier.

Dunlop, John B. 1973. "The Odyssey of a Skeptic: Gleb Nerzhin." In Dunlop 1973: 241–59.

Dunlop, John B., Richard S. Haugh, and Michael Nicholson, eds. 1985. *Solzhenitsyn in Exile: Critical Essays and Documentary Materials.* Stanford, Calif.: Hoover Institution Press.

Eagle, Herbert. 1977. "Existentialism and Ideology in *The First Circle.*" *Modern Fiction Studies* 23: 47–61.

Eakin, Paul John. 1985. *Fictions in Autobiography: Studies in the Art of Self-Invention.* Princeton: Princeton University Press.

Eliade, Mircea. 1963. *Myth and Reality.* New York: Harper and Row.

Epstein, Mikhail. 1992. "Labor of Lust." *Common Knowledge* 1, no. 3: 91–107.

Erlich, Victor. 1973. "The Writer as Witness: The Achievement of Aleksandr Solzhenitsyn." In Dunlop 1973: 16–27. Reprinted from *Slavic Forum: Studies in Language and Literature* (The Hague: Mouton).

Esipov, V. V., ed. 1994. *Shalamovskii Sbornik* [*A Shalamov Collection*]. Vologda: Teachers' Training Institute.

———. 1996. *Shalamovskii Sbornik II* [*A Shalamov Collection, Vol. 2*]. Vologda: Teachers' Training Institute.

Etkind, Efim. 1978. *Notes of a Non-Conspirator.* Trans. Peter France. Oxford: Oxford University Press. Russian original: *Zapiski nezagovorshchika* (London: Overseas Publications Interchange, 1977).

———. 1986. "Ispoved' shenapana." *Vremia i my* 91: 230–36.

Ezrahi, Sidra DeKoven. 1980. *By Words Alone: The Holocaust in Literature.* Chicago: University of Chicago Press.

Fainsod, Merle. 1970. *How Russia Is Ruled.* Cambridge, Mass.: Harvard University Press. First published in 1953.

Fanger, Donald. 1986. "Conflicting Imperatives in the Model of the Russian Writer: The Case of Terz/Sinyavsky." In Morson 1986: 111–24.

Fautré, Willy, and Guido De Latte. 1980. *Nos prisonniers du Goulag.* Verrieres: Église du Silence.

Fedotov G. P. 1966. *The Russian Religious Mind.* 2 vols. Cambridge, Mass.: Harvard University Press.

Felman, Shoshana, and Dori Laub. 1992. *Testimony: Crises of Witnessing in Literature, Psychoanalysis, and History.* New York: Routledge.

Fireside, Harvey. 1979. *Soviet Psychoprisons.* New York: Norton.

Frankel, Edith Rogovin. 1975. "Russians, Jews and Solzhenitsyn." *Soviet Jewish Affairs* 5/2: 48–68.

Frankl, Victor. 1962. *Man's Search for Meaning: An Introduction to Logotherapy.* Trans. Ilse Lasch. Boston: Beacon. First version published as *Ein Psycholog erlebt das Konzentrationslager* in 1946.

Friedlander, Albert H., ed. 1968. *Out of the Whirlwind: A Reader of Holocaust Literature.* Garden City, N.Y: Doubleday.

Galler, Meyer. 1994. *Soviet Camp Speech.* Jerusalem: Magnes Press.

Geller, Mikhail. 1974. *Kontsentratsionnyi mir i sovetskaia literatura* [*The World of Concentration Camps and Soviet Literature*]. London: Overseas Publications Interchange.

———. 1978. "Predislovie" ["Introduction"]. In Shalamov 1978: 5–16.

———. 1989a. *Aleksandr Solzhenitsyn: K 70-letiyu so dnia rozhdeniia* [Aleksandr Solzhenitsyn: In Honor of His 70th Birthday]. London: Overseas Publications Interchange.

———. 1989b. "*Kolymskie rasskazy* ili *Levyi bereg?*" ["*Kolyma Tales* or *The Left Bank?*"]. *Russkaia mysl'* (September 22): 10.

Geller [Heller], Mikhail, and Aleksandr Nekrich. 1986. *Utopia in Power: The History of the Soviet Union from 1917 to the Present.* Trans. Phyllis B. Carlos. New York: Summit Books, 1986. Original: *Utopiia u vlasti* (London: Overseas Publications Interchange, 1982).

Genette, Gérard. 1980. *Narrative Discourse: An Essay in Method.* Trans. Jane E. Lewin. Ithaca: Cornell University Press.

Genis, Aleksandr. 1994. "Luk i kapusta" ["Onion and Cabbage"]. *Znamia,* no. 6: 188–200.

Getty, J. Arch, Gåbor, T. Rittersporn, and Viktor N. Zemskov. 1993. "Les Victimes de la répression pénale dans l'U.R.S.S. d'avant-guerre: Une première enquête (partir du témoinage des archives." *Revue des Études Slaves* 65: 361–70.

Gibian, George. 1980. "Surviving the Gulag." *New Leader* 63: 17–18.

Ginsburg, Ruth. 1989. "Karneval und Fasten: Exzess und Mangel in der Sprache des Körpers." *Poetica* 21: 26–42.

Ginzburg, Aleksandr. 1967. *Belaia kniga o dele Siniavskogo i Danielia: Moskva 1966* [*White Book on the Trial of Sinyavsky and Daniel: Moscow 1966*]. Frankfurt: Possev.

Gluzman, Semyon. 1989. *On Soviet Totalitarian Psychiatry.* Amsterdam: International Association on the Political Use of Psychiatry.

Gluzman, Semyon, and Vladimir Bukovsky. 1989. "Manual of Psychiatry for Dissenters." In Gluzman 1989: 70–87.

Goffman, Erving. 1961. *Asylums: Essays on the Social Situation of Mental Patients and Other Inmates.* Garden City, N. Y.: Doubleday.

Goldhagen, Daniel Jonah. 1996. *Hitler's Willing Executioners: Ordinary Germans and the Holocaust.* New York: Knopf.

Gorbanevskaya, Natalia. 1972. *Red Square at Noon.* Trans. Alexander Lieven. New York: Holt, Rinehart and Winston.

Gorchakov, G. 1989. "Trudnyi khleb pravdy." *Voprosy literatury,* no. 9: 105–17.

Gorcheva, Alla Iur'evna. 1996. *Pressa Gulaga, 1918–1955* [*The Press of the Gulag, 1918–1955*]. Moscow: Moscow University Press.

Gorelik, Gennady. 1997. "The Top-Secret Life of Lev Landau." *Scientific American* 277/2: 52–57.

Grossman, Vasilii. 1985. *Life and Fate.* Trans. Robert Chandler. New York: Harper and Row. Original: *Zhizn' i sudba* (Moscow: Knizhnaia palata, 1989).

Groys, Boris. 1987. "Stalinizm kak esteticheskii fenomen" ["Stalinism as an Aesthetic Phenomenon"]. *Sintaksis* 17: 98–110.

Gruenewald, Oskar. 1987. "Yugoslav Camp Literature: Rediscovering the Ghost of a Nation's Past-Present-Future." *Slavic Review* 46: 513–28.

Guthrie, Ramon. 1947. "Preface." In David Rousset, *The Other Kingdom,* trans. Ramon Guthrie. New York: Reynal and Hitchcock.

Halperin, David M. 1973. "The Role of Lie in *The First Circle.*" In Dunlop 1973: 260–76.

———. 1985. "Continuities in Solzhenitsyn's Ethical Thought." In Dunlop 1985: 267–83.

Harman, Gilbert. 1977. *The Nature of Morality: An Introduction to Ethics.* New York: Oxford University Press.

Harris, Jane G. 1990. *Autobiographical Statements in Twentieth-Century Russian Literature.* Princeton: Princeton University Press.

Harrison, Bernard. 1989. "Morality and Interest." *Philosophy* 64: 303–22.

———. 1991. *Inconvenient Fictions: Literature and the Limits of Irony.* New Haven: Yale University Press.

———. 1993/94. "Gaps and Stumbling-Blocks in Fielding: A Response to Černy, Hammond and Hudson." *Connotations* 3.2: 147–72.

———. 1994. "Sterne and Sentimentalism." In Toker 1994: 63–100.

Hartman, Geoffrey H. 1991. *Minor Prophecies: The Literary Essay in the Culture Wars.* Cambridge, Mass.: Harvard University Press.

Heller. *See* Geller.

Hemingway, Ernest. 1940. *For Whom the Bell Tolls.* New York: Charles Scribner's Sons.

Hochhuth, Rolf. 1964. *The Deputy.* Trans. Richard and Clara Winston. New York: Grove Press.

Hoffman, Frederick J. 1964. *The Mortal No: Death and the Modern Imagination.* Princeton: Princeton University Press.

Holmgren, Beth. 1991. "The Transfiguring of Context in the Work of Abram Terts." *Slavic Review* 50: 965–77.

Hosking, Geoffrey. 1980. *Beyond Socialist Realism: Soviet Fiction since Ivan Denisovich.* London: Granada.

Howe, Irving. 1963. "Predicaments of Soviet Writing." *New Republic* (May 11): 19.

———. 1980. "Beyond Bitterness." *New York Review of Books* 27 (August 14): 36–37.

———. 1986. "Writing and the Holocaust." *New Republic* (October 27): 27–39.

Iakovich, Elena. 1990. "Demidov i Shalamov: Zhitie Georgiia na fone Varlama" ["Demidov and Shalamov: The Life of Georgii against the Background of Varlam"]. *Literaturnaia gazeta* 11 (April): 7.

Iakubov, V. 1987. "V kruge poslednem: Varlam Shalamov i Aleksandr Solzhenitsyn" ["In the Last Circle: Varlam Shalamov and Aleksandr Solzhenitsyn"]. *Vestnik russkogo studencheskogo khristianskogo dvizheniia*, no. 137: 156–61.

Ikramov, Kamil. 1991. *Delo moego otsa* [*My Father's File*]. Moscow: Sovetskii pisatel'.

Isaev, Ivan. 1996. "Pervye i poslednie vstrechi" ["The First and the Last Meetings"]. In Esipov 1996: 89–97.

Iser, Wolfgang. 1980 [1978]. *The Act of Reading: A Theory of Aesthetic Response.* Baltimore: Johns Hopkins University Press.

———. 1993. *The Fictive and the Imaginary: Charting Literary Anthropology.* Baltimore: Johns Hopkins University Press.

Istrati, Panaït. 1929. *Vers l'autre flamme: Apres seize mois dans l'U.R.S.S.* Paris: Rieder.

Izard, Georges. 1949. *Kravchenko contre Moscou.* Paris: Paris-Vendôme.

Jakobson, Michael. 1993. *Origins of the GULAG: The Soviet Prison Camp System 1917–1934.* Lexington: University Press of Kentucky.

Jakobson, Roman. 1971. "On Realism in Art." In *Readings in Russian Poetics: Formalist and Structuralist Views*, ed. Ladislav Matejka and Krystyna Pomorska. Cambridge, Mass.: MIT Press.

Kaminski, Andrzej J. 1990. *Konzentrationslager 1896 bis heute: Geschichte, Funktion, Typologie.* Munich: Piper. Earlier version published in 1982.

Karner, Stefan. 1995. *Im Archipel GUPVI: Kriegsgefangenschaft und Internierung in der Sowjetunion 1941–1956.* Vienna: Oldenburg.

Kaufmann, Walter. 1976. "Solzhenitsyn and Autonomy." In *Solzhenitsyn: A Collection of Critical Views*, ed. Kathryn Feuer. Englewood Cliffs, N. J.: Prentice Hall.

Kennan, George. 1973. "Between Earth and Hell." In Dunlop 1973: 501–11.

Kern, Gary. 1975. "The Case of Kostoglotov." *Russian Literature Triquarterly* 11: 406–34.

Khmelnitskii, Sergei. 1986. "Iz chreva kitova" ["From the Belly of the Whale"]. *Dvadtsat' dva*, no. 48: 151–80.

Kline, Laura Anne. 1998. "'Novaja Proza': Varlam Šalamov's *Kolymskie rasskazy.*" Ph.D. dissertation, University of Michigan.

Koestler, Arthur. 1941. *Scum of the Earth.* London: Jonathan Cape.

———. 1952a. *Arrow in the Blue.* New York: Macmillan.

———. 1952b. Preface to Weisberg 1952: vii–xv.

———. 1965 [1945]. *The Yogi and the Commissar and Other Essays.* London: Hutchinson.

———. 1966. Preface to Buber-Neumann 1966: 9–11.

Kopelev, Lev. 1978. *I sotvoril sebe kumira* [*And He Made Himself an Idol*]. Ann Arbor: Ardis. English translation by Gary Kern: *The Education of a True Believer* (New York: Harper and Row, 1980).

Korallov, M. 1989. "Iz Voronezha i Berlaga" ["From Voronezh and Berlag"]. *Voprosy literatury*, no. 9: 118–49.

Kornblith, Hilary. 1993. *Inductive Inference and Its Natural Ground: An Essay in Naturalistic Epistemology.* Cambridge, Mass.: MIT Press.

Krasnov, Vladislav. 1980. *Solzhenitsyn and Dostoevski: A Study in the Polyphonic Novel.* Athens: University of Georgia Press.

Kravchenko, Victor. 1946. *I Chose Freedom*. New York: Scribner.

―――. 1950. *I Chose Justice*. New York: Scribner.

Krook, Dorothea. 1959. *Three Traditions of Moral Thought*. Cambridge: Cambridge University Press.

Kublanovskii, Iu. 1984. "Tomov premnogikh tiazhelei" ["Heavier Than Volumes"]. *Russkaia mysl'* (January 5): 12.

Kundera, Milan. 1981. *The Book of Laughter and Forgetting*. Trans. Michael Henry Heim. New York: Knopf.

Kuraev, Mikhail. 1990. *Nochnoi dozor: Povesti [Night Patrol: Tales]*. Moscow: Sovremennik.

Lang, Berel. 1990. *Act and Idea in the Nazi Genocide*. Chicago: University of Chicago Press.

Langer, Lawrence L. 1975. *The Holocaust and the Literary Imagination*. New Haven: Yale University Press.

―――. 1982. *Versions of Survival: The Holocaust and the Human Spirit*. Albany: State University of New York Press.

Le Procès des camps de concentration Soviétiques. 1951. Paris: Wapler.

Lefort, Claude. 1976. *Un Homme en trop: Réflexions sur "L'Archipel du Gulag."* Paris: Seuil.

Leggett, George. 1981. *The Cheka: Lenin's Political Police*. Oxford: Clarendon.

Lejeune, Philippe. 1989. *On Autobiography*. Ed. Paul John Eakin, trans. Katherine Leary. Minneapolis: University of Minnesota Press.

Lenin, V. 1970. *Polnoe sobranie sochinenii [Complete Works]*. 55 vols. Moscow: Politicheskaia literatura.

Levi, Primo. 1987 [1981]. *Moments of Reprieve*. Trans. Ruth Feldman. London: Abacus.

―――. 1988. *The Drowned and the Saved*. Trans. Raymond Rosenthal. Harmondsworth: Penguin.

―――. 1990. *If This Is a Man/The Truce*. Trans. Stuart Woolf. London: Abacus. First published in English by Bodley Head, 1965.

Levitt, Marcus C. 1991. "Siniavskii's Alternative Autobiography: *A Voice from the Chorus*." *Canadian Slavonic Papers* 33: 46–61.

Liapunov, Vadim. 1973. "Limbo and the Sharashka." In Dunlop 1973: 231–40.

Lie, Arne Brun, with Robby Robbinson. 1990. *Night and Fog*. New York: Norton.

Longinus. 1985. *On the Sublime*. Trans. James A. Arieti and John M. Crossett. New York: Edwin Mellen.

Loseff, Lev. 1984. *On the Beneficence of Censorship: Aesopian Language in Modern Russian Literature*. Munich: Sagner.

Losskii, Nikolai. 1957. *Kharakter russkogo naroda [The Character of the Russian People]*. Frankfurt: Possev.

Lotman, Yu. M., and B. A. Uspensky. 1984. *The Semiotics of Russian Culture*. Ann Arbor: Ardis.

Lourie, Richard. 1975. *Letters to the Future: An Approach to Sinyavsky-Terz*. Ithaca: Cornell University Press.

Lukacs, Georg. 1969. *Solzhenitsyn*. Trans. William David Graf. London: Merlin Press.

313

Luplow, Richard. 1971. "Narrative Style and Structure in *One Day in the Life of Ivan Denisovich.*" *Russian Literature Triquarterly* 1: 399–412.

MacIntyre, Alasdair. 1981. *After Virtue: A Study in Moral Theory.* Notre Dame, Ind.: University of Notre Dame Press.

Maggs, Peter B. 1996. *The Mandelstam and "Der Nister" Files: An Introduction to Stalin-Era Prison and Labor-Camp Records.* Armonk, N.Y.: M. E. Sharpe.

Mäkinen, Ilkka. 1993. "Libraries in Hell: Cultural Activities in Soviet Prisons and Labor Camps from the 1930's until the 1950's." *Libraries and Culture* 28: 117–42.

Malia, Martin. 1994. *The Soviet Tragedy: A History of Socialism in Russia, 1917–1991.* New York: Free Press.

Mandelstam, Nadezhda. 1970. *Hope against Hope: A Memoir.* Trans. Max Hayward. New York: Atheneum. Russian original: *Vospominaniia [Memoirs]* (New York: Chekhov Publishing House, 1970).

———. 1974. *Hope Abandoned.* Trans. Max Hayward. New York: Atheneum. Russian original: *Vtoraia kniga [Second Book]* (Paris: YMCA Press, 1972).

Mannheim, Karl. 1955. *Ideology and Utopia: An Introduction to the Sociology of Knowledge.* Trans. Louis Wirth and Edward Shils. New York: Harcourt, Brace.

Mansell, Darrel. 1976. "Unsettling the Colonel's Hash: 'Fact' in Autobiography." *Modern Language Quarterly* 37: 115–31.

Margolin, Julius. 1965–66. "Kniga o zhizni: Vosem' glav o detstve" ["A Book of Life: Eight Chapters on Childhood"]. *Novyi zhurnal* 81: 37–78, and 82: 56–96.

———. 1970. *Parizhskii otchet [Paris Report].* Tel Aviv: Maoz.

———. 1973. *Povest' tysiacheletii [A Tale of Millennia].* Tel Aviv: Society for the Preservation of the Memory of Dr. Julius Margolin.

———. 1975. *Nesobrannoe [Uncollected Works].* Tel Aviv: Society for the Preservation of the Memory of Dr. Julius Margolin.

Marsh, Rosalind. 1989. *Images of Dictatorship: Portraits of Stalin in Literature.* London: Routledge.

———. 1995. *History and Literature in Contemporary Russia.* New York: New York University Press.

Matich, Olga. 1988. "Vasilii Aksenov and the Literature of Convergence: Ostrov Krym as Self-Criticism." *Slavic Review* 47: 642–51.

———. 1989. "*Spokojnoj noči:* Andrej Sinjavskij's Rebirth as Abram Terz." *Slavic and East European Journal* 33: 50–63.

McCarthy, Mary. 1973. "The Tolstoy Connection." In Dunlop 1973: 332–50.

McDowell, Deborah E. 1991. "In the First Place: Making Frederick Douglass and the Afro-American Narrative Tradition." In William Andrews, ed., *Critical Essays on Frederick Douglass.* Boston: G. K. Hall.

McLean, Hugh. 1982. "Walls and Wire: Notes on the Prison Theme in Russian Literature." *International Journal of Slavic Linguistics and Poetics* 24–25: 253–63.

Medvedev, Roy. 1974. *K sudu istorii: Genezis i posledstviia stalinizma.* New York: Knopf. English translation by George Shriver: *Let History Judge: The Origins and Consequences of Stalinism* (revised and expanded edition, New York: Columbia University Press, 1989). First English version published in 1971.

————. 1985. "On Solzhenitsyn's *The Gulag Archipelago*." In Dunlop 1985: 461–62.

Medvedev, Zhores A. 1973. *Ten Years after Ivan Denisovich*. Trans. Hilary Sternberg. New York: Knopf.

Mikhailik, Elena. 1996. "V kontekste literatury i istorii" ["In the Context of Literature and History"]. In Esipov 1996: 105–29.

Miletich, Nicolas. 1986. "Postface" to Varlam Chalamov, *La Nuit: Récits de Kolyma*. Trans. Catherine Fournier. Paris: Decouverte/Fayard.

Milosz, Czeslaw. 1953. *The Captive Mind*. Trans. Jane Zielonko. New York: Knopf.

Morand, Bernadette. 1976. *Les Écrits des prisonniers politiques*. Paris: Presses Universitaires de France.

Morson, Gary Saul. 1981. "Tolstoy's Absolute Language." In Gary Saul Morson, ed., *Bakhtin: Essays and Dialogues on his Work*. Chicago: University of Chicago Press.

————, ed. 1986. *Literature and History: Theoretical Problems and Russian Case Studies*. Stanford, Calif.: Stanford University Press.

Muchnic, Helen. 1973. "*Cancer Ward:* Of Fate and Guilt." In Dunlop 1973: 277–94.

Mukařovský, Jan. 1970. *Aesthetic Function, Norm and Value as Social Facts*. Trans. Mark E. Suino. Michigan Slavic Contributions. Ann Arbor: University of Michigan.

Nabokov, Vladimir. 1957. *Pnin*. London: Heinemann.

————. 1962. *Pale Fire*. London: Weidenfeld and Nicolson.

————. 1979. *The Gift*. Trans. Michael Scammell with the collaboration of the author. New York: Putnam.

Naidich, Larisa. 1995. *Sled na peske: Ocherki o russkom iazykovom uzuse* [*A Trace on the Sand: Sketches on Russian Linguistic Usage*]. St. Petersburg: St. Petersburg State University.

Nekliudov, Sergei. 1994. "Tret'ia Moskva" ["The Third Moscow"]. In Esipov 1994: 162–66.

Nekrasov, Viktor. 1984. "Lev Konson. 'Korotkie povesti'" ["Lev Konson: 'Short Tales'"]. *Novoe russkoe slovo* (December): 2.

Nepomnyashchy, Catharine Theimer. 1995. *Abram Tertz and the Poetics of Crime*. New Haven: Yale University Press.

Nietzsche, Friedrich. 1968a. *Basic Writings of Nietzsche*. Trans. and ed. Walter Kaufman. New York: Modern Library.

————. 1968b. *The Will to Power*. Trans. Walter Kaufmann and R. J. Hollingdale. New York: Random House.

Nivat, Georges. 1980. *Soljenitsyne*. Paris: Seuil.

Nove, Alec. 1964. *Was Stalin Really Necessary? Some Problems of Soviet Political Economy*. London: Allen and Unwin.

————. 1989. *Glasnost' in Action: Cultural Renaissance in Russia*. Boston: Unwin Hyman.

Nussbaum, Andrew J. 1990. "Literary Selves: The Tertz-Sinyavsky Dialogue." In Harris 1990: 238–59.

Nussbaum, Martha. 1986. *The Fragility of Goodness: Luck and Ethics in Greek Tragedy and Philosophy*. Cambridge: Cambridge University Press.

———. 1990. *Love's Knowledge: Essays in Philosophy and Literature*. New York: Oxford University Press.

Oja, Matt F. 1985. "Shalamov, Solzhenitsyn, and the Mission of Memory." *Survey* 125, 62–69.

———. 1989. "Toward a Definition of Camp Literature." *Slavic Review* 48: 272–74.

Okudzhava, Bulat. 1993. *Zaeizzhyi muzykant* [*A Traveling Musician*]. Moscow: Olimp.

———. 1995. *Uprazdnennyi teatr: Semeinaia khronika* [*Abolished Theatre: A Family Chronicle*]. Moscow: Rusanov Publishing.

O'Neill, William L. 1982. *A Better World: The Great Schism—Stalinism and the American Intellectuals*. New York: Simon and Schuster.

Orlov, Alexander. 1953. *The Secret History of Stalin's Crimes*. New York: Random House.

Orlova, Raissa, and Lev Kopelev. 1990. *My zhili v Moskve 1956–1980* [*We Lived in Moscow 1956–1980*]. Moscow: Kniga. First published in English in 1987 (Ann Arbor: Ardis).

Orwell, George. 1949. *Nineteen Eighty-Four.* New York: Harcourt, Brace and World.

Ozick, Cynthia. 1990 [1980]. *The Shawl*. New York: Vintage Books.

Panin, Dimitri. 1982. *Teoriia gustot* [*Theory of Densities*]. Paris: Chois.

Parrau, Alain.1995. *Écrire les camps*. Paris: Belin.

Pervukhin, Natalia. 1991. "The 'Experiment in Literary Investigation' (Čexov's *Saxalin* and Solzenitsyn's *Gulag*)." *Slavic and East European Journal* 35: 489–502.

Pike, David.1977. "A Camp through the Eyes of a Peasant: Sozhenitsyn's *One Day in the Life of Ivan Denisovich*." *California Slavic Studies* 10: 193–223.

Pipes, Richard, ed. 1996. *The Unknown Lenin: From the Secret Archive*. New Haven: Yale University Press.

Plyushch, Leonid. 1979. *Na karnavale istorii* [*History's Carnival*]. London: Overseas Publications Interchange.

Pomerants, G. 1993. "Urok medlennogo chteniia" ["A Lesson in Slow Reading"]. *Oktiabr'*, no. 6: 178–83.

Pomerantsev, Vladimir. 1953. "Ob iskrennosti v literature" ["On Sincerity in Literature"]. *Novyi mir,* no. 12: 218–45.

Pontuso, James F. 1990. *Solzhenitsyn's Political Thought*. Charlottesville: University of Virginia Press.

Porter, Robert. 1987. "Animal Magic in Solzhenitsyn, Rasputin, and Voynovich." *Modern Language Review* 82/3: 675–84.

Pour la vérité sur les camps concentrationnaires. 1951. Paris: Éditions du Pavois.

Prianishnikov, Boris. 1979. *Nezrimaia pautina* [*The Invisible Web*]. New York: B. Prianishnikov.

Proffer, Carl. 1987. *The Widows of Russia*. Ann Arbor: Ardis.

Rancour-Laferriere, Daniel. 1985. "The Deranged Birthday Boy: Solzhenitsyn's Portrait of Stalin in *The First Circle*." *Mosaic* 18/3: 61–72.

Rapoport, Natal'ia. 1988. "Pamiat'—eto tozhe meditsina" ["Memory Is Also Medicine"]. *Sputnik* (Israel), May 16: 10–11, May 23: 10–10. Reprinted from *Iunost'*.

Remnick, David. 1994 [1993]. *Lenin's Tomb: The Last Days of the Soviet Empire.* New York: Random House.

Richards, Susan. 1985. *"The Gulag Archipelago* as 'Literary Documentary.'" In Dunlop 1985: 145–63.

Rigoulot, Pierre. 1991. *Les Paupières lourdes: Les Français face au goulag: aveuglements et indignations.* Paris: Editions Universitaires.

Rigoulot, Pierre, with Geoffroi Crunelle. 1984. *Les Français au Goulag (1917–1984).* Paris: Fayard.

Rorty, Richard. 1989. *Contingency, Irony, and Solidarity.* Cambridge: Cambridge University Press.

Rosefielde, Steven. 1980. "The First 'Great Leap Forward' Reconsidered: Lessons of Solzhenitsyn's *Gulag Archipelago." Slavic Review* 39: 559–87.

———. 1981. "An Assessment of the Sources and Uses of Gulag Forced Labor 1929–56." *Soviet Studies* 33: 51–87.

———. 1987. "Incriminating Evidence: Excess Deaths and Forced Labor under Stalin—A Final Reply to Critics." *Soviet Studies* 39/2: 292–313.

Rosenfeld, Alvin H. 1980. *A Double Dying: Reflections on Holocaust Literature.* Bloomington: Indiana University Press.

———. 1995. "Primo Levi: The Survivor as Victim." In James S. Pacy and Alan P. Wertheimer, eds., *Perspectives on the Holocaust: Essays in Honor of Raul Hilberg.* Boulder: Westview.

Rossi, Jacques. 1987. *Spravochnik po GULagu: Istoricheskii slovar' sovetskikh penitentsiarnykh institutsii i terminov, sviazannykh s prinuditel'nym trudom.* Preface by Alain Besançon. London: Overseas Publications Interchange. English translation by William A. Burbans: *The Gulag Handbook: An Encyclopedic Dictionary of Soviet Penitentiary Institutions and Terms Related to the Forced Labor Camps* (New York: Paragon House, 1989).

Rothberg, Abraham. 1971. *Aleksandr Solzhenitsyn: The Major Novels.* Ithaca: Cornell University Press.

Rousset, David. 1947. *The Other Kingdom.* Trans. Ramon Guthrie. New York: Reynal and Hitchcock. Original: *L'Univers concentrationnaire* (Paris: Pavois, 1946).

———. 1947. *Les Jours de notre mort.* Paris: Pavois.

Rovner, Adam. 1997. "Risk and Appeal: Hannah Arendt, the Eichmann Trial and Ka-Tzetnik." Master's thesis, The Hebrew University of Jerusalem.

Roziner, Felix. 1991. *A Certain Finkelmeyer.* Trans. Michael Henry Heim. (New York: Norton). Original: *Nekto Finkelmaier* (London: Overseas Publications Interchange, 1981).

Rubenstein, Joshua. 1980. *Soviet Dissidents: Their Struggle for Human Rights.* Boston: Beacon Press.

———. 1996. *Tangled Loyalties: The Life and Times of Ilya Ehrenburg.* London: I. B. Tauris.

Ruttner, Eckhard. 1975. "The Names in Solzhenitsyn's Short Novel *One Day in the Life of Ivan Denisovich." Names: Journal of the American Name Society* 23: 103–11.

Rzhevsky, Leonid. 1978. *Solzhenitsyn: Creator and Heroic Deed.* Trans. Sonja Miller. University: University of Alabama Press. Original: *Tvorets i podvig* (Frankfurt: Possev, 1972).

Samoilova, G. V., ed. 1996. *Zapoliarnaia tochka Gulaga: Nizhnekolymskii muzei istorii i kul'tury* [*An Arctic Point of the Gulag: The Lower Kolyma Museum of History and Culture*]. Moscow: Vozvrashchenie.

Sarolea, Charles. 1926. "Introduction." In Doubassoff 1926: vii–xvii.

Saunders, George, ed. 1974. *Samizdat: Voices of the Soviet Opposition.* New York: Monad Press.

Saunders, Kate. 1996. *Eighteen Layers of Hell: Stories from the Chinese Gulag.* London: Cassell.

Scammell, Michael. 1984. *Solzhenitsyn: A Biography.* New York: Norton.

Scarry, Elaine. 1985. *The Body in Pain: The Making and Unmaking of the World.* New York: Oxford University Press.

Schmemann, Alexander. 1973. "On Solzhenitsyn." In Dunlop 1973: 28–44.

Segal, Dimitri. 1981. "Literatura kak okhrannaia gramota" ["Literature as Safe Passage"]. *Slavica Hierosolymitana* 5–6: 151–244.

Senfeld, I. 1979. "Krugi zhizni i tvorchestva Iuriia Dombrovskogo" ["The Circles of Iurii Dombrovskii's Life and Work"]. *Grani* 111–12: 351–77.

Shalamov, Varlam. 1985a. "Chetvertaia Vologda." Ed. Mikhail Geller. In Shalamov 1985: 19–216. Text edited by I. Sirotinskaia printed, with some minor changes, in Shalamov 1994a: 9–174 and in Shalamov 1998, 4: 7–148.

———. 1986b [1967]. "Pis'mo staromu drugu" ["Letter to an Old Friend"]. *Russkaia mysl',* no. 3608 (14 February): 10–11. Also printed in E. M. Velikanova, ed., *Tsena metafory ili Prestuplenie i nakazanie Siniavskogo i Danielia* [*The Cost of Metaphor, or the Crime and Punishment of Sinyavsky and Daniel*] (Moscow: Kniga, 1989). First appeared anonymously in Ginzburg 1967.

———. 1987b. "Dvadtsatye gody" ["The Twenties"]. *Iunost',* no. 11: 37–43, no. 12: 28–37.

———. 1989c. "Novaia proza" ["New Prose"]. *Novyi mir,* no. 12: 3–71. Includes "O moei proze" ["On My Prose: letter to I. P. Sirotinskaia"], 58–66.

———. 1992b. "Perepiska Varlama Shalamova i Nadezhdy Mandel'shtam" ["Correspondence of Varlam Shalamov and Nadezhda Mandelstam"]. Ed. I. Sirotinskaia. *Znamia,* no. 2: 158–77.

———. 1993b. "Iz perepiski" ["From Correspondence"]. *Znamia,* no. 5: 110–60.

———. 1994a. *Chetvertaia Vologda.* Vologda: Grifon.

———. 1994b. "Pava i drevo" ["The Peahen and the Tree"]. First published in *Literaturnyi sovremennik* 3 (1937). In Shalamov 1994a: 175–79.

———. 1995. "Iz zapisnykh knizhek" ["From Notebooks"]. *Znamia,* no. 6: 134–75.

Shentalinsky, Vitaly. 1996. *Arrested Voices: Resurrecting the Disappeared Writers of the Soviet Regime.* Trans. John Crowfoot. New York: Free Press. Published in Great Britain under the title *The KGB Literary Archive.*

Shklovskii, E. A. 1991. *Varlam Shalamov.* Moscow: Znanie.

Shneerson, Mariia. 1984. *Aleksandr Solzhenitsyn: Ocherki tvorchestva* [*Essays on the Works of Aleksandr Solzhenitsyn*]. Frankfurt: Possev.

Shreider, Iulii. 1989. "Varlam Shalamov o literature" ["Varlam Shalamov on Literature"]. *Voprosy literatury,* no. 5: 225–48.

Shteppa, Konstantin (W. Godin). 1957. "Feliks Dzerzhinskii: Creator of the Cheka and Founder of 'Chekism.'" In Wolin and Slusser 1957: 65–95.

Shtokman, Igor'. 1989. "Strela v polete: Uroki biografii Iu. Dombrovskogo" ["An Arrow in Flight: Lessons of Iu. Dombrovskii's Biography"]. *Voprosy literatury,* no. 12: 84–109.

Shturman, Dora. 1988. *Gorodu i miru: O publitsistike A. I. Solzhenitsyna* [*Urbi et orbi: The Publicistics of A. I. Solzhenitsyn*]. Paris–New York: Third Wave Publishing House.

Shur, Anna. 1984. "V. T. Shalamov i A. I. Solzhenitsyn: Sravnitel'nyi analiz nekotorykh proizvedenii" ["V. T. Shalamov and A. I. Solzhenitsyn: A Comparative Analysis of Some Works"]. *Novyi zhurnal* 155: 92–101.

Sinyavsky, Andrey. 1990. *Soviet Civilization: A Cultural History.* Trans. Joanne Turnbull with the assistance of Nikolai Formozov. New York: Little, Brown.

Sirotinskaia, I. P. 1992. "Zhizn' i smert' Varlama Shalamova" ["The Life and Death of Varlam Shalamov"]. Interview given to John Glad. *Vremia i my* 119: 204–20.

———. 1994. "Dolgie-dolgie gody besed" ["Long, Long Years of Conversations"]. In Esipov 1994: 109–46. Partly reprinted in Shalamov 1996: 448–60.

———. 1996. "Vospominaniia o V. Shalamove" ["Recollections of V. Shalamov"], in Shalamov 1996: 448–49.

Skinner, B. F. 1972. *Beyond Freedom and Dignity.* New York: Knopf.

Slote, Ben. 1996. "Revising Freely: Frederick Douglass and the Politics of Disembodiment." *a/b: Autobiography Studies* 11: 19–37.

Smirnov, Konstantin. 1991. "Zhertvoprinoshenie: Istoriia odnoi sem'i" ["Sacrifice: The History of a Family"]. *Ogonek* 2: 18–21.

Sokhriakov, Iu. 1993. "Nravstvennye uroki lagernoi prozy" ["The Moral Lessons of Camp Prose"]. *Moskva,* no. 1: 175–83.

Sokolov, Sasha. 1980. *Mezhdu sobakoi i volkom* [*Between Dog and Wolf*]. Ann Arbor: Ardis.

Solzhenitsyn, Aleksandr. 1980. *The Oak and the Calf: Sketches of the Literary Life in the Soviet Union.* Trans. Harry Willetts. London: Collins; New York: Harper and Row. Original: *Bodalsia telenok s dubom: Ocherki literaturnoi zhizni* (Paris: YMCA Press, 1975).

———. 1981b. "Zhit' ne po lzhi!" ["Live Not by Lies!"]. In *Sobranie sochinenii* [*Collected Works*], vol. 9. Vermont/Paris: YMCA Press.

———. 1995. *Invisible Allies.* Trans. Alexis Klimov and Michael Nicholson: Washington, D.C.: Counterpoint.

———. 1998–99. "Ugodilo zernyshko promezh dvukh zhernovov: Ocherki izgnaniia" ["Caught between Two Millstones: Sketches on Exile"]. *Novyi mir,* no. 9 (1998): 47–125; 11 (1998): 93–153; 2 (1999): 67–140.

———. 1999. "S Varlamom Shalamovym" ["With Varlam Shalamov"]. *Novyi mir,* no. 4: 163–69.

Sommer, Robert. 1976. *The End of Imprisonment.* New York: Oxford University Press.

Spengemann, William C. 1979. *The Forms of Autobiography.* New Haven: Yale University Press.

Spiegelman, Art. 1991. *MAUS.* New York: Pantheon.

Stephan, John. 1978. *Russian Fascists: The Tragedy and Farce in Exile 1925–1945.* New York: Harper and Row.

Sternberg, Meir. 1982. "Point of View and the Indirections of Direct Speech." *Literature and Style* 15: 67–117.

Strugatskii, A. N., and B. N. Strugatskii. 1980. *The Snail on the Slope*. Trans. Alan Meyers. London: V. Gollancz. Original: *Ulitka na sklone* (Frankfurt: Possev, 1972; Moscow: Text, 1997).

Sudoplatov, Pavel, and Anatoli Sudoplatov. 1994. *Special Tasks: The Memoirs of an Unwanted Witness—a Soviet Spymaster*, with Jerrold L. and Leona P. Schechter. Boston: Little, Brown.

Suleiman, Susan Rubin. 1983. *Authoritarian Fictions: The Ideological Novel as a Literary Genre*. New York: Columbia University Press.

———. 1996. "Monuments in a Foreign Tongue: On Reading Holocaust Memoirs by Emigrants." *Poetics Today* 17: 639–57.

Terrée, Emmanuel. 1982. *L'Affaire Kravchenko: Paris 1949, le Goulag en correctionnelle*. Paris: Robert Laffont.

Tertz, Abram/Andrey Sinyavsky. 1964. *Liubimov*. Washington: B. Filipoff. English translation by Manya Harari: *The Makepeace Experiment* (New York: Pantheon, 1965).

———. 1965. *"The Trial Begins" and "On Socialist Realism."* Trans. Max Hayward. New York: Vintage.

———. 1966. *Mysli vrasplokh*. New York: Rausen. Reprinted in Tertz/Sinyavsky 1992a, 1: 313–38. English translation by Manya Harari: *Unguarded Thoughts* (London: Collins and Harvill, 1972).

———. 1975a. *Progulki s Pushkinym*. London: Overseas Publications Interchange in association with Collins. Reprinted in Tertz/Sinyavsky 1992a, 1: 339–436. English translation by Catharine Theimer Nepomnyashchy and Slava I. Yastremski: *Strolls with Pushkin* (New Haven: Yale University Press, 1993).

———. 1975b. *V teni Gogolia*. London: Overseas Publications Interchange in association with Collins. Reprinted in Tertz/Sinyavsky 1992a, 2: 3–336.

———. 1976b. "The Literary Process in Russia." Trans. Michael Glenny. In *Kontinent 1: The Alternative Voice of Russia and Eastern Europe*. London: Andre Deutsch. The original, "Literaturnyi protsess v Rossii," was published in the journal *Kontinent*, no. 1 (1974): 143–90.

———. 1986. *Fantastic Stories*. Trans. Max Hayward, Ronald Hingley, and Manya Harari. Evanston: Northwestern University Press. Original: *Fantasticheskie povesti* (Paris: Institut literacki, 1961).

———. 1990. "Liudi i zveri: Po knige G. Vladimova *Vernyi Ruslan*" ["People and Animals: According to G. Vladimov's book *The Faithful Ruslan*"]. *Voprosy literatury*, no. 1: 61–86.

Thomas, D. M. 1998. *Alexander Solzhenitsyn: A Century in His Life*. New York: St. Martin's Press.

Thoreau, Henry David. 1986. *"Walden" and "Civil Disobedience."* Ed. Owen Thomas. New Delhi: Prentice-Hall of India.

Timofeev, Lev. 1991. "Poetika lagernoi prozy: Pervoe chtenie 'Kolymskikh rasskazov' Varlama Shalamova" ["The Poetics of Camp Prose: The First Reading of 'Kolyma Tales' by Varlam Shalamov"]. *Russkaia mysl'* 3859–63 (8 March– 5 April). Also published that same year in *Oktiabr'*, no. 3.

Todorov, Tzvetan. 1970. *Introduction à la littérature fantastique*. Paris: Seuil.

———. 1996. *Facing the Extreme: Moral Life in the Concentration Camps.* Trans. Arthur Denner and Abigail Pollak. New York: Henry Holt. First published in the original French in 1991.

Toker, Leona. 1989. "Stories from Kolyma: The Sense of History." *Hebrew University Studies in Literature and the Arts* 17: 188–220.

———. 1993a. "Who Was Becoming Seasick? Cincinnatus." *Cycnos* 10: 81–90.

———. 1993b. "Varlam Shalamov's Kolyma." In *Between Heaven and Hell: The Myth of Siberia in Russian Culture,* ed. Galya Diment and Yury Slezkine. New York: St. Martin's Press.

———. 1994. "'The Snake Charmer' by Varlam Shalamov." In *Reference Guide to Short Fiction,* ed. Noelle Watson. Detroit: St. James Press.

———. 1995. "Versions of Job: Some Jewish Characters in the Stories of Varlam Shalamov." In *Jews and Slavs,* vol. 4: *Judeo-Slavic Interactions in the Modern Period,* ed. Wolf Moskovich, Samuel Shwarzband, and Anatoly Alekseev. Jerusalem: FPL.

———. 1996. "Awaiting Translation: Lev Konson's Gulag Stories." *Judaism* 45: 119–27.

———. 1997a. "Contra Schopenhauer: Varlam Shalamov and the *Principium Individuationis.*" REAL 13: 257–69.

———. 1997b. "Towards a Poetics of Documentary Prose: From the Perspective of Gulag Testimonies." *Poetics Today* 18: 187–222.

———. 2000. "Kafka's 'The Hunger Artist' and Shalamov's 'The Artist of the Spade': The Discourse of Lent." In *Cold Fusion: Aspects of the German Cultural Presence in Russia,* ed. G. Barabtarlo. Oxford: Berghahn.

Tolstoy, Nicholas. 1977. *Victims of Yalta.* London: Hodder and Stoughton.

Tolszyk, Dariusz. 1999. *See No Evil: Literary Cover-Ups and Discoveries of the Soviet Camp Experience.* New Haven: Yale University Press.

Trifonov, Iurii. 1978. "Dom na naberezhnoi." In *Povesti* [*Tales*]. Moscow: Sovetskaia Rossiia. English translation by Michael Glenny in *Another Life and House on the Embankment* (New York: Simon and Schuster, 1983).

———. 1988. "Ischeznovenie." In *Otblesk kostra. Ischeznovenie.* Moscow: Sovetskii pisatel'. English translation by David Lowe: *Disappearance* (Ann Arbor: Ardis, 1981).

Tsvetkov, E. 1978. "Khranitel' drevnostei" ["The Keeper of Antiquities"]. *Vremia i my* 30: 113–24.

Turkov, A. 1989. "Chto zhe sluchilos' s Zybinym?" ["What Has Happened to Zybin?"]. *Znamia,* no. 5: 226–28.

Venclova, Tomas. 1979. "Prison as Communicative Phenomenon: The Literature of Gulag." *Comparative Civilization Review* 2: 65–73.

Vihavainen, Timo. Forthcoming. "Finnish Memoirs from Stalin's Russia."

Vladimov, Georgii. 1975. *Vernyi Ruslan: Istoriia karaul'noi sobaki.* Frankfurt: Possev. English translation by Michael Glenny: *The Faithful Ruslan: The Story of a Guard Dog* (New York: Simon and Schuster, 1979).

Voinovich, Vladimir. 1977. *Life and Extraordinary Adventures of Private Ivan Chonkin.* Trans. Richard Lourie. New York: Farrar, Straus and Giroux. Original: *Zhizn' i neobychainye prikliucheniia soldata Ivana Chonkina* (Paris: YMCA Press, 1975).

————. 1987. *Moscow 2042.* Trans. Richard Lourie. San Diego: Harcourt Brace Jovanovich. Original: *Moskva 2042* (Ann Arbor: Ardis, 1987).

Volkov, Oleg. 1990. "O perezhitom, dozvolennom i nedozvolennom" ["On the Experienced, Allowed, and Banned" (Interview given to D. Urnov)]. *Voprosy literatury,* no. 3: 54–72.

Volkova, Elena. 1998. *Tragicheskii paradoks Varlama Shalamova* [*The Tragic Paradox of Varlam Shalamov*]. Moscow: Respublika.

Vulfovich, Teodor. 1997. "Razgovory s Iuriem Dombrovskim" ["Conversations with Iurii Dombrovskii"]. *Znamia,* no. 6: 123–47.

Werth, Nicolas. 1997. "Un État contre son people: Violences, répressions, terreurs en Union soviétique." In Stéphane Courtois, Nicolas Werth, Jean-Louis Panné, Andrzej Paszkowsku, Karel Bartosek, and Jean-Louis Margolin, *Le Livre noir du communisme: Crimes, terreur et répression,* with the collaboration of Rémi Kauffer, Pierre Rigoulot, Pascal Fontaine, Yves Santamaria et Sylvain Boulouque. Paris: Robert Laffont.

Wheatcroft, Stephen G. 1981. "Assessing the Size of Forced Concentration Camp Labour in the Soviet Union, 1929–56." *Soviet Studies* 33/2: 265–95.

————. 1983. "Towards a Thorough Analysis of Soviet Forced Labour Statistics." *Soviet Studies* 35: 223–37.

————. 1990. "More Light on the Scale of Repression and Excess Mortality in the Soviet Union in the 1930s." *Soviet Studies* 42: 355–67.

White, Hayden. 1992. "Historical Emplotment and the Problem of Truth." In Saul Friedlander, ed., *Probing the Limits of Representation.* Cambridge, Mass.: Harvard University Press.

Wiesel, Elie. 1989. *Night.* New York: Bantam Books.

Williams, Bernard. 1985. *Ethics and the Limits of Philosophy.* London: Fontana/Collins.

Wilson, Raymond J. III. 1989. "The Misreading of Solzhenitsyn's *Cancer Ward:* Narrative and Interpretive Strategies in the Context of Censorship." *Journal of Narrative Technique* 19: 175–96.

Wolin, Simon, and Robert M. Slusser, eds. 1957. *The Soviet Secret Police.* New York: Praeger.

Woodward, James. 1992a. "A Russian Stoic? A Note on the Religious Faith of Jurij Dombrovskij." *Scando-Slavica* 38: 33–45.

————. 1992b. "The 'Cosmic' Vision of Jurii Dombrovskii: His Novel *Fakul'tet nenuzhnykh veshchei.*" *Modern Language Review* 87: 896–908.

Wordsworth, William. 1974. "Essays upon Epitaphs." In *The Prose Works of William Wordsworth,* ed. W. J. B. Owen and Jane Worthington Smyser, vol. 2. Oxford: Clarendon.

Wu, Hongda Harry. 1992. *Laogai: The Chinese Gulag.* Trans. Ted Slingerland. Boulder: Westview Press. Composed mainly in 1989.

Zakharova, Elena. 1988. "Poslednie dni Varlama Shalamova" ["The Last Days of Varlam Shalamov"]. *Russkaia mysl'* (January 8): 12–13.

Zamiatin, Evgenii. 1952. *My.* New York: Chekhov Publishing House. English translation by Gregory Zilboorg: *We* (New York: Dutton, 1959).

Zamorski, Kazimierz (alias Sylvester Mora) and Pietro Zwierniak. 1945. *La Justice Soviétique.* Rome: Magi-Spinetti.

Zamoyska, Hélène. 1986. "Pis'mo Elen Zamoiska (Pel'tie) Andreiu Siniavskomu" ["Letter of Hélène Zamoiska (Peltier) to Andrei Siniavskii"]. *Vremia i my* 91 (1986): 222–23.

Zholkovsky, Alexander. 1988. "Three on Courtship, Corpses, and Culture: Tolstoj, 'Posle bala'—Zoshchenko, 'Dama s cvetami'—E. Ginzburg, 'Raj pod mikroskopom'." *Wiener slavistischer Almanach* 22: 7–24.

Zorin, Libushe. 1980. *Soviet Prisons and Concentration Camps: An Annotated Bibliography 1917–1980.* Newtonville, Mass.: Oriental Research Partners.

Index

Esenin, Sergei, 57, 275
Esenin-Volpin, Aleksandr, 57
Essad-Bey (Leo Nussbaum), 254
exile, 48, 103, 104, 126–27, 189, 236, 251, 252

falsification of records, 4–5, 17, 274, 284
famine in the Ukraine, 24, 37, 64, 117, 212, 264
Fautré and De Latte, 258
Fedorov E., 274, 289–90
Feuchtwanger, Lion, 17
Filshtinskii, Isaak, 22, 67, 68, 96, 180, 255, 265
Fisher, Lipa, 61, 255
focal character, focalizer (defined), 77
Frankl, Victor, 162, 164, 266, 281, 286
Frisher, Hella, 256

Gagen-Torn, Nina, 274
Galanskov, Yury, 24
Galler, Meyer, 271
Gazarian, Suren, 258, 289
Geller (Heller), Mikhail, xiii, 7, 29, 30, 49, 149, 160–62, 251, 284; and Nekrich, 12, 24
Gendlin, Leonard, 275
Genette, Gérard, 132, 266, 276, 285
Genis, Aleksandr, 242, 292
Gilboa, Joshua, 34, 43, 96, 255, 256, 269, 270, 271, 274, 282
Ginzburg, Aleksandr, 235, 262
Ginzburg, Evgenia, 52–55, 57–75 *passim*, 76–77, 79–102 *passim*, 108, 128, 129–35 *passim*, 179, 186, 220, 236, 243, 260–61, 263, 267, 268, 271, 274–75, 279, 281–82
glasnost and perestroika, 26, 55, 66–69, 70–72, 83–84, 150, 161, 196, 221, 224, 225, 253, 260, 280
Gliksman, Jerzy, 38, 42–43, 74, 78, 79, 251, 255
Gluzman, Semyon, 25, 266
Goffman, Erving, 282
Gogol, Nikolai, 163, 283
goners (*dokhodiagi*), 138, 145, 166, 171, 173–76, 184, 199
Gorbachev, Mikhail, 26, 52, 185, 253
Gorbanevskaya, Natalia, 57, 262
Gorbatov, A. V., 73
Gorchakov, G., 265

Gorky, Maxim, 16, 251–52
Grankina, Nadezhda, 68
Grigorenko, Petro G., 57, 59, 60, 78, 84, 250, 266
Grin, Aleksandr, 217
Grossman, Vasilii, 67, 221
grotesque, 222, 227–31
Guberman, Igor, 25, 61, 292
Guevara, Che, 160
Gulag language x, 21, 107–109, 192, 226, 271, 274, 289–90
Gulag locations: Arkagala, 146; Arkhangelsk, 14; Ashkhabad, 44; Baragon, 147; Barashevo, 24; Belichie, 146, 277, 279; Butugychag, 70–71; Chukotka, 258; Debin, 147; Ekibastuz, 78, 91, 189; Jelgalla, 146; Karaganda, 40–41, 189, 266; Karelia, 38; Kargopol, 35; Kazakhstan, 20, 40–41, 104, 147, 190; Kem, 30; Kengir, 65, 92, 127, 252; Kholmogory, 14, 251; Kolyma, 11, 17, 21, 42, 53–55 *passim*, 57, 68, 70–72, 73, 74, 77, 79–80, 86, 94, 111, 127–29, 135, 136, 138–40, 145–46, 190, 212, 222, 236, 272, 282, 285, 289; Komi Republic, 90; Kotlas, 38; Magadan, 128–29, 146, 170; Marfino, 189; Medvezhegorsk, 31, 35, 38; Mordovia, 25, 58; Novaya Zemlya, 270; Partizan mine, 145; Perm, 25, 26; Pertominsk, 14; Popov Island, 30; Potma, 25; Sekirnaia Hill, 15, 29, 32; Serpantinnaia, 166, 277; Solovetsky islands 14, 15, 29, 30, 55, 68, 97, 106, 132, 251, 252, 254, 265, 274; Spokoinyi mine, 277, 279; Susuman, 146; Svirlag, 31; Taishet, 51, (Ozerlag) 258, 289; the Urals, 20, 25, 26, 144; Viatka, 66, 90; Vishera, 144; Vorkuta 20, 44, 47, 90, 92, 136–37, 271; Yagodnoe, 146; Yertsevo 35, 255
Gulag narratives: admonitory significance 6, 10; artistic merit, 6, 8, 124; call for the readers' self-scrutiny 6; congruence of content and stance, 39, 72, 74, 124; consciousness-raising function, 6, 8, 32, 46, 76, 101, 123, 244; deniability, 103; ethics and aesthetics, 9, 74–76, 101, 209, 240; heteroglossia, 65, 98, 102, 106, 271; historical significance 6, 123; individual and communal concerns, 39, 74, 76–82, 87, 97, 101–102,

Schopenhauer, Arthur, 172, 176–77
Second Russian Revolution, 26, 226, 263
secondary adaptation, 167
self-mutilation, 165, 168–70, 243, 290
semiotic proficiency, 124, 152, 172, 211
Sentaurens, Andrée, 268
Serebriakova, Galina, 52
Serge, Victor, 30, 45
Shalamov, Varlam, xiii, 6, 7, 9, 21, 55, 59,
    69, 78, 79, 85, 90, 95, 96, 98, 99, 126,
    129–30, 141–87, 188, 190, 195, 198–99,
    211, 218, 219, 221, 232–33, 235, 237,
    238, 242, 243, 244, 249, 250, 255, 256,
    261, 262, 273, 276–84, 285, 289; *Koly-
    ma Tales,* xiii, 67, 123, 125, 149–52,
    160–73, 241
—cycles: *AL,* xiii, 160–61, 167–71, 267;
    KR ("Pervaya Smert"), xiii, 160–67;
    KR-2, xiii, 125, 161, 177, 179, 183–85,
    251, 283; *LB,* xiii, 160–61, 170–73;
    "Sketches of the Criminal World," 161,
    177, 283; *VL,* 160, 161, 173–76, 177;
    "Vishera," xiii, 144, 161, 184, 246
—longer works: "Anna Ivanovna," 138–40,
    161; "The Fourth Vologda," 143, 161,
    277, 281; "The Twenties," 143–44, 277
—short stories: "Aleksandr Gogoberidze,"
    180; "The Almaznyi Spring," 146; "The
    Artist of the Spade," 146; "Berdy
    Onzhe," 277; "Berries," 180–81, 277;
    "The Best Praise," 287; "Boris Iuzha-
    nin," 276; "Bread," 128–29, 134; "The
    Bug," 142–43, 276; "The Businessman,"
    165, 168–70; "The Butyrskaia Prison
    [1929]," 177; "Captain Tolly's Love,"
    282; "Carpenters," 164, 167, 282, 283;
    "Chase of Locomotive Smoke," 147;
    "Cherry Brandy," 151; "The Chess
    Set of Doctor Kuzmenko," 183–84;
    "The City on the Hill," 146; "Con-
    densed Milk," 133, 164, 181–83, 199;
    "Courses," 146, 157, 279–80; "The
    Cross," 144; "A Day Off," 153–59, 162,
    173; "The Descendant of a Decem-
    brist," 282; "Dominoes," 146, 180, 186,
    199; "Dry Rations," 157; "The Duck,"
    279; "Engineer Kiselev," 180; "An
    Epitaph," 281; "Evening Prayer," 165;
    "The First Chekist," 277; "The First
    Death," 162; "Galina Pavlovna Zyba-
    lova," 130, 279; "The Glove," 186; "The
    Golden Taiga," 146; "Graphite," 277;

"The Green Procurator," 86, 146;
    "Handwriting," 145–46; "How It Be-
    gan," 145, 156; "In the Night," 164;
    "An Individual Assignment," 151–52,
    163; "Ivan Bogdanov," 185–86; "Ivan
    Fyodorovich," 272; "Khan-Girei," 178;
    "The Lawyers' Plot," 138, 146, 165–66;
    "Lazarson," 178; "Lend-Lease," 127;
    "Lesha Chekanov," 277; "Lida," 163;
    "The Life of Engineer Kipreev," 180,
    276; "Major Pugachev's Last Battle,"
    146, 199; "Marcel Proust," 119; "The
    Monk Josif Shmaltz," 144; "My First
    Tooth," 156, 170; "The Necklace of
    Princess Gagarin," 258; "The Necktie,"
    159; "On Tick," 162–64, 283; "Pain,"
    180, 217, 279; "The Parcel," 162; "The
    Path," 173; "Pava I drevo," 280; "Per-
    mafrost," 184, 255, 285; "A Piece
    of Meat," 286; "The Procurator of
    Judea," 170–71; "Prosthetic Appli-
    ances," 178, 227; "Quiet," 173–76, 283;
    "Rain," 162, 164–65; "The Red Cross,"
    170; "The Revival of the Larch," 148;
    "Riabkon," 142; "A Seizure," 148, 167,
    170; "Sententia," 96, 161, 162, 171–73;
    "Seraphim," 162; "Shock Therapy,"
    162, 279; "The Snake Charmer," 109,
    134, 164, 186, 278–79; "The Stukov
    Affair," 178; "Such'ia voina," 22; "The
    Tatar Mullah and the Fresh Air," 151;
    "There Are No Guilty Ones in the
    Camps," 246, 273; "Through the
    Snow," 5–6, 151, 162; "To the Hospi-
    tal," 277; "Train," 147, 161, 170, 289;
    "Typhoid Quarantine," 146, 166–67;
    "Vishera" 177–78; "Vstavnaia novella,"
    278; "The Weizmanist," 180, 279–80;
    "Wheelbarrow I," 179; "Wheelbarrow
    II," 179; "Yakov Ovseevich Zavodnik,"
    184–85
Shapiro, Maria, 83, 98, 252
Sharansky, Natan, 57, 61, 75, 84, 85, 86,
    92, 270, 271
sharashka, 64, 91, 104, 130, 189, 200–208,
    285
Shaw, Bernard, 17
Shelest, G., 284
Shentalinsky, Vitaly, 59
Shifrin, Abram, 268
Shiriaev, Boris, 46, 97, 251, 258
Shreider, Yulii, 149, 186

LEONA TOKER is a professor in the Department of English
at the Hebrew University in Jerusalem.